Type and Archetype in Late Antique and Byzantine Art and Architecture

Art and Material Culture in Medieval and Renaissance Europe

Edited by

Sarah Blick
Laura D. Gelfand

VOLUME 19

The titles published in this series are listed at *brill.com/amce*

Type and Archetype in Late Antique and Byzantine Art and Architecture

Edited by

Jelena Bogdanović
Ida Sinkević
Marina Mihaljević
Čedomila Marinković

BRILL

LEIDEN | BOSTON

Cover Illustration: *Christ Pantokrator with Prophets*, dome of the former church of Theotokos Pammakaristos, Istanbul (Constantinople), *c.*1310. © Photo: Marina Mihaljević

Library of Congress Cataloging-in-Publication Data

Names: Bogdanović, Jelena, 1973- editor. | Sinkević, Ida, 1960- editor. | Mihaljević, Marina, 1960- editor. | Marinković, Čedomila, editor.
Title: Type and archetype in late antique and Byzantine art and architecture / edited by Jelena Bogdanović, Ida Sinkević, Marina Mihaljević, Čedomila Marinković.
Description: Leiden ; Boston : Brill, [2023] | Series: Art and material culture in Medieval and Renaissance Europe, 2212-4187 ; volume 19 | Includes bibliographical references and index.
Identifiers: LCCN 2022060646 (print) | LCCN 2022060647 (ebook) | ISBN 9789004527201 (hardback) | ISBN 9789004537781 (ebook)
Subjects: LCSH: Art, Byzantine—Themes, motives. | Architecture, Byzantine. | Architecture—Composition, proportion, etc. | Art, Byzantine—Historiography. | Architecture, Byzantine—Historiography.
Classification: LCC N6250 .T97 2023 (print) | LCC N6250 (ebook) | DDC 709.02/14—dc23/eng/20230103
LC record available at https://lccn.loc.gov/2022060646
LC ebook record available at https://lccn.loc.gov/2022060647

Typeface for the Latin, Greek, and Cyrillic scripts: "Brill". See and download: brill.com/brill-typeface.

ISBN 2212-4187
ISBN 978-90-04-52720-1 (hardback)
ISBN 978-90-04-53778-1 (e-book)

Copyright 2023 by Koninklijke Brill NV, Leiden, The Netherlands.
Koninklijke Brill NV incorporates the imprints Brill, Brill Nijhoff, Brill Hotei, Brill Schöningh, Brill Fink, Brill mentis, Vandenhoeck & Ruprecht, Böhlau, V&R unipress and Wageningen Academic.
All rights reserved. No part of this publication may be reproduced, translated, stored in a retrieval system, or transmitted in any form or by any means, electronic, mechanical, photocopying, recording or otherwise, without prior written permission from the publisher. Requests for re-use and/or translations must be addressed to Koninklijke Brill NV via brill.com or copyright.com.

This book is printed on acid-free paper and produced in a sustainable manner.

Contents

Acknowledgments VII
List of Illustrations IX
Notes on Contributors XV

Introduction 1
*Jelena Bogdanović, Ida Sinkević, Marina Mihaljević,
and Čedomila Marinković*

1 Type and Archetype in Late Antique Empress Imagery in the
Central Balkans 15
Jelena Anđelković Grašar

2 The *Hodegetriai*: Replicating the Icon of the Hodegetria by Means of
Church Dedications 43
Anna Adashinskaya

3 The Body of Christ as Relic Archetype 72
Ljubomir Milanović

4 From Earth to Heaven: Transcendental Concepts of Architecture in
Late Roman and Early Byzantine Art (*c*.300–700) 101
Cecilia Olovsdotter

5 Representation of the Temple in the Sarajevo Haggadah: Type or
Archetype? 144
Čedomila Marinković

6 Type and Archetype: Echoing Architectural Forms of the Church of
Nea Moni 163
Marina Mihaljević

7 In Search of Archetype: Five-Domed Churches in Middle and Later
Byzantine Architecture 189
Ida Sinkević

VI

8 The Canopy as 'Primitive Hut' in Byzantine Architecture 210
Jelena Bogdanović

Conclusion: Highlighted Themes, Explanatory Terms, and Critical Mechanisms 233
Jelena Bogdanović, Ida Sinkević, Marina Mihaljević, and Čedomila Marinković

Bibliography 241
Index 288

Acknowledgments

This book is the result of collegiate friendship and shared long-term interests in late antique and Byzantine art and architecture. Trained in various disciplines from art history to architectural engineering, we often have to deal with the inconsistency of the terminology we use when discussing various kinds of cross-cultural artistic accomplishments in the wider Mediterranean. *Type and Archetype in Late Antique and Byzantine Art and Architecture* grew out of a panel discussion about typology and meanings of relevant terms. The panel was originally conceived in 2012 and presented within the communication session at the 23rd International Congress of Byzantine Studies, held in Belgrade, Serbia, in August 2016. As often happens in academia, while some participants at the conference were not able to continue the pursuit of publication of our deliberations and findings due to family and professional obligations, other contributors became involved. Years later, at the moment when this book is approaching its publication, we would love to thank individuals and institutions that provided stalwart support.

Our first thanks go to the conference participants and contributors to this volume for their friendship, kindness, patience, collegiality, and expertise. We also thank the organizers of the Congress of Byzantine Studies, who gave us an opportunity to present the relevance of the topic of type and archetype to the wider scholarly audience. Additional thanks are due to the leadership of the College of the Liberal Arts and Sciences at Vanderbilt University for logistic and financial support. Above all, we thank the Dean of the College of Arts and Sciences, John G. Geer; Associate Provost for Faculty Affairs and Finances, Kamal Saggi; Chair of Classical and Mediterranean Studies, William Caferro; Chair of History of Art and Architecture, Kevin Murphy; and administrative coordinator Julia Kamasz. At Brill, we are immensely grateful to Sarah Blick and Laura D. Gelfand, editors of the series *Art and Material Culture in Medieval and Renaissance Europe*, Kate Hammond, acquisition editor, and Marcella Mulder, editor. We cannot ever be grateful enough for their time, focus, promptness, expertise, professionalism, cheer, and genuine support of this project. The expert guidance of the editorial team at Brill, strengthened by the erudite and constructive assessment by the anonymous reviewer, helped us refine and prepare the manuscript for publication. Copyediting and various stages of the book production were carried out by Joe Hannan, Marianne Noble, and Fem Eggers. For illustrative material we thank the Blago Fund, the Foundation of the Holy Monastery Hilandar, the Jewish Community of Bosnia and Herzegovina, Nebojša Stanković, Alexandar (Alex) Blum, Ivan Drpić, Joshua Schwartz, and Yehoshua Peleg. Our families supported this project with grace and love.

Jelena Bogdanović, Ida Sinkević, Marina Mihaljević, and
Čedomila Marinković
September 2022

Illustrations

1.1   *Felix Romuliana*, imperial palace (1a) and imperial tumuli on the hill Magura (1b). Photo: After Popović, "Sakralno-funerarni kompleks na Maguri" [Sacral and funerary complex at Magura], fig. 105, and Milka Čanak-Medić and Brana Stojković-Pavelka, *Felix Romuliana—Gamzigrad* (Belgrade: Arheološki institut, 2010), fig. 27   21

1.2   Jewelry (2a) and golden foils of the diadem (2b) from the crypt of the mausoleum in Šarkamen. Photo: Nebojša Borić, documentation of the Institute of Archaeology   22

1.3   Early Byzantine oil lamp from the Belgrade City Museum (Helena and Constantine?). Photo: Documentation of the Belgrade City Museum   25

1.4   Aureus of Empress Galeria Valeria from the National Museum in Belgrade (4a) and cameo with female bust from *Horreum Margi* (Galeria Valeria?) (4b). Photo: After Anđelković Grašar, "Image as a Way of Self-Representation," figs. 1a and 1b   27

1.5   Cameos in medallions from Remesiana (Fausta?) (5a, 5b). Photo: After Anđelković Grašar, "Image as a Way of Self-Representation," figs. 2a and 2b   29

1.6   Steelyard weight from the National Museum in Belgrade (Ariadne?). Photo: After *Starinar* 64/2014, book cover   32

1.7   Portrait of Byzantine empress (Euphemia?). Photo: *Arheološko blago Niša* [Archaeological Treasure of Niš] (Belgrade: Srpska akademija nauka i umetnosti, 2004), inside book cover   34

1.8   Obverse of the coin of Emperor Justin II. Photo: Documentation of the National Museum of Leskovac, Numismatics collection I/2 (inv. NI/2, 78)   36

3.1   Dečani monastery, church of the Christ Pantokrator, Serbia, 14th century, viewed from the southwest. Photo: Ljubomir Milanović   73

3.2   Dečani monastery, church of the Christ Pantokrator, Serbia, 14th century, sarcophagi in the west bay of the south aisle. Photo: Ljubomir Milanović   73

3.3   Dečani monastery, church of the Christ Pantokrator, Serbia, 14th century, original iconostasis with fresco surrounding it and the coffin of Saint Stefan Dečanski. Photo: Ljubomir Milanović   76

3.4   Dečani monastery, church of the Christ Pantokrator, Serbia, 14th century, original iconostasis with fresco surrounding it and the coffin of Saint Stefan Dečanski, oblique view. Photo: Ljubomir Milanović   84

3.5   Coffin of the holy king Stefan Dečanski, about 1340, Museum of the Serbian Orthodox Church, Belgrade. Photo: Aleksandar Radosavljević   85

3.6   Coffin of the holy king Stefan Dečanski, about 1340, detail, Museum of the Serbian Orthodox Church, Belgrade. Photo: Aleksandar Radosavljević   86

X ILLUSTRATIONS

3.7 Dečani monastery, church of the Christ Pantokrator, Serbia, 14th century, old position of the reliquary, picture taken *c*.1941. Photo: After Petković and Bošković, *Dečani* 87

3.8 Dečani monastery, church of the Christ Pantokrator, Serbia, 14th century, relics of the holy king Stefan Dečanski. Photo: Dečani monastery (Serbian Orthodox Church) 89

3.9 Dečani monastery, church of the Christ Pantokrator, Serbia, 14th century, the holy king Stefan Dečanski, fresco, south face of the northeast pier. Photo: Ljubomir Milanović 90

3.10 Dečani monastery, church of the Christ Pantokrator, Serbia, 14th century, the holy king Stefan Dečanski, fresco, south face of the northeast pier, detail. Photo: Ljubomir Milanović 92

3.11 Dečani monastery, church of the Christ Pantokrator, Serbia, 14th century, holy king Stefan Dečanski, fresco, south face of the northeast pier, detail. Photo: Ljubomir Milanović 93

3.12 Dečani monastery, church of the Christ Pantokrator, Serbia, 14th century, Saint Stephen Protomartyr, fresco, west wall of the south bay of the naos. Photo: Ljubomir Milanović 94

3.13 Dečani monastery, church of the Christ Pantokrator, Serbia, 14th century, Christ Pantokrator from Deesis, fresco, west wall of the south bay of the naos. Photo: Ljubomir Milanović 95

3.14 Dečani monastery, church of the Christ Pantokrator, Serbia, 14th century, iconostasis, viewed from the back, picture taken *c*.1941. Photo: After Petković and Bošković, *Dečani* 96

4.1 Consular diptych of Probus; Rome or northern Italy, 406; Aosta, Tesoro della Cattedrale. Photo: Diego Cesare, Regione autonoma Valle d'Aosta, Archivi dell'Assessorato Beni culturali, Turismo, Sport e Commercio della Regione autonoma Valle d'Aosta—fondo Catalogo beni culturali 105

4.2 Consular diptych of Areobindus; Constantinople, 506; Paris, Musée national du Moyen Âge—Cluny, inv. Cl. 13135. Photo: © RMN-Grand Palais (musée de Cluny—musée national du Moyen Âge) / Thierry Ollivier 107

4.3 Consular diptych of Clementinus; Constantinople, 513; Liverpool, National Museums Liverpool—World Museum, inv. M10036. Photo: Courtesy National Museums Liverpool, World Museum 108

4.4 Christ and Mary diptych; Constantinople, mid-6th century; Berlin, Staatliche Museen, Skulpturensammlung und Museum für Byzantinische Kunst, inv. 564–565. Photo: Fotonachweis: Staatliche Museen zu Berlin, Skulpturensammlung und Museum für Byzantinische Kunst / Antje Voigt 111

4.5 Chronography of 354, fol. 7 *Natales Caesarum*; Rome, 354; Vatican, Biblioteca Apostolica Vaticana, inv. Romanus 1 MS, Barb.lat. 2154. Photo: © Biblioteca Apostolica Vaticana 112

ILLUSTRATIONS

XI

4.6   Rabbula Gospels, fol. 9v Matthew and John; Syria, 586; Florence, Biblioteca
       Medicea Laurenziana inv. cod. Plut. I, 56. Photo: © Firenze, Biblioteca Medicea
       Laurenziana, MS Plut. 1.56, f. 9v. Su concessione del MiC. È vietata ogni ulteriore
       riproduzione con qualsiasi mezzo   116

4.7   Ashburnham Pentateuch, fol. 2r Genesis; Italy (Rome?), 6th century; Paris,
       Bibliothèque nationale de France, inv. MS nouv. acq. lat. 2334. Photo:
       Bibliothèque nationale de France   118

4.8   Ravennese sarcophagus, 3rd–4th century; Ravenna, Museo Arcivescovile.
       Photo: After Kollwitz and Herdejürgen, *Die Sarkophage*, fig. 19.1, cat. A 49   120

4.9   Coptic funerary stela; Egypt, 5th–8th century; Los Angeles, Los Angeles County
       Museum of Art, inv. 47.8.10. Photo: Museum Associates/LACMA   121

4.10   Silver plaque with representation of Saint Paul; Syria, 550–600; New York,
       Metropolitan Museum of Art, inv. 50.5.1. Photo: Fletcher Fund, 1950   123

4.11   Ambo from Hagios Georgios; Thessaloniki, 500–550; Istanbul, İstanbul
       Arkeoloji Müzeleri, inv. 1090 T. Photo: Cecilia Olovsdotter   125

4.12   Votive bronze *situla*; Constantinople (?), 6th century; Istanbul, İstanbul
       Arkeoloji Müzeleri, inv. 852. Photo: Cecilia Olovsdotter   126

4.13   Gold bracelet with representation of a temple to Isis; Egypt (Alexandria?),
       4th century; Paris, Bibliothèque nationale de France, inv. Seyrig.1972.1318.
       Photo: Bibliothèque nationale de France   128

4.14   Chronography of 354, fol. 13 Constantius II as consul; Rome, 354; Vatican,
       Biblioteca Apostolica Vaticana, inv. Romanus 1 MS, Barb.lat. 2154.
       Photo: © Biblioteca Apostolica Vaticana   130

4.15   Consular diptych of Boethius, Rome or northern Italy 487; Brescia, Museo di
       Santa Giulia. Photo: Su concessione della Fondazione Brescia Musei   132

4.16   Consular diptych of Anastasius; Constantinople, 517; Paris, Bibliothèque
       nationale de France, MMA, inv. 55. Photo: Bibliothèque nationale
       de France   133

4.17   Funerary stela of a couple; Byzantium/Constantinople (?),
       3rd–4th century; Istanbul, İstanbul Arkeoloji Müzeleri (courtyard).
       Photo: Cecilia Olovsdotter   136

4.18   Lead sarcophagus; Roman Syria (mod. Baabda), 3rd century; Istanbul, İstanbul
       Arkeoloji Müzeleri, inv. 1149 M. Photo: Cecilia Olovsdotter   137

4.19   Silver *missorium* of Theodosius I; Constantinople (?), 388; Madrid, Real
       Academia de la Historia. Photo: After Delbrueck, *Die Consulardiptychen*,
       plate 62   140

4.20   'David' silver plate, (3/9) David before Saul; Constantinople, 613/629–630;
       New York, Metropolitan Museum of Art, inv. 17.190.397. Photo: Gift of
       J. Pierpont Morgan, 1917   142

XII ILLUSTRATIONS

5.1   Representation of the Jerusalem Temple on the silver tetradrachm of Bar Kochba, undated issue, year 134/5 CE. Obverse: representation of the Temple with the rising star. Photo: Public domain Classical Numismatic Group, Inc. http://www.cngcoins.com [Accessed June 16, 2022] 149

5.2   Synagogue, Dura-Europos, 3rd century. Torah Shrine. Photo: © Alamy 151

5.3   Hammat Tiberias 4–5th century synagogue. Detail of the mosaic floor depicting the holy Ark surrounded by two large candelabra and other ceremonial objects. Photo: Zev Radovan/Bible Land Pictures © Alamy 152

5.4   Representation of the Temple in the Sarajevo Haggadah (14th century CE), National Museum of Bosnia and Herzegovina. Photo: © Jewish community of Bosnia and Herzegovina 155

5.5   Tentative reconstruction of the Herodian Temple facade. Drawing: Schwartz and Peleg, "Notes on the Virtual Reconstruction of the Herodian Period Temple and Courtyards," 81, illustration 7. Courtesy of Prof. Joshua Schwartz and Yehoshua Peleg 157

6.1   Nea Moni, Chios, 11th century. Exterior view. Photo: Marina Mihaljević 164

6.2   Nea Moni, Chios, 11th century. Plan. Drawing: Marina Mihaljević 165

6.3   Nea Moni, Chios, 11th century. Reconstruction of the interior. Drawing: Marina Mihaljević after Anastasios Orlandos (in Bouras, *Nea Moni*, figs. 57 and 78) 166

6.4   Nea Moni, Chios, 11th century. Reconstruction of the west elevation Drawing: Marina Mihaljević (after Bouras, *Nea Moni*, figs. 104 and 115) 167

6.5   Nea Moni, Chios, 11th century. Reconstruction of the dome. Drawing: Marina Mihaljević after Bouras, *Nea Moni*, figs. 89–90 and 107 168

6.6   Küçükyalı (Maltepe), 9th century, Istanbul (Constantinople). Plan of the church. Drawing: Marina Mihaljević after Ricci, "Reinterpretation of the 'Palace of Bryas'" 170

6.7a   Panagia Mouchliotissa (Theotokos Panagiotissa), Istanbul (Constantinople), 10th–11th century. Drawing: Marina Mihaljević after Bouras, "Hē Architektonikē tēs Panagias ton Mouchliou stēn Kōnstantinoupoli" [The architecture of Panagia Mouchliou in Constantinople], figs. 8 and 43 171

6.7b   Theotokos Eleousa, Veljusa, 11th century. Plan. Drawing: Marina Mihaljević 171

6.8   Theotokos Eleousa, Veljusa, 11th century. Domes. Photo: Marina Mihaljević 172

6.9   Panagia Mouchliotissa (Theotokos Panagiotissa), Istanbul (Constantinople), 10th–11th century. Dome. Photo: Marina Mihaljević 173

6.10   The Tomb and the Ascension of Christ, ivory, *c.*400, Bayerisches Nationalmuseum, Munich, Inv. Nr. MA 157. Photo: Andreas Praefcke. Wikimedia Commons, https://en.wikipedia.org/wiki/File:Reidersche_Tafel_c_400_AD.jpg [Accessed July 9, 2022] 178

6.11   Tetradrachm of Bar Kochba, undated issue, year 134/5 CE. Obverse: representation of the Temple with the rising star. Photo: Public domain

ILLUSTRATIONS

XIII

Classical Numismatic Group, Inc. http://www.cngcoins.com [Accessed June 9, 2022]   181

6.12   Synagogue, Dura-Europos, 3rd century. Torah Shrine. Photo: © Alamy   182

6.13   Surb Prkitch, Ani, 11th century. Exterior, from the south. Photo: Marina Mihaljević   186

6.14   Surb Prkitch, Ani, 11th century. Interior from the southeast. Photo: Marina Mihaljević   187

6.15   Pilgrim's ampulla no. 18, reverse. Photo: © Dumbarton Oaks, Byzantine Collection, Washington, DC   188

7.1   Homilies of James Kokkinobaphos, Vat. gr. 1162, fol. 2v, 12th century. Photo: © Universal History Archive/UIG/Bridgeman Images   192

7.2   Church of the Virgin Kosmosoteira, Pherrai, 1152, southwest view. Photo: https://commons.wikimedia.org/wiki/File:Monastery_of _Panagia_Kosmosotira,_Ferres,_Evros.JPG [Accessed June 6, 2022]   195

7.3   Church of St. Panteleimon, Nerezi, 1164, south view. Photo: Ida Sinkević   195

7.4   Church of St. Panteleimon, Nerezi, 1164, floor plan. Drawing: Ida Sinkević   196

7.5   Church of St. Panteleimon, Nerezi, 1164, southeast dome, fresco, Ancient of Days. Photo: Ida Sinkević   198

7.6   Church of St. Panteleimon, Nerezi, 1164, southwest dome, fresco, Christ Priest. Photo: Ida Sinkević   199

7.7   Church of the Virgin of Ljeviška, 1306/1307, floor plan. Drawing: After Ćurčić, *Gračanica: King Milutin's Church*, fig. 101D   201

7.8   Church of the Mother of God, Gračanica monastery, 1321, floor plan Drawing: After Ćurčić, *Gračanica: King Milutin's Church*, fig. 101F   203

7.9   Church of the Mother of God, Gračanica monastery, 1321, central dome, interior view. Photo: Courtesy BLAGO Fund, Inc.   205

7.10   Church of the Mother of God, Gračanica monastery, 1321, fresco, Evangelist John, southeast dome. Photo: Courtesy BLAGO Fund, Inc.   207

7.11   Church of the Mother of God, Gračanica monastery, 1321, fresco, Evangelist Luke, northeast dome. Photo: Courtesy BLAGO Fund, Inc.   208

7.12   Gospel Book, MS E.D. Clarke 10, f. 2v, 11th century, Oxford, Bodleian Library. Photo: © Bodleian Library Oxford   209

8.1   Primitive hut, engraving, Charles Eisen, frontispiece of Marc-Antoine Laugier, *Essai sur l'architecture*, 2nd ed., 1755. Photo: Public domain image from DOME, digitized content from the MIT Libraries' collections, dome.mit.edu [Accessed June 3, 2022]   212

8.2   Presentation of Christ in the Temple, mosaic, *katholikon* of the Hosios Loukas monastery, Greece, 11th century. Photo: Public domain image by Hans A. Rosbach from Wikimedia commons https://commons.wikimedia

.org/wiki/File:Hosios_Loukas_Katholikon_(nave,_North-West_squinch) _-_Presentation_02.jpg [Accessed June 3, 2022]   221

8.3   Presentation of the Mother of God in the Temple (also known as the Entry of the Ever Virgin Mary and Most Holy Mother of God Theotokos into the Temple; *Vavedenije*), icon, Hilandar, Mt. Athos, 14th century. Photo: Courtesy of the Foundation of the Holy Monastery Hilandar   222

8.4   Hagia Sophia, Constantinople, modern Istanbul, Turkey, 6th century, analysis showing light penetration in the central canopy. Drawing: Alex Blum created by using Rhinoceros, Autodesk Revit, and Photoshop   227

8.5   Process from volume to canopy to nine-square design based on canopied *parti* in Byzantine churches. Drawing: Alex Blum created by using Autodesk Revit and Adobe Illustrator   228

8.6   Five-domed *katholikon* of the Matejič monastery, Skopska Crna Gora, Northern Macedonia, 14th century. Photo: Ivan Drpić   228

8.7   'Windblown' capital with acanthus leaves, Hagios Demetrios, Thessaloniki, Greece, 5th century. Photo: Nebojša Stanković   230

Notes on Contributors

Anna Adashinskaya

(PhD, Central European University, Budapest-Vienna) is a research fellow at the Oriental Studies Institute of the Russian Academy of Sciences, Moscow. Between 2020 and 2021, she was a postdoctoral member of the ERC project Art Historiographies in Central and Eastern Europe: An Inquiry from the Perspective of Entangled Histories. She completed her PhD in Medieval Studies with a dissertation on practices of ecclesiastic foundation, sponsorship, and patronage. Her main research interests concern monasticism in the Balkans and the interaction between Slavic Balkan States and Byzantium during the late medieval period.

Jelena Anđelković Grašar

(PhD, University of Belgrade) is a senior research associate at the Institute of Archaeology in Belgrade, Serbia. Her research interests are the history of art and visual culture in antiquity, late antiquity, early Christianity, and early Byzantium, as well as gender studies and women's history within these periods. Her secondary field of interest is cultural heritage, its educational potential, management, presentation, interpretation and popularization. Anđelković Grašar is secretary of the editorial board of the journal *Starinar*. She was an associate in several EU-funded projects and manager in three: TRAME—Tracce di memoria (2020–2023) and COOLTOUR-Millennials for cultural heritage (2022–2024) from the ERASMUS+ program and SHELeadrersVR (2022–2025) from the Creative Europe program. She has co-organized international conferences at Viminacium Archaeological Park, Serbia, the exhibition *Itinerarium Romanum Serbiae* in Santiago de Chile, and was the president of the national organization committee of the Fifteenth Annual International Conference on Comparative Mythology—Sacred Ground: Place and Space in Mythology and Religion held in Belgrade and Viminacium. She is the author of the book *Femina Antica Balcanica* and numerous scholarly articles.

Jelena Bogdanović

(PhD, Princeton University) is Associate Professor at Vanderbilt University. She specializes in cross-cultural and religious themes in the architecture of the Balkans and Mediterranean. Among her authored and edited books are *The Framing of Sacred Space: The Canopy and the Byzantine Church* (2017), *Icons of Space: Advances in Hierotopy* (2021, paper edition 2023), *Perceptions of the Body and Sacred Space in Late Antiquity and Byzantium* (2018, paper edition 2020), *Space of the Icon: Iconography and Hierotopy* (2019, with Michele Bacci and Vladimir Sedov), *Political Landscapes of Capital Cities* (2016, with Jessica Christie and Eulogio Guzmán), and *On the Very Edge: Modernism and Modernity in the Arts and Architecture of Interwar Serbia (1918–1941)* (2014, with Lilien Robinson and Igor Marjanović).

Čedomila Marinković

(PhD, University of Belgrade) is an independent researcher from Belgrade. Trained as an art and architectural historian, she specializes in Serbian medieval and Byzantine art. Marinković has published several books including monographs *Petar Omčikus* (1998), *Slika podignute crkve* [Image of the completed church] (2007), *Jews in Belgrade 1521–1942* (2020), and *Synagogues in Vojvodina* (2022). Among her publications are peer-reviewed articles: "Founder's Model—Representation of a Maquette or the Church?" (2007), "A Live Craft: The Architectural Drawings on the Façade of the Church of the Holy Virgin Evergetis in Studenica (Serbia) and the Architectural Model from Červen (Bulgaria)" (2008), and "Principles of the Representation of the Founder's Architecture in Serbian Medieval and Byzantine Art" (2013). Marinković's second field of expertise is Jewish art. She is currently preparing for publication of her dissertation, "Constructing the Stage for Narrative: Representations of Architecture in the Sarajevo Haggadah and Illuminated Sephardic Haggadot of the 14th Century." Marinković has received fellowships and grants from the University of Belgrade, the Italian Government, and Athens University, and was awarded the Ženi Lebl award for the best scientific work on a Jewish topic for her PhD thesis.

Marina Mihaljević

(PhD, Princeton University) is Assistant Professor of Art and Architectural History at the State University of Novi Pazar, Serbia. Her specialization is in the field of architectural exchange within the broader Byzantine sphere, especially in the regions of the Balkans and the Mediterranean. She is the author of several articles on Byzantine architecture, including "Religious Architecture" (2021), "Change in Byzantine Architecture" (2016) and "Üçayak: A Forgotten Byzantine Church" (2014).

Ljubomir Milanović

(PhD, Rutgers University) is a research associate at the Institute for Byzantine Studies at the Serbian Academy for Sciences and Arts, Belgrade. Trained as an art historian, he specializes in late antique, early Christian, and medieval art with a focus on Byzantine and post-Byzantine production. Milanović is the author of numerous articles and book chapters, including "On the Threshold of Certainty: The Incredulity of Thomas in the Narthex of the Katholikon of the Hosios Loukas Monastery" (2013), "Cover Girl: Envisioning the Veil in the Work of Milena Pavlović-Barilli" (2014), "Illuminating Touch: Post-Resurrection Scenes on the Diptych from the Hilandar Monastery" (2015), "The Path to Redemption: Reconsidering the Role of the Image of the Virgin above the Entrance to the Church of the Virgin Hodegetria" (2016), and "Delivering the Sacred: Representing *Translatio* on the Trier Ivory" (2018). Milanović is currently preparing for publication of his dissertation, "The Politics of *Translatio*: The Visual Representation of the Translation of Relics in the Early Christian and Medieval Period, The Case of St. Stephen." He has received fellowships and grants from the Andrew W. Mellon Foundation, the École française de Rome, the Delaware Valley Medieval Association, and the Studenica Foundation.

Cecilia Olovsdotter
(PhD, University of Gothenburg) is a classical archaeologist and art historian affiliated as senior research fellow to the Swedish Institute of Classical Studies in Rome. She specializes in Roman and late antique art and architecture, with an emphasis on triumphal iconographies of commemorative and religious art. Among her publications are *The Consular Image: An Iconological Study of the Consular Diptychs* (2005), "Representing Consulship: On the Conception and Meanings of the Consular Diptychs" (2011), "'To Illustrate the History of Art.' John Brampton Philpot's Photographic Collection and the Study and Mediation of Late Antique Ivories in the Mid Nineteenth Century" (2016), and the edited volume *Envisioning Worlds in Late Antique Art: New Perspectives on Abstraction and Symbolism in Late-Roman and Early-Byzantine Visual Culture* (2019), including her own contribution "Architecture and the Spheres of the Universe in Late Antique Art." She is currently finishing a monograph on *Victoria* and the cosmic conception of victory in the art of the Late Roman Empire.

Ida Sinkević
(PhD, Princeton University) is the Arthur J. '55 and Barbara Rothkopf Professor of Art History at Lafayette College, in Easton, Pennsylvania. Her research is focused on Byzantine art and on the impact of medieval visual culture on later periods. Her publications include a number of articles, a book on the church of St. Panteleimon at Nerezi in the Republic of North Macedonia, and an edited volume, *Knights in Shining Armor: Myth and Reality 1450–1650* (2006).

Introduction

Jelena Bogdanović, Ida Sinkević, Marina Mihaljević, and Čedomila Marinković

This book, *Type and Archetype in Late Antique and Byzantine Art and Architecture*, aims to renew interest in typology within late antique and Byzantine art and architectural history. In particular, it suggests paths for revising approaches to typology as a way of organizing our knowledge about visual and representational aspects of art and architecture in the Mediterranean region. Instead of aiming for a comprehensive treatment of historical developments of visual types and their diversity, the authors focus rather on selected examples of art and architecture that offer historical specificity and provide relevant frameworks for a more nuanced understanding of concepts of type and archetype in late antiquity and Byzantium as well as their relevance to typology as a scholarly method.

Art historians usually associate types with easily identifiable and visually recognizable artistic forms. In the medieval religious context, the most prevalent typological investigations of art forms start with textual references in the Bible, as, for example, in the work of the English monk and scholar Bede (*c.*673–735).[1] Biblical typology is framed by the relationship between the Old and New Testaments and is articulated already in the texts of the New Testament. In such a construct, Old Testament prophetic narratives and forms are understood as types (τύπος, plural τύποι) which, based on some kind of likeness, prefigure New Testament fulfillment in antitypes (ἀντίτυπα): as when Adam is the type that prefigures Christ as antitype, or the human-made sanctuary is the antitype of the true heavens (cf. Romans 5:14; Hebrews 9:24). Such theological typology is highly suggestive of an analogue approach to contemporaneous religious visual arts and architecture.[2] Even if not specifically named

---

1   See, for example, Bede, *Bedae Venerabilis opera, Pars II: Opera exegetica, 2A: De Tabernaculo, De Templo, In Ezram et Nehemian*, ed. David Hurst (Turnhout: Brepols, 1969), and, in particular, the section on the Tabernacle and the Temple. Biblical typology is particularly discussed in Jean Danielou, *From Shadows to Reality: Studies in Biblical Typology of the Fathers* (Westminster: Newman Press, 1960) and Leonhard Goppelt, *Typos: Die typologische Deutung des Alten Testaments im Neuen; Anhang, Apokalyptik und Typologie bei Paulus* (1939; repr. Darmstadt: Wissenschaftliche Buchgesellschaft, 1990).

2   See, for example, Sabine Schrenk, *Typos und Antitypos in der frühchristlichen Kunst* (Münster: Aschendorffsche Verlagsbuchhandlung, 1995) and the review of her book by Albert Dietl, "Sabine Schrenk, Typos und Antitypos in der frühchristlichen Kunst (Jahrbuch für Antike

---

© KONINKLIJKE BRILL NV, LEIDEN, 2023 | DOI:10.1163/9789004537781_002

as such, visual typology became one of the major principles of representation and referentiality in Judeo-Christian arts and has been particularly utilized in iconographical studies.[3] The repetitive use of various visual types and their reproducibility solidify recognizable forms and confer familiar meanings that point beyond themselves to the ultimate source: the archetype (ἀρχέτυπον).[4] The universality of such an approach builds upon the idea of type as a fixed expression of the all-encompassing action of God as the Creator. Yet, when detailed through historical, regional, and cultural frameworks and investigated through differing modes of creative expression, the typological method is complicated. Defining and clearly classifying types and then studying them in a systematic way proves to be inconsistent and quite complex.[5]

---

und Christentum, Erg.-Bd.21), Münster 1995," *Journal für Kunstgeschichte* 2, no. 2 (1998), 121–25.

3 The visual typology of religious images is deeply rooted in the iconographical and iconological studies prevalent in art historical scholarship. For good overviews, see Maria Cristina Carile and Eelco Nagelsmit, "Iconography, Iconology," in *Encyclopedia of the Bible and Its Reception*, vol. 12, ed. Constance Furey, Steven Linn McKenzie, Thomas Chr. Römer, Jens Schröter, Barry Dov Walfish, and Eric Ziolkowski (Berlin: De Gruyter, 2016), 778–783, and Christine Hasenmueller, "Panofsky, Iconography, and Semiotics," *Journal of Aesthetics and Art Criticism* 36, no. 3 (1978), 289–301. A plethora of art historical works approach visual typology from within iconographical studies. One representative work that clearly presents the relevance of typology for the systematization of knowledge about religious icons, even if again not specifically using the term typology, is Alfredo Tradigo, *Icons and Saints of the Eastern Orthodox Church* (Los Angeles: J. Paul Getty Museum, 2006). Richard Krautheimer effectively introduced iconographical studies and relevant methods of typology in medieval architecture in Krautheimer, "Introduction to an 'Iconography of Mediaeval Architecture'," *Journal of the Warburg and Courtauld Institutes* 5 (1942), 1–33, repr. in Krautheimer, *Studies in Early Christian, Medieval, and Renaissance Art* (London: University of London Press, 1969), 115–150. In another text, Krautheimer, "The Carolingian Revival of Early Christian Architecture," *Art Bulletin* 24, no. 1 (1942), 1–38, which can be understood as an attempt to provide an iconology of architecture or to bridge the gap between formalist and sociopolitical studies of architecture, Krautheimer aimed to contextualize the type of specific architectural form transmitted by identifying the critical sociopolitical moments in their historical and cultural reception.

4 The philosophical considerations of type and archetype go back to Plato and his theory of forms. Additional definitions of type and archetype can be found in the writings of Aristotle, Plutarch, Polybius, Xenophon, Sophocles, Lucian, Cicero, and Dionysius of Halicarnassus, to mention but a few. See Henry George Liddell and Robert Scott, *A Greek-English Lexicon* (Oxford: Clarendon Press, 1940), entries for "archetype" and "type," also at http://www.perseus.tufts.edu/hopper/text?doc=Perseus%3Atext%3A1999.04.0057%3Aentry%3Da%29rxe%2Ftupos and http://www.perseus.tufts.edu/hopper/text?doc=Perseus%3Atext%3A1999.04.0057%3Aentry%3Dtu%2Fpos (accessed January 22, 2021).

5 Architectural historians and theoreticians, who are often architects by training, are especially concerned with typology due to the rise of the sociopolitical history of art that aims to supplant and to some extent simultaneously deny formalist studies that center on the role of form and typology in architectural design. In his unpublished dissertation, "The Concept

INTRODUCTION

In this volume, we reassess methodologies that address type and archetype, as its ultimate source, by contextualizing questions of typology within the scope of Judeo-Christian primary textual sources and evidence emerging from selected art and architectural examples in the Mediterranean region. Prevailing general definitions of type and typology distinguish between the two related concepts, whereby a type is a grouping (class) based on common features, while typology is the systematic classification of types according

of Type in Architecture: An Inquiry into the Nature of Architectural Form," (PhD diss., ETH Zurich, 1995), Leandro Madrazo Agudin, details no less than twelve historical definitions of type used in architecture and the theory of architecture. It seems relevant to enumerate all twelve definitions of type, as defined by numerous intellectuals and practitioners from Plato to Eisenman, which are extrapolated by Madrazo, and at the same time to acknowledge that the list is not exhaustive. Madrazo highlights the following definitions of type relevant for architectural studies: (1) as an ideal, primeval form; as archetype (Platonic idea); (2) as an idea in the mind, with aesthetic, epistemological, and metaphysical connotations (Renaissance idea, or *disegno*); (3) as an idea in the mind, with aesthetic and epistemological connotations (Morris's idea; Boullée's conception of architectural form as geometric solids); (4) as a sensible model; as prototype (Vitruvius's wooden hut; Quatremère's threefold model of hut, tent, and cave; Quatremère's *modele*); (5) as a fundamental principle inherent both to natural forms and to art forms (Quatremère's *type*); a variant of this is the idea of type as primitive principle subjected to the influence of outward factors (Semper's notion of type in the context of his doctrine of style); (6) as a taxonomic category, used in classification of buildings according to form, function, or other criteria (Durand's diagrams; typological studies in the 1960s and 1970s; functional and morphological classifications in general); this approach includes the notion of type as fundamental to the creation of an epistemology of architecture (Rossi's notion of type); (7) as a two-dimensional geometric figure or diagram (Serlio's drawings of temples; Palladio's plan drawings of villas; Durand's geometric diagrams); (8) as a geometric solid (Boullée, Le Corbusier, Eisenman); (9) as a mental image (Laugier's *cabane*; Arnheim's 'structural skeleton'); (10) as a patterned process of design, amenable to systematization (Durand's method of composition; Eisenman's transformational process); (11) as a theme, or conceptual space, which makes creativity possible (Leonardo's sketches; Palladio's villas; Wright's Prairie houses; Quatremère's *type*; Arnheim's 'structural skeleton'; as well as concepts formulated in the realms of information theory and artificial intelligence, like 'frame,' 'schema,' 'script,' and others); and (12) as an impediment to creativity (Van Doesburg's notion of form-type; Alexander's pattern theory; Eisenman's transformational process). Madrazo suggests that despite diverse and occasionally contrasting definitions, the type remains useful for organizing the knowledge of architecture based on functional, morphological, or progressive forms in architecture. Additionally, according to Madrazo and other scholars, such as Anthony Vidler and Werner Oechslin, type remains critical for the creation of an epistemology of architecture. See Anthony Vidler, "The Third Typology," *Oppositions* 7 (1977), 13–16, repr. in *Architecture Theory Since 1968*, ed. K. Michael Hays (Cambridge, MA/London: MIT Press, 1998), 284–294; Anthony Vidler, "The Idea of Type: The Transformation of the Academic Ideal: 1750–1830," *Oppositions* 8 (Spring 1977), 95–115; and Werner Oechslin, "Premises for the Resumption of the Discussion of Typology," *Assemblage* 1 (1986), 36–53. See also Sam Jacoby, "Typal and Typological Reasoning: A Diagrammatic Practice of Architecture," *The Journal of Architecture* 20, no. 6 (2015), 938–961. See also nn. 3 and 4 above.

to their shared characteristics.[6] The typological approach in studies of late antique and Byzantine visual arts and architecture predominantly stems from taxonomic classification of formal, representational features of art and architecture. The methods of typological investigation are rooted in iconographical studies, interchangeably used for the visual arts and architecture. By looking at 'typical' visual elements we discuss various types of images and icons, through examination of their content, formal characteristics, inscriptions, placement, or historical styles. Some art historians focus on shared iconographic, representational, and above all visual features of various types of religious icons, as when discussing various classes of saints—military saints, ascetic or monastic saints.[7] Yet, as scholars continually raise the question of likeness, Katherine Marsengill effectively argues that Byzantine icons were true portraits that conformed to religious prototypes (from ancient Greek πρωτότυπον, meaning original, primitive form), rather than actually resembling the person portrayed.[8] These questions of likeness and mimetic qualities of types complicate the applicability of iconographical methods within the considerations of typology and its relevance within image theory.

Similarly, by examining 'typical' floor plans, construction techniques, stylistic features, and functions of the buildings we study, we establish a variety of architectural types. While iconographical approaches used for studying typology in the visual arts are akin to those employed in architecture in considering shared representational and functional features of architectural examples, they are also diverging. In prevailing studies of late antique and Byzantine architecture, the type often encompasses the idea of a planning type—a distinct scheme of the building layout. This notion of architectural type includes general outline and its proportions as well as the division of inner spaces of a building by means of the masonry walls, masonry piers, or stone monoliths.

---

6   See, for example, definitions of type and typology at https://en.wiktionary.org/wiki/type and https://en.wiktionary.org/wiki/typology (accessed April 12, 2022).

7   See, for example, Henry Maguire, *The Icons of Their Bodies: Saints and Their Images in Byzantium* (Princeton: Princeton University Press, 1996). See also n. 3 above.

8   Katherine Marsengill, "The Influence of Icons on the Perception of Living Holy Persons," in *Perceptions of the Body and Sacred Space in Late Antiquity and Byzantium*, ed. Jelena Bogdanović (Abingdon: Routledge, 2018), 87–103. See also Marsengill, *Portraits and Icons: Between Reality and Spirituality in Byzantine Art* (Turnhout: Brepols, 2013); Michele Bacci, *The Many Faces of Christ: Portraying the Holy in the East and West, 300 to 1300* (London: Reaktion Books, 2014); Charles Barber, *Figure and Likeness: On the Limits of Representation in Byzantine Iconoclasm* (Princeton: Princeton University Press, 2002); and Hans Belting, *Likeness and Presence: A History of the Image before the Era of Art*, 2nd ed. (Chicago: Chicago University Press, 1996).

INTRODUCTION   5

Accordingly, the basilica, one of the most common architectural types, can be described as an oblong building divided in its interior by longitudinal rows of columns placed symmetrically to the building major axis. The interior is comprised of elongated subspaces—the middle space, the nave, is wider than the lateral aisles. Because this type of building can accommodate large groups of people, it was used in antiquity for civic structures and then reappropriated for religious functions in late antiquity and medieval times. Among centrally planned buildings, in which at least two sides are of equal length and the main central space is symmetrical when bisected laterally and longitudinally, are those based on the circle, the square, and polygons, often hexagons and octagons. These centrally planned buildings were often used in late antiquity and Byzantium for funerary and commemorative structures, such as mausolea and martyria, as well as for baptisteries. An architectural planning type characteristic of Middle Byzantine church architecture that developed after the mid-9th century is the so-called cross-in-square. This architectural type represents the building with a centralized, usually square, naos preceding the tripartite sanctuary. The interior space of the naos is divided in nine equal portions by means of four vertical columns which support the church's upper structure.

The categorization of buildings presented here points to their horizontal layout, but the 'planning type' unavoidably includes three-dimensional spatial characteristics. In the case of churches of the basilican type, it is supposed that the nave is not only wider but also higher than the lateral aisles. As a result, the light is introduced into the interior of the building by a tier of openings, the clerestory, placed in the masonry above the line of vertical supports between the lower lateral and higher central roofs. In centrally planned structures, the core space developed around its vertical axis is the major defining element in understanding the structure. If it lacks openings and windows, the dark interior would be suggestive of tomb architecture as used in pagan traditions. If the central open space is defined as light-filled by window openings, it would indicate an early Jewish or Christian building, because light is an attribute of God in these two monotheistic religions in the late antique Mediterranean. Likewise, the four interior columns of the more complex cross-in-square Byzantine churches carry the central dome. The dome is supported by pendentives (curved triangles) positioned between the barrel vaultings surmounting the four arms of the cross bays. The corner compartments are much lower and are frequently covered by domical or cross vaults. On the exterior, this system bears the recognizable pyramidal composition of the main architectural volumes, with the crowning dome above the central portion of the building, the four cross arms just below the dome drum, and the lowest peripheral corner compartments.[9] In view of the close relationship between the ground plan and the structural, three-dimensional appearance of the building, the term 'structural type,' is more pertinent to the idea of type in late antique and Byzantine architecture and is practically interchangeable with the term 'planning type.'

In religious architecture, the naos most often defines the type, while the sanctuary and the narthex are secondary spaces in terms of architectural feasibility. Symmetry emerges as critical for architectural and structural ordering. For example, the tri-partite sanctuary of a distinctly Byzantine church has three separate spaces of the prothesis, altar space and diaconicon, of which the first two are actually required for the performance of liturgical rites. Likewise, the narthex, the exonarthex, and other auxiliary spaces can be understood more as additions rather than primary spaces in terms of defining the church type.

The advantages of utilizing typology as a major methodological device in the study of church buildings had been justified by the correlation between the changes in the predominant building types and the occurrence of new ones in accordance with the liturgical changes that had affected the Byzantine rite between the 7th and early 9th centuries.[10] The changes in church architecture and the appearance of the novel planning types in the Middle Byzantine period has been seen as a result of the standardization of rite and related functional demands.[11] This in effect means that the typology has been considered as concordant both with functional and chronological categories.[12]

---

9 For a characteristic Middle Byzantine composition of the church exterior, see Robert Ousterhout, *Master Builders in Byzantium* (Princeton: Princeton University Press, 1999), 112. Marina Mihaljević, "Constantinopolitan Architecture of the Komnenian Era (1080–1180) and its Impact in the Balkans" (PhD diss., Princeton University, 2010), 123–124, presents the hierarchical treatment of the church parts as a widely assimilated metropolitan element in Byzantine architecture.

10 Richard Krautheimer, *Early Christian and Byzantine Architecture*, 4th ed. (New Haven/London: Yale University Press, 1986), 297–300. Vasileios Marinis, "Liturgy and Architecture in the Byzantine Transitional Period (7th–8th centuries)," in *Transforming Sacred Spaces: New Approaches to Byzantine Ecclesiastical Architecture from the Transitional Period*, ed. Sabine Feist (Wiesbaden: Reichert Verlag, 2020), 189–198, analyses liturgical changes and the architectural impact.

11 Marina Mihaljević, "Religious Architecture," in *The Oxford Handbook of Byzantine Art and Architecture*, ed. Ellen C. Schwartz (New York, NY: Oxford University Press, 2021), 307–328, esp. 312–314, outlines historical and cultural changes affecting Byzantine ecclesiastical architecture.

12 For further remarks on the relationship between the typological and functional approach to Byzantine architecture, see Cyril Mango, "Approaches to Byzantine Architecture," *Muqarnas* 8 (1991), 40–44, esp. 42–43; Krautheimer, *Early Christian and Byzantine Architecture*, 295–297; Hans Buchwald, "The Concept of Style in Byzantine Architecture," in *Form, Style and Meaning in Byzantine Church Architecture* (Aldershot: Ashgate, 1999), 1–4; Robert Ousterhout, "The Architecture of Iconoclasm," in *Byzantium in the Iconoclastic*

INTRODUCTION 7

In her work on the regional reception of Constantinopolitan 12th-century architecture, Mihaljević elucidates the art historical constructs regarding the much debated transition from the old to the new types in Byzantine architecture.[13] She analyzes methodological approaches to the category of type in Middle Byzantine architecture, particularly the cross-in-square, which had been evaluated as an 'ideal' type, fully concomitant not only with the functional-ritual requirements but also with the other artistic and architectural aspects of wider religious meanings, including the interior decorative system and the exterior appearance of the church building.[14]

The fundamental change in the search for the 'ideal' church type that affected building planning between the 7th and 9th centuries was in dramatic opposition to the later continuation of the Middle Byzantine planning formulas, especially the cross-in-square architectural type.[15] This example posits the transition from the basilica to the centrally planned churches as a fundamental problem in tracing the historical development of Byzantine architecture.

The long-standing evolutionist approach involved preserved monuments essentially being lined up and assigned a position in the sequence of the evolution of the ideal cross-in-square church type.[16] The so-called cross-domed church type played a particularly important role in this methodological model, because it was recognized as a turning point in the transition from axial to centrally planned church types.[17] In Byzantine architecture, the chronological

---

Era (ca. 680–850): The Sources, ed. Leslie Brubaker and John Haldon (Burlington, VT: Ashgate, 2001), 3–36, esp. 16–17.

13   Mihaljević, "Constantinopolitan Architecture," 16–23.

14   In his seminal study, "The Ideal Iconographic Scheme of the Cross-in-Square Church," in *Byzantine Mosaic Decoration: Aspects of Monumental Art in Byzantium* (Boston: Boston Book & Art Shop, 1955), 14–16, Otto Demus observes the 'ideal' Middle Byzantine decorative programs as pertaining to the cross-in-square church type. For the analysis of the church exterior hierarchical composition, in which the dome and the apse received special treatment in accordance with the sanctity of the spaces, see Mihaljević, "Constantinopolitan Architecture," 47–49, 123–124, 197–199.

15   This narrative led to the depreciation of Late Byzantine architectural practice and its omnipresent evaluation as non-innovative, which is a question beyond the scope of this study. See Cyril Mango, *Byzantine Architecture* (New York: Rizzoli, 1985), 252–295; Krautheimer, *Early Christian and Byzantine Architecture*, 415–450.

16   For the evolutionist method, see Mihaljević, "Constantinopolitan Architecture," 17–20.

17   The mid-8th-century reconstruction of Hagia Eirene in Constantinople, featuring the cross-domed arrangement on the gallery level, is most often used as an example of the cross-domed church: Krautheimer, *Early Christian and Byzantine Architecture*, 285–300. More recently, see Sabine Feist, "The Impact of Late Antique Churches on the Ecclesiastical Architecture during the Transitional Period: The Case Study of St. Irene in Constantinople," in *Transforming Sacred Spaces: New Approaches to Byzantine*

series, based primarily upon the church planning type, regularly included the Constantinopolitan cross-domed churches today known as Gül and the Kalenderhane Camii, which were long considered to be transitional monuments in the period between the 7th and 9th centuries. The archaeological discoveries in both edifices and the resulting redating of the churches to the 12th century finally revealed the full scope of misconceptions inherent in the linear, evolutionist approach in architectural typology.[18] In his analysis of the sustained use of basilica plans and adaptations of the cross-in-square church type beyond Byzantine architecture in the territories of medieval Bulgaria, Serbia, Rus', the Vento, and the Norman Kingdom of southern Italy, Mark Johnson additionally points to two major themes of hybridity of architectural types and relationships in architectural typology in religious and civic architecture.[19]

It is not possible to distinguish the architectural type from the ground plan (planar design) as it is inherently tied to the consideration of structure and tectonic articulation, nor how the interior relates to the exterior of the building. The building plan, stripped of other relevant architectural evidence, often does not offer the possibility of recognizing the upper construction and distinguishing the structural type. Byzantine buildings quite regularly display an incongruity in plans and structural systems of their substructure and superstructure.[20] Buildings known by their ground-level plans preserve only fragmentary evidence about the overall design, which can be interpreted in various ways.[21] This is especially relevant for the distinction between massive

---

Ecclesiastical Architecture from the Transitional Period, ed. Sabine Feist (Wiesbaden: Reichert Verlag, 2020), 129–145, esp. 132–139.

18 Cecil L. Striker, "The Findings at Kalenderhane and Problems of Method in the History of Byzantine Architecture," in *Byzantine Constantinople, Monuments, Topography, and Everyday Life*, ed. Nevra Necipoğlu (Leiden/Boston/Cologne: Brill 2001), 107–116.

19 Mark Johnson, "Acceptance and Adaptation of Byzantine Architectural Types in the 'Byzantine Commonwealth'," in *The Oxford Handbook of Byzantine Art and Architecture*, ed. Ellen C. Schwartz (New York: Oxford University Press, 2021), 373–388.

20 Örgü Dalgıç and Thomas F. Mathews, "A New Interpretation of the Church of Peribleptos and Its Place in Middle Byzantine Architecture," in *The First International Sevgi Gönül Byzantine Studies Symposium, Istanbul 2007* (Istanbul: Vehbi Koç Vakfı, 2010), 424–431, esp. 426–429. Mihaljević, "Constantinopolitan Architecture," 25–26 considers such a discrepancy to be a result of the different function of the substructure spaces, and a reasonable reduction of unnecessary construction expenses for the erection of the vaults of great spans.

21 The archaeological evidence from many important Byzantine monuments, such as the famous church of St. George in Mangana, introduces doubts about their structural system despite substantial physical remains of their lower parts. Mihaljević, "Constantinopolitan Architecture," 26–28.

structural walls and the linear supports, which in effect defines the difference in architectural types in Byzantine architecture.

The prevailing typological approach in architecture has been broadened and substituted by more nuanced approaches. A number of additional factors, such as regional developments, also change the appearance of linear narrative of late antique and Byzantine architecture.[22] For example, the questions of building scale and availability of construction materials can be connected with the origins, dissemination, and endurance of particular planning types.[23] Despite its historic grounding in the liturgical function of the church, the idea of type in ecclesiastical architecture demonstrates only loose connections, or even absolute disjunction, with the mimetic qualities and variety of functions of church buildings—parish churches, cemetery churches, private chapels, or monastic churches. Mihaljević emphasizes the flexibility of Byzantine masters in resolving the particular structural, functional, and formal demands of the architectural design of the church. She proposes that in the process of design the Byzantine architects operated with spatial compartments, segments of the church building, and treated them as three-dimensional spatial units—blocks—suitable for combining. Such a procedure in effect resulted in myriad, ever-changing design solutions in Byzantine churches.[24]

In her previous work on architectural taxonomy, Bogdanović also offers an alternative approach to the consideration of type in late antiquity and Byzantium. She suggests a more plastic and integrated approach that starts directly with the three-dimensional building type and an understanding of architecture beyond the function of shelter to include the concept of the space that a building frames. The plastic treatment of the interior space and the consideration of light and acoustics as architectural elements of design suggest a more integrated understanding of Byzantine architectural typology. Based on the analysis of hundreds of churches, she reveals the relationships between the three-dimensional module, the canopy, and the design of the Byzantine church, most often recognized for its dome.[25] Instead of following the prevailing

---

22   Striker, "The Findings at Kalenderhane," 107–116; Robert Ousterhout, "Problems of Architectural Typology during the Transitional Period (Seventh to Early Ninth Century)," in *Transforming Sacred Spaces: New Approaches to Byzantine Ecclesiastical Architecture from the Transitional Period*, ed. Sabine Feist (Wiesbaden: Reichert Verlag, 2020), 147–158.

23   Slobodan Ćurčić, *Architecture in the Balkans from Diocletian to Süleyman the Magnificent* (New Haven/London: Yale University Press, 2010), 328–337.

24   Marina Mihaljević, "Change in Byzantine Architecture," in *Approaches to Byzantine Architecture and Its Decoration*, ed. Mark Johnson, Robert Ousterhout, Amy Papalexandrou (Farnham, Surrey/Burlington, VT: Ashgate 2012), 99–119.

25   Jelena Bogdanović, *The Framing of Sacred Space: The Canopy and the Byzantine Church* (Oxford/New York: Oxford University Press, 2017).

typologies used to explain church design (such as the cross-in-square church), this approach considers a generative but non-imitative system instead—the nine-square grid design spatially articulated by a three-dimensional module of a canopy, a four-columned structure with a domical roof.

Today recognized as cross-domed, cross-in-square, or domed-octagon churches, these various building types associated with Byzantine architecture were all achieved by utilizing the opportunities of the nine-square grid diagram.[26] The use of the canopied building module allowed for flexibility of design and applications in various types of buildings, civic or religious, and for various types of church, whether they were basilicas or more centralized in plan. Such an approach also challenges the linear evolutionist narrative of Byzantine architecture that positions the period between the 7th and 9th centuries as a major historical threshold for the transition from longitudinal to more centralized planning of churches.

The experimentations with the domical bay as a building module are highlights of 6th-century Byzantine architecture, as a point of mature transition from late antique precedents.[27] The paradigmatic canopied bay opened up possibilities for technical and creative innovations, including the sophisticated application of geometry and optics in architectural design beyond the Constantinopolitan Hagia Sophia. The square-based domical bay of the Chalke (Bronze) Gate is an exemplar of these experimentations. Emperor Justinian's historian Procopius described the Chalke Gate, once the main vestibule of the Great Palace, in his invaluable text *Buildings*.[28] The central structural part of the Chalke Gate was a canopy-like structure with a dome on pendentives, a key feature of Byzantine churches in 6th-century Constantinople. Procopius's description of the interior decoration of the Chalke Gate also summarizes the major aesthetic principles of 6th-century architectural design, which were also used and attested on a larger scale for numerous Byzantine church edifices. All interior floors and vertical walls, up to the string course, were covered with marble revetments, while arches and vaults were covered with mosaics.

---

26   Bogdanović, *The Framing of Sacred Space*, 251–263.

27   Bogdanović, *The Framing of Sacred Space*, 251–263. See also Ćurčić, *Architecture in the Balkans*, 187–201, 231–238; Jelena Bogdanović, "Byzantine Constantinople: Architecture," in *Routledge Handbook of Istanbul*, ed. Kate Fleet (forthcoming).

28   Procopius, *Buildings*, trans. Henry Bronson Dewing and Glanville Downey, Loeb Classical Library, vol. 7 (Cambridge, MA: Harvard University Press, 1979), I, x, 11–12; Bogdanović, *The Framing of Sacred Space*, 243–251.

INTRODUCTION   11

Of the more than 20 churches and shrines Emperor Justinian rebuilt or built in Constantinople, as mentioned by Procopius in his text, all three of the buildings which are still standing, Hagia Sophia, Hagia Eirene, and Ss. Sergios and Bakkos, have a domed canopy as the central structural unit.[29] These structures are well lit and acoustically sound. The interior decoration of these buildings includes delicate architectural sculpture, marble carvings, golden mosaics, and monumental inscriptions with historical and religious content. These elements of architectural design and decoration, even if not always all used comprehensively, would remain aspirational criteria for numerous other Byzantine accomplishments.

Bogdanović argues that the canopy was a guiding idea for architectural design, which unified its material and non-material aspects, and that such an approach supersedes the current typology used in Byzantine studies. The main argument here is that diagrammatic reasoning is also typological and specific for architectural theory.[30] At the same time, the recognizable design principles articulated in Byzantine architecture over a thousand years of its existence, rather than geographical or chronological distinctions, characterize certain accomplishments as late antique and Byzantine.

Again, as in the studies of visual arts, scholars occasionally delve into the mechanisms of articulation and ultimate sources of architectural types beyond somewhat generic, metaphoric, and metonymic references to the Heavenly Jerusalem or biblical architecture mentioned in texts. By using iconographical methodology, the architectural historian Richard Krautheimer linked an architectural structure, studied as a 'type' or a 'copy,' to its original, or architectural, prototype.[31] His initial analysis employed three major criteria—floor plan, execution, and dedication of the building—which he derived from selected medieval texts that discuss religious architecture and from actual architectural examples.[32] To test his thesis, for the major prototype of medieval religious architecture he chose the church of the Holy Sepulchre in Jerusalem, because as the most iconic building of medieval Christian world it was frequently 'copied.' He examined architectural reproductions of the Holy Sepulchre in western European churches and baptisteries; two different types of buildings based on their function. Krautheimer concluded that medieval architects

---

29   Bogdanović, "Byzantine Constantinople: Architecture," (forthcoming), with reference to churches and shrines discussed by Procopius, *Buildings*, chapters 1–11.
30   See also relevant text by Jacoby, "Typal and Typological Reasoning: A Diagrammatic Practice of Architecture," 938–961.
31   Krautheimer, "Introduction," 1–33.
32   Krautheimer, "Introduction," 1–33, esp. 7, 16.

did not intend to imitate the likeness of the prototype, but to reproduce it "*typice* and *figuraliter* [by type and symbolically—translation ours] as a memento of a venerated site and simultaneously as a symbol of promised salvation," while maintaining "the relation between pattern and symbolical meaning ... as being determined by a network of reciprocal half-distinct connotations."[33] As with recent studies focusing on the visual arts that question the concept of likeness,[34] further analysis of the mechanisms for the transmission of the architectural form and meaning of the Holy Sepulchre in Byzantium confirms that the emphasis was not on the mimetic qualities nor on the reproduction of a likeness of the Holy Sepulchre. The prototype for Byzantine religious architecture is not the Holy Sepulchre, but rather the visionary architecture of several biblical constructs—the Ark of the Covenant, the Tabernacle, and the Temple, as well as the Heavenly Jerusalem—while the ultimate archetype is divine beauty, toward which humans reach by using various material and non-material aspects of their creations.[35]

The type and extremely relevant archetype in late antique and Byzantine contexts have proved to be critical concepts for understanding the mechanisms of artistic creativity. However, they are largely undertheorized, and discussions of them remain wrapped in inconsistent terminology. Should we therefore abandon typological studies? And if so, what would be an alternative? Or should we revise current typological approaches, which privilege and single out the concept of type at the expense of other inseparably related and relevant concepts, above all, that of archetype? And if so, how should we then consider typology? These are the main questions we raise in our investigations, to ultimately suggest that typological approaches remain extremely useful in studies of art and architecture but that innovative methodologies beyond iconographical studies that rely heavily on formal and visual likeness are needed. In order to propose scholarly approaches to understanding of type and its ultimate source, the archetype, we turn to the definitions and use of these concepts in late antique and medieval contexts in the Mediterranean and investigate their referentiality.[36] We reconsider the relevance of intellectual

---

33   Krautheimer, "Introduction," citation notes on pp. 9 and 17.

34   See n. 8.

35   Jelena Bogdanović, "The Rhetoric of Architecture in the Byzantine Context: The Case Study of the Holy Sepulchre," *Zograf* 38 (2014), 1–21; Bogdanović, *The Framing of Sacred Space*, 266, 299; Filip Ivanović, "Images of Invisible Beauty in the Aesthetic Cosmology of Dionysius the Areopagite," in *Perceptions of the Body and Sacred Space*, ed. Jelena Bogdanović (Abingdon: Routledge, 2018), 11–21.

36   This approach, which relates to the reasoning about type and archetype from within late antique and Byzantine intellectual discourse, rather than considering them in retrospect

INTRODUCTION 13

theoretical discourse on type and archetype, whereby the selected case studies test the applicability of proposed hypotheses.

Late antique and Byzantine theologians and philosophers discussed type and archetype extensively. Starting with (Pseudo-)Dionysius the Areopagite, self-identified student of the apostle Paul and an enigmatic intellectual,[37] the concepts of type (τύπος, model or pattern) and archetype (ἀρχέτυπον, the original type from which the physical replicas are made) were recurringly used in religious texts.[38] As in Platonic tradition, within late antique and Byzantine culture the type and archetype provide sophisticated tools for understanding both idea (εἶδος, ἰδέα) and form (εἰκών, σχῆμα, μόρφωσις) in art and architecture on multiple levels.[39] Yet while related, the two notions are often different and even opposing, though not necessarily mutually exclusive. What we find is that the discourse articulated by members of the intellectual elite living in the late antique and medieval Mediterranean permits a more nuanced approach to their artistic and architectural expression.

The use of case studies in this volume needs clarification. The authors are fully aware that the selected case studies presented here cannot be utilized to extract universally shared collective forms in order to suggest historical trajectories, and that neither can they be used without question as self-contained entities that confirm comprehensively all conceptual aspects of typology. Here, we mostly use case studies to understand individual examples of a type within a given category and to provide insight into historical, geographical, and cultural specificities of typology in the visual arts and architecture.

---

of the post-18th-century articulation of typology within epistemological theories, is a critical premise in this volume.

37 On the polemical discussions about identity of (Pseudo-)Dionysius the Areopagite and relevance of his texts for late antique and Byzantine studies, see Ronald F. Hathaway, *Hierarchy and the Definition of Order in the Letters of Pseudo-Dionysius: A Study in the Form and Meaning of the Pseudo-Dionysian Writings* (The Hague: Martinus Nijhoff, 1969), 31–36, and Maximos Constas, "Dionysius the Areopagite and the New Testament," in *The Oxford Handbook of Dionysius the Areopagite*, ed. Mark Edwards, Dimitrios Pallis, and Georgios Steiris (New York: Oxford University Press, 2022), 48–63.

38 Dionysius Areopagita, *Corpus Dionysiacum*, 2 vols., ed. Beate Regina Suchla, Günter Heil, and Adolf M. Ritter (Berlin: De Gruyter, 1990–1991), including *De coelesti hierarchia* (*Celestial Hierarchy*, henceforth CH), in which (Pseudo-)Dionysius the Areopagite defines the terms of type and archetype.

39 Bogdanović touches upon this theme of type and archetype in architecture in Jelena Bogdanović, "Rethinking the Dionysian Legacy in Medieval Architecture: East and West," in *Dionysius the Areopagite: Between Orthodoxy and Heresy*, ed. Filip Ivanović (Newcastle upon Tyne: Cambridge Scholars, 2011), 109–134. See also chapter by Bogdanović in the present volume.

In particular, in this volume on type and archetype in visual arts and architecture in late antiquity and Byzantium, the interrelations between the material and non-material, the representational and conceptual are probed further. There are two major goals. One is to investigate typology as a scholarly tool used in visual arts and architecture, including whether and to what extent the criteria used to approach typology can be interchangeably used in these two artistic domains. The other is to provide a more nuanced comprehension of type and its ultimate source, the archetype, set against the cultural and intellectual values that come from within late antique and Byzantine medieval realms.

By focusing on selected examples of art and architecture from the late antique and medieval Balkans and the wider Mediterranean, we consider intellectual thought on type and archetype but start from the objects themselves and seek their ultimate archetypes. The notion of type and archetype is related to objects of various physical scales, from recognizable visual elements in icons, to architectural features of individual buildings (chapels, churches, palaces), and to distinct aspects of built and natural environments. By juxtaposing well-known and new material about icons and iconic imagery, religious and civic structures, including churches built in late antiquity and Byzantium, the book aims to initiate debate on methodological approaches that include typology within Byzantine and Byzantine-related architecture, art, and archaeology. In the process, we additionally clarify the use of relevant terminology associated with typological methodologies within the field of late antique and Byzantine studies. Therefore, type and its derivative terms, such as archetype, prototype, antitype, and stereotype, are all discussed. A particular emphasis is placed on human scale and nonverbal communicative features employed in the conceptual and actual designs of studied examples. Ultimately, enriched by the theoretical framework that stems from within late antique and Byzantine culture itself, this book aims to contribute to the research and methodologies used in the broader field of Mediterranean studies and to contribute to image theory and theory of architecture.

CHAPTER 1

Type and Archetype in Late Antique Empress Imagery in the Central Balkans

Jelena Anđelković Grašar

1 Introduction

Located at the crossroads of different civilizations, the territory of the Central Balkans displays rich and diverse cultural, social, and religious heritage. The geopolitical complexity of the region shaped every aspect of its material culture and is also evident in the versatile types of visual representations of imperial women. Usually based on the archetype of the divine heiress and intended for imperial propaganda, the most common female imperial image types include an empress as paired ruler, an independent sovereign, and a religious figure evocative of a maternal or virginal ideal. Rooted in historical stereotypes of noble women and based on the archetype of the divine one, empress image types influenced representations of ordinary women and, as such, they constructed the idea of a prototype which it was desirable to imitate.[1]

---

1   Negative images of empresses of non-noble origin culminated in Procopius's *Sacred History*, and legends about the empress Theodora later continued to inspire the imaginations of researchers and writers, and even today have remained present in academic research which is oriented toward methodologies that can help in the creation of an accurate image of the empress. Pauline Allen, "Contemporary Portrayals of the Byzantine Empress Theodora (of AD 527–48)," in *Stereotypes of Women in Power: Historical Perspectives and Revisionist Views*, ed. Barbara Garlick, Suzanne Dixon, and Pauline Allen (New York/London: Greenwood Press, 1992), 93–104; Leslie Brubaker, "Sex, Lies and Textuality: The Sacred History of Prokopios and the Rhetoric of Gender in Sixth-Century Byzantium," in *Gender in the Early Medieval World: East and West, 300–900*, ed. Leslie. Brubaker and Julia M.H. Smith (Cambridge: Cambridge University Press, 2004), 83–101. On the influence and mutual relationship between various image types, specifically in the territory of the Central Balkans, see Jelena Anđelković Grašar, *Femina Antica Balcanica* (Belgrade: Arheološki institut, Evoluta, 2020); Jelena Anđelković Grašar, "Image as a Way of Self-Representation, Association and Type Creation for Late Antique Women in the Central Balkans," in *Vivere Militare Est: From Populus to Emperors—Living on the Frontier*, vol. 1, ed. Snežana Golubović and Nemanja Mrđić (Belgrade: Institute of Archaeology, 2018), 333–364.

© KONINKLIJKE BRILL NV, LEIDEN, 2023 | DOI:10.1163/9789004537781_003

2 Theoretical Background of Archetype and Type(s) in the Creation of Empress Imagery

Among several possible uses of the archetype concept, in this study the most important is the idea of the archetype developed from Jungian psychology, because of its consideration of the collectively inherited unconscious idea, or, in this case, an image universally present in the psyche of any individual. In order to explore the archetypes and then types of an empress image, the image should not be simplified to its iconic form, reduced to a representation modelled in selected material,[2] but rather considered as a mental image, shaped in people's minds and influenced by many social, cultural, religious, and political factors.[3] Mental images are related to mental models, which are personal, internal representations of external reality; they are constructed by individuals based on their unique life experiences, perceptions, and understandings of the world.[4] Thus mental images can be reshaped under other circumstances and be subject to various interpretations over time and can be followed in their recurring use in various forms of art.

The most prominent female archetype in psychoanalysis is the Great Mother. Carl Gustav Jung and supporters of psychoanalysis considered the Great Mother image as an archetype which appears in the human collective unconscious realm and mythological patterns of Greek and Roman goddesses.[5] Michael Carroll considers psychological archetypes of the Great Mother as important factors in the creation of the Christian Marian (Theotokos) cult.[6]

---

2 The Latin terms *typus, effigiesi, figura, forma, idolum, pictura, repraesentation* can be related to the English cognates depiction and representation.

3 The Latin term *imago* stands for the image related to imitate, imagine, an iconic mental representation, or mental image.

4 Natalie A. Jones, Helen Ross, Timothy Lynam, Pascal Perez, and Anne Leitch, "Mental Models: An Interdisciplinary Synthesis of Theory and Methods," *Ecology and Society* 16, no. 1 (2011), 46 [available at http://www.ecologyandsociety.org/vol16/iss1/art46/].

5 Carl Gustav Jung, "Approaching the Unconscious," in *Man and His Symbols*, ed. Carl Gustav Jung (Garden City, NY: Doubleday 1964), 18–103; Carl Gustav Jung, *Analytical Psychology: Its Theory and Practice: The Tavistock Lectures* (New York: Pantheon, 1968); Carl Gustav Jung, "Psychological Aspects of the Mother Type," in *Collected Works of C.G. Jung*, vol. 9:1, *The Archetypes and the Collective Unconscious*, trans. R.F.C. Hull (London: Routledge and Kegan Paul, 1981), 75–110; Erich Neumann, *The Great Mother: An Analysis of the Archetype*, trans. Ralph Mannheim (Princeton, NJ: Princeton University Press, 1970); Sylvia B. Perera, *Descent to the Goddess: A Way of Initiation for Women* (Toronto: Inner City Books, 1981); Edward C. Whitmont, *Return of the Goddess* (New York: Crossroad Publishing, 1992); David Adams Leeming and Jake Page, *Goddess: Myths of the Female Divine* (Oxford: Oxford University Press, 1996).

6 Michael P. Carroll, *The Cult of the Virgin Mary: Psychological Origins* (Princeton: Princeton University Press, 1992).

The archetype itself comprehends two sides of the 'archetypal feminine' providing its dual nature, i.e., maternal and virginal (spiritual) aspects to be identified in the creation of goddess types. Based on archetypes well known in the spheres of religion and various pagan cults, over time forms of the maternal—virginal types of pagan goddesses—began to be transferred to the profane sphere as well.[7] In such a construct, various (anti)types of the late antique empress images can be interpreted by using a classification—typology—which often depends on the context, but the very same image might become the original model—prototype—for late antique women of high social status.

Various typologies can be employed to recognize types in late antique empress imagery. Although typologies of race, depending on the socio-political context, can be considered outdated, anthropology can provide thought-provoking insight towards some sort of typology of 'otherness' relating to ancient cultures and people.[8] Similarly, Jung's personality typology based on two attitudes and four functions can be helpful in the analysis of a particular person, even a historic figure, but, as critics argue, there is no pure type but rather a "conglomeration, an admixture of the attitudes and functions that in their combination defy classification."[9] In considering a specific archaeological artifact, archaeological or stylistic typology can be very helpful to determine not only the object's features but additional external factors which influenced its shape, facture, color, and decoration, while ultimately keeping in mind that no typology can be considered entirely consistent and final.[10] According to the philosophy of essentialism, an artifact's form and attributes are seen as a consequence of the imperfect realization of the template (exemplar type), which is often attributed to differences in raw material properties or the creator's

---

7   Anđelković Grašar, "Image as a Way of Self-Representation," 333–364.

8   Goran Štkalj, Aleksandar Bošković, and Željka Buturović, "Attitudes of Serbian Biological Anthropologists toward the Concept of Race," *Anthropologie* LVII/3 (2019), 287–297; Aleksandar Bošković, *Kratak uvod u antropologiju* [A brief introduction to anthropology] (Zagreb: Naklada Jesenski i Turk, 2010), 19–37. Contemporary anthropology places the question of identity at the center of its research, focusing on gender, race, and ethnic identities. Ibid. 188–189.

9   Carl Gustav Jung, *Collected Works of C.G. Jung*, vol. 6, *Psychological Types*, trans. R.F.C. Hull (Princeton: Princeton University Press [1921] 1976); Daryl Sharp, *Personality Types: Jung's Model of Typology* (Toronto: Inner City Books 1987), 89.

10 William Y. Adams, "Archaeological Classification: Theory Versus Practice," *Antiquity* 62 (1988), 40–56; Robert Whallon and James A. Brown, eds., *Essays on Archaeological Typology* (Evanston: Center for American Archaeology Press, 1982); William Y. Adams and Ernest W. Adams, *Archaeological Typology and Practical Reality: A Dialectical Approach to Artifact Classification and Sorting* (Cambridge: Cambridge University Press, 2007); John C. Whittaker, Douglas Caulkins, and Kathryn A. Kamp, "Evaluating Consistency in Typology and Classification," *Journal of Archaeological Method and Theory* 5, no. 2 (1998), 129–164.

individual technical competence.[11] These essential forms are often considered as 'mental templates' similar to the mental images analyzed in this study, which may be materialized more or less successfully. Typology in Christian theology represents the theory of making connections between Old Testament types and events or persons from the New Testament.[12] Types as prefiguration correspond to antitypes, events, or aspects of Christ in the New Testament. The Virgin Mary within the holy marriage with the Holy Spirit refers to an old sabbatical institution whereby she, as a figure for Israel, the representative of God's people, symbolizes their deepest hope for salvation which is about to be realized.[13] In considering the image of an empress, it can be said that in forming a religious image of an emperor a similar concept of theological typology was used whereby an earthly ruler becomes an antitype of the heavenly king. The same type of associative relationships can be applied for the relationship between the Queen of Heaven and a terrestrial empress.

Ideal type is the most important for the creation of an empress image and its social recognition. According to Max Weber:

> An ideal type is formed by the one-sided accentuation of one or more points of view and by the synthesis of a great many diffuse, discrete, more or less present and occasionally absent concrete individual phenomena, which are arranged according to those one-sidedly emphasized viewpoints into a unified analytical construct [German word *Gedankenbild*—'mental image']. In its conceptual purity this mental construct cannot be found empirically anywhere in reality. It is utopia. Historical research faces the task of determining in each individual case the extent to which this ideal-construct approximates to or diverges from reality.[14]

---

11   Francis A. Grabowski, *Plato, Metaphysics and the Forms* (New York/London: Continuum 2008).

12   Patrick Fairbairn, *Typology of Scripture: Two Volumes in One* (Grand Rapids, MI: Kregel Publications, 1960); Leonhard Goppelt, *Typos: The Typological Interpretation of the Old Testament in the New* (Grand Rapids, MI: Wm. B. Eerdmans Publishing, 1982); Piotr Łabuda, "Typological Usage of the Old Testament in the New Testament," *The Person and the Challenges* 1, no. 2 (2011), 167–182.

13   Fairbairn, *Typology of Scripture*, 255–263; Sarah Jane Boss, *Empress and Handmaid: On Nature and Gender in the Cult of the Virgin Mary* (London/New York: Cassel 2000), 217–218.

14   Max Weber, "Objectivity in Social Science and Social Policy," in *The Methodology of the Social Sciences*, trans. and ed. E.A. Shils and H.A. Finch (Illinois: Free Press of Glencoe 1949), 90.

For Weber, mental images are directly linked with ideal types as ideal-constructs, which do not have to be associated with any perfection or moral ideals but rather the subjective accentuation of certain elements of the phenomena in question.

Using typology in classification, analysis, and understanding of images can be misleading, thus involving typification as a process of creating a standard social construction based on assumptions, and even discrimination based upon it, is known as typism.[15] Closely related to typification is the stereotype, which signifies something that lacks individual markers and generalization in a social construction of reality, and is often associated with individuals belonging to a particular group, often a social one.[16] Stereotypes usually have a negative connotation which is based on prejudice and can lead to, for example, racism or sexism. From the contemporary point of view, the latter can be easily recognized in the ancient sources, especially those which provide testimonies about imperial women.[17]

3   Type and Archetype in Late Antique Empress Imagery

Depending on the idea and message to be communicated with the public, there were various image types suitable for promoting imperial interests, dynastic legitimacy, or religious notions, and among all of these types, two figures are distinctive: empress as mother and empress as wife. The territory of present-day Serbia is known as the homeland of 18 Roman emperors, and during the Tetrarchy significant building activity is associated not only with emperors, but with their mothers as well.[18] An important aspect of the impact of these women was their noble origin; if this was absent, it had to be fabricated. For example, according to myth, the mother of the Roman emperor Galerius (r. 305–311), Romula, conceived the divine son with the god Mars, thus providing him with the noble origin which he did not have as the son of a

---

15   Kwang-ki Kim and Tim Berard, "Typification in Society and Social Science: The Continuing Relevance of Schutz's Social Phenomenology," *Human Studies* 32, no. 3 (2009), 263–289.

16   C. Neil Macrae, Charles Stangor, and Miles Hewstone, eds., *Stereotypes and Stereotyping* (New York/London: The Guilford Press, 1996).

17   Jelena Anđelković Grašar and Emilija Nikolić, "Stereotypes as Prototypes in the Perception of Women: A Few Remarks from History and Folk Tradition," *Archaeology and Science* 13 (2018), 89–107.

18   Aleksandar Jovanović, *Tlo Srbije: zavičaj rimskih careva* [Serbia: Homeland of the Roman Emperors] (Belgrade: Princip-Bonart Press, 2006).

herdsman.[19] Neglecting the figure of the father in favor of glorification of the mother was important in the political ideology of the Tetrarchy. In the case of Romula, this is indicated by the building of a residential palace in her honor, named for her *Felix Romuliana*, as well as having her funerary tumulus next to the emperor's one (Figure 1.1).[20] According to the archaeological excavations conducted in Šarkamen, it seems that another woman from the Tetrarchy had a prominent place in this imperial ideology. It is supposed that Maximinus Daia (r. 310–313) followed Galerius's example of glorification of the mother figure when he started the construction of the palace, honoring the place of his birth. A set of jewelry discovered during the excavations of the crypt of the mausoleum located within the palatial complex suggests the funeral of a female member of the imperial family (Figure 1.2),[21] possibly the funeral of the empress, the unknown mother of Maximinus Daia and sister of Galerius, who was honored in Šarkamen together with her son.[22]

Unlike Romula, who directly influenced Galerius's persecution of Christians by worshiping mountain deities, the mother of Constantine the Great (r. 306–337), Helena, followed the lead of her son in supporting Christians.[23] Like

---

19   Through this legend Galerius glorified himself as the new Romulus or Alexander the Great. Lactantius, *De mortibus persecutorum*, in *Corpus Scriptorum Ecclesiasticorum Latinorum*, vol. 19, ed. Samuel Brandt and Georgius Laubmann (Prague/Vienna/Leipzig: F. Tempsky, G. Freytag, 1890), 9:9; Sexti Aurelii Victoris, *Liber de Caesatibus, praecedunt Origogentis Romanae et Liber de virisillustaburbis Romae, subsequitur Epitome de Caesaribus*, ed. F. Pichlmayr (Leipzig: B.G. Teubneri, 1911), 40:16.

20   The idea that the architectural complex in Gamzigrad was actually sacred Romula's house was confirmed with the excavations conducted in 1984 when a fragment of the archivolt with the inscription *Felix Romuliana* was discovered. Dragoslav Srejović, "Felix Romuliana, Galerijeva palata u Gamzigradu" [Felix Romuliana, Galerius's palace in Gamzigrad], *Starinar* 36 (1985), 51, fig. 1; Dragoslav Srejović and Čedomir Vasić, "Diva Romula—Divus Galerius, Imperial Mausolea and Consecration Memorials in Felix Romuliana (Gamzigrad, East Serbia)," in *The Age of Tetrarchs*, ed. Dragoslav Srejović (Belgrade: University of Belgrade, Centre for Archaeological Research, Faculty of Philosophy, 1994), 141–156; Dragoslav Srejović, "Diva Romula—Divus Galerius. Poslednje apoteoze u rimskom svetu" [Diva Romula—Divus Galerius. The last apotheoses in the Roman world], *Sunčani sat* 5 (1995), 17–30; Ivana Popović, "Sakralno-funerarni kompleks na Maguri" [Sacral and funerary complex at Magura], in *Felix Romuliana—Gamzigrad*, ed. Ivana Popović (Belgrade: Arheološki institut, 2010), 141–158.

21   Ivana Popović, "The Find of the Crypt of the Mausoleum: Golden Jewellery and Votive Plaques," in *Šarkamen (Eastern Serbia): A Tetrarchic Imperial Palace: The Memorial Complex*, ed. Ivana Popović (Belgrade: Arheološki institut, 2005), 59–82.

22   Miodrag Tomović, "Conclusion," in *Šarkamen (Eastern Serbia): A Tetrarchic Imperial Palace: The Memorial Complex*, ed. Ivana Popović (Belgrade: Archaeological Institute, 2005), 107–109.

23   *De Vita Imp. Constantini*, in "Eusebii Pamphili Caesareae Palaestinae Episcopi," *Opera omnia quaeexistant*, Tomus II (Paris: 1837), 3.47.

FIGURE 1.1 *Felix Romuliana*, imperial palace (1a) and imperial tumuli on the hill Magura (1b)
PHOTO: AFTER POPOVIĆ, "SAKRALNO-FUNERARNI KOMPLEKS NA MAGURI" [SACRAL AND FUNERARY COMPLEX AT MAGURA], FIG. 105, AND MILKA ČANAK-MEDIĆ AND BRANA STOJKOVIĆ-PAVELKA, *FELIX ROMULIANA—GAMZIGRAD* (BELGRADE: ARHEOLOŠKI INSTITUT, 2010), FIG. 27

FIGURE 1.2 Jewelry (2a) and golden foils of the diadem (2b) from the crypt of the mausoleum in Šarkamen
PHOTO: NEBOJŠA BORIĆ, DOCUMENTATION OF THE INSTITUTE OF ARCHAEOLOGY

Galerius and Maximinus Daia, who dedicated their palaces to memories of their mothers, Constantine had several cities renamed Helenopolis in honor of his mother, Helena.[24] Empress mother Helena gained the political verification of power with the status *nobilissima femina* in 318 and the rank of Augusta in 324. Alongside her social and political image, Helena also had a significant reputation as a good Christian who was a patron and in Christian spirit took care of poor people. Owing to this powerful religious image that was created, all other Christian women during the Byzantine Empire were encouraged spiritually by the fact that Helena was the mother of the first Christian emperor.[25] Helena Augusta is represented on the obverse side of the golden solidus that is kept in the National Museum in Belgrade, minted in Thessaloniki in 324.[26] The reverse side reveals an image of Securitas, as is typical of empress gold coins, implying an idea of the empress as *SECVRITAS REIPVBLICAE* reminiscent of former representations of *PAX AUGUSTA*.[27] This symbol of imperial virtue aims to emphasize the complex role of Helena as empress mother who, within the empire in which her son is the supreme ruler, provides peace, security, and happiness. The portrait of Helena is rendered in the style of Tetrarchian art, where all forms are more abstract than realistic. Since the empress is depicted with the diadem, many iconographical similarities between mother and son are apparent when comparing this image with Constantine's golden medallion, also held in the National Museum in Belgrade.[28]

---

24   Cyril Mango, "The Empress Helena, Helenopolis, Pylae," *Travaux et Mémoires. Centre de recherche d'histoire et civilisation byzantine* 12 (1994), 143–158.

25   Julia Valeva, "Empresses of the Fourth and Fifth Centuries: Imperial and Religious Iconographies," in *Niš I Vizantija* 7, ed. Miša Rakocija(Niš: Kulturni centar Niša, 2009), 67–76.

26   Dragoslav Srejović, "Kasnoantički i ranovizantijski portret" [Late antique and early Byzantine portrait] in *Antički portret u Jugoslaviji*, ed. Nenad Cambi, Emilio Marin, Ivana Popović, Ljubiša B. Popović, and Dragoslav Srejović (Belgrade: Narodni muzej Beograd, Muzeji Makedonije Skopje, Arheološki muzej Zagreb, Arheološki muzej Split, Narodni muzej Ljubljana, 1987), 244, cat. 245; Angela Donati and Giovanni Gentili, eds., *Constantino Il Grande. La civiltà antica al bivio tra Occidente e Oriente* (Milan: Silvana Editoriale, 2005), cat. 17; Miloje Vasić, *Gold and Silver Coins of Late Antiquity (284–450 AD) in the Collection of National Museum in Belgrade* (Belgrade: National Museum, 2008), cat. 242.

27   Patrick M. Bruun, "Constantine and Licinius A.D. 313–337," in *The Imperial Roman Coinage* 7, ed. Carol Humphrey, Vivian Sutherland, and Robert A. Carson (London: Spink and Son Ltd., 1966), 323, 514 no. 134.

28   Cf. Srejović, "Kasnoantički i ranovizantijski portret," 244, cat. 244, 245.

From the end of the 4th century, Helena's name and religious type of image were associated with the *inventio crucis* legend, as they are still.[29] Iconography of Helena and Constantine with the True Cross is suggestive; thus two figures with the motif of the cross between them on the discus of an early Byzantine lamp from Singidunum are recognized as Helena and Constantine (Figure 1.3).[30] The figures are depicted schematically, in festive, imperial costume and in orans position, while the cross is placed between them with the opening for oil above.[31] In such a reduced scene, the figure of a woman is recognizable only by the accentuated breasts.[32] Representations of biblical figures, as well as Christian symbols, on oil lamps have been known since the 4th century when they replaced mythological figures and scenes.[33] As already mentioned, the first source for this scene can be found in the legend of the True Cross. Yet since artistic solutions in applied arts were based upon the

---

29 Jan Willem Drijvers, *Helena Augusta: The Mother of Constantine the Great, and the Legend of her Finding of the True Cross* (Leiden: Brill, 1992), 79–180; Jan Willem Drijvers, "Helena Augusta: Cross and Myth. Some New Reflections," in *Millennium 8. Yearbook on the Culture and History of the First Millennium C.E.* ed. Wolfram Brandes (Berlin: De Gruyter Mouton, 2011), 125–174; Barbara Baert, *A Heritage of Holy Wood: The Legend of the True Cross in Text and Image* (Leiden: Brill, 2004), 15–41.

30 This oil lamp probably was produced in some local workshop in the period between the 6th and 9th century. Marija Birtašević, "Jedan vizantijski žižak iza a rheološke zbirke Muzeja grada Beograda" [An early Byzantine oil lamp from the archaeological collection of the Belgrade City Museum], *Godišnjak Muzeja grada Beograda* 2 (1955), 43–46. Another interpretation of the scene is that the figures represent Saint Thecla and Saint Menas. See Branka Gugolj and Danijela Tešić-Radovanović, "A Lamp from the Belgrade City Museum with a Representation of ss. Constantine and Helen," in *Symbols and Models in the Mediterranean: Perceiving through Culture*, ed. Aneilya Barnes and Mariarosaria Salerno (Newcastle upon Tyne: Cambridge Scholars Publishing 2017), 124–135.

31 Decoration of imperial garments suggests *loros* which appeared on coins in the period between the 7th and 9th century. Ornament on the head of the female figure indicates *stemma* with *pendilia*, characteristic for representations of early Byzantine empresses, and such an image could have been seen during official court ceremonies. Ioannis Malalae, "Chronographia," in *Corpus Fontium Byzantinae* 35, ed. Ioannes Thurn (Berlin/New York: Walter de Gruyter, 2000), 17.9; Agathias, *The Histories*, in *Corpus fontium historiae Byzantinae* 2A, trans. and ed. Joseph D. Frendo (Berlin: De Gruyter, 1975), 3.15; Maria Parani, *Reconstructing the Reality of Images: Byzantine Material Culture and Religious Iconography (11th–15th Centuries)* (Leiden: Brill, 2003), 18–26.

32 The accentuated breasts on the female figure indicate the skill of the craftsman of the local workshop and this type of 'gender label' is also known from a fresco-painted tomb in Osenovo. Renate Pillinger, Vania Popova-Moroz, and Barbara Zimmermann, *Corpus der spätantiken und frühchristlichen Wandermalereien Bulgariens* (Vienna: Verlag der Österreichischen Akademie der Wissenschaften, 1999), 14, fig. 4.

33 Slavica Krunić, *Antičke svetiljke iz Muzeja grada Beograda* [Ancient lamps from the Belgrade City Museum] (Belgrade: Muzej grada Beograda, 2011), 380–381.

FIGURE 1.3   Early Byzantine oil lamp from the Belgrade City Museum (Helena and Constantine?)
PHOTO: DOCUMENTATION OF THE BELGRADE CITY MUSEUM

iconographic patterns on coins, there was a considerable practice of depicting co-rulers on coins during the 6th and 7th centuries, which often had the aim of propaganda, supporting certain heirs to the throne. When women were represented, their images could be considered as those of real co-rulers, as is the case with Empress Sophia, wife of Emperor Justin II (r. 565–574), or Empress Martina, wife of Emperor Heraclius (r. 610–641), honored with these coins as the mother who provided the succession of the imperial throne.[34] The motif of the cross on the coins between the imperial couple can be also considered as a scepter, which from the 5th century onwards was a symbol of the source of the ruler's power; that is, coming from the God.[35] Given the knowledge that utilitarian objects were often used to promote imperial propaganda, it might be possible that the iconographical pattern from coinage was transferred on to the lamp.[36] Because the figures are shown in orans position and the male

---

34   Philip Grierson, *Byzantine Coinage* (Washington, DC: Dumbarton Oaks Research Library and Collection 1982, 2nd edition, 1999), 25–27.
35   Grierson, *Byzantine Coinage*, 29; Suzanne Spain, "The Translation of Relics Ivory, Trier," *Dumbarton Oaks Papers* 31(1977), 285.
36   The custom of representation of the imperial couple on coins meant the imitation of imperial protocol, when the person with the higher rank stood on the right side of the one with lower rank, i.e., from the perspective of an observer, the emperor would be on the left and co-ruler on the right. If the couple is represented with the cross, the emperor would

figure with the nimbus, this representation possesses religious character and eschatological significance. Thus this image can be understood as having the function of honoring Helena and Constantine as saints, patrons of the True Cross and protectors of the ideal state.[37]

Political interests often affected the choice of empress, and politically arranged marriages were very common. Therefore, in search of noble origin, Emperor Galerius gave a lot of respect to his wife Galeria Valeria, daughter of Augustus Diocletian.[38] Valeria was proclaimed Augusta in 308 even though she was already an empress daughter and her influence on the dynastic propaganda and ideology can be supposed with particular certainty. Hence Valeria's image was distinctive on coinage minted in her honor (Figure 1.4a).[39] This image type became the ideal and a sort of prototype in the creation of the visual identity of noble Roman ladies of high social rank, who aspired to imitate this paradigm of imperial appearance. Such an empress image can be seen on a cameo made of two-layered agate and opal from the first decade of the 4th century from *Horreum Margi* (Figure 1.4b). Here, a female bust is depicted in right profile, which could be associated with the image of Galeria Valeria.[40] According to the stylistic characteristics which suggest the art of the Tetrarchic period, this work of art can be dated to the period between 300 and 311. The coiffure is characteristic of the 3rd century and can be seen on several representations from the beginning of the 4th century as well, when it was worn by Galeria Valeria, Helena, and Fausta.[41] According to the facial features, this

---

be to the right of the cross and the empress would be on the left side. Leslie Brubaker and Helen Tobler, "The Gender of Money: Byzantine Empresses on Coins," *Gender & History* 12, no. 3 (2000), 573–574; Grierson, *Byzantine Coinage*, 26. Since on this oil lamp the female figure is positioned on the left, that could indicate Helena's importance within the scene, which is based on the legend, mostly associated with the empress.

37 Baert, *A Heritage of Holy Wood*, 125–126.

38 Timothy D. Barnes, *The New Empire of Diocletian and Constantine* (London: Harvard University Press, 1982), 38, 156.

39 Srejović, "Kasnoantički i ranovizantijski portret," 242; Carol Humphrey and Vivian Sutherland, *The Roman Imperial Coinage* 6 (London: Spink and Son Ltd., 1967), 562 br. 53.

40 Ivana Popović, *Rimske kameje u Narodnom muzeju u Beogradu*, [Roman cameos in the National Museum Belgrade] (Belgrade: Narodni muzej Beograd, 1989), 36–37, cat. 49; Ivana Popović, "Roman Cameos with Representation of Female Bust from Middle and Lower Danube," in *Glyptique romaine*, ed. Hélène Guiraud and Antony Andurand (Toulouse: Presses Universitaires Mirail, 2010), No. 38, Pl. XIII, 38; Aleksandrina Cermanović-Kuzmanović, "Jedna kameja iz Ćuprije" [A cameo from Ćuprija], *Zbornik Filozofskog fakulteta* 7, no. 1 (1963), 119–125.

41 Angelina Raičković and Bebina Milovanović, "Development and Changes in Roman Fashion Showcase Viminacium" *Archaeology and Science* 6 (2011), 83.

FIGURE 1.4
Aureus of Empress Galeria Valeria from the National Museum in Belgrade (4a) and cameo with female bust from *Horreum Margi* (Galeria Valeria?) (4b)
PHOTO: AFTER ANĐELKOVIĆ GRAŠAR, "IMAGE AS A WAY OF SELF-REPRESENTATION," FIGS. 1A AND 1B

28   ANĐELKOVIĆ GRAŠAR

portrait is recognized as Galeria Valeria owing to likenesses in engravings and on coinage.[42]

Connections to the imperial origin did not help Empress Fausta to escape *damnatio memoriae*, even though she was the daughter of Emperor Maximianus, sister of Maxentius, wife of Constantine the Great and mother of their three sons, future emperors Constantine II, Constantius II, and Constans I. She married Constantine in 307, and this marriage was arranged as a political alliance of the two emperors.[43] Although she had the same titles as Helena—*nobillisima femina* (318) and Augusta (324)—she was not remembered in history, and not only because she was murdered in 326[44] but because traces of her were erased. The majority of representations of Fausta are associated with known types of public image on coins. After she gained the status of Augusta, coins with this title were minted in the short period between 324 and 326. The empress is depicted on the obverse side in profile, according to the fashion of the time, with characteristic coiffure, wavy hair and a bun at the back. In these portraits, unlike those of Helena, Fausta is depicted without a diadem, which some authors interpret as her inferiority with regard to Helena's stronger influence,[45] while others consider this to be specificity of adornments, with only practical significance.[46]

This iconographical pattern can be seen on two cameos from Remesiana made in agate and opal, which are today housed in the National Museum in Belgrade and generally accepted to represent portraits of Empress Fausta, produced around 320 (Figure 1.5a/b).[47] Previous identifications were associated

---

42   For analogies, see Popović, *Rimske kameje u Narodnom muzeju u Beogradu*, 36–37; Popović, "Roman Cameos," 210–211.

43   Barnes, *The New Empire of Diocletian and Constantine*, 42–43; Jan Willem Drijvers, "Flavia Maxima Fausta: Some Remarks," *Historia* 41 (1992), 501–503.

44   David Woods, "On the Death of the Empress Fausta," *Greece & Rome* 45, no. 1 (1998), 70–86.

45   Patrick M. Bruun, "Constantine and Licinius A.D. 313–337," in *The Imperial Roman Coinage* 7, ed. Carol Humphrey, Vivian Sutherland, and Robert A. Carson (London: Spink and Son Ltd., 1966), 45.

46   Drijvers, "Flavia Maxima Fausta: Some Remarks," 503.

47   Ivana Kuzmanović Novović, "Portreti cara Konstantina i članova njegove porodice na gliptici u Srbiji" [Portraits of Emperor Constantine and members of his family on glyptic in Serbia], in *Niš i Vizantija* 7, ed. Miša Rakocija (Niš: Kulturni centar Niša, 2009), 85–86, fig. 20; Ivana Popović, "Inventar grobnica iz Dola kod Bele Palanke (*Remesiana*)" [Inventory of tombs from Dol near Bela Palanka (*Remesiana*)], in *Niš i Vizantija*7, ed. Miša Rakocija (Niš: Kulturni centar Niša, 2009), 56–61, figs. 1–5; Ivana Popović, "Kameje iz kasnoantičke zbirke Narodnog muzeja u Beogradu" [Cameos from late antique collection of the National Museum in Belgrade], *Zbornik Narodnog muzeja* 14, no. 1 (1992), 402–403, cat. 1, 2; Popović, "Roman Cameos," cat. 39, 40, pl. XIII; Ivana Popović, *Kasnoantički i ranovizantijski nakit od zlata u Narodnom muzeju u Beogradu* [Late antique and early

FIGURE 1.5
Cameos in medallions from Remesiana (Fausta?) (5a, 5b)
PHOTO: AFTER ANĐELKOVIĆ GRAŠAR, "IMAGE AS A WAY OF SELF-REPRESENTATION," FIGS. 2A AND 2B

with the empresses of the Antonine dynasty, namely Annia Galeria Faustina (130–176) or Bruttia Crispina (164–188),[48] but according to the archaeological context of finds and Fausta's image on coins, it is more likely that these are the images of Constantine's wife.[49] The type of coiffure is characteristic of empress images on coins, like the one seen on the bronze medallion minted in Sirmium after 316/17 when Fausta was in the zenith of her beauty.[50] This visual similarity could be a confirmation of the relationship between this type of portrait and its use for specific purposes. Craftsmen used direct models of portraits on coinage, because often glyptic workshops were in the vicinity of court mints and were probably moved in accordance with the mints. This analysis might lead toward a conclusion that imperial representations on cameos, as on coins, could express political ideas and purposes.

Empress Ariadne was on the imperial throne for more than 40 years, and influenced political and state affairs, directly or otherwise, with her choices and decisions. With a strong sense for imperial propaganda, she is one of the most visually depicted empresses. Ariadne was the oldest daughter of Emperor Leo I and Empress Verina, and after her father's death in 474 she had a crucial role in the inheritance of the imperial throne, first as an empress mother of young Leo II and later as holder of the imperial throne.[51]After the death of her first husband, Emperor Zeno, in 491, election of the new emperor depended on the choice of Adriane's new spouse, making Anastasius emperor.[52] Her image can be seen in various examples of official art throughout the empire, on coins[53] and on ivory consular diptychs,[54] as well as in sculpture.[55] The image of the imperial couple on the reverse side of coins

---

Byzantine golden jewelry in the National Museum in Belgrade] (Belgrade: Narodni muzej Beograd, 2001), cat. 71, 80; Dragoslav Srejović, ed., *Rimski carski gradovi i palate u Srbiji* [Roman imperial towns and palaces in Serbia] (Belgrade: Srpska akademija nauka i umetnosti, 1993), 81, cat. 119.

48   Popović, "Kameje iz kasnoantičke zbirke Narodnog muzeja u Beogradu," 402–403; Popović, "Roman Cameos," 216.

49   Popović, "Inventar grobnica iz Dola kod Bele Palanke (*Remesiana*)," 55–66; Srejović, *Rimski carski gradovi i palate u Srbiji*, 81.

50   Raissa Calza, *Iconografia romana imperiale da Carausio a Giuliano (287–363 d. C.)* (Rome: L'Erma di Bretschneider, 1972), 248–256, 301, 304; Francesco Gnecchi, *I medaglioni romani* I (Milan: Vlrico Hoepli, editore libraio della real casa, 1912), 22, table. 8, 10–12.

51   Cyril Mango and Roger Scott, trans., *The Chronicle of Theophanes Confessor: Byzantine and Near Eastern History AD 284–813* (Oxford: Clarendon Press, 1997), AM 5965, A.D. 472/73, 119.

52   Mango and Scott, *The Chronicle of Theophanes Confessor*, AM 5983, A.D. 490/91, 209.

53   Grierson, *Byzantine Coinage*, 176.

54   Diliana Angelova, "The Ivories of Ariadne and Ideas about Female Imperial Authority in Rome and Early Byzantium" *Gesta* 43, no. 1 (2004), 1–15.

55   Anne McClanan, *Representations of Early Byzantine Empresses: Image and Empire* (New York: Palgrave Macmillan US, 2002), 83–87, figs. 3.6–3.9.

and on consular diptychs assured the legitimacy of the inherited throne for the new emperor, Anastasius, since Ariadne possessed the status of Augusta and via marriage made Anastasius not only the August but, after her death, the successor of the previous three emperors, Zeno, Leo II, and Leo I.[56] On the steelyard weight from the National Museum in Belgrade an early Byzantine empress is depicted, and it could be Ariadne from the period of her reign with Zeno (Figure 1.6).[57] The plastically modeled bust of an empress is adorned with rich imperial ornate detail, in one hand there is a scroll and the other hand is in the gesture of blessing. Since the costume of the empress was in accordance with that of the emperor, the purple *chlamys-paludamentum* and *loros* as well were the most important parts of the imperial ceremonial ensemble, likewise several examples of depictions of empresses from the 6th century testify that golden embroidery on the *palla* and *stola* were part of the costume, although these were mostly associated with the fashion of ladies of high social rank.[58] This type of garment, along with the scroll in the hand and particular type of crown (a tall hat with diadem, both decorated with jewels, pearls and precious stones), can be seen in numerous depictions on steelyard weights from the 5th century from the territory of the eastern Mediterranean,[59] with the steelyard weight held in the *Kunsthistorisches Museum* in Vienna[60] being most similar in manner and style to the one from Belgrade. Costume, crown, and facial features can be associated with three marble sculptures of Empress Ariadne from the Louvre, Lateran, and Capitoline museums, and they are different from her depictions from diptychs where she is dressed in *paludamentum* with fibula, richly adorned collar, and crown with *pendilia*, dated to the period of her reign with Anastasius. Dating of the Belgrade weight can be assigned to the period between 474 and 491, which is supported by the stylistic characteristics

---

56   Brubaker and Tobler, "The Gender of Money: Byzantine Empresses on Coins," 580–582; McClanan, *Representations of Early Byzantine Empresses*, 82.

57   Mirjana Tatić-Ðurić, "Bronzani teg sa likom vizantijske carice" [Steelyard weight with an image of Byzantine empress], *Zbornik Narodnog muzeja* 3 (1962), 115–126, T. I, II a, III b–g; Srejović, "Kasnoantički i ranovizantijski portret," 248, cat. 254; Miroslav Vujović, "Ranovizantijskik kantar iz Beograda" [Early Byzantine steelyard weight from Belgrade], *Starinar* 64 (2014), 171–172, fig. 7a–g.

58   Maria Parani, "Defining Personal Space: Dress and Accessories in Late Antiquity," in *Objects in Context, Objects in Use: Material Spatiality in Late Antiquity*, ed. Luke Lavan, Ellen Swift, and Toon Putzeys (Leiden/Boston: Brill, 2007), 510–511; Herbert Norris, *Ancient European Costume and Fashion* (Toronto: J.M. Dent and Sons (1927), reissued Dover Publications, 1999), 148, 151–153.

59   Richard Delbrueck, *Spätantike Kaiserporträts* (Berlin: Walter de Gruyter, 1933), 229–231, pls. 122–123; McClanan, *Representations of Early Byzantine Empresses*, 29–64, figs. 2.3–2.8, 2.11–2.13, 2.16.

60   Rudolf Noll, *Von Altertum zum Mittelalter* (Vienna: Kunsthistorisches Museum, 1958), 14, cat. 16.

FIGURE 1.6
Steelyard weight from the National Museum in Belgrade (Ariadne?)
PHOTO: AFTER *STARINAR* 64/2014, BOOK COVER

of dualism of late antique and early Byzantine art, halfway between Hellenistic illusionism and oriental expressionism.[61] Because of such a rendering, it should be supposed that the artistic manner was not directed toward the copying of a real portrait but rather the convincing expression of an idea of power and authority that a specific person represents. Namely, the image of the empress on this weight can be considered as belonging to the typified representations which were in use within the imperial cult. Like bronze coins, oil lamps, and other utilitarian objects, weights were useful for spreading imperial propaganda and available to the wider audience throughout the empire. Since the empress's image was on the weights of small mass, it can be supposed that they were used for measuring valuable goods, which could have represented the figurative and spiritual presence of an empress, and her guaranty of good measure and precise balance.[62]

The wife of Emperor Justin I, Empress Euphemia, was Byzantine empress in the period between 518 and 523/524. Although in historical sources she was

---

61 Tatić-Đurić, "Bronzani teg sa likom vizantijske carice," 118–122.
62 Judith Herrin, "The Imperial Feminine in Byzantium," *Past & Present* 169 (2000), 9.

TYPE AND ARCHETYPE IN LATE ANTIQUE EMPRESS IMAGERY

described as a prostitute,[63] during her reign she was known as a pious and honored Christian.[64] According to Procopius, Empress Euphemia was not involved in state affairs,[65] which accounts for the absence of her image on coins and the fact that only one representation associated with this empress is preserved.[66] A bronze portrait from Balajnac, now housed in the National Museum in Niš, is considered to depict Euphemia (Figure 1.7).[67] This head was found in the center of the city's square, in the place where the forum was probably located, where Justinian erected statues of Justin I and Euphemia in their honor.[68] The portrait features asymmetry of face and neck, whereby the head can be considered as part of a statue, which was not positioned frontally but turned to the left, probably toward the imperial pair.[69] Ornament on the head suggests a *stemma* with *pendilia*, characteristic for the end of the 5th and first half of the 6th century.[70] The portrait is rendered idealistically with

---

63   Prokopije iz Cezareje [Procopius], *Tajna istorija* [Historia arcana], trans. Albin Vilhar, ed. Radivoj Radić (Belgrade: Dereta, 2004), 6, 17.

64   Alexander A. Vasiliev, *Justin the First: An Introduction to the Epoch of Justinian* (Cambridge, MA: Harvard University Press, 1950), 91.

65   Prokopije iz Cezareje [Procopius], *Tajna istorija* [Historia arcana], 9, 49.

66   A small gilded statue of Empress Euphemia was placed in the church of St. Euphemia, which was founded by the empress and is the place of her burial. Vasiliev, *Justin the First*, 91.

67   Srejović, "Kasnoantički i ranovizantijski portret," 248, cat. 255; Dragoslav Srejović and Aleksandar Simović, "Portret vizantijske carice iz Balajnca" [A portrait of a Byzantine empress from Balajnac], *Starinar* 9–10 (1959), 77–86; Elisabeth Alföldi-Rosenbaum, "Portrait Bust of a Young Lady of the Time of Justinian," *Metropolitan Museum Journal* 1 (1968), 26, figs. 17, 18; , Kurt Weitzmann, ed., *Age of Spirituality: Late Antique and Early Christian Art, Third to Seventh Century* (Catalogue of the exhibition at The Metropolitan Museum of Art, November 19, 1977, through February 12 1978) (New York: The Metropolitan Museum of Art, 1979), 32, cat. 26. Some scholars believe this portrait represents Empress Ariadne. McClanan, *Representations of Early Byzantine Empresses*, 87–88, fig. 3.10; Dagmar Stutzinger, "Das Bronzbildnis einer spätantiken Kaiserin aus Balajncim Museum von Nis," *Jahrbuch für Antike und Christentum* 29 (1986), 146–165.

68   Srejović and Simović, "Portret vizantijske carice iz Balajnca," 77, 85. Another opinion considers the possibility that this head was part of some hoard. Mihailo Milinković, "Neka zapažanja o ranovizantijskim utvrđenjima na jugu Srbije" [Some remarks on early Byzantine fortresses in southern Serbia], in *Niš i Vizantija* 3, ed. Miša Rakocija (Niš: Kulturni centar Niša 2005), 167.

69   Since the back of the sculpture was not finished in detail, it could be supposed that this statue was placed in some sort of niche. Srejović and Simović, "Portret vizantijske carice iz Balajnca," 79–80. Group statues of early Byzantine empresses were placed all over Constantinople. Averil Cameron and Judith Herrin, *Constantinople in the Early Eighth Century: The Parastaseis Syntomoi Chronikai* (Leiden: Brill, 1984), 29–37.

70   Holes where *pendilia* were fastened can be seen behind the ears. Srejović and Simović, "Portret vizantijske carice iz Balajnca," 79. This type of ornament is very well known from the representation of Empress Theodora from the church San Vitale. Ann M. Stout, "Jewelry as a Symbol of Status in the Roman Empire," in *The World of Roman Costume*, ed.

FIGURE 1.7
Portrait of Byzantine empress (Euphemia?)
PHOTO: *ARHEOLOŠKO BLAGO NIŠA* [ARCHAEOLOGICAL TREASURE OF NIŠ] (BELGRADE: SRPSKA AKADEMIJA NAUKA I UMETNOSTI, 2004), INSIDE BOOK COVER

a spiritual facial expression, which is in accordance with the artistic manner of early Byzantine art. The empress is represented as a younger woman and according to the crown this portrait can be dated to between 520 and 530.[71] Since the empress's death had occurred during this period, and according to Procopius she was raised to the imperial throne in 518, when she was in the late years of life,[72] it should be supposed that at the time of the portrait's production Euphemia was of a certain age, while the portrait from Balajnac represents her as a young women.[73] Identification of this portrait as Euphemia can be supported by coins of Justin I and Justinian I discovered at the same site.[74] The youthfully rendered portrait testifies to the usual aspirations in early Byzantine art. Idealized images of rulers were created, with individualism reduced on

Judith Lynn Sebesta and Larissa Bonfante (Madison: The University of Wisconsin Press, 2001), 85–86.
71 Srejović and Simović, "Portret vizantijske carice iz Balajnca," 85.
72 Prokopije iz Cezareje, *Tajna istorija*, 6, 17.
73 Weitzmann, *Age of Spirituality*, 32, cat. 26.
74 Milinković, "Neka zapažanja o ranovizantijskim utvrđenjima na jugu Srbije," 166–167.

the details. Attention was paid instead to factors which accentuated imperial dignity and improved the impression of the imperial cult image.

Empress Sophia, wife of Emperor Justin II, was on the throne between 565 and 578. As a niece of Empress Theodora, she considered herself an important factor in inheritance of the imperial throne. From 565, she was understood to be the emperor's paired ruler and partner, while a relationship with the previous empresses of the Theodosian dynasty was established via the title *Aelia*.[75] Sophia's strong personality influenced public perception of her. Unlike Theodora, she was supported and recognized as ruler by the citizens. She actively participated in many state affairs, including financial and religious politics, as when she, together with Justin, strongly supported Chalcedon Christianity.[76] She expressed her power and influence very openly, especially in the years after Justin became mentally ill and after his death.[77] All these circumstances led to her significant role in the choice of the new emperor.[78] Sophia's dominant personality can also be observed in visual culture of this period. She was represented in a pair with the emperor, Justin, on public monuments in Constantinople[79] and, in light of her piety, on the reliquary cross *Crux Vaticana*, again with Justin.[80] Although Ariadne had an important role in state politics, beyond those on diptychs, there are no surviving images where she is represented on the throne.[81] Empress Sophia was credited for everything that occurred within the empire. Therefore, it was her privilege to be represented on the throne and holding of one of the most important ruler's insignia, the *globus cruciger*. She is the first empress represented as the emperor's co-ruler in such a way, on the obverse side of bronze coins, as the most prominent and

---

75   Averil Cameron, "The Empress Sophia," *Byzantion* 45 (1975), 5–21; Lynda Garland, *Byzantine Empresses: Women and Power in Byzantium, AD 527–1204* (London: Routledge, 1999), 40–42, 47.

76   Garland, *Byzantine Empresses*, 43–47.

77   John of Ephesus, *Iohannis Ephesini Historiae Ecclesiasticae Pars Tertia*, ed. Ernest Walter Brooks, CSCO 106, Scr. Syr. 54–55 (Louvain: L. Durbecq, 1935–36, repr. 1952), 1.22, 2.4–7, 3.3.4; Evagrius, *The Ecclesiastical History of Evagrius*, ed. Joseph Bidez and Léon Parmentier (London: Methuen, 1898, repr. Amsterdam: Hakkert, 1964), 5.1, 5.11.

78   Since her son died in 565, the choice of new emperor depended on Sophia's acts and choices, this, firstly, was Tiberius and, after his death, Maurice. Mango and Scott, *The Chronicle of Theophanes Confessor*, AM 6061 (AD 568/9); John of Ephesus, *Iohannis Ephesini Historiae Ecclesiasticae Pars Tertia*, 3.5; Evagrius, *The Ecclesiastical History of Evagrius*, 5.13.

79   Averil Cameron, "The Artistic Patronage of Justin II," *Byzantion* 50 (1980), 70–71.

80   McClanan, *Representations of Early Byzantine Empresses*, 163–168, fig. 7.5.

81   Although consular ivory diptychs are identified as Empress Ariadne in most of the cases, there is also an opinion that these diptychs depict Empress Sophia. See McClanan, *Representations of Early Byzantine Empresses*, 168–178, figs. 7.6, 7.7.

FIGURE 1.8 Obverse of the coin of Emperor Justin II
PHOTO: DOCUMENTATION OF THE NATIONAL MUSEUM OF LESKOVAC, NUMISMATICS COLLECTION I/2 (INV. NI/2, 78)

convenient medium for the spreading of imperial propaganda.[82] The image contributed to the dynastic legitimacy of inheritance of the imperial throne, as well as the creation of associations with the most significant models for Christian rulers—Constantine and Helena.[83] This type of empress image can be seen on five bronze half-folles minted in Thessaloniki, discovered within the coin hoard in Caričin Grad-*Iustiniana Prima* (Figure 1.8),[84] as well as on copper coins minted in Nicomedia, from the same site.[85]

82 Grierson, *Byzantine Coinage*, 27.
83 This practice was continued by other imperial couples, such as Tiberius II Constantine and Ino Anastasia, Maurice and Constantina, Phocas and Leontia, while with Heraclius and Martina Caesars are depicted as well. Brubaker and Tobler, "The Gender of Money," 583–587.
84 Vladimir Kondić and Vladislav Popović, *Caričin Grad, utvrđeno naselje u vizantijskom Iliriku* [Caričin Grad, fortified settlement in the Byzantine Illyricum] (Belgrade: Srpska akademija nauka i umetnosti, 1977), 226, cat. 189. Alfred R. Bellinger, *Catalogue of the Byzantine Coins in the Dumbarton Oaks Collection and in the Whittemore Collection*, vol. 1, *Anastasius I to Maurice (491–602)* (Washington, DC: Dumbarton Oaks, 1966), 221, no. 66.1; 22, no. 67. 1–3.
85 Miodrag Grbić, "Vizantijski novci iz Caričina Grada" [Byzantine coins from Caričin Grad], *Starinar* 14 (1939), 109–110.

4 Conclusion

One of the best known and most intriguing archetypes is the one related to the Mother of God. For decades, scholars have argued about the existence of this religious archetype, which was supposedly spread throughout the prehistoric world, as well as whether the majority of ancient goddesses have their origin in this single figure and concept of the Mother of God.[86] Common representations of empresses are depictions of her on the throne, as sole figure or together with an emperor. The type of this representation might be based exactly on the idea of the archetype of the enthroned goddess. The iconographic pattern of the sitting goddess with child in her arms is known from the 5th millennium BC in the art of prehistoric cultures of the Danube basin.[87] Enthroned goddesses are known during antiquity, with the trappings of maternity, but also without a child. Among the most characteristic figures are Hera-Juno, Cybele, and most specifically Isis. This type of representation remains significant for the representation of the Byzantine Christian Theotokos (Mother of God) as well.[88] Thus it is not surprising that this image type was desirable for the representation of an heiress in the terrestrial realm, as a reference to the divine ones. The relationship sometimes went in the opposite direction, and it can be said that the specific image type of the Virgin Mary known as Maria Regina was created according to the iconography of early Byzantine empresses, represented

---

86 On the archetype of the goddess as source of life, death, and procreation, as a unique entity of earth and nature, and her manifestations through goddesses from the period of the Paleolithic to Greek and Roman goddesses, see Leeming and Page, *Goddess: Myths of the Female Divine*. On the origin of the Thetokos cult and its connections with the archetype of the Mother of God, see Carroll, *The Cult of the Virgin Mary*; Johanna H. Stuckey, "Ancient Mother Goddess and Fertility Cults," *Journal of the Association for Research on Mothering* 7, no. 1 (2005), 32–44, with bibliography. See also n. 5.

87 Dragoslav Srejović, *Praistorija* [Prehistory] (Belgrade: Izdavački zavod Jugoslavije, 1967), 5–23, figs. 1, 4, 8, 9, 13, 14, 16–17, and 30.

88 Iconography of mother and child, from the earliest paintings in catacombs, and later of the Theotokos and Christ on the throne, had in their focus the idea of maternity, which became even more important in the context of Incarnation and in the period after the Iconoclasm. Nikodim P. Kondakov, *Iconographia Bogomateri*, vol. 1 (St. Petersburg: Typography of the Imperial Academy of Sciences, 1914); Ioli Kalavrezou, "Images of the Mother: When the Virgin Mary Became Meter Theou," *Dumbarton Oaks Papers* 44 (1990), 165–172. On associations between Goddess Isis and the Theotokos, see Thomas F. Mathews and Norman Muller, "Isis and Mary in Early Icons," in *Images of the Mother of God: Perceptions of the Theotokos in Byzantium*, ed. Maria Vassilaki (Aldershot: Ashgate, 2005), 3–12.

with rich imperial ornate detail.[89] Over centuries, empresses had followed this maternal, enthroned type of representation which reflected their ways of life via imagery. For Christian empresses and especially for the iconography of their religious image, models of exemplary religious image besides the maternal type comprehended the idea of virginity, another important aspect of the Theotokos, which were actually exalted functions of previous virginal goddesses. For these reasons, the gesture of orans position can be associated not only with ancient female prayers but also with the type of the Theotokos and archetypes known from the iconography of ancient and prehistoric goddesses.[90] Relationships between empresses and goddesses, and later the Theotokos, in order to express political and ideological messages as well as to contribute to imperial and dynastic propaganda remained strong. These certainly resulted in the empress as antitype of this millennial heritage. Besides the same or similar iconographic patterns, attributes, and symbols associated with their images, connections between goddess and empress images were explicit, especially on coins.[91] The image of Galeria Valeria on the obverse side of coins was paired with Venus Vitrix on the reverse side, indicating the empress's role as a good mother. Because her image can be seen on cameos from *Horreum Margi*, it can be said that the important female role in the Tetrarchic system was seen in this maternal type of women who were becoming mothers to Augustus's adopted sons—Caesars.[92] Helena's role as mother was strengthened

---

89   Bissera Pentcheva, *Icons and Power: The Mother of God in Byzantium* (University Park, PA: Pennsylvania State University Press, 2010), 21–26; Maria Lidova, "The Earliest Images of Maria Regina in Rome and the Byzantine Imperial Iconography," in *Niš i Vizantija* 8, ed. Miša Rakocija (Niš: Kulturni centar Niša, 2010), 231–243.

90   Virginal aspects are characteristic for Athena and Artemis, as well as Tyche-Fortuna, which suggests protective functions, known from prehistoric cults of Near Eastern mother goddesses, while the vestiges of cults of Tyche and the Mother of God can be found even in the Akathist Hymn. Elizabeth A. Gittings, "Civic Life: Women as Embodiments of Civic Life," in *Byzantine Women and Their World*, ed. Ioli Kalavrezou (New Haven/London: Yale University Press, 2003), 36–37; Vasiliki Limberis, *Divine Heiress: The Virgin Mary and the Making of Christian Constantinople* (London: Routledge, 2002), 123–130; Bissera Pentcheva, "The Supernatural Defender of Constantinople: The Virgin and Her Icon in the Tradition of the Avar Siege," *Byzantine and Modern Greek Studies* 26 (2002), 2–41.

91   Another legend associated with Romula's mausoleum in Gamzigrad, points to the idea that Galerius created his relationship to the mother figure based on the model of Dionysus, who divinized his mother, Semele. Maja Živić, "Umetnička ostvarenja u carskoj palati" [Artistic achievements in the Imperial Palace], in *Felix Romuliana—Gamzigrad*, ed. Ivana Popović (Belgrade: Arheološki institut, 2010), 117.

92   Srejović, "Kasnoantički i ranovizantijski portret," 242, cat. 239; Popović, "Roman Cameos," 220. On the relationship between empresses and the goddess Venus, as well as the

by her image associated with *PIETAS AVGUSTES* and *SECVRITAS REIPVBLICAE* on coins. These formulas emphasized the empress's political power given to her by her son as well as the complex role of the empress mother, who provides peace, security, and happiness in the state where her son is a ruler.[93] Helena was honored as the greatest Christian mother. She became the model for future Byzantine empresses, who through their acts and images aspired to a resemblance and wished to become 'New Helenas.'[94] Just like Helena, Fausta's image was based on the maternal type, representing her as careful mother of future emperors of the Constantine dynasty, with legends on coins such as *SALVS REIPVBLICAE, SPES REIPVBLICAE*, or *PIETAS AVGVSTAE*.[95] These legends were associated with the idea of hope, security, and safety, which had been transferred via the empress's maternal image type.[96] In later times, these epithets were superseded by those of *ΕΛΠΙC* (hope) or *BEBAIA ΕΛΠΙC* (certain hope) and directly related to the Theotokos.[97]

Stereotypes of humble origins and negative attitudes toward empresses of non-noble origin which were created in ancient sources were followed and negated by glorification of the imperial maternal figure. This practice started with Galerius. With Helena, the mother of the first Christian emperor, the

---

symbolism of maternity, see Julie Langford, *Maternal Megalomania: Julia Domna and the Imperial Politics of Motherhood* (Baltimore: Johns Hopkins University Press, 2013).

93 Kalavrezou, "Images of the Mother," 166; John. P.C. Kent, *Roman Coins* (New York: Abrams, 1978), nos. 639–40, pl. 162; Drijvers, *Helena Augusta*, 41–42.

94 Jan Willem Drijvers, "Helena Augusta: Exemplary Christian Empress," *Studia Patristica* 24 (1993), 85–90; Leslie Brubaker, "Memories of Helena: Patterns in Imperial Female Matronage in the Fourth and Fifth Centuries," in *Women, Men and Eunuchs: Gender in Byzantium*, ed. Liz James (London/New York: Routledge, 1997), 52–75; Liz James, *Empresses and Power in Early Byzantium* (London: Leicester University Press, 2001), 14, 149–150, 153–154; Lynda L. Coon, *Sacred Fictions: Holy Women and Hagiography in Late Antiquity* (Philadelphia: University of Pennsylvania Press, 1997), 97–103, 118–119, 134–135; Judith Herrin, *Women in Purple: Rulers of Medieval Byzantium* (Princeton: Princeton University Press, 2001), 1–2, 21. On Constantine as an ideal Christian emperor and about his image as model for "New Constantines," see Paul Magdalino, ed., *New Constantines: The Rhythm of Imperial Renewal in Byzantium, 4th to 13th centuries: Papers from the Twenty-sixth Spring Symposium of Byzantine Studies, St Andrews, March 1992* (Cambridge: Variorum, 1994).

95 Kent, *Roman Coins*, nos. 641–642, pl. 162; Maria R. Alföldi, *Die constantinische Goldprägung: Untersuchungen zu ihrer Bedeutung für Kaiserpolitik und Hofkunst* (Mainz: Philipp von Zabern, 1963), nos. 503, 506, pl. 10, figs. 153, 154.

96 Kalavrezou, "Images of the Mother," 166.

97 Kalavrezou, "Images of the Mother," 166.

practice had a new flywheel in Christian society.[98] Empresses as spouses usually tried to discover ways of fighting these stereotypes.[99]

Stylized cameos of Fausta represent prototypes of empress images known from the Danube region, and were probably made based on patterns created in workshops along the Danube Limes.[100] Prototype here refers to the idea of the imperial mother or wife; both important for dynastic politics and propaganda.[101] Cameos, together with coins, remained as one of the most convenient means of promotion of the imperial cult. They are rendered in the style of Roman classicism, referring to the models of the 'good emperors,' in this case empresses like Faustina Minor, suggesting the relationship between Constantine and Marcus Aurelius, and an idea that Constantine's dynasty is the legitimate successor of the glory of the previous ones.[102]

Likewise, successors of Constantine's dynasty, empresses of the Theodosian house, continued to be dominant female figures, not only in affairs associated with the court and the Empire but mostly in religious issues.[103] Like Helena, they were considered models of exemplary Christian behavior. Their images could have been seen throughout the Empire. These empresses are usually represented on steelyard weights. Moreover, such representations of empresses from steelyard weights can be considered again as image (proto)types rather than images of real persons and, together with images on coins, were subjugated to the goal of promotion and spreading of the imperial cult. The last empress who could possibly have been represented on these weights is Ariadne, since after her reign minting of coins with the empress image

---

98   The gradual appearance of a female figure in politics, or in general public affairs within the empire, could probably be interpreted as a reaction to the dominant male figure and military atmosphere during the era of military emperors. Valeva, "Empresses of the Fourth and Fifth Centuries: Imperial and religious iconographies," 67–76. The negative attitude of contemporaries to Constantine's origins as "the son of a harlot" is evidenced by the ridicule from rival Maxentius on being proclaimed Caesar. Noel Lenski, "The Reign of Constantine," in *The Cambridge Companion to the Age of Constantine*, ed. Noel Lenski (New York: Cambridge University Press, 2012), 59–90, 62.

99   For more on stereotypes in historical sources, see Anđelković Grašar and Nikolić, "Stereotypes as Prototypes in the Perception of Women," 89–95, 101–102.

100   Ivana Popović, "Jewellery as an Insigne of Authority, Imperial Donation and as Personal Adornment," in *Constantine the Great and the Edict of Milan 313: The Birth of Christianity in the Roman Provinces on the Soil of Serbia*, ed. Ivana Popović and Bojana Borić-Brešković (Belgrade: National Museum Belgrade, 2013), 188–195.

101   Anđelković Grašar, "Image as a Way of Self-Representation," 333–364.

102   Popović, "Roman Cameos," 220–221.

103   Kenneth G. Holum, *Theodosian Empresses: Women and Imperial Domination in Late Antiquity* (Berkeley, Los Angeles: University of California Press, 1982).

stopped, which corresponds to the end of the distribution of weights with the empress image.[104]

An alleged monumental sculpture of Justin I and Euphemia, based on the fragmented empress's head, can be compared with fragments of the sculpture that probably represented Emperor Justinian discovered at Caričin Grad, and which possibly stood at the Roman forum.[105] This find suggests that after a time, in the territory of the central Balkans, monumental sculpture appeared in the service of imperial propaganda, signifying Justinian's golden age—*renovatio imperii*. The visual poetics of the empress Euphemia's face confirms this hypothesis, since the youthful freshness could be transferred to the image of an older empress during the restoration of the Roman Empire in the first half of the 6th century. The ideal type of ruler is achieved by using the ideology of rejuvenated emperors and empresses in visual arts, with the idea that for the whole of humankind there began a new spring.[106]

One of the most important types of imperial image was the type of co-ruler, as can be seen on coins of Justin II and Sophia. These coins represent the only known instance of an emperor and an empress seated side by side on a throne, with the *globus cruciger* and the scepter signifying Christian rulership and victory.[107] Bronze coins with such an image were widely distributed across the Empire, promoting the unity of this imperial couple. It was important for empresses that in the eyes of the public they could be distinguished as co-rulers. Hence, the type of *Koinōnia* (partner in the imperium) was created via the use of imperial tokens such as the diadem, the imperial cloak, the scepter, the *globus cruciger*, and the throne, implying that the empress's authority was comparable to that of a male co-emperor.[108]

Ultimately, it can be said that in the representation of the empress's ideological image, concepts of both type and archetype were important. The archetype could be traced all the way back to the enthroned goddesses of the prehistoric world. Via imperial attributes of the Greco-Roman goddesses it was mutually intertwined with the image of the Theotokos, with both known inherited aspects—maternal and virginal. Such a constructed empress image could be considered as a sort of antitype which refers to the goddess archetype.

---

104 McClanan, *Representations of Early Byzantine Empresses*, 29–64.

105 Perica Špehar, "The Imperial Statue from Iustiniana Prima," *Archaeology and Science* 9 (2014), 43–49.

106 Srejović, "Kasnoantički i ranovizantijski portret," 102–103, 248–249, cat. 255.

107 Diliana Angelova, *Sacred Founders: Women, Men, and Gods in the Discourse of Imperial Founding, Rome through Early Byzantium* (Berkeley: University of California Press, 2015), 191.

108 Angelova, *Sacred Founders*, 194.

Furthermore, it is clear that in accordance with dynastic legitimacy and imperial propaganda, the ideal type was the most desirable for the imperial image and as such it holds the right to promote only certain aspects of the ruler, whether male or female. By neglecting non-desirable aspects and therefore individualism, usually simplified, a unified ideal type can thus become the prototype of an imperial image—an original model which can later be replicated or imitated. The relationship between mental templates, mental models, and mental images can be traced in a non-material model which, when it enters the material world, may or may not follow the mental exemplar, as the variety in the empress imagery confirms. Typification and stereotypes again depend on the 'other,' or rather subjectification or generalization, which is directly linked with the social construct, as is clearly visible in comparing historical sources and visual testimonies about the late antique empresses. Despite the barriers and derogatory stereotypes associated with female rulers in late antiquity, images of empresses were so distinctive in terms of the ideas and ideals they possessed in public that they became prototypes for representative images of respectable noble women who wished to resemble the most important image type—that of the empress.[109]

109　On empress type and prototype, see also Anđelković Grašar, *Femina Antica Balcanica*, 25–56, 153–160; Anđelković Grašar, "Image as a Way of Self-Representation," 333–364; Sofija Petković, Milica Tapavički-Ilić, and Jelena Anđelković Grašar, "A Portrait Oil Lamp from Pontes—Possible Interpretations and Meanings within Early Byzantine Visual Culture," *Starinar* 65 (2015), 79–89.

CHAPTER 2

The *Hodegetriai*: Replicating the Icon of the Hodegetria by Means of Church Dedications

Anna Adashinskaya

To Dr. Alexei Lidov, my mentor and teacher

∴

Being proud of their history and ancient church, the inhabitants of Vasilopoulo, a village near Aetos, published on the webpage of RadioAetos[1] the early 20th-century notes of the local priest George Papaspyros, collected by the village schoolteacher Athanasios Tragomalos. Accordingly, the local Hodegetria church, called Holy Tuesday (*Agia Triti*) and erected during the Byzantine period, celebrated on the Holy Tuesday after Easter with a gathering of people from all the neighboring villages. Legend explains this strange name in the following way: More than a thousand years ago, there was a bishopric in the town of Aetos and the local bishop discovered that his flock was extremely illiterate, "distinguished from animals only by their ability to speak." He tried, therefore, to find a way to approach them and established a fair (*panagyris*), where locals, occupied normally with pasturing and hunting, could come and stay together. The fair started on the Holy Monday and continued until the Holy Tuesday when the bishop came to preach and instruct his gathered flock. Due to the multitude of people, a place slightly outside the village was chosen for the fair, and because this was conducted by the bishop, the inhabitants decided to build a church dedicated to the Hodegetria (the Virgin Guide), who was supposed to "direct the flock" to the location of the fair. The church also

---

1 Athanasios Tragomalos, "Naos Panagias Odēgētrias sto Basilopoulo Xēromerou" [The Church of Hodegetria at Basilopoulo Xeromerou] in *XeromeroPress*—https://xiromeropress.gr /εντυπωσιακό-οδοιπορικό-αφιέρωμαναό/ (accessed November 7, 2021).

© KONINKLIJKE BRILL NV, LEIDEN, 2023 | DOI:10.1163/9789004537781_004

received the name "of the Holy Tuesday," because of the time set for the gathering, and it became famous for numerous miracles of curing blind people and sterile women.

A fascinating mash-up of historical and invented elements, this folkloric story nevertheless bears ancient motifs typically encountered in Byzantine narratives associated with the miracle-working icon of the Hodegetria in Constantinople.[2] First, it recounts a fair held on a Tuesday due to a holy event, which echoes the Tuesday miracle happening amidst a fair held next to the walls of the Hodegon monastery in Constantinople. Further, the dedication of the village church to the Hodegetria is explained through her guiding qualities.[3] Like its Constantinopolitan prototype, the Hodegetria sanctuary in the village can cure blindness and sterility. Finally, the villagers' collective efforts to erect the church recall the brotherhood serving the icon in the Hodegon.

The fame of the Constantinopolitan icon generated many replicas which were venerated in a way similar to their prototype. The presence of these Hodegetria copies in different provinces and towns of the Byzantine Empire and beyond its borders led to the emergence of numerous Hodegetria-dedicated foundations, which were usually described in sources as churches or monasteries made "for the name of the Most Holy Mother of God Hodegetria." They were probably established for the purpose of imitating the Byzantine capital's veneration practices and for housing the copies of the Constantinopolitan icon. This can be inferred on the basis of their dedication, which reflects a shift in the focus of the Hodegon cult from the curing water-fountain to the icon, presumed to be painted by Evangelist Luke.[4]

Such foundations were aimed mainly at the transfer of a part of the famous icon's miracle-working power through the veneration of copies of

---

2 Of numerous studies dedicated to the Constantinopolitan Hodegetria and her veneration, the most recent and significant are: Christine Angelidi and Titos Papamastorakis, "The Veneration of the Virgin Hodegetria and the Hodegon Monastery," in *Mother of God: Representations of the Virgin in Byzantine Art*, ed. Maria Vassilaki (Athens: Benaki Museum, 2000), 373–387; Bissera Pentcheva, "The Activated Icon: The Hodegetria Procession and Mary's Eisodos," in *Images of the Mother of God: Perceptions of the Theotokos in Byzantium*, ed. Maria Vassilaki (Aldershot: Ashgate, 2005), 195–208; Alexei Lidov, "The Flying Hodegetria. The Miraculous Icon as Bearer of Sacred Space," in *The Miraculous Image in the Late Middle Ages and Renaissance*, ed. Erik Thunø and Gerhard Wolf (Rome: "L'Erma" di Bretschneider, 2004), 291–321; Bissera Pentcheva, *Icons and Power: The Mother of God in Byzantium* (University Park, PA: Pennsylvania State University Press, 2006), 109–143.

3 In the Byzantine legends, the monastery of Hodegon received its name due to the guides who directed the blind people to the miracle-working source, see Pentcheva, *Icons and Power*, 126.

4 Angelidi and Papamastorakis, "The Veneration of the Virgin Hodegetria," 377–378.

THE HODEGETRIAI 45

the icon and the imitation of rituals and religious practices associated with the Hodegetria (confraternities, processions, etc.). The existing sources and monuments more often than not offer only faint traces of these practices. The present study therefore analyzes the sizeable amount of known evidence about Hodegetria-associated foundations in an attempt to understand how the transfer of the icon-veneration functioned.[5] Moreover, this inquiry into the connections between the miracle-working image and its various imitations may shed some light on the understanding of the 'archetype—prototype—types' relationship in Byzantine pious practices and icon veneration.

Scholars have often examined these relationships within the framework of Byzantine image theory, influenced particularly by the iconoclasm controversies.[6] In fact, in the course of the controversies, the iconophiles—represented by such theologians as John of Damascus, Theodore the Studite, and Patriarch Nikephoros I—detailed particular argumentation regarding the relationship between an icon and its holy prototype as grounded in the notion of likeness. The resemblance to the prototype became the key factor for the veneration of an image, since every icon was ultimately an imprint (*typos*) of the holy figures depicted. Just as a wax seal is an impression of its seal matrix, so an icon and its prototype shared a number of common properties (the name, the appearance), though they differed in their essence.[7] In this way, the corporality of a holy figure contained all potential imprints made, whereas

---

5   A similar study concerning the Italian replicas of the Hodegetria was conducted by Michele Bacci, "The Legacy of the Hodegetria: Holy Icons and Legends between East and West," in *Images of the Mother of God: Perceptions of the Theotokos in Byzantium*, ed. Maria Vassilaki (Aldershot: Ashgate, 2005), 321–336.

6   Marie-José Baudinet, "La relation iconique à Byzance au IXe siècle d'après les Antirrhétiques de Nicéphore le Patriarche: un destin de l'aristotélisme," *Études philosophiques* 1 (1978), 85–106; Hans Georg Thümmel, *Bilderlehre und Bilderstreit: Arbeiten zur Auseinandersetzung über die Ikone und ihre Begründung vornehmlich im 8. und 9. Jahrhundert* (Würzburg: Augustinus, 1991), esp. 46–51; Kenneth Parry, *Depicting the Word: Byzantine Iconophile Thought of the Eighth and Ninth Centuries* (Leiden/Boston: Brill, 1996), 22–43; Charles Barber, *Figure and Likeness: On the Limits of Representation in Byzantine Iconoclasm* (Princeton: Princeton University Press, 2002); Kenneth Parry, "Theodore the Stoudite: The Most 'Original' Iconophile?" *Jahrbuch der Österreichischen Byzantinistik* (2018), 261–75; Kenneth Parry, "The Theological Argument about Images in the 9th Century," in *A Companion to Byzantine Iconoclasm*, ed. Mike Humphreys (Leiden/Boston: Brill), 425–463; Jaś Eisner, "Iconoclasm as Discourse: From Antiquity to Byzantium," *The Art Bulletin* 94, no. 3 (2012), 368–394; Bissera Pentcheva, *The Sensual Icon: Space, Ritual, and the Senses in Byzantium* (University Park, PA: Pennsylvania State University Press, 2014), 57–88.

7   Barber, *Figure and Likeness*, 78–80, 102, 121–123.

the imprints participated in the prototype's grace which was mediated by their likeness and could be venerated to honor the depicted figure.[8]

The iconophile grouping in the controversies, however, engineered a concept of visual hierarchy that went beyond the relationship between the icons and the holy figures, namely it pertained to the sacral superiority manifested in some images in comparison to others. If, according to Patriarch Nikephoros, "the prototypes are more honorable, and themselves are more worthy of honor,"[9] then the icons honored with divine grace through their miracle-working power become the images, worthy of further multiplication. Thus, simultaneously with the theological development of image theories, the pious practices started to distinguish the visual objects for special veneration.[10] Usually, these were the images possessing the status of *acheiropoieta*[11] or produced by the holy artists such as Evangelist Luke.[12] If, in the theological argumentation, Christ's incarnation validated the production and veneration of images, the miraculous abilities of some icons provided further historical and physical proof for their participation in the divine grace. In the attempt to acquire a part of the grace, these representations became the subjects of reproduction, since copies could retain some spiritual power of the original.

However, the Byzantines appreciated the verisimilitude of images in a different manner from a postmodern beholder.[13] The copies resembled the originals via a number of portrait features, poses, or even their names and inscriptions, whereas the actual media (wooden panel, mural painting) seemed to be irrelevant. Moreover, as the following investigation will detail, the concept of iconic resemblance included not only, and not always, the replication of visual formulas (i.e., iconography), but also the similarity of the devotional rituals, the dedication of the church spaces, and the arrangement of other church images entering into the interplay with the emulated miraculous icon. Thus the present research delves into the non-iconographic means facilitating the spread of

---

8   Barber, *Figure and Likeness*, 121–123, 138–139; Parry, "The Theological Argument," 438–441, 451.

9   Barber, *Figure and Likeness*, 99.

10   Hans Georg Thümmel, *Die Frühgeschichte der ostkirchlichen Bilderlehre: Texte und Untersuchungen zur Zeit vor dem Bilderstreit* (Berlin: De Gruyter, 1992), 174–198.

11   Michele Bacci, *The Many Faces of Christ: Portraying the Holy in the East and West, 300 to 1300* (London: Reaktion Books, 2014), 30–46.

12   Michele Bacci, *Il pennello dell'Evangelista* (Pisa: GISEM, 1994), 33–96; Michele Bacci, "With the Paintbrush of the Evangelist Luke," in *Mother of God: Representations of the Virgin in Byzantine Art*, ed. Maria Vassilaki (Athens: Benaki Museum, 2000), 79–89.

13   Alexander Kazhdan and Henry Maguire, "Byzantine Hagiographical Texts as Sources on Art," *Dumbarton Oaks Papers* 45 (1991), 1–22.

THE HODEGETRIAI   47

the Hodegetria veneration and enabling the imitation and veneration of the
famous prototype through its replicas.

The earliest and most famous case of veneration transfer is the Hodegetria
of Thessaloniki, a miraculous icon housed in a chapel of St. Sophia, which,
like its archetype, was taken daily in a solemn procession to the ambo of the
church for participation in the service, and became a palladium for the city,
possessing supernatural powers.[14] During the Norman siege of 1185, the icon
alerted the citizens about the approaching conquest by refusing to return to
its chapel.[15] In this episode, a brotherhood (η αδελφότης) carrying the icon
during the procession is also mentioned, making the similarity with the
Constantinopolitan prototype even closer.[16] Thus the prototype and replica
shared a number of common features: participation in Tuesday processions,
the icon's brotherhood, its function as a palladium, and its involvement in city
politics,[17] as well as its miraculous powers.

Even though the Constantinopolitan veneration of the Hodegetria emerged
in the post-iconoclast period,[18] it passed through several formative stages with

---

14   Jean Darrouzès, "Sainte-Sophie de Thessalonique d'après un rituel," *Revue des études byz-
      antines* 34 (1976), 45–78, concerning the placement of the chapel, see pp. 71–72. See also
      Bacci, "The Legacy of the Hodegetria," 323.
15   *Patrologia Graeca* (167 vols.), ed. J.-P. Migne (Paris, 1857–1866) [hereafter *PG*], 136, 125–127.
16   For the confraternity of the Hodegon, see Barbara Zeitler, "Cults Disrupted and Memories
      Recaptured: Events in the Life of the Icon of the Virgin Hodegetria in Constantinople," in
      Memory and Oblivion: Proceedings of the XXIX International Congress of the History of Art,
      ed. Wessel Reinink and Jeroen Stumpel (Amsterdam: Comité international d'histoire de
      l'art, 1999), 701–708; Nancy Patterson Ševčenko, "Servants of the Holy Icon," in *Byzantine
      East, Latin West: Art Historical Studies in Honor of Kurt Weitzmann*, ed. Christopher Moss
      and Katherine Kiefer (Princeton: Princeton University, 1995), 547–555.
17   Concerning politicians' appeals to the abilities of the icon in Thessaloniki, see *PG* 136, 41.
      As an expression of the political might of the icon and its protective power, Michael VIII
      introduced the procession with the Hodegetria during the triumphal entrance in the
      capital in 1261: George Pachymeres, *Relations historiques*, ed. Albert Failler and Vitalien
      Laurent, vol. 1 (Paris: Belles Lettres, 1984), 216–217; Georgios Akropolites, *Annales*, ed.
      Immanuel Bekker (Bonn: E. Weber, 1837), 196–197; Nikephoros Gregoras, *Historia byzan-
      tina*, ed. Ludwig Schopen, vol. 1 (Bonn: E. Weber, 1829), 87–88. Annmarie Weyl Carr, "Court
      Culture and Cult Icons in Middle Byzantine Constantinople," in *Byzantine Court Culture
      from 829 to 1204*, ed. Henry Maguire (Washington, DC: Dumbarton Oaks Research Library,
      1997), 97–99.
18   For the veneration of the Icon of the Hodegetria and its development during Palaiologan
      times, see Gordana Babić, "Les images byzantines et leurs degrés de signification: l'exemple
      de l'Hodigitria," in *Byzance et les images: Cycle de conferences organisé au musée du Louvre
      par le Service culturel du 5 octobre au 7 décembre 1992*, ed. André Guillou and Jannic Durand
      (Paris: Musée du Louvre, 1994), 189–222; Angelidi and Papamastorakis, "The Veneration of
      the Virgin Hodegetria," 373–387; Christine Angelidi and Titos Papamastorakis, "Picturing
      the Spiritual Protector: From Blachernitissa to Hodegetria," in *Images of the Mother of*

emphases on different aspects of the veneration practices: a place centered around the blindness-curing water source, the palladium-housing monastery, or a pilgrimage center, where the brotherhood served the Virgin's miraculous image. During the Palaiologan period, the veneration of the Hodegetria icon became widespread, the origin and supernatural power of the icon having been described in a corpus of miracle stories.[19] It is possible that after the dedication of the month of August to the Hodegetria icon (1297) and the re-establishment of its public cult under the Palaiologoi,[20] the veneration of the image spread throughout the empire, leading to the establishment of numerous churches dedicated to the Hodegetria. These foundations varied in size and importance from family chapels on the distant Byzantine periphery to rich and spacious complexes as in Mystras.

It is impossible to consider all cases of churches dedicated to the Hodegetria across the Byzantine Commonwealth within the framework of a single article. Instead, I will analyze a number of selected examples representing the Byzantine urban milieu and rural periphery, and the Serbian and Bulgarian states, as well as foreign-ruled Greek territories. In doing so, I shall try to find the motivations behind the practice of dedicating ecclesiastic institutions to the Hodegetria.

The earliest monastery with such a dedication attested outside of Constantinople is a convent in Jerusalem.[21] Its dedication was first mentioned in 1353/54 by an anonymous Byzantine pilgrim,[22] who was also the first to account for the holy event marked by this foundation, that is to say its establishment

---

God: Perceptions of the Theotokos in Byzantium, ed. Maria Vassilaki (Aldershot: Ashgate, 2005), 209–223.

19 Published by Christine Angelidi, "Un texte patriographique et édifiant: Le 'Discours narratif' sur les Hodègoi," Revue des études byzantines 52 (1994), 113–149.

20 On the dedication of the entire month of August to the Virgin, see Venance Grumel, "Le mois de Marie des Byzantins," Échos d'Orient 31 (1932), 257–269. The decree of Andronikos II concerning this legislation came down to us from works of Nikephoros Choumnos, see Jean François Boissonade, ed., Anecdota Græca e codicibus regiis descripsit annotatione illustravit, vol. 2 (Paris: Ex Regio Typographeo, 1830), 107–136. Concerning the veneration of the image in the Palaiologan era, see Angelidi and Papamastorakis, "The Veneration of the Virgin Hodegetria," 83–85.

21 Denys Pringle, The Churches of the Crusader Kingdom of Jerusalem, vol. 3, The City of Jerusalem (Cambridge: Cambridge University Press, 1993), 314–316.

22 Afanasios Papadopoulos-Kerameus and Gabriil Destunis, "Kratkij rasskaz o svjatyh mestah Ierusalima i o Strastjah Gospoda nashego Iisusa Hrista i o drugih bezymjannogo, napisannyj v 1253/4 g." [A short narration about the holy places of Jerusalem and about the Passions of our Lord Jesus Christ and about other things, anonymous, written in 1253/4], Pravoslavnyj palestinskij sbornik 40 (1895), 7. Translation in Denys Pringle, Pilgrimage to Jerusalem and the Holy Land, 1187–1291 (New York: Routledge, 2012), 193.

THE HODEGETRIAI

on the site where the Virgin stood during the Crucifixion.[23] This is confirmed by another anonymous Byzantine pilgrim, who visited the city between 1250 and 1350. This source is somewhat more specific about the place, calling it the monastery "where the nuns are living" and ascertaining that it is found at "one stadium from the holy Sepulcher."[24] In the 15th century, the Russian deacon Zosima mentioned the church of the Hodegetria in Jerusalem, adding that, in his time, it was situated inside a monastery inhabited by monks.[25] A number of 16th-century Greek travelers, namely the authors of the *Narration about the Holy Sepulchre*, of the poetic *Proskynetarion*, and of the *Narration about Jerusalem*, noted that the monastery was in fact a Greek nunnery placed to the west of the Holy Sepulchre.[26] They all confirmed that it was the place from where the Theotokos viewed the Passion, and added that it was destroyed by the Arabs in the middle of the 16th century. Nowadays, the place is associated with the nunnery of Megale Panagia (Dair al-Banat), dedicated to the Presentation of the Virgin.[27] However, Gustav Kühnel[28] has suggested that the nunnery was dedicated initially to the Hodegetria as it might have had a copy of the famous icon.

One fact should be underlined: the connection established between the monastery's dedication to the Hodegetria and the evangelic event commemorated in that place of the Holy City. As all the pilgrims agree, the nunnery was built on the spot from which the Virgin witnessed the suffering and death of her son on Golgotha. According to Alexei Lidov's observation, as a bilateral icon with a Crucifixion on its back, the two images of the Constantinopolitan Hodegetria merged during the Tuesday processions into a complex spatial

---

23   Information about the Greek monastery as standing on the place occupied by the Virgin during the Crucifixion is given only by the authors belonging to the Orthodox tradition. The Western travelers referred to the location of the Virgin during the Crucifixion as being situated "on the very spot where the altar of the church" of Mary Latina is. See Saewulf's account in Robert Willis, *The Architectural History of the Church of the Holy Sepulchre at Jerusalem* (London: Parker, 1849), 144–146. On the church of Mary Latina, see Pringle, *The Churches of the Crusader Kingdom of Jerusalem*, vol. 3, 236–243.

24   *PG* 133, 981; Pringle, *Pilgrimage to Jerusalem*, 383.

25   Nikolai Prokofiev, ed., *Kniga hozhenij. Zapiski russkih puteshestvennikov XI–XV vv.* [The book of pilgrimages. Narrations of the Russian travelers in the 14th to 15th centuries] (Moscow: Sovetskaya Rossiya, 1984), 310.

26   Afanasios Papadopoulos-Kerameus, "Vosem' grecheskih opisanij svjatyh mest XIV, XV i XVI vv." [Eight Greek descriptions of the holy places of the 14th, 15th and 16th centuries], *Pravoslavnyj palestinskij sbornik* 56 (1903), 28, 71, 123.

27   Pringle, *The Churches of the Crusader Kingdom of Jerusalem*, vol. 3, 314.

28   Gustav Kühnel, *Wall Painting of the Latin Kingdom of Jerusalem* (Berlin: Mann Verlag, 1988), 27–28.

image perceived by beholders "as a single one."[29] This complex image served as the model for several bilateral icons with the Hodegetria on the front panel and the Crucifixion or the Man of Sorrows on the back.[30]

In this sense, one may suggest that the dedication to the Hodegetria of the Jerusalem monastery was motivated by its legendary location inside the city's Bible-related topography (the place from where the Virgin witnessed the Crucifixion), and by the link between this location and the theological concept expressed by the double-sided icon of the Hodegetria (juxtaposition of the Mother's and Christ's sacrifices). An earlier description of the Virgin's monastery in the same location, made in 1106 by the Russian abbot Daniel,[31] coincides in all details with the known facts about the foundation; the only difference is that Daniel does not mention the Hodegetria dedication. This may suggest that the Jerusalem convent received its appellation after the image of Constantinople, between 1106 and 1253/54, on account of the similarity between topographic and iconographic theological concepts.

A number of images bearing the epithet 'Η ΟΔΗΓΗΤΡΙΑ' (A Guide) appeared in the empire's different regions at about the same time as the icon in Constantinople started to receive imperial and aristocratic donations, to participate in royal commemorative ceremonies in the Pantokrator monastery, to protect the capital's walls, to witness imperial oaths, and to be considered

---

29   Lidov, "The Flying Hodegetria," 286–288.

30   Demetrios Pallas, *Die Passion und Bestattung Christi in Byzanz. Der Ritus—das Bild* (Munich: Institut für Byzantinistik und neugriechische Philologie der Universität, 1965), 308–323.

31   Gelian Prochorov, ed., "'Hozhdenie' igumena Daniila" [The 'pilgrimage' of the Hegoumenos Daniil], in *Pamjatniki literatury Drevnej Rusi. XII vek* (Moscow: Chudozhestvennaya Literatura, 1980), 25–114 (Published at Elektronnye publikacii Instituta russkoj literatury, http://lib.pushkinskijdom.ru/Default.aspx?tabid=4934# (accessed on June 16, 2021)): "И ту есть мѣсто на пригории; … И пришедше на мѣсто то святаа Богородица, и узрѣ с горы тоя сына своего распинаема на крестѣ, и видѣвши, ужасеся, и согнуся, и сѣде, печалию и рыданиемъ одръжима бѣаше … И то мѣсто есть подаль от Распятия Христова, яко полутораста сажень есть на запад лиць мѣсто то от Распятия Христова. Имя мѣсту тому Спудий, иже ся протолкуеть Тщание Богородично. И есть на мѣстѣ томъ нынѣ манастырь, церкви Святаа Богородица клѣтьски верхъ въсперенъ." Translation: "And here on a rise is the place … And when the holy mother of God came to this place and saw from this hill her son crucified on a cross she was horror-stricken at what she saw and sank down and was overcome with grief and sobbing … And this place is a little way from the (place of) Christ's crucifixion, about 150 fathoms to the west; the name of the place is Spudii (gr. *spoudē*) which is translated as 'the hastening of the Mother of God.' And there is now a monastery on that place and a very fine tall square church built in honour of the holy Mother of God." The translation is published in John Wilkinson, Joyce Hill, and William Francis Ryan, eds., *Jerusalem Pilgrimage, 1099–1185* (London: Hakluyt Society, 1988), 129–130.

THE HODEGETRIAI

to have been painted by Evangelist Luke.[32] It is precisely this shift from simple replication of the icon in the same medium (wooden board) to the depiction of Mary in mural decoration, labeled as Hodegetria, that indicates a new stage in the cult's development. This is when the Hodegetria icon started to be understood not only as miracle-working object, but also as a concept, as a reference to certain qualities of the Theotokos.

By the late 11th or early 12th century, both mural images and icons of the Hodegetria were starting to be venerated in southern Italy. The crypt of Santa Maria delle Grazie, situated below the Sicilian Cappella Palatina, dates back to 1105–1130. It was the place of Roger II's coronation as king of Sicily,[33] but its main purpose was to contain royal burials.[34] The Enthroned Virgin with Child on the northeastern wall is the only piece of original decoration.[35] The Virgin's depiction bears the identifying inscription 'Ἡ ΟΔΗΓΙ[ΤΡΙΑ]' and, stylistically, belongs to Byzantine-Sicilian art of around 1100.

Bearing the same epithet, the image of the Virgin found its place among the mosaic decoration in the upper chapel as well. On the northern side of the eastern wall, above the balcony arranged by Roger II for himself in the northern aisle, there is the standing figure of the Virgin Ἡ ΟΔΗΓΗΤΡΙΑ with the Child, whose blessing is addressed to Saint John the Baptist. The scroll in this depiction with the text "Ἴδε ὁ ἀμνός του Θ(εο)ύ ὁ αἴρων τὴν ἁμαρτίαν του κόσμου" (Look, the Lamb of God, who takes away the sin of the world, Jh. 1:29)[36] creates, thus, a kind of dialogue between these figures, which brings to mind the sacrifice of Christ taking place in the proscomidion below.

Even though the two full-length images of the Virgin from the Cappella Palatina do not strictly belong to the type of Hodegetria, they testify nonetheless to the presence of the veneration of this particular image in Sicily during this period. The replica of the Hodegetria was brought there by Batholomew di

---

32   Angelidi and Papamastorakis, "The Veneration of the Virgin Hodegetriai," 377–385.

33   Thomas Dittelbach, "La chiesa inferiore," in *La Cappella Palatina a Palermo*, ed. Beat Brenk (Modena: Panini Editore, 2010), 283–293, esp. 283, considers that the church was built immediately after the royal court was moved from Messina to Palermo, while William Tronzo, "L'architettura della Cappella Palatina," in *La Cappella Palatina a Palermo*, ed. Beat Brenk (Modena: Panini Editore, 2010), 79–99 argues for 1102–1115 as the construction dates of the Palatine chapel.

34   Dittelbach, "La chiesa inferiorei," 284, considers that it was intended for William II, while Tronzo, "L'architettura," 93, suggests that it was a burial place for Roger II.

35   Antonina Testa, "L'affresco dell' Odigitria nella Cappella Palatina di Palermo," *Sicilia archeologica* 28, no. 87/88/89 (1995), 125–128.

36   Ernst Kitzinger, "The Mosaics of the Cappella Palatina in Palermo: An Essay on the Choice and Arrangement of Subjects," *The Art Bulletin* 31 (Dec. 1949), 269–292 (273, 285).

Simeri, who founded a monastery dedicated to the Hodegetria (Nea Odigitria)[37] and placed it under Roger II's royal patronage.[38] Thus the appearance in the royal frescoes and mosaics of the Virgin with this epithet was motivated by the veneration of the mobile image which replicated the Constantinopolitan prototype. Simultaneously, the Virgin's epithet can be explained through the theological understanding of the Hodegetria icon: in both the crypt and upper chapel, the Hodegetria image is placed near the proskomedia, where preparation of bread and wine for liturgical sacrifice takes place. Hence, as pointed out previously, the central concept of redemptive sacrifice unifies the iconography of the Hodegetria with the rituals taking place in the prothesis.

The veneration of the Hodegetria in Cyprus, too, dates back to the 12th century, when an image of the Virgin inscribed 'Η ΟΔΙΓΙΤΡΗΑ' appeared in the murals of the church of St. Nicholas tis Stegis.[39] Nowadays, there are no widely venerated replicas of the Constantinopolitan icon in Cyprus, but traces of its veneration are preserved in the dedications of churches, in icons belonging to the Hodegetria iconographic type (e.g., the icon from the Panagia Moutoullas church),[40] and in a later veneration of the Kykkotissa icon,[41] which was invested with the Hodegetria's power and meaning. In the 1422 narrative on the Kykkos icon created by the Cypriot hieromonk Gregory of Kykkos, many features and miracles echo the much-venerated Hodegetria.[42]

Even though it was built during the Lusignan and Venetian periods,[43] the main cathedral of the Orthodox population in Leukosia/Nicosia, known today as Bedestan, was dedicated to the Hodegetria, starting at least from

---

37 Bacci, "The legacy of the Hodegetria," 324; Walther Holtzmann, "Die altesten Urkunden des Klosters S. Maria del Patir," *Byzantinische Zeitschrift* 26 (1926), 328–351.

38 Alessandro Pratesi, "Per un nuovo esame della 'Carta di Rossano'," *Studi Medievali* 11 (1970), 209–235, esp. 216–217.

39 Andreas Stylianou and Judith Stylianou, *The Painted Churches of Cyprus: Treasures of Byzantine Art* (Nicosia: A.G. Leventis Foundation, 1985), 62.

40 Doula Mouriki, *Thirteenth Century Icon Painting in Cyprus* (Athens: Gennadius Library, 1986), 63ff. fig. 26.

41 The Kykkos icon's cult was developed starting from the 15th century, though the icon itself is mentioned for the first time in 1365. John Hackett, *A History of the Orthodox Church of Cyprus* (London: Methuen and Co., 1901), 331–335; Annmarie Weyl Carr, "Reflections on the Life of an Icon: The Eleousa of Kikkos," *Epetērida Kentrou Meletōn Ieras Monēs Kykkou* 6 (2004), 103–162.

42 Bacci, "With the Paintbrush of the Evangelist Luke," 87.

43 Michalis Olympios, "Resting in Pieces: Gothic Architecture in Cyprus in the Long Fifteenth Century," in *Medieval Cyprus: A Place of Cultural Encounter*, ed. Sabine Rogge and Michael Grünbart (Münster: Waxmann, 2015), 340–343; Tassos Papacostas, "In Search of a Lost Byzantine Monument: Saint Sophia of Nicosia," *Epetērida tou Kentrou Epistimonikōn Ereunōn* 31 (2005), 11–37.

the 14th century. The notes in the *Parisinus graecus* 1589 indicate that, during the 14th century, the Greek Orthodox priests George, Basil, and Stylianos Horkomosiates inherited the office in the cathedral of the Hodegetria in Leukosia,[44] whereas a note in the *Vaticanus graecus* 2194 testifies that the Cathedral of the Hodegetria at about the same time also had its confraternity (συναδέλφοι τῆς ἁγίας ἐκκλησίας),[45] typically established in cases of veneration of Hodegetria copies.[46]

The parochial church in Arediou, known as the church of the Hodegetria, celebrates the Presentation of the Theotokos as its patron feast. Even though no wooden icons of the Virgin are preserved in the church, there is a depiction of a Hodegetria-type figure on the southern wall, which can be dated to the 14th century. This image reproduces the iconographic pattern of an earlier fresco discovered underneath.[47] As the focus of local veneration of the Virgin, the church is surrounded by numerous folkloric legends associated with the protection of Cyprus by the Mother of God.[48] Similar legends are connected with the 15th-century Hodegetria church in the village of Choli, which is furnished with a contemporary icon of the Hodegetria type.[49] Finally, a 16th-century chapel added to the 13th-century main church of Panagia Katholiki in the village of Kouklia[50] was possibly dedicated to the Hodegetria as well.[51]

---

44 Jean Darrouzès, "Notes pour servir à l'histoire de Chypre (premier article)," *Kypriakai Spoudai* 17 (1953), 89–90; Erich Trapp, Rainer Walther, and Christian Gastgeber, eds., *Prosopographisches Lexikon der Palaiologenzeit*, CD-Rom Version (Vienna: Verlag der Österreichischen Akademie der Wissenschaften, 2001) [hereafter *PLP*], nos. 21106, 21107, 21109.

45 Jean Darrouzès, "Notes pour servir à l'histoire de Chypre (deuxième article)," *Kypriakai Spoudai* 20 (1956), 55.

46 Ševčenko, "Servants of the Holy Icon," 547–551.

47 M. Loulloupis, *Annual Report of the Director of the Department of Antiquities, Cyprus, for the year 1988* (Nicosia: Department of Antiquities, 1990), 18.

48 Georgios Paganes, "Ekklesia tēs Panagias tēs Odēgētrias," [Church of Panagia Hodegetria] at *Koinotiko Symboulio Aredou*—http://arediou.com/portfolio-item/thriskeftiki-zoi/#toggle -id-2 (accessed November 7, 2021).

49 Gwynneth der Parthog, *Medieval Cyprus: A Guide to the Byzantine and Latin Monuments* (Lefkosia: Moufflon Publications, 2006), 101.

50 Stylianou and Stylianou, *The Painted Churches of Cyprus*, 233. The authors mention the church under its present-day name as Panagia Katholikē and date it entirely within the 16th century. M. Loulloupis (*Annual Report*, 27) distinguishes several stages in the building of the church and dates the additional chapel to the 16th century.

51 The present-day tradition mentions that the chapel of the Katholikē church was associated with the Hodegetria icon. See the official site of the Kouklia village—http://www.kouk lia.org.cy/churches_odigitria.shtm (accessed June 14, 2021). However, the tradition also mentions several other epithets for the venerated Virgin in this village: Chrysopolitissa,

Like Thessaloniki, the main urban centers of the Byzantine Empire must have had their own replicas of the Protectress of the City, at least as it can be understood from the known church dedications.

One of the most important Byzantine towns of the Palaiologan period,[52] Mystras, had a *katholikon* of the Brontocheion monastery dedicated to the Hodegetria. Initially, the monastery was dedicated to Sts. Theodores, whose church was the first *katholikon*:[53] in 1296, a note in the *Parisinus graecus* 708 mentions Pachomios,[54] the future founder of the Hodegetria church, as the *hegoumenos* of Sts. Theodores.[55] The first mention of the Brontocheion monastery as associated with the Virgin may have come from the period of the second patriarchate of Athanasios I (1303–1309), when Pachomios received the titles of *archimandrite* and *protosynkellos*.[56] The note of Nikephoros Moschopoulos

---

Galaktophorousa, Aphroditissa (Franz Georg Maier and Vassos Karageorghis, *Paphos: History and Archaeology* (Nicosia: A.G. Leventis Foundation, 1984), 354–355).

52   On the history and development of Mystras and its importance in the Palaiologan epoch, see Manolis Chatzidakis, *Mystras: The Medieval City and the Castle* (Athens: Ekdotikē Athenēs, 1981); Despoina Evgenidou, ed., *The City of Mystras*, Mystras, August 2001–January 2002, exhibition catalogue (Athens: Hellenic Ministry of Culture, 2001); Titos Papamastorakis, "Myzithras of the Byzantines / Mistra to Byzantinists," in *Byzantines poleis 8os–15os aiōnas. Prooptikes tēs ereunas kai nees ermēneutikes prosengiseis*, ed. Tonia Kiousopoulou (Rethymnon: Panepistēmiou Krētēs, 2012), 277–196; Sophia Kalopissi-Verti, "Mistra. A Fortified Late Byzantine Settlement," in *Heaven and Earth*, vol. 2, *Cities and Countryside in Byzantine Greece*, ed. Jenny Albani and Eugenia Chalkia (Athens: Hellenic Ministry of Culture, 2013), 224–239.

53   Anastasios Orlandos, "Daniēl o prōtos ktitōr tōn Hagiōn Theodōrōn tou Mystra," [Daniel, the first founder of Saints Theodore of Mystras], *Epetēris Etaireias Byzantinōn Spoudōn* 12 (1936), 443–448.

54   *PLP*, no. 22220.

55   Rhodoniki Etzeoglou, *O naos tēs Odēgētrias tou Brontochiou ston Mystra. Oi toichographies tou narthēka* [The church of the Hodegetria of Vrontochion in Mystras. The murals of the narthex] (Athens: Akademia Athenōn, 2013), 30. Pachomios is mentioned in the epigram and dedicatory colophon of a manuscript with homilies by Saint John Chrysostom, which was copied by the nomikos Basilakes in 1296, see Spyridon Lampros, "Lakedaimónioi vivliográfoi kaí ktítores kodíkon katá toús mésous aiónas kaí epí tourkokratías" [Lacedaemonian bibliographers and commissioners of codices during the Middle Ages and Turkish domination], *Neos Hellēnomnēmōn* 4, no. 2 (1907), 152–187, 160–160b.

56   The *sigillion* of Athanasios is not preserved, but is mentioned in another document of 1366 (Vitalien Laurent, *Les regestes des actes du Patriarcat de Constantinople*, vol. 1, fasc. 4, *Les Regestes de 1208 à 1309* (Paris: Institut français d'études byzantines, 1971), 464–465, no. 1672; Franz Miklosich and Josef Müller, eds., *Acta et Diplomata graeca medii aevi sacra et profana* (Vienna: Carolus Gerold, 1860), vol. 1, 479–483) with a possible quotation of the earlier text, see Titos Papamastorakis, "Reflections of Constantinople: The Iconographic Program of the South Portico of the Hodegetria Church, Mystras," in *Viewing the Morea: Land and People in the Late Medieval Peloponnese*, ed. Sharon Gerstel (Washington, DC: Harvard University Press, 2013), 372–374; Etzeoglou, *O naos tēs Odēgētrias*, 31.

THE HODEGETRIAI

on the Gospel book[57] given to "the monastery of the Most Holy Theotokos Brontocheion" can establish with certainty the year 1311 as the *terminus ante quem* for the new dedication of the foundation. However, neither source refers to Brontocheion as the Hodegetria monastery, but rather as a foundation dedicated to the Virgin. Subsequently, the first reference to Brontocheion as the monastery "ἐπ' ὀνόματι ... τῆς πανυπεράγνου ὑπεραγίας Θεοτόκου τῆς ὁδηγήτριας" [in the name ... of the most pure and holy Theotokos Hodegetria][58] appears in the chrysobull of 1314–1315 by Andronikos II, which is inscribed on the wall of the southern chapel of the church's narthex.

Even though they are well preserved, the murals of the church do not contain any image of the Virgin inscribed as Hodegetria. In the frescoes of the narthex, there is a depiction of the Virgin belonging to the Zoodochos Pege type,[59] while in the southern gallery there are the extended cycles of Christ's Childhood and the Virgin's Dormition.[60] These may be associated with the famous Constantinopolitan cults of the Virgin from Zoodochos Pege monastery, Chalkoprateia, and Blachernai. There is also an image of the Virgin with Child, both accepting the model of the foundation from the hands of a monk (presumably Pachomios himself) in the arcosolium of the northern chapel.[61] This funerary image of the Virgin preserves the iconographic type of the Hodegetria, but it is not labeled in this way. One may, therefore, assume that

---

57 Athanasios Papadopoulos-Kerameus, "Nikēphoros Moschopoulos," *Byzantinische Zeitschrift* 12 (1903), 220.

58 Gabriel Millet, "Inscriptions byzantines de Mistra," *Bulletin de correspondence hellénique* 23 (1899), 102. For the same expression encountered in the chrysobulls of 1319, 1320, 1322, see Millet, "Inscriptions byzantines de Mistra," 108, 113, 114, 115, 116.

59 Rhodoniki Etzeoglou, "The Cult of the Virgin Zoodochos Pege at Mistra," in *Images of the Mother of God: Perceptions of the Theotokos in Byzantium*, ed. Maria Vassilaki (Aldershot: Ashgate, 2005), 239–250.

60 Papamastorakis, "Reflections of Constantinople," 371–395, proposes to date the frescoes of the southern gallery to the same period as the frescoes of the chrysobull chapel, i.e., soon after 1322. Chatzidakis, *The Medieval City and the Castle*, 67, proposed a date *c.*1366; while Anastasios Tantsis ("Ē chronologēsē tou naou tēs Odēgētrias sto Mystra" [The dating of the Hodegetria church in Mystras], *Byzantiaka* 31 (2014), 179–204) proposes to date the entire gallery to *c.*1407.

61 Titos Papamastorakis, "Epitymbies parastaseis kata tē mesē kai ysterē byzantine periodo" [Funeral representations in the Middle and Late Byzantine periods], *Deltion tēs Christianikēs Archaiologikēs Hetaireias* 19 (1996–1997), 290–293; Ursula Weissbrod, *"Hier liegt der Knecht Gottes," Gräber in byzantinischen Kirchen und ihr Dekor (11. bis 15. Jahrhundert)* (Wiesbaden: Harrassowitz Verlag, 2003), 106–108. Rhodoniki Etzeoglou, "Quelques remarques sur les portraits figurés dans les églises de Mistra," *Jahrbuch der Österreichischen Byzantinistik* 32, no. 5 (1982), 514–515. However, Anastasios Tantsis ("Ē chronologēsē tou naou," 190–193) considers that the depicted monk is the *despotes* of Mystras Theodore I Palaiologos (*PLP*, no. 21460).

the *katholikon* was initially dedicated simply to the Virgin, and, perhaps, celebrated the Dormition as its patron feast, while the dedication to the Hodegetria appeared around 1315. A possible explanation for this could be the presence of a movable and much-venerated replica of the Constantinopolitan prototype, which was kept in the *katholikon*, but is no longer preserved. Moreover, one may even agree with the hypothesis of Elias Anagnostakis who, regarding one case of litigation initiated by the nun Euphrosyne-Marina over a Hodegetria icon, suggested that this icon (which was appropriated by Nikephoros Moschopoulos) was housed in the Brontocheion monastery and prompted the Hodegetria veneration there.[62]

The presence of a church dedicated to the Hodegetria in another important urban center, Monembasia, is attested by several sources which call the foundation 'H OΔHΓHTPIA.' The earliest mention of the church is found in the Life of Saint Martha, the monastery's *hougoumene*, written in the 10th century by Archbishop Paul.[63] A note by Ioannes Likinios dated to 1606 in the Kutlumus 220 manuscript recounts that the Hodegetria church was then 456 years old so, consequently, it was built in 1150.[64] Finally, compiling in the 16th century the genealogy of his wife, Carola Kantakouzene de Flory, Hugues Busac mentions that a certain ruler was buried in the Hodegetria church on the hill.[65] One can add to this the evidence of a graffito that Haris Kalligas suggested identified the Hodegetria church in Monembasia as the one currently dedicated to Saint Sophia.[66] According to local tradition preserved in the *Synaxarion* of Zakynthos, Andronikos II sent a lavishly-decorated Hodegetria icon, later

---

62 Elias Anagnostakes, "Apo tēn eikona tēs monachēs Euphrosynēs ston bio tōn Hosiōn tou Megalou Spēlaiou: Ē istoria mias kataskeuēs" [From the image of the nun Euphrosyne to the Life of the saints of Megale Spelaion: The History of one foundation], in *Monachismos stēn Peloponnēso, 40s–150s ai.* [The monasticism at Peloponnesus, the 4th to the 15th century], ed. Boula Konti (Athens: Institute for Byzantine Research, 2004), 179–189. The hypothesis is supported by Titos Papamastorakis ("Reflections of Constantinople," 393).

63 "περὶ τῆς μακάριας Μάρθας, τῆς Ἡγουμένης τοῦ πανσέπτου ναοῦ τῆς ὑπεραγίας Θεοτόκου ἐν τῇ θεοφρουρήτῳ πόλει Μονεμβασίας, κάτωθεν τῆς Ὀδηγητρίας τοῦ αὐτοῦ κάστρου"—Athanasios Kominis, "Paolo di Monembasia," *Byzantion* 29/30 (1959–1960), 247; Haris Kalligas, "The Church of Haghia Sophia at Monemvasia: Its Date and Dedication," *Deltion tēs Christianikēs Archailogikēs Hetaireias* 9 (1977–1979), 218.

64 Peter Schreiner, *Die Byzantinischen Kleinchroniken*, Corpus Fontium Historiae Byzantinae 12/1, vol. 1 (Vienna: Österreichische Akademie der Wissenschaften, 1975), 320, no. 41.6.

65 "vasilef ehi enan thamenon is ton goulan tis Monovasias is tin Odiitrian eclisian Omorfi"—Edith Brayer, Paul Lemerle, and Vitalien Laurent, "Le Vaticanus latinus 4789: histoire et alliances des Cantacuzènes aux XIVe–XVe Siècles," *Revue des études byzantines* 9 (1951), 71, 74.

66 Kalligas, "The Church of Haghia Sophia;" Haris Kalligas, *Monemvasia: Byzantine City State* (London: Routledge, 2010), 19–21, 118–121.

THE HODEGETRIAI   57

called 'Monembasiotissa,' to the city as its guardian in the absence of the ruler.[67] Therefore, the city had a church dedicated to the Hodegetria icon by the second half of the 10th century. This church was probably rebuilt around 1150. It was used to house the copy of the Constantinopolitan palladium and it contained at least one royal burial. The presence of the Hodegetria icon was a matter of identity for the inhabitants of Monembasia. In the composite manuscript Kutlumus 220 (its different parts are dated to the 15th–17th centuries) dedicated in large part to the history of the city,[68] one can find the narration about Pulcheria and the discovery of the Hodegetria icon.[69] This 10th-century church which dominates the town from the top of a hill can be considered the earliest known Hodegetria foundation. One cannot be sure that it was established for housing an icon, as the latter appears only in a story from Palaiologan times; however, it is possible to state that the legend of the miracle-working palladium was a part of the self-identity of the inhabitants of Monembasia as well as local history.

Even though no material evidence has yet been found, the Proceedings of the Patriarchal Synod attest in 1340 that another important imperial town, Didymoteichon,[70] had its own monastery "in the glorious name of the Most Holy Mistress and Mother of God Hodegetria."[71]

The cult could be transferred from the center to the periphery by exiled clergy and refugees. This was the case of Neilos Erichiotes, initially a monk of the Stoudios monastery,[72] who was forced to leave the capital after opposing the unionist policies of Michael VIII. After his pilgrimage to the Holy Land, Neilos settled in Epiros, where he established a monastery dedicated to the Hodegetria (Geromeri), as is testified by his last will of 1337, confirmed by *despotes* John II Orsini.[73] Replicating the setting of Constantinopolitan

---

67   Kalligas, *Monemvasia*, 32; Nikolaos Katramis, *Philologika analekta ek Zakynthou* [Philological collection from Zakynthos] (Zakynthos, 1880), 188.

68   For the history and composition of the manuscript, see Paul Lemerle, "La Chronique improprement dite de Monemvasie: le contexte historique et légendaire," *Revue des études byzantines* 21 (1963), 6.

69   Spyridon Lampros, "Treis paradoxographikai diēseis" [Three Mirabilia narrations about Peloponnesos], *Neos Hellēnomnēmōn* 4, no. 2 (1907), 129–151.

70   For the history and importance of the town, see Peter Soustal, *Thrakien* (*Thrake, Rhodope und Haimimontos*) (Vienna: Österreichische Akademie der Wissenschaften, 1991), 240–244.

71   Miklosich and Müller, *Acta et Diplomata*, vol. 1, 198–199.

72   Donald M. Nicol, *The Despotate of Epiros, 1267–1479: A Contribution to the History of Greece in the Middle Ages* (Cambridge: Cambridge University Press, 1984), 243–244.

73   *Geromeri: Testament of Neilos Erichiotes for the Monastery of the Mother of God Hodegetria in Geromeri*, trans. George Dennis, in *Byzantine Monastic Foundation Documents: A*

veneration, he himself might have introduced a copy of the miracle-working icon: judging by its double-sided format, the preserved 14th-century replica inscribed as 'Η ΟΔΗΓΗΤΡΙΑ,'[74] was a processional icon. This icon is still venerated in the *katholikon* dedicated to the Dormition of the Theotokos. In addition to the Dormition, the monastery also celebrates the Tuesday of the Holy Week,[75] which nowadays no longer has a connection with the Hodegetria (it celebrates instead Ss. Raphael, Nicholas, and Eirine of Lesbos). Therefore, the monastery preserved not only the dedication and replica of the icon but also some pious customs connected with the Hodegetria prototype and the Tuesday miracle.

The empire's distant, rural areas developed their own practices associated with the Hodegetria cult. There are two monasteries on Crete with this dedication. The oldest one, dating back to the early 14th century, is situated in the Asterousia Mountains and, besides its dedication, its mural decoration reminds one of the power of the Hodegetria by showing the complete Akathistos cycle, which depicts the icon's miracles.[76] The second foundation, in Gonia, has a dedicatory inscription from 1634,[77] but some of the icons kept there are much older.[78] The church in Meronas, dedicated nowadays to the Dormition,[79] was possibly once associated with the Hodegetria as well. Here, the murals in the naos (northern nave) contain the Akathistos cycle,

---

    Complete Translation of the Surviving Founders' Typika and Testaments, ed. John Thomas and Angela Constantinides Hero (Washington, DC: Dumbarton Oaks Research Library, 2000) [hereafter *BMFD*], 1396–1403, esp. 1402.

74   Varvara Papadopoulou, "Amphigraptē eikona tou 14ou aiōna stē monē Gēromeriou Thesprōtias" [A double-sided icon from the 14th century in the monastery of Geromerion, Thesprotia], *Byzantina* 25 (2005), 375–389, esp. 389.

75   *Selida tēs Ieras Monēs Gēromeriou sto Diadiktyo. Ē monē sēmera* https://www.monigiromeriou.gr/el/shmera.htm (accessed November 7, 2021).

76   Ioannis Spatharakis, *The Pictorial Cycles of the Akathistos Hymn for the Virgin* (Leiden: Alexandros Press, 2005), esp. 35–46. For the connection of the Akathistos with the miracles of the Hodegetria, see Lidov, "The Flying Hodegetria," 286–288, 291–321.

77   Giuseppe Gerola, *Monumenti Veneti dell'isola di Creta*, vol. 4 (Venice: Istituto Veneto di Scienze, 1932), 412.

78   Manuel Chatzidakis and Manuel Borboudakis, *Eikonēs tēs krētikēs technē: apo ton Chandaka ōs tēn Moscha kai tēn Hagia Patroupolē* [Icons of the Cretan School from Candia to Moscow and St. Petersburg], exhibition catalogue (Herakleion: Vikelea Dimotiki vivliothiki, 2004 [1993]), 126–127, no. 17.

79   Manuel Borboudakis, "Oi toichographies tēs Panaias tou Merōna kai mia synkekrimenē tasē tēs krētikēs zōgraphikēs" [The murals of Panagia Meronas and one specific tendency in Cretan painting], in *Pepragmena E' Diethnous Krētologikou Synedriou* (Herakleion: Hetairia Krētikōn Historikōn Meletōn, 1986), 396–412; Spatharakis, *The Pictorial Cycles of the Akathistos Hymn for the Virgin*, 8–44.

THE HODEGETRIAI

whereas the main icon of the church, dated to the middle of the 14th century,[80] depicts the Hodegetria.

A small rural foundation on Chalki Island celebrates the Apodosis of the Dormition (23 August) as its patron feast and is dedicated, according to its inscription, to the Hodegetria.[81] Painted in 1367, the church was the collective foundation of three men (Michael the deacon, *kyr* Niketas, and Manouel) and two nuns (Agnese and Magdalene). They had such an extreme fascination for the supernatural power of the famous Hodegetria that they ordered the labeling of two different iconographies (the Blachernitissa in the apse and the Brephokratousa on the northern wall)[82] with the epithet 'Η ΩΔΗΗΤΡΑ.' The same strategy was applied by the inhabitants of Tigani (Mesa Mani). Here, in the Agitria (Hodegetria) Church, celebrating 23 August as its patron feast, the villagers during the 13th century inscribed the Virgin of the Blachernitissa in the apse and the Glykophilousa in the narthex with the Hodegetria labels.[83] This phenomenon of mislabeling the Hodegetria occurred in both cases in village foundations in very remote areas. Moreover, the labeling pattern is repeated in both cases: one image is in the altar and another one is in the publicly accessible space. One may assume, therefore, that these poor communities, not having been able to order adequate replicas of the icon in Constantinople, used the murals produced by local masters to indicate the presence of the miracle-working Virgin in the liturgical rite, as well as to display her image for public veneration.

The fame of the miracle-working icon spread beyond the borders of the Byzantine Empire and reached the neighboring Orthodox states. One of the most important examples is the Hodegetria church of the Peć Patriarchate, built by the Serbian Archbishop Danilo II[84] in 1332–1337 as a foundation for his burial.[85] After his visit to the Byzantine capital and in gratitude for delivering

---

80 Chatzidakis and Borboudakis, *Eikonēs tēs krētikēs technē*, 493, no. 137.

81 Maria Sigala, "Ē Panagia ē Odēgētria ē Enniameritissa stē Chalkē tēs Dōdekanēsou" [Panagia Hodegetria Enniameritissa in Chalki, Dodecanese islands], *Archaiologikon Deltion* 55, no. 1 (2000) [2004], 329–381, esp. 133.

82 Sigala, "Ē Panagia ē Odēgētria ē Enniameritissa," 335, 362.

83 Nikolaos Drandakis, *Byzantines toichografies tēs Mesa Manēs* [Byzantine murals of Inner Mani] (Athens: Archaiologikē Hetaireia, 1995), 238, 247 and 252, 254.

84 There is a solid corpus of literature devoted to this church, however, thanks to a recently defended dissertation, Anđela Gavrilović, "Zidno slikarstvo crkve Bogorodice Odigitrije u Peći" [Wall paintings of the church of the Virgin Hodegetria in Peć] (PhD diss., University of Belgrade, Faculty of Philosophy, Art History Department, 2012), accessible at http://doiserbia.nb.rs/phd/fulltext/BG20130419GAVRILOVIC.pdf, with older bibliography.

85 Gavrilović, "Zidno slikarstvo," 37–42. On the iconographic features connected with the allocation of the church for burial purposes, see Danica Popović, "Grob arhiepiskopa

him from many dangers,[86] Danilo dedicated the church to 'the Most Pure Mother of God Hodegetria,' as the inscription above the votive portrait relates.[87] In this composition situated on the western wall, the *ktetor* with the church model is led by Prophet Daniel toward the depiction of the Enthroned Virgin. Although the text above Danilo II's portrait reads that the foundation is brought to the Hodegetria, the image of the Virgin does not bear this label and does not match the iconographic type. Vojislav Đurić noted that the iconographic program of the church contains unusually numerous depictions of the Virgin belonging to different iconographic types,[88] which brings to mind different aspects of the adoration of the Virgin, like the iconographic program in the Hodegetria in Mystras.

The written sources confirm this hypothesis: according to the Life of Danilo II written by one of his students, the *ktetor* established a Greek brotherhood in the church and "ordered that at any time in that holy church *parakleseis* should be sung continuously on Tuesdays and Fridays."[89] It is precisely on these same days that the two famous miracle-working icons of the Virgin, i.e., the Hodegetria and the Blachernitissa in Constantinople, produced their miracles.[90] In this way, Danilo imitated the liturgical time of the Byzantine capital in his Serbian church with prayers read in the Greek language.

Concerning the dedication of this church, the Life of Danilo II notes that he "started to build a church in the name of the Most Holy One, who is called

---

Danila II" [The Tomb of the Archbishop Danio II], in *Arhiepiskop Danilo II i njegovo doba* [The Archbishop Danilo II and His Time], ed. Vojislav Đurić (Belgrade: SANU, 1991), 329–344.

86 For motives for the foundation, see Gavrilović, "Zidno slikarstvo," 29–32.

87 For the inscription and the discussion of the composition, see Gavrilović, "Zidno slikarstvo," 278–282.

88 Vojislav Đurić, "Sveti pokroviteli arhiepiskopa Danila II i njegovih zadužbina" [Holy Patrons of the Archbishop Danilo II and his foundations], in *Arhiepiskop Danilo II*, 284.

89 Đure Dančić, ed., *Životi kraljeva i arhiepiskopa srpskih napisao arhiepiskop Danilo i drugi* [The Lives of Kings and Archbishops, written by Archbishop Danilo and the Others] (Zagreb: Svetozar Galec, 1866), 369—оустави же вь тои светѣи црькьви вь вьторьникь и вь петькь вьсегда непрѣмѣно пѣти параклисы (the translation is mine).

90 For the discussion of the Friday miracle of the Blachernai icon, see Eustratios N. Papaioanou, "The 'Usual Miracle' and an Unusual Miracle: Psellos and the Icons of Blachernai," *Jahrbuch der Österreichischen Byzantinistik* 51 (2001), 177–188; Bissera Pentcheva, "Rhetorical Images of the Virgin: The Icon of the 'Usual Miracle' at the Blachernai," *Revue des études slaves* 38 (2000), 35–54; Charles Barber, *Contesting the Logic of Painting: Art and Understanding in Eleventh-Century Byzantium* (Leiden: Brill, 2007), 80–98. Concerning the Tuesday miracle of the Hodegetria icon, see Lidov, "The Flying Hodegetria," 291–321; Pentcheva, *Icons and Power*, 109–143.

THE HODEGETRIAI

Hodegetria of Constantinople, namely, to the feast of Dormition."[91] This passage underlines two important points. First, by dedicating his foundation to the Hodegetria, Danilo had in mind the Constantinopolitan monastery which he wished to imitate. Second, the text equates the Hodegetria dedication of the church with the feast of the Dormition, which was probably the patron feast of the Hodegon *katholikon*.

Besides Danilo II, two other noblemen built Hodegetria churches in Serbia. Jovan Dragoslav, the *kaznac* (treasurer) of King Milutin, erected a foundation in Mušutište in 1315.[92] In 1345, nobleman Rudl from Strumica decided to pass the Hodegetria church he built and some nearby possessions to the Hilandar monastery on Mount Athos.[93]

The capital of the Bulgarian Empire also replicated the famous Byzantine foundation. However, there is no material evidence preserved from this institution, while the main source about the Hodegetria monastery in Veliko Tarnovo[94] is a Greek Life of Saint Romylos, written by his disciple Gregorios,[95] and its Slavic translation.[96] Composed about 20 years after the saint's death in 1382–1391,[97] the Greek text says that when Saint Romylos grew old enough to leave his parents he "entered the fortified town called Trinovon in this same province, and made his home in one of the monasteries there, and the monastery had its name after the Mother of God and Hodegetria." The only

---

91 Dančić, *Životi kraljeva i arhiepiskopa*, 368: "начеть здати цръковь вь име прѣсветыіє яже зовома Одигитрия цариградьска, праздьникь оуспеніє."

92 Branislav Todić, *Serbian Painting: The Age of King Milutin* (Belgrade: Draganić, 1999), 340 with older bibliography.

93 Information about the nobleman, his church, and property are given in a chrysobull by Stefan Dušan of 1345 for Hilandar: Siniša Mišić, "Hrisovulja kralja Stefana Dušana Hilandaru kojom prilaže vlastelina Rudla" [The chrysobull by King Stefana Dušana to Hilandar, by which he endows the nobleman Rudle], *Stari Srpski arhiv* 9 (2010), 75–86.

94 Bistra Nikolova, *Monasi, manastiri i manastirski zhivot v Srednovekovna Balgariya*, vol. 1, *Manastirite* [Monks, monasteries and monastic life in medieval Bulgaria, vol. 1, Monasteries] (Sofia: Algraf, 2010), 453–456.

95 François Halkin, "Un ermite des Balkans au XIVᵉ siecle. La vie grecque inedite de St. Romylos," *Byzantion* 31 (1961), 117: "καταλαμβάνει τὴν Ζαγοράν εἴς τε τὸ Τρίνοβον λεγόμενον κάστρον τῆς αὐτῆς ἐπαρχίας εἰσὼν ἐν ἑνὶ τῶν ἐκεῖσε μοναστηρίων τὴν οἴκεσιν ἐποιήσατο, τῆς θεομήτορος Ὁδηγητρίας τὴν ἐπωνυμίαν ἔχων τὸ μοναστήριον."

96 Though the Slavic translation is preserved in the 16th-century manuscript, it was probably contemporary with the Greek original: "и постигаеть загоріе въ торвонь прѣж(д)е гл(а)голюмыи градь, иакиіаже трѭновь тоеж(д)е епархіе въходить въ единь ѿ иже тамо монастыреи селюніе сътвараеть. Б(о)гом(а)тери и одигитріе именованіе имаше монастырь"—Polichronij Syrku, *Monaha Grigorija zhitije prepodobnogo Romila* [The Life of venerable Romyl by Monk Gregory] (St. Petersburg: Tipografija Imperatorskoj Akademii Nauk, 1900), 5.

97 Halkin, "Un ermite des Balkans," 113.

information one can deduce from the text is that the foundation was situated within the borders of Tarnovo city, close to the location of the Holy Mount.[98]

As in Slavic countries, the popularity of the Hodegetria continued in Greek-inhabited territories under foreign rule. In 1311, Gregory Pachymeres,[99] with the help of his family members, built a church dedicated to the Hodegetria on the island of Euboia (village of Spelies),[100] a territory ruled by the Venetians since 1204.[101] Judging by its iconographic program, the church was intended for burial purposes,[102] precisely like the foundation of Serbian Archbishop Danilo II. Likely during the Komnenian and Palaiologan periods, the Hodegon monastery in Constantinople started to be used for private[103] and royal[104] burials; in connection with this practice, the protective power of the Hodegetria was understood as extending to the afterlife as well. This could explain both the dedication of burial churches to the Hodegetria and the appearance of the Hodegetria-like images of the Virgin in funerary portraits.[105]

Another aspect of the Constantinopolitan veneration, namely, the Hodegetria's confraternity, was also replicated in foreign-ruled territories. A

---

98   Syrku, *Monaha Grigorija*, xxv.

99   *PLP*, no. 22205.

100   The date, the name of the founder, and the original dedication of the church to the Hodegetria survived in the dedicatory inscription, see Johannes Koder, *Negroponte: Untersuchungen zur Topographie und Siedlungsgeschichte der Insel Euboia während der Zeit der Venezianerherrschaft* (Vienna: Österreichische Akademie der Wissenschaften, 1973), 167. For discussion of the style and iconography of the murals, see Melita Emmanuel, "Die Fresken der Muttergottes-Hodegetria-Kirche in Spelies auf der Insel Euboia (1311). Bemerkungen zu Ikonographie und Stil," *Byzantinische Zeitschrift* 83, no. 2 (1990), 451–467.

101   Koder, *Negroponte*, 45–55.

102   Emmanuel, "Die Fresken der Muttergottes-Hodegetria-Kirche," 459–461.

103   In the 12th century, Theodore Balsamon described at least two tombs situated on the monastery's territory (one of them belonged to Stephanos Komnenos), see Konstantin Horna ed., "Die Epigramme des Theodoros Balsamon," *Wiener Studien* 25 (1903), 181–183. A donation act of the Sanianoi couple (1390) shows that even members of the low nobility could expect to be buried in the Hodegon. Not having children, the Sanianoi passed to the monastery their house in Constantinople expecting the brotherhood to build in return a tomb for the couple and commemorate them twice a week. Albert Failler, "Une donation des époux Sanianoi au monastère des Hodègoi," *Revue des études byzantines* 34 (1976), 111–117.

104   According to the Short Chronicles, two emperors died inside of the Hodegon monastery and were buried there, Andronikos III in 1341 (Schreiner, *Die Byzantinischen Kleinchroniken* vol. 1, 64, 81; vol. 2, 251) and John V Palaiologos in 1391 (Schreiner, *Die Byzantinischen Kleinchroniken* vol. 1, 69; vol. 2, 345).

105   For the funerary portraits with the Hodegetria-like iconographies, see Papamastorakis, "Epitymbies parastaseis," 285–304.

THE HODEGETRIAI 63

church of the Hodegetria in Agraphoi (Corfu),[106] was attested for the first time by a document of 1286[107] containing a dedicatory inscription listing 91 church founders belonging to ten different neighboring villages. On the basis of this and later documents attesting the activities of the Hodegetria confraternity in Agraphoi, Spyros Karydis concluded that the confraternity was the initial founder of this parochial church which later (in 1744) was converted into a monastery. The members of the confraternity, who in a later document are called brothers and founders,[108] had rights for burial in the church or on its grounds, and managed the income from the Hodegetria dependencies.[109] As in all other cases, the church is not called Hodegon in documents, but rather "of the Mother of God Hodegetria" or "of the Mother of God called Hodegetria."[110]

Finally, the support expressed by non-Greek rulers for the Hodegetria cult may testify to their belief in the military and political power of the icon and its replicas. According to the dedicatory inscription above the entrance gate, the *katholikon* of the Hodegetria in Apolpaina (Leukas) was rebuilt by Jacopo Ruffo or Rosso[111] and his wife Zampia (?) in 1449–1450.[112] A close associate

---

106   Spyros Karydis, *Ē Odēgētria Agraphōn Kerkyras. Psēphides apo tē makraiōnē istoria tēs* [The Hodegetria of Agraphoi in Kerkyra. Pieces of its long history] (Kerkyra/Corfu: Hieros Naos Hyperagias Theotokou Hodegetrias Agraphon, 2011).

107   Karydis, *Ē Odēgētria Agraphōn Kerkyras*, 15–18. For publication of the document and the discussion of its date, see Spyros Karydis, "Syllogikes Chorēgies stēn Kerkyra kata tēn Prōimē Latinokratia. Epigrafika Tekmēria" [Collective sponsorship in Corfu during the early Latin rule. Epigraphic evidence], *Byzantina Symmeikta* 26 (2016), 167–172.

108   Karydis, *Ē Odēgētria Agraphōn Kerkyras*, 109–111.

109   Karydis, *Ē Odēgētria Agraphōn Kerkyras*, 55–56, 101–106.

110   Karydis, *Ē Odēgētria Agraphōn Kerkyras*, 15–51.

111   Under 1436, a certain Jacobo Ruffo is mentioned as a governor of Leukas by Cyriacus of Ancona, who spent some time with him in Aktio (Preveza) in 1436 (Erich Ziebarth, "Kyriakos o ex Ankōnos en Ēpeirō" [Ciriaco of Ancona in Epirus], *Ēpeirōtika Chrōnika* 1 (1926), 114–115; Nicol, *The Despotate of Epiros*, 206). On the other hand, a certain Jacopo Rosso is mentioned among *governatori* of Leonardo III Tocco in 1449 (Riccardo Predelli and Pietro Bosmin, eds., *I libri commemoriali della Republica di Venezia: Regestri*, vol. 5 (Venice: A spese della Società, 1901), 37, no. 96), precisely when the residence of Leonardo was moved to Leukas after the fall of Arta (Walter Haberstumpf, "Dinasti italiani in levante. I Tocco duchi di Leucade: regesti (secoli XIV–XVII)," *Studi veneziani* NS 45 (2003), 205).

112   Peter Soustal and Johannes Koder, *Nikopolis und Kephallenia* (Vienna: Österreichische Akademie der Wissenschaften, 1981), 162–163; Panos Rontogiannes, "Ē Christianikē Technē stēn Leukada" [The Christian art in Lefkada], *Epetēris Etaireias Leukadikōn Meletōn* 3 (1973), 27–57, esp. 29; Maro Philippa-Apostolou, "Ē Odēgētria tēs Leukadas, istorikes phaseis" [The Hodegetria of Lefkada, historical phases], *Praktika D' Synedriou "Eptanēsiakou Politismou," Leukada 8–12 Septembriou 1993*, ed. P. Rontogiannis (Athens: Etaireia Leukadikōn Meletōn, 1996), 133–159.

of the Tocco family, Jacopo was Italian in origin; he nonetheless built, or rather reconstructed, the monastery belonging probably to the Orthodox rite. According to a colophon found in the manuscript *Vaticanus graecus* 2561, the Hodegetria monastery existed on the island from the 11th century (1025?),[113] but it was continuously supported, particularly in the turbulent 15th century. After the marriage between Leonardo III Tocco and Milica Branković in 1463, Helena, the daughter of the *despotes* of Mystras, Thomas Palaiologos, and wife of the deceased *despotes* of Serbia Lazar Branković, accompanied Milica and stayed on Leukas.[114] After the death of her daughter, Helena Palaiologina settled in the Hodegetria monastery, took the name Ypomone, and became the *hegoumene* (until her death in 1474), also commissioning the mural decoration of the church.[115]

In addition to preserved foundations, there are several churches and monasteries of the Hodegetria which are known only from written sources. From appeals made by the Metropolitans of Methymna and Mytilene to the Patriarchal Court in 1331[116] and 1324,[117] respectively, one can find out about the Hodegetria monasteries on Lesbos: one was situated inside the Agioi Theodoroi *kastron*, and another, built by a certain Gidon, in the Mytilene metropolis. A village church with the same dedication is known from the Menoikeion act of 1321 as placed near the River Angista and the village of Kouvouklia,[118] while another Hodegetria church, with some houses in its possession, was ceded in 1323 to Vatopedi by its founder, *Sebastos* Manouel Kourtikes.[119] Around the mid-14th century, a monk by the name of Ioannitzopoulos donated his own foundation of the Hodegetria in Maurochorion, inside Palaiokastron (Lemnos),

---

113   Peter Schreiner, "Das Hodegetria-Kloster auf Leukas im 11 Jahrhundert: Bemerkungen zu einer Notiz im Vat. Gr. 2561," *Byzantinische Forschungen* 12 (1987), 57–64.

114   Nicol, *The Despotate of Epiros*, 211.

115   Immanuel Bekker, ed., *Chronicon* in *Georgius Phrantzes, Joannes Cananus, Joannes Anagnostes* (Bonn: E. Weber, 1838), 450; Demetrio Petrizzopulo, *Saggio storico sull' et à di Leucadia: sotto il dominio de' Romani e successivi conquistatori* (Florence: Stamp. di Piatti, 1814), 49–50; Philippa-Apostolou, "Ē Odēgētria tēs Leukadas," 138ff.

116   Miklosich and Müller, *Acta et Diplomata*, vol. 1, 164–166, no. 73; Jean Darrouzès, *Les regestes des actes du Patriarcat de Constantinople*, vol. 1, fasc. 5, *Les regestes de 1310 à 1376* (Paris: Institute Français d'études Byzantines, 1977), 122–124, no. 2164.

117   Miklosich and Müller, *Acta et Diplomata*, vol. 1, 115–118, no. 59; Darrouzès, *Les regestes*, vol. 1, fasc. 5, 88–89, no. 2118.

118   André Guillou, *Les Archives de Saint-Jean-Prodrome sur le mont Mènécée* (Paris: Presses universitaires de France, 1955), 53–55, no. 9.

119   *Actes de Vatopédi*, vol. 1, *des origines à 1329*, ed. J. Bompaire, J. Lefort, V. Kravari and Ch. Giros (Paris: Lethielleux, 2001), 327–332, no. 61.

THE HODEGETRIAI   65

to the Athonite monastery of Lavra.[120] Finally, the monastery of Xenophon
had a small *metochion* (*eukterios*) of the Hodegetria in Phournia (Longos).[121]
Such evidence indicates that the popularity of the Hodegetria was so immense
that this topographic attribute of the Virgin, connected with a precise location, replaced those characteristic epithets, such as Eleousa, Kecharitomene,
etc. Consequently, the focus in the veneration of the Theotokos turned from
the speculative concepts of mercy, grace, and advocacy toward a more engag-
ing and material approach. Thus the veneration of the Hodegetria provided
believers with a material object (icon) invested with miraculous power, and
this object could be communicated with by addressing it or its replicas via a
number of prayers and pious actions.

In this sense, one document appears to be the most important for the present investigation, as it demonstrates the mechanism of establishing a foundation dedicated to the Hodegetria. It is a synodal decision of 1316[122] given
on behalf of a Laconian nun, Euphrosyne-Marina. The nun addressed the
Patriarchal Synod concerning an icon of the Theotokos Hodegetria, which was
possessed in common by her and the deceased Bishop of Kernitsa, Malotaras.
However, Malotaras started to take more than half of the icon's revenues, and,
despite an earlier court decision, he withheld the entire income. Malotaras
turned to the *proedros* of Lacedaimonia Metropolitan of Crete, Nikephoros
Moschopoulos,[123] who initially decided to remove the icon from Euphrosyne,
but later regretted this and returned it to her.

The document reads further: "The nun, having received the icon of this
[Theotokos], built a holy church in her [the icon's] name, and with no little
zeal and help provided for this deed by the beloved nephew of the mighty and
holy *autokrator*, *kyr* Andronikos Palaiologos Asanes,[124] who happened to be
in the position of *kephale* of Peloponnese. And she held it having hired the
presbyters and giving to it [the icon] a proper holy veneration through them
[the priests]."[125] Yet, circa 1315, the Metropolitan of Patras and *proedros* of
Lacedaimonia, Michael, took the icon from Euphrosyne again on the pretext

---

120   *Actes de Lavra*, vol. 3, *de 1329 à 1500*, ed. P. Lemerle, A. Guillou, N. Svoronos and
       D. Papachryssanthou (Paris: Lethielleux, 1979), 57–66, esp. 62, no. 136.
121   *Actes de Xénophon*, ed. D. Papachryssanthou (Paris: Lethielleux, 1986), 36.
122   Darrouzès, *Les regestes*, vol. 1, fasc. 5, 45–46, no. 2064. Miklosich and Müller, *Acta et
       Diplomata*, vol. 1, 52–53, no. 30.
123   *PLP*, no. 19376; on identification of the metropolitan of Crete, see Darrouzès, *Les regestes*,
       vol. 1, fasc. 5, 46; Anagnostakes, "Apo tēn eikona tēs monachēs Euphrosynēs," 172.
124   *PLP*, no. 1489; Erich Trapp, "Beiträge zur Genealogie der Asanen in Byzanz," *Jahrbuch der
       Österreichischen Byzantinistik* 25 (1976), 167.
125   Miklosich and Müller, *Acta et Diplomata*, vol. 1, 52.

that it was held by his predecessor. This fact made Euphrosyne address the Synodal Court, which decreed that the icon should be returned to the church built by the nun, and that its revenues should be divided between Euphrosyne and the successors of Malotaras.[126]

Concerning this case,[127] Elias Anagnostakis proposed several important conclusions related to the persons involved, state policies, and ecclesiastic foundations.[128] He assumed that the church erected by Euphrosyne was the monastery of Mega Spelaion in Kalavryta, while the time when the Metropolitan of Patras took the icon coincided with the period when the Hodegetria church was constructed in the Brontocheion monastery, and it might have housed the contested icon.

It is important to underline, above all, the fact that the icon had its own assets, even before being housed in a church. This indicates that the icon was perceived as an independent, legal entity, a kind of ecclesiastic institution in itself, supplied with the right of ownership. Moreover, Euphrosyne built the church in the name (ἐπ' ὀνόματι) of the Hodegetria icon itself, whereby the clergy was hired to provide the proper veneration for the image. The majority of churches dedicated to the Hodegetria in the Byzantine Commonwealth, especially the parochial and rural ones, might have been organized on the basis of a similar principle, i.e., they could have been built in order to house a venerated image that was a copy or replica of the Constantinopolitan miracle-working Virgin. Whenever local replicas of the Hodegetria became famous and received their own, separate cults, secondary replicas emerged and these bore names connected to the location of their prototypes, which themselves were copies of the famous Constantinopolitan icon. These secondary replicas, although they received new names according to their derived prototypes, preserved the iconography of the Hodegetria, as is the case of the images of the Virgin Megaspelaiotissa.[129]

Not only documents but also ethnographic observations can assist with tracing the spread of practices associated with the Hodegetria of Constantinople. On the island of Kimolos, in its central village of Chorio, the main church was

---

126   For more details about identification of the actors and the chronology, see Anagnostakes, "Apo tēn eikona tēs monachēs Euphrosynēs," 171–182.

127   The case is also considered by Nicolas Oikonomides, "The Holy Icon as an Asset," *Dumbarton Oaks Papers* 45 (1991), 40.

128   Anagnostakes, "Apo tēn eikona tēs monachēs Euphrosynēs," 178–179.

129   For more details about the image from the Mega Spelaion and its funereal use, see Papamastorakis, "Epitymbies parastaseis," 298–302; Weissbrod, *"Hier liegt der Knecht Gottes,"* 137–138.

THE HODEGETRIAI   67

renovated in 1867–1874 with funds collected from all the islanders[130] and was dedicated to the Hodegetria, celebrating the Presentation of the Virgin as its patron feast. Even though the church building is relatively new (16th–17th century), the church houses a Hodegetria icon that, under a 17th-century layer of painting, preserves some features of its Byzantine base.[131] Several legends about personal recoveries of inhabitants and the salvation of the entire island from death are associated with this image.[132] The most striking element is the custom of a festal procession carried out on the feast of the Presentation of the Virgin with the participation of the local bishop, mayor, members of the coast guard, and all the island's clergy and laics. On this day, the icon is taken around the entire village and followed by other adorned images of the Theotokos, in the same way the Hodegetria was surrounded by other Marian icons, according to the description from the 11th century.[133]

In connection with the phenomenon of the emergence of churches dedicated to the Hodegetria, it is worth turning now to the question of the patron feasts of these Hodegetria-dedicated foundations. The majority of churches and monasteries which have survived until the present day celebrate as their patron feast the Dormition of the Virgin (Choli, Kouklia, Geromeri, Agraphoi, Peć, Asterousia, Gonia), its Apodosis (Enniameritissa on Chalki, Agitria on Mesa Mani), or the Presentation of the Theotokos (Jerusalem, Arediou, Kimolos). This means that the dedication of a foundation to the Hodegetria is not equated with a precise feast or, better said, it implies several feasts associated with the Virgin (the Dormition, its Apodosis, and the Presentation of the Virgin).[134] Theoretically, the day of the Hodegetria could coincide with the memory of Empress Pulcheria, who was associated with the icon's discovery, and the miracle of the Virgin saving the capital from the Avar siege (August 4, 626).[135] However, the text of the Constantinopolitan *Synaxarion* directly indicates that the celebration of this day happened in the Blachernai

---

130 Despoina Athanasiadou-Bentoure and Georgos Bentoures, *Kimōlos: Ho topos. Hoi ekklēsies. Hosia Methodia* [Kimolos: The place. The churches. Holy Methodia] (Kimolos: Dēmos Kimōlos, 2013), 5.

131 Ioannes Ramphos, "Ta christianika mnēmeia tēs Kimōlou kai tōn perix nēsidōn" [The Christian monuments of Kimolos and the neighboring islands], *Kimōliaka* 2 (1972), 231–232, see also p. 204 for another Hodegetria icon from the same village, dated c.1500.

132 Ioannes Ramphos, *Ta 'Sōtēria' tēs Kimōlou eis tēn Hagian Barbaran* [The 'Salvation' of Kimolos in Agia Varvara] (Athens: n.p., 1954), 5–6.

133 Pentcheva, "The 'Activated' Icon,"198–199.

134 Pentcheva, "The 'Activated' Icon," 200–201; Pentcheva, *Icons and Power*, 136–143.

135 *Synaxarium Ecclesiae Constantinopolitanae e Codice Sirmondiano Nunc Berolinensi*, ed. Hippolyte Delehaye (Brussels: Socios Bollandianos, 1902), cols. 872–876.

68   ADASHINSKAYA

monastery ("and that's why we all celebrate the present yearly commemoration in Her venerable house in Blachernai").[136]

Further, in the 14th-century *Narration of the Hodegon Monastery*, the anonymous author describes two icons of the Hodegetria: one in the naos of the church, accessible to visitors,[137] and the true Hodegetria icon, painted by Saint Luke, set in the prothesis. The latter was probably isolated from the main church space by a ciborium with a grille, as it is seen in the frontispiece of the Hamilton Psalter.[138] From this story, it appears that the icon being exhibited in the naos, in a place typical for the patron icon of the church, is actually an image of the Dormition.[139] This seems to be supported by the example of the Serbian Archbishop Danilo II, who dedicated his church to "Hodegetria of Constantinople, namely, to the feast of Dormition."[140] One can inquire, therefore, what was the patron feast associated with the Hodegetria? The Dormition or, maybe, the Presentation?

If one looked at regulations concerning patron feasts in the Byzantine *typika*, one would discover that the celebration of a group of feasts associated with a certain saint or a holy person was the most common practice and thus the purpose of a dedication was to indicate the person of a holy patron, and not a particular calendar feast.

Seemingly, the practice of establishing a certain patron feast started to appear in the Palaiologan period, and foundations were generally dedicated to a holy personage and celebrated all feasts connected with that individual. However, precisely during this period, some monasteries started to celebrate certain feasts more solemnly than others. In the *typikon* for the monastery of the Archangel Michael on Mount Auxentios near Chalcedon, Michael VIII pointed to the *Synaxis* of the Archangel Michael (November 8) as the main feast (κυρία μέντοι τῶν ἑορτῶν); he also ordered the celebration of the Miracle of the Archangel Michael at Colossae (September 6), however, less splendidly.[141] Similarly, in the *typikon* for the Machaira foundation (1210), Neilos, the Bishop of Tamasia, appoints the Presentation of the Virgin at the

---

136   *Synaxarium Ecclesiae*, 876: Διὰ ταῦτα τὴν παροῦσαν ἀνάμνησιν ἐτησίως πανηγυρίζομεν ἐν τῷ σεβασμίῳ αὐτῆς οἴκῳ, τῷ ὄντι ἐν Βλαχέρναις.
137   Angelidi, "Un texte patriographique et édifiant," 139.
138   Helen C. Evans, ed., *Byzantium: Faith and Power (1261–1557)* (New York: Metropolitan Museum of Art/New Haven: Yale University Press, 2004), 153–154 with older bibliography.
139   Angelidi, "Un texte patriographique et édifiant," 130.
140   Dančić, *Životi kraljeva i arhiepiskopa*, 368.
141   Alexei Dmitrievsky, *Opisanie liturgicheskih rukopisej, hranjashhihsja v bibliotekah Pravoslavnogo Vostoka* [Description of the liturgical manuscripts kept in the libraries of the Orient], vol. 1, *Typika* (Kiev: Tipogrsfija Korchak-Novitskag, 1895), 788–789; *BMFD*, 1229–1230.

THE HODEGETRIAI   69

Temple as the most splendid celebration, while the Dormition was slightly less pompous, and other Marian feasts should be "lavishly feasted."[142] The monastery of Theotokos Evergetis had the Dormition as "the feast of feasts and the festival of festivals," but other Marian days were to be celebrated "differently from the rest."[143] The foundation of Empress Eirene Doukaina Komnene, dedicated to the Theotokos Kecharitomene, emphasized the feast of the Dormition in the same way as the Nativity, Epiphany, and Passion days, while the Birth of the Virgin, Entry to the Temple, and Presentation of the Lord in the Temple were holy days of second rank.[144] *Sebastokrator* Isaak Komnenos ordered the celebration of all feasts of the Mother of God with bell-ringing, hymnody, illumination, and food distributions at the gates; however, he especially emphasized the preparations for the Dormition.[145] John, the *ktetor* of St. John the Forerunner Phoberos monastery, prescribed church illumination, hymns, and psalmodies for all feasts associated with the monastery's 'patron' (δεσπότης), Saint John the Baptist.[146]

Yet, several of the *typika*'s festival regulations remained outside of this paradigm. The foundation of the 11th century dedicated to the Virgin Eleousa celebrated the Entrance of the Virgin to the Temple as the most solemn feast.[147] The monastery of the Mother of God tou Roidiou had the Dormition as "the feast that it is the custom to celebrate."[148] Similarly, the foundation of the Synadenoi family, the Bebaia Elpis monastery, had only the Dormition to be celebrated in a special manner,[149] which is called by the foundress Theodora "*The* feast of the Virgin." In connection with the last example, one shouldn't forget that it was precisely the Dormition which was considered the main Marian feast in the Palaiologan period, since the Decree of Adronikos II of 1297[150] established the month-long celebration of the Dormition, which should

---

142   *BMFD*, 1132.
143   Paul Gautier, "Le typikon de la Théotokos Évergétis," *Revue des études byzantines* 40 (1982), 45; *BMFD*, 482.
144   Gautier, "Le typikon de la Théotokos Kécharitôménè," 109–111; *BMFD*, 696–697.
145   Louis Petit, "Typikon du monastère de la Kosmosotira près d'Aenos (1152)," *Izvestiya Russkogo arheologicheskogo instituta v Konstantinopole* 13 (1908), 23–25; *BMFD*, 802–803.
146   Afanasios Papadopoulos-Kerameus, *Noctes Petrapolitana* [The nights of Petropolis] (St. Petersburg: Tip. V.F. Kirshbauma, 1913), 50; *BMFD*, 918.
147   Louis Petit, "Le monastère de Notre-Dame de Pitié en Macédoine," *Izvestiya Russkogo arheologicheskogo instituta v Konstantinopole* 6 (1900), 86; *BMFD*, 184.
148   *BMFD*, 433.
149   Hippolyte Delehaye, *Deux typica byzantins de l'époque des Paléologues* (Brussels: M. Lamertin, 1921), 79–80, 99; *BMFD*, 1555, 1565.
150   Grumel, "Le mois de Marie des Byzantins," 257–269; Boissonade, *Anecdota Græca*, 107–136.

"begin on the beginning and the first day of the month in which this mystery is, and is prolonged to the end, and ends at the very end of the month."[151]

Taking the above into consideration, one may assume that generally foundations dedicated to the Virgin named with different epithets (Eleousa, Kecharitomene, Hodegetria, etc.) celebrated all Marian feasts, with particular attention given to one or two of them (usually the Dormition and the Presentation). However, in conjunction with the special emphasis on the Dormition in Constantinople during the Palaiologan era, this feast started to dominate among Marian days. Consequently, modern-day patron feasts in historical foundations dedicated to the Hodegetria can vary within the framework of Marian celebrations, which does not indicate any deviation from the initial concept of replicating the Constantinopolitan sanctuary.

•••

In conclusion, I underline several important aspects of the dedications of ecclesiastic foundations to the Virgin Hodegetria. It is not always a particular icon that was the object of imitation, but a complex set of pious practices, rituals, beliefs, and customs associated with the Hodegetria, which could be borrowed wholesale or in part. Specifically, this set of practices consisted of the miracle-working image of the Virgin, a foundation dedicated to this particular image of the Virgin, a confraternity serving the image, weekly processions with the image, visual recollection of the icon's story in murals (Akathistos cycle), a patron feast celebrating the Virgin and her advocacy, and private veneration of the icon and/or images of the Virgin bearing the same designation in funeral contexts. All or only some of these aspects could be imitated in order to invoke the Virgin in her quality of conductress and protectress in a particular foundation, as well as to denote the presence of the miracle-working power primarily associated with the venerated image in the Byzantine capital.

If one returns to the very beginning of this study, to the case of the village of Vasilopoulou, one would discover that the venerated image of the Virgin occurs neither in the legendary narrative, nor in the veneration practices of the foundation, but at the same time other features such as celebration of the Holy Tuesday, the holding of a fair together with the pious event, the miracles which occurred, the dedication of the church and its patron feast are enough to recreate, at least in part, the image of the Constantinopolitan icon, its cult and its shrine.

---

151   Boissonade, *Anecdota Græca*, 126.

In some other cases, like in the story of the nun Euphrosyne-Marina, the replica of the Hodegetria plays the main role in the organization of the cult. The recognition of the icon's importance and its spiritual and economic power determined the erection of a foundation and the establishment of an organized veneration. Moreover, being perceived as an entity, the icon may gain the right of possession (as in the Euphrosyne-Marina story), it can participate in dialogue relations, as happened between the Thessalonikian Hodegetria and the city's inhabitants, or it can 'attend' services and respond to the prayers of its worshippers, as happened on the island of Kimolos.

The theological meaning concentrated in the visual program of the image (the Mother's sacrifice juxtaposed with the sacrifice of Christ) could also prompt the use of the icon's designation as 'the Hodegetria' in the development of an iconographic or hierotopic program, as was the case in Jerusalem and the Cappella Palatina.

The practice of veneration of the Hodegetria by organized confraternities could additionally prompt some church dedications (Agraphoi, Leukosia) as an economically acceptable strategy for communal ecclesiastic establishments.

The choice of the dedication of an important urban foundation to the Hodegetria can be a matter of recreating the topography and political might of the capital in the competing provincial centers of the Empire (Monembasia, Thessaloniki, Mystras, Didymoteichon) and the neighboring states (Bulgaria, the Crusader entities), while *ktetors* of numerous small private foundations could bring them under the auspices of the Hodegetria, expecting Her guidance and protection in earthly matters and the afterlife.

Thus the relationship between the Constantinopolitan Hodegetria and its replicas cannot be explained simply in terms of iconographic method and the 'original-copies' paradigm. As the examples brought forth suggest, the veneration of the Hodegetria can appear in different forms and employ numerous and various practices. Simultaneously, one can see that in Byzantine cases the replication of images is performed in terms of the relationship between an archetype and its embodiment, when a miraculous image retains some of its original characteristics after replication. In this way, the resemblance between the prototype (the miraculous image) and its imprints (copies) went beyond the visual characteristics and encompassed the names, the devotional practices, the similarity of locations, and the dedication of the sacral space.

CHAPTER 3

The Body of Christ as Relic Archetype

Ljubomir Milanović

King Stefan Uroš III Dečanski (1321–1331) began the construction of his endowment, the church dedicated to Christ Pantokrator in Dečani, in 1327 (Figure 3.1).[1] Following the example set by his ancestors, he created a place for his remains and hoped thereby to gain spiritual salvation.[2] The ideological conception of his royal tomb was modeled after the Studenica monastery, the prototype for all the mausoleums of the Nemanjić dynasty.[3] Here, the tomb of Stefan Nemanja, the founder of the holy Nemanjić dynasty, was marked by a sarcophagus located in a western bay of the church.[4] Where Dečani differs from the Studenica model is in the placement of the tomb in the southwest part of the nave as a freestanding structure, which is unique among Serbian sepulchres (Figure 3.2).[5] According to Danica Popović, the freestanding position

---

1 For the date of the construction of the monastery and its architecture, see Vladislav R. Petković and Đurđe Bošković, *Dečani* (Belgrade: Academia Regalis Serbica, 1941), vol. 1, 19–37; Bratislav Pantelić, *The Architecture of Dečani and the Role of Archbishop Danilo II* (Wiesbaden: Reichert, 2002), 25; Branislav Todić and Milka Čanak-Medić, *Manastir Dečani* [Dečani monastery] (Priština: Muzej u Prištini, 2005), 17 with extended bibliography. See also Milka Čanak-Medić, *Manastir Dečani. Saborna crkva. Arhitektura* [Dečani monastery. Cathedral church. Architecture] (Belgrade: Republički zavod za zaštitu spomenkika kulture Beograd, 2007), 19ff. Early sources recorded two dedications of the church, both to Christ Pantokrator and to the Ascension of Christ. For the double dedication, see Todić and Čanak-Medić, *Manastir Dečani*, 19, n. 24. On the completion of the church construction, see Todić and Čanak-Medić, *Manastir Dečani*, 28.

2 In the founding charter of the monastery of Dečani (1330), the king expresses his desire to continue the tradition of building monasteries as a final resting place established by his forefathers. See Pavle Ivić and Milica Grković, *Dečanske hrisovulje* [Charters from Dečani] (Novi Sad: Institut za lingvistiku, 1976), 304; see also Arhiepiskop Danilo, *Životi kraljeva i arhiepiskopa srpskih* [Lives of Serbian kings and archbishops], trans. Lazar Mirković (Belgrade: Srpska književna zadruga, 1935), 151–156.

3 Todić and Čanak Medić, *Manastir Dečani*, 22.

4 Danica Popović, "Grob svetog Simeona u Studenici" [The tomb of St. Simeon in Studenica], in *Osam vekova Studenice. Zbornik radova*, ed. Episkop Žički Stefan et al. (Belgrade: Sveti arhijerejski sinod srpske pravoslavne crkve, 1986), 155–166. On royal tombs in medieval Serbia, see Danica Popović, *Srpski vladarski grob u srednjem veku* [The Serbian ruler's tomb in the Middle Ages] (Belgrade: Institut za istoriju umetnosti, Filozofski fakultet, 1992), 175–187.

5 Following the tradition of the royal tombs established by Stefan Nemanja in Hilandar monastery and developed by Saint Sava in the Studenica monastery, the body of the ruler was

FIGURE 3.1 Dečani monastery, church of the Christ Pantokrator, Serbia, 14th century, viewed from the southwest
PHOTO: LJUBOMIR MILANOVIĆ

FIGURE 3.2 Dečani monastery, church of the Christ Pantokrator, Serbia, 14th century, sarcophagi in the west bay of the south aisle
PHOTO: LJUBOMIR MILANOVIĆ

74 MILANOVIĆ

of the tomb in Dečani reflects a new royal ideology that emphasized, as she puts it, "a strengthening of dynamic self-consciousness."[6]

According to the early 15th-century biography of Grigorije Camblak (Gregory Tsamblak), Stefan Dečanski received a formal burial organized by his son, King Stefan Uroš IV Dušan (1331–1355), who moved his father's body from Zvečan, where he died, to the Dečani monastery.[7] Dečanski's relics were elevated and King Stefan Uroš III was canonized c.1343.[8] After the invention and

---

placed in a prepared underground tomb in the southwestern corner of the church nave on top of which a sarcophagus would be placed with its rear end against the wall. On the tomb of Stefan Nemanja in Hilandar Monastery, see Danica Popović, "Sahrane i grobovi u srednjem veku" [Burials and graves in the Middle Ages], in *Manastir Hilandar*, ed. Gojko Subotić (Belgrade: Publikum, 1998), 205–214; Jelena Bogdanović, "The Original Tomb of St Simeon and its Significance for the Architectural History of Hilandar Monastery," *Hilandarski zbornik* 12 (2008), 35–56; see also Dimitrije Bogdanović, Vojislav J. Đurić, and Dejan Medaković, *Manastir Hilandar* [Hilandar monastery] (Belgrade: Jugoslovenska revija, 1997). For the Studenica monastery, see Popović, "Grob svetog Simeona u Studenici," 155–166; Popović, *Srpski vladarski grob*, 176–278. See also Todić and Čanak-Medić, *Manastir Dečani*, 22.

6   Danica Popović, "Srednjovekovni nadgrobni spomenici u Dečanima" [Medieval tombstones in Dečani], in *Dečani i vizantijska umetnost sredinom XIV veka: međunarodni naučni skup povodom 650 godina manastira Dečana*, ed. Vojislav J. Đurić (Belgrade: Srpska akademija nauka i umetnosti, 1989), 225–237, 236. For more on the use of freestanding sarcophagi as grave markers, especially in the West, see Josef Deér, *The Dynastic Porphyry Tombs of the Norman Period in Sicily* (Cambridge: Harvard University Press, 1959), 27–41.

7   Grigorije Camblak, "Žitije Stefana Dečanskog" [The Life of Stefan Dečanski], in Grigorije Camblak, *Knjiīževni rad u Srbiji*, trans. Lazar Mirković (Belgrade: Prosveta, 1989), 49–87, 72. On the king's death in Zvečan, see Pantelić, *The Architecture*, 23. Many scholars have proposed a date for the translation of the king's body from Zvečan to Dečani as having occurred in 1332. Dušan Korać has suggested that the translation could not have taken place before the monastery church was completed and consecrated, which, according to the inscription, happened in 1334–1335. For other opinions and a recent bibliography on this topic, see Dušan Korać, "Kanonizacija Stefana Dečanskog i promene na vladarskim portretima u Dečanima" [Stefan Dečanski's canonization and changes in the ruling portraits in Dečani], in *Dečani i vizantijska umetnost sredinom XIV veka: međunarodni naučni skup povodom 650 godina manastira Dečana*, ed. Vojislav J. Đurić (Belgrade: Srpska akademija nauka i umetnosti, 1989), 287–295, 290–291.

8   Aleksandar Solovjev first proposed the date of the canonization and translation of the king's body to the reliquary casket broadly as between 1339 and 1343. He based his conclusion on literary sources, especially late ones such as that of the king's biographer Grigorije Camblak and Konstantin Mihajlović iz Ostrovice from the 17th century. Both biographies placed the translation of the king's body at seven and nine years, respectively, after his burial. If the burial occurred in 1331 or 1332, as Solovjev has suggested, a date falling between 1339 and 1341 may be taken as the *terminus post quem*. Korać, however, has argued for a canonization date in 1343 based on the preamble in the charter issued by King Stefan Dušan to the monastery of Saints Peter and Paul on the River Lim in Debreštu near Prilep on October 25, 1343 in which King Stefan Dečanski was described as holy for the first time. Korać pointed out that the king's body could not have been laid in the prepared tomb in the Dečani before the end of

THE BODY OF CHRIST AS RELIC ARCHETYPE   75

elevation, the body of the king was translated in a solemn ceremony, deposited in a wooden coffin, and placed in a prominent place in the church to be venerated.[9] Unfortunately, we have no recorded evidence as to the original position of King Stefan's shrine after it was displayed in the church. Today, the reliquary is located in front of the icon of Christ, perpendicular to the iconostasis (Figure 3.3).

Relics and icons have a long history of association.[10] While theologians and scholars have largely used theories of archetype or prototype to understand the origin of icons, this is not the case with the origin of relics. According to theologian John of Damascus (c.675–749), a defender of icons during the iconoclastic controversies, icons are representations of the invisible, intangible models of incomprehensible essence that bring man closer to the glory of God.[11] The question of the origin of icons is directly connected with the dogmatic question of Christ's Incarnation. As Vladimir Lossky has stated, "it is in the context of the Incarnation (say rather: it is by the fact, by the event of the Incarnation) that the creation of man in the image of God receives all its theological value."[12] The Incarnation of the Son of God is at the core of Damascus's thought, which justifies the representation of Christ's human figure.[13] Worshipping representations of Christ was not idolatry since, in the

---

      1334 or the beginning of 1335, when construction of the church was completed. Based on the date of the second burial of the king, the date of canonization should be in 1343, which corresponds to the date found in the literary sources, see Aleksandar Solovjev, "Kad je Dečanski proglašen za sveca? Kralja Dušanova povelja Limskom manastiru" [When was Dečanski declared a saint? King Dušan's charter to the Lim monastery], *Bogoslovlje* 4 (1929), 284–298; Korać, "Kanonizacija Stefana Dečanskog," 290–291. For the charter, see Žarko Vujošević, "Hrisovulja kralja Stefana Dušana manastiru Sv. Petra i Pavla na Limu" [The Chrysobull of King Stefan Dušan to the monastery of ss. Peter and Paul on Lim], *Stari srpski arhiv* 3 (2004), 45–69. For the literary sources, see Konstantin Mihajlović iz Ostrovice, *Janičarove uspomene ili turska hronika* [Janissary's memories or Turkish chronicle] (Belgrade: Prosveta, 1986), 95–96.

9   Camblak, "Žitije Stefana Dečanskog," 73.

10   This relationship between icons and relics was especially an issue during the iconoclastic controversies, see John Wortley, "Icons and Relics: A Comparison," *Greek, Roman and Byzantine Studies* 43 (2002–2003), 161–174; Ljubomir Milanović, "Encountering Presence: Icon/Relic/Viewer," in *Icons of Space: Advances in Hierotopy*, ed. Jelena Bogdanović (Abingdon, Oxon/New York: Routledge, 2021), 239–259.

11   *Patrologia Graeca* (167 vols.), ed. J.-P. Migne (Paris, 1857–1866) [hereafter PG], 94, 1232–1420. John of Damascus, *Three Treatises on the Divine Images*, trans. Andrew Louth (Crestwood, NY: St. Vladimir's Seminary Press, 2003), 19–59, esp. 21–23.

12   Vladimir Lossky, *In the Image and Likeness of God*, trans. John Erickson, Thomas E. Bird, intro. John Meyendorff (Crestwood, NY: St. Vladimir's Seminary Press, 1974), 136.

13   Jelena Bogdanović, "The Performativity of Shrines in a Byzantine Church: The Shrine of St. Demetrios Performativity in Byzantium and Medieval Russia," in *Spatial Icons:*

FIGURE 3.3　Dečani monastery, church of the Christ Pantokrator, Serbia, 14th century, original iconostasis with fresco surrounding it and the coffin of Saint Stefan Dečanski
PHOTO: LJUBOMIR MILANOVIĆ

words of Basil of Caesarea (330–379) "the honor given to the image [the Son] passes to the prototype [the Father]."[14]

Through icons, one can recognize the human impulse to materialize the ineffable and make it available to the senses. The Incarnation was the foundation for the contemplation of the archetype and the miracles that took place by means of icons were, for the faithful, evidence of the omnipresence of God. Likewise, saints' bodies were materialized evidence through which the believer was able to address a glorified saint and, by extension, God. Through divine grace, bodies became similar to the archetypal body of Christ, immortal and incorruptible.[15] In this manner, the body of Christ can be viewed as the archetype of all bodily relics.

Byzantine commentaries likened altars to the holy tomb of Christ. The placing of the body of the saint in proximity to the altar materialized this connection between the body of the saint and the body of Christ.[16] Some theologians believed that the body of Christ was a holy relic during the three days it spent in the tomb and, consequently, was a prototype for holy relics.[17] Because Christ's body did not decay while entombed, the uncorrupted bodies of the saints likewise took on special meaning and were treated as being blessed with divine power.[18] According to the first letter of Saint Paul to the Corinthians (1 Cor. 15:53), the earthly body of a saint was sanctified or transfigured: "For this corruptible must put on incorruption and this mortal must put on immortality." Thiofrid of Echternach, an early 12th-century monastic writer on relics, stated that, because of the merits achieved during the saint's lifetime, their

---

      Performativity in Byzantium and Medieval Russia, ed. Alexei Lidov (Moscow: Indrik, 2011), 275–301, 298–299.

14   Saint Basil the Great, *On the Holy Spirit* (Crestwood, NY: St. Vladimir's Seminary Press, 1980), 18.45, 72.

15   Elizabeth A. Fisher, "Life of the Patriarch Nicephoros I of Constantinople," in *Byzantine Defenders of Images: Eight Saints' Lives in English Translation*, ed. Alice-Mary Talbot (Washington, DC: Dumbarton Oaks Papers, 1998), 25–143, 54–56; Jaroslav Pelikan, *Jesus Through the Centuries: His Place in the History of Culture* (New Haven/London: Yale University Press, 1999), 87.

16   In his interpretation of the liturgy of the altar, Saint Germanus, the Patriarch of Constantinople (d. 733) said that it corresponded with the Holy Grave of Christ, see Saint Germanus of Constantinople, *On the Divine Liturgy*, trans. Paul Meyendorff (Crestwood, NY: St. Vladimir's Seminary Press, 1999), 59.

17   Sergius Bulgakov, *Relics and Miracles: Two Theological Essays*, trans. Boris Jakim (Grand Rapids, MI: William B. Eerdmans Publishing Company, 2011), 1–43.

18   Arnold Angenendt, "Relics and Their Veneration," in *Treasures of Heaven: Saints, Relics, and Devotion in Medieval Europe*, ed. Martina Bagnoli et al. (New Haven: Yale University Press, 2011), 19–29, 19.

bodies were considered bodies in Christ who "transmitted His own incorruptibility to their dead flesh."[19]

Before turning to the main theme of this chapter, to better grasp the connection between Christ's body and that of a saint it is important to understand the nature of saints' bodies. As relics, saints' bodies provided material evidence through which we are able to address a glorified saint. The efficacy of a given saint's relics depended on Christian faith; they were the medium through which saints interceded on behalf of humanity. The veneration of saints' relics and their frequent discovery in an uncorrupted state affirms that the physical world has the potential for being transfigured and resurrected, as it participates in the restoration of humanity to the beauty of the divine image and likeness.[20] The notion that God was able to preserve the bones or the entire corpse of a saint led to the legend of the indestructible life, according to which the

---

19   Thiofrid of Echternach, *Flores epytaphii sanctorum* 1.3, in *Corpus Christianorum. Continuatio Mediaevalis* 133 (Turnholt: Brepols, 1996), 16, l. 23 and 1. 4, 20, l. 80, see also Angenendt, "Relics and Their Veneration," 22; Julia M.H. Smith, "Relics: An Evolving Tradition in Late Christianity," in *Saints and Sacred Matter: The Cult of Relics in Byzantium and Beyond*, ed. Cynthia Hahn and Holger A. Klein (Washington, DC: Dumbarton Oaks Research Library and Collection, 2015), 41–60, 52.

20   On relics and the development of their cult, see Hippolyte Delehaye, *The Legends of the Saints* (London: Longman, 1907); André Grabar, *Martyrium. Recherches sur le culte des reliques et l'art Chrétien antique* (Paris: Collège de France, 1946); Andrey Frolow, *La relique de la Vraie Croix. Recherches sur le développement d'un culte* (Paris: Institut français d'études byzantines, 1961); Nicole Herrmann-Mascard, *Les reliques des saints. Formation coutumière d'un droit* (Paris: Klincksieck, 1975); Peter Brown, *The Cult of the Saints: Its Rise and Function in Latin Christianity* (Chicago: Chicago University Press, 1981); Sergei Hackel, ed., *The Byzantine Saint* (Crestwood, NY: St. Vladimir's Seminary Press, 2001); David Sox, *Relics and Shrines* (London: G. Allen & Unwin, 1985); Barbara Abou-El-Haj, *The Medieval Cult of Saints: Formations and Transformations* (Cambridge: Cambridge University Press, 1994); Anton Legner, *Reliquien in Kunst und Kult: zwischen Antike und Aufklärung* (Darmstadt: Wissenschaftliche Buchgesellschaft, 1995); Godefridus J.C. Snoek, *Medieval Piety from Relics to the Eucharist: A Process of Mutual Interaction* (Leiden/New York: E.J. Brill, 1995); Arnold Angenendt, *Heilige und Reliquien. Die Geschichte ihres Kultes vom frühen Christentum bis zur Gegenwart* (Munich: Nikol, 1997); Edina Bozóky and Anne-Marie Helvétius, eds., *Les reliques: objets, cultes, symboles: actes du colloque international de l'Université du Littoral-Côte d'Opale, Boulogne-sur-Mer, 4–6 septembre 1997* (Turnhout: Brepols, 1999); James Howard-Johnston and Paul Antony Hayward, eds., *The Cult of the Saints in Late Antiquity and the Middle Ages: Essays on the Contribution of Peter Brown* (Oxford: Oxford University Press, 1999); Anneke B. Mulder-Bakker, ed., *The Invention of Saintliness* (London/New York: Routledge, 2002); Alexei Lidov, ed., *Vostochnokhristianskie relikvii* [Eastern Christian relics] (Moscow: Progress-traditsiia, 2003); Irina A. Shalina, *Relikvii v vostochnokhristianskoĭ ikonografii* [Relics in Eastern Christian iconography] (Moscow: Indrik, 2005); Martina Bagnoli et al., eds., *Treasures of Heaven: Saints, Relics, and Devotion in Medieval Europe* (New Haven: Yale University Press, 2011); Cynthia Hahn and Holger A. Klein, eds., *Saints and Sacred Matter: The Cult of Relics in Byzantium and Beyond* (Washington, DC: Dumbarton Oaks Research Library and Collection, 2015).

bodies of the martyred were miraculously restored, and the bodies of certain saints remained in an incorrupt state.[21] The phenomenon of the whole and uncorrupted body rested on sporadic cases of bodies remaining intact long after burial.

That the power of the saints was still active even after their death gave them a paradoxical status of being neither fully dead nor alive. This allowed them to continue to remain an active presence in everyday life. As Caroline Bynum has observed, "the saints do not decay, in life or in death. They appear to us in visions, whole and shining ..."[22] Every saint has already begun the process of sanctification once they make a place for God in themselves.[23] This is best explained by Saint Paul, who writes to the Corinthians (2 Cor.3:18): "But we all with open face, beholding as in a glass the glory of the Lord, are changed into the same image from glory to glory, even as by the Spirit of the Lord." For Paul, Christ endowed saints' bodies with His power, and by creating a sanctified body at the moment of death, inanimate flesh was given new, immortal life.

Christ experienced death. Luke the Evangelist (Luke 23:46) described His soul departing His body as the giving of His spirit to the Father: "Father into thy hands I commend my spirit." However, the decomposition of His body was prevented by its connection with the divine spirit. In the words of Sergius Bulgakov, Christ's body did not see corruption "but found itself, as it were, in the state of a sleep."[24] Similarly, saints' relics sanctified by the divine spirit were akin to Christ's body during its three days and nights as a holy relic, which would be resurrected. This correlation makes Christ's body an archetype of the saintly body, a proto relic. As we have seen, by taking on human flesh God gives an ontological foundation for the sanctification of man and thereby establishes a basis for the veneration of relics. Saints' holy bodies preserve the divine power that dwelt in them and become a model of universal resurrection.

As holy relics, the uncorrupted bodies of saints became conduits between earth and heaven, humanity and the divine. In the words of Gregory of Nazianzus (c.329–390): "The bodies of the martyrs have the same power as their holy souls, whether one touches them or just venerates them."[25] Thus

---

21 Arnold Angenendt, "Corpus incorruptum: Eine Leitidee der mittelalterlichen Reliquien-verehrung," *Saeculum* 42 (1991), 320–346.

22 Caroline W. Bynum, *The Resurrection of the Body in Western Christianity, 200–1336* (New York: Columbia University Press, 1995), 220.

23 Bulgakov, *Relics and Miracles*, 21.

24 Bulgakov, *Relics and Miracles*, 103.

25 Gregory of Nazianzus, *Against Julian* 1 (Oration 4) 69, as cited by Derek Kruger; see Derek Kruger, "The Religion on Relics in Late Antiquity and Byzantium," in *Treasures of Heaven: Saints, Relics, and Devotion in Medieval Europe*, ed. Martina Bagnoli et al. (New Haven: Yale University Press, 2011), 5–17, 5.

saints were able to intercede with God on behalf of humankind since there was continuous communication between saints in heaven and Christians on earth.

Theologians often refer to a saint's death as being a transitional phase, which they liken to falling asleep. Confirming their ambivalent status of being in a liminal state of living death, Saint Jerome (347–420) wrote: "The truth is that the saints are not called dead, but are said to be asleep. Wherefore Lazarus, who was about to rise again, is said to have slept."[26] Paulinus of Nola (c.354–431) considered Saint Felix "buried, but not dead" and claimed that from his "temporary tranquil sleep" in his "gleaming" tomb, the saint monitored the courtyard of his church and delighted in the crowd who came to visit.[27]

Glorified bodies of saints that had already been transfigured were understood as altars on the earth, while according to the Book of Revelation (Rev. 6:9) their souls were placed under heavenly altars.[28] In order to establish the link between heaven and earth, and to connect bodies under earthly altars with souls under their heavenly counterparts, it was necessary for saints' relics to be placed either beneath, or in close proximity to, an altar.[29]

The translation of relics is a crucial element in scholarly studies analyzing the cult of relics and their function.[30] In the West, Ambrose (337/340–397), bishop of Milan, was a pioneer in the discovery and translation of saints' bodies to the altar of a church.[31] A 4th-century translation ceremony is described in a hymn that celebrates the memory of three martyrs—Felix, Victor, and Nabor—who were Moorish soldiers belonging to the garrison of Milan.[32]

---

26   Saint Jerome, *Against Vigilantius*, 6 in *St. Jerome: Letters and Selected Works. A Select Library of Nicene and Post-Nicene Fathers of the Christian Church*, 2nd series, vol. 6, trans. W.H. Fremantle, G. Lewis and W.G. Martley, ed. Philip Schaff and Henry Wace (New York: The Christian Literature Company, 1893), 419.

27   Paulinus of Nola, *The Poems of St. Paulinus of Nola*, trans. P.G. Walsh (New York: Newman Press, 1975), 194.

28   Alan T. Thacker, "The Making of a Local Saint," in *Local Saints and Local Churches in the Early Medieval West*, ed. Alan Thacker and Richard Sharpe (Oxford: Oxford University Press, 2002), 45–75, 51; see also, Richard Krautheimer, *Rome: Profile of a City, 312–1308* (Princeton, NJ: Princeton University Press, 1980), 112–113.

29   Bulgakov, *Relics and Miracles*, 29.

30   On the translation of relics with a detailed bibliography, see Ljubomir Milanović, "The Politics of Translatio: The Visual Representation of the Translation of Relics in the Early Christian and Medieval Period, The Case of St. Stephen" (PhD diss., Rutgers University, New Brunswick, 2011), 8–58.

31   Patricia Cox Miller, "Figuring Relics: A Poetics of Enshrinement," in *Saints and Sacred Matter: The Cult of Relics in Byzantium and Beyond*, ed. Cynthia Hahn and Holger A. Klein (Washington, DC: Dumbarton Oaks Research Library and Collection, 2015), 99–109, 100.

32   Ambrose, *Hymns x*, "*Victor Nabor Felix pii.*" For a French translation with commentary, see Pierre Dufraigne, *Adventus Augusti, Adventus Christi: recherche sur l'exploitation idéologique et littéraire d'un cérémonial dans l'Antiquité tardive* (Paris: Institut d'études augustiniennes, 1994).

THE BODY OF CHRIST AS RELIC ARCHETYPE   81

They were executed in Lodi in 304, during the great persecution of Diocletian. Their bodies were returned to this city under the episcopate of Maternus between the years 316 and 328 in what was, as far as we know, the first official translation.[33] The Second Council of Nicaea of 787 insisted, with special urgency, that relics were to be used in the consecration of churches and that their absence was to be remedied if any church had been consecrated without them.[34]

One of the important stages in the translation of relics was the relics' elevation. *Elevatio* was usually performed after the invention of relics in preparation for the moving of the body to a new location. It routinely took place inside the church and involved the disinterment of a saint from his tomb and relocation to the most prominent position in the building. The coffin was placed on an elevated platform behind the altar and oriented at right angles to it. The saint's head therefore came to lie in the west, in order that he would face Christ as He came again from the east.[35] This kind of solemn translation (*elevatio corporis*) was treated as the outward recognition of sanctity and was analogous to canonization in the period prior to the 13th century, when the Holy See in the West reserved for itself the passing of a final judgement upon the merits of the deceased servants of God.[36]

Following the 13th century, translations usually occurred only after official papal canonization.[37] The opening of the saint's tomb was preceded by a three-day fast since the clergy who were to carry out the ceremony required abundant spiritual preparation for the task ahead. Sometimes, as part of the preliminaries, the tomb was opened in private the night before the translation so that the bones could be inspected and old rotten garments replaced by new wrappings.[38] In the East, official canonization required the vigorous examination of the saint in the late 13th and early 14th centuries. The earliest records

---

33   Alban Butler, *The Lives of the Fathers, Martyrs, and Other Principal Saints*, vol. 1 (Dublin: H. Coyne, 1833), 94; Pierre Dufraigne, *Adventus Augusti, Adventus Christi*, 298.

34   Snoek, *Medieval Piety*, 185.

35   Arnold Angenendt, "Zur Ehre der Altäre erhoben: Zugleich ein Beitrag zur Reliquienverehrung," *Römishe Quartalschrift für christliche Altertumskunde* 89 (1994), 221–244.

36   Milanović, "The Politics of Translatio," 30.

37   In the early Middle Ages, a bishop and synod controlled canonization. Around 1200, the Pope asserted exclusive rights for the canonization of saints. Jill Raitt, ed., *Christian Spirituality: High Middle Ages and Reformation*, in collaboration with Bernard McGinn and John Meyendorff (New York: Crossroad, 1987), 94.

38   Ronald C. Finucane, "Sacred Corpse, Profane Carrion: Social Ideals and Death Rituals in the Later Middle Ages," in *Mirrors of Mortality: Studies in the Social History of Death*, ed. Joachim Whaley (London: Europa, 1981), 53.

of the ritual date from this period.[39] According to the historian Pachymeres (1242–c.1310) in his *De Michaele et Andronico Paleologis*, the uncorrupted relics of the patriarch of Constantinople Arsenius were translated to Constantinople in 1284 and deposited in the Hagia Sophia in a coffin placed to the right of the bema.[40] Pachymeres reports that the emperor, senate, patriarch, and clergy sang hymns and pronounced panegyrics at the ceremony.[41]

Once translated, saints' relics were deposited and presented in different ways. According to early Christian sources, relics were placed within the altar during its consecration. This, however, made them inaccessible for veneration.[42] There were other places in Western and Byzantine churches designated for saints' relics. Smaller reliquaries, containing body fragments, were usually kept inside the bema, on the altar, or nearby.[43] Intact bodies were positioned so that they were easily accessible for veneration on a daily basis.[44]

There are few surviving sources about the translation of relics and their location and display in medieval Serbia.[45] Existing sources emphasize the signs by which sanctity might be recognized, such as the working of miracles,

39 Ruth Macrides, "Saints and Sainthood in the Early Palaiologan Period," in *The Byzantine Saint*, ed. Sergei Hackel (Crestwood, NY: St. Vladimir's Seminary Press, 2001), 67–88, 83–87. See also Alice-Mary Talbot, "The Relics of New Saints: Deposition, Translation, and Veneration in Middle and Late Byzantium," in *Saints and Sacred Matter: The Cult of Relics in Byzantium and Beyond*, ed. Cynthia Hahn and Holger A. Klein (Washington, DC: Dumbarton Oaks Research Library and Collection, 2015), 215–231, esp. 218.

40 For the translation of relics, see George Pachymeres, *De Michaele et Andronico Palaeologis libri tredecim*, ed. Immanuel Bekker (Bonn: 1835), ii. 83.14–84.7; for more details on the translation of Patriarch Arsenius, see Macrides, "Saints and Sainthood," 73–79.

41 Pachymeres, *De Mich.* ii. 84.18–85.14.

42 See n. 26. See also Vasileios Marinis and Robert Ousterhout, "'Grant Us to Share a Place and Lot with Them,' Relics and the Byzantine Church Building (9th–15th Centuries)," in *Saints and Sacred Matter: The Cult of Relics in Byzantium and Beyond*, ed. Cynthia Hahn and Holger A. Klein (Washington, DC: Dumbarton Oaks Research Library and Collection, 2015), 153–173, esp. 154–155.

43 Marinis and Ousterhout, "Grant Us to Share a Place," 153–173, esp. 154–155, 160–161, with older bibliography.

44 Talbot, "The Relics of New Saints," 216.

45 Lazar Mirković, "Uvrštenje despota Stefana Lazarevića u red svetitelja [Inclusion of Despot Stefan Lazarevic in the order of saints]," *Bogoslovlje* 2 (1927), 163–177; Vladimir Ćorović, "Prilog proučavanju načina sahranjivanja i podizanja nadgrobnih spomenika u našim krajevima u srednjem veku" [Contribution to the study of the method of burial and erecting of gravestones in our region in the Middle Ages], *Naše starine* 3 (1956), 127–147. Đorđe Trifunović, "Stara srpska crkvena poezija" [Old Serbian church poetry], in *O Srbljaku*, ed. Dimitrije Bogdanović et al. (Belgrade: Srpska književna zadruga, 1970), 11–17; Danica Popović, "Srpska vladarska *translatio* kao trijumfalini *adventus*" [The Serbian ruler's *translatio* as triumphant *adventus*], in *Pod okriljem svetosti, Kult svetih vladara i relikvija u srednjovekovnoj Srbiji* (Belgrade: Balkanološki institut SANU, 2006), 233–253.

THE BODY OF CHRIST AS RELIC ARCHETYPE 83

incorruption of the body, exudation of oil (myron), or the emission of a fragrant odor.[46] Most likely, there was no formal canonization of the saints in the Serbian medieval state. Sainthood was achieved by living a life with holiness and virtue. The opening of the grave and the finding of an uncorrupted body was one of the conditions for the recognition of a saint.[47]

The tradition of moving saints' bodies in medieval Serbia probably started in the first half of the 13th century with the body of Saint Sava at Mileševa monastery. In his biography of Saint Sava, Domentijan describes the invention of his body after its burial in Mileševa.[48] Saint Sava appears in a dream to a monk, demanding the removal of his body and that it be placed in a wooden reliquary "in the middle of the church, for everyone to behold."[49] After the translation of Saint Sava's relics, the body was placed in a prominent place "in the midst of the holy and great church," a location now unknown to us.[50]

Depositing of the relics before the chancel barrier and in front of the icon of Christ seems not to have been established until the 14th century. According to the Serbian Archbishop Danilo II (1324–1337), the body of the Serbian queen, Helen (d. 1314), was removed from her tomb in the 14th century and displayed in a wooden coffin in front of the altar screen, below the icon of Christ the Savior, in the church of the Holy Virgin in the Gradac monastery.[51] The same source informs us that the relics of King Milutin (1282–1321) were transferred from his tomb in the Banjska monastery and placed in a wooden reliquary before the icon of Christ on the chancel barrier, outside the royal doors.[52]

I will now return to the case of King Stefan Dečanski and his relics in the church of Christ Pantokrator in Dečani. The Dečani monastery is the only Serbian royal mausoleum in which the material traces of the cult of Stefan

---

46 Mirković, "Uvrštenje despota Stefana Lazarevića," 168.

47 Trifunović, "Stara srpska crkvena poezija,"12.

48 Domentijan, *Životi Sv. Save i Sv. Simeona* [The Lives of St. Sava and St. Simeon], trans. Lazar Mirković (Belgrade: Srpska književna zadruga, 1938), 27–221, 216–217.

49 Domentijan, *Životi Sv. Save i Sv. Simeona*, 217.

50 Translation in Pantelić, *The Architecture*, 31, n. 105. On the location of Saint Sava's original tomb, see Popović, *Srpski vladarski grob*, 55–57; Danica Popović, "Mošti Svetog Save" [The relics of Saint Sava], in *Pod okriljem svetosti, Kult svetih vladara i relikvija u srednjovekovnoj Srbiji* (Belgrade: Balkanološki institut SANU, 2006), 75–97, esp. 85–88.

51 According to Archbishop Danilo II, the elevation of the queen occurred in 1317, three years after her death. The relics were moved from the sarcophagus tomb in the southwest corner of her mausoleum church at the Gradac monastery to their new position near the altar, see Arhiepiskop Danilo, *Životi kraljeva*, 75–76.

52 Arhiepiskop Danilo, *Životi kraljeva*, 120–121.

FIGURE 3.4 Dečani monastery, church of the Christ Pantokrator, Serbia, 14th century, original iconostasis with fresco surrounding it and the coffin of Saint Stefan Dečanski, oblique view
PHOTO: LJUBOMIR MILANOVIĆ

Dečanski are well preserved.[53] Currently, his relics are displayed on the northeast side, in front of the icon of Christ and perpendicular to the iconostasis (Figure 3.4). The king's face is oriented toward the altar and the east. The reliquary is positioned on an elevated platform, allowing visitors to lie under his sarcophagus in order to receive a blessing from the saint. During the Middle Ages, however, the reliquary of the body of Saint Stefan Dečanski was in a different location.

As we have seen, the elevation and translation of the king's body occurred in the summer or autumn of 1343 and was an official translation in the presence of church dignitaries and other nobility.[54] The body was placed in a

53   Danica Popović, "Sveti kralj Stefan Dečanski" [Holy king Stefan Dečanski], in *Pod okriljem svetosti. Kult svetih vladara i relikvija u srednjovekovnoj Srbiji* (Belgrade: Balkanološki institut SANU, 2006), 143–183, 156; Smilja Marjanović-Dušanić, *Sveti kralj* [Holy king] (Belgrade: Clio, 2007), 342.

54   The accepted *terminus post quem* for the portraits is the spring or summer of 1343; as we have seen, the king is identified as holy in the inscription. The year 1345 may be taken as a *terminus ante quem* because in the inscription of prayer, Dušan is called a young king, and the last written charter bearing his signature dates back to 1345. Gojko Subotić, "Prilog

FIGURE 3.5 Coffin of the holy king Stefan Dečanski, about 1340, Museum of the Serbian Orthodox Church, Belgrade
PHOTO: ALEKSANDAR RADOSAVLJEVIĆ

specially prepared reliquary for the occasion. The Dečani monastery preserves a reliquary casket from the first half of the 14th century (Figure 3.5).[55] The coffin is rectangular, with a lid in the shape of a hipped roof. This reliquary is made of wood and was covered in layers of gesso before being painted. The front, right side, and lid of the coffin are decorated with a relief of interlaced, predominantly floral motifs. The central rectangular panel on the front side depicts interwoven animals with ornamental forms (Figure 3.6). The frames that surround the decoration may have once been sheathed with gilded silver.[56] The lavish design indicates its precious contents. Notably, the addition of the silver framing evokes paradise as an ideal final resting place for the body

hronologiji dečanskog zidonog slikarstva" [Contribution to the chronology of Dečani wall paintings], *Zbornik radova vizantološkog instituta* 20 (1981), 111–138, 124; Dragan Vojvodić, "Portreti vladara, crkvenih dostojanstvenika i plemića u naosu i prirpati" [Portraits of rulers, ecclesiastical dignitaries and noblemen in the naos and narthex], in *Zidno slikarstvo manastira Dečana: građa i studije*, ed. Vojislav J. Djurić (Belgrade: Srpska akademija nauka i umetnosti, 1995), 265–298, 278–280.

55 For more about the reliquary, see Petković and Bošković, *Dečani*, 105–106; Mirjana Ćorović-Ljubinković, *Srednjovekovni duborez u istočnim oblastima Jugoslavije* [Medieval woodcut sculpture in the eastern regions of Yugoslavia] (Belgrade: Arheološki institut-posebna izdanja 5, 1965), 54–59; Mirjana Šakota, *Dečanska riznica* [Treasury of Dečani monastery] (Belgrade: BIGZ, 1984), 287–289; Todić and Čanak-Medić, *Manastir Dečani*, 32–33, 235–236; Danica Popović, "Shrine of King Stefan Uroš III Dečanski," in *Byzantium: Faith and Power (1261–1557)*, ed. Helen C. Evans (New York: The Metropolitan Museum of Art, 2004), 114–115; Miljana Matić, "Kivot za mošti svetog kralja Stefana Dečanskog" [Kivot with the remains of the holy king Stefan Dečanski], in *Srpsko umetničko nasleđe na Kosovu i Metohiji. Identitet, značaj, ugroženost*, ed. Miodrag Marković and Dragan Vojvodić (Belgrade: SANU, Kragujevac: Grafostil, 2017), 414–415.

56 There are traces of nails that probably held silver decoration that is now lost. Ćorović-Ljubinković, *Srednjovekovni duborez*, 56.

FIGURE 3.6 Coffin of the holy king Stefan Dečanski, about 1340, detail, Museum of the Serbian Orthodox Church, Belgrade
PHOTO: ALEKSANDAR RADOSAVLJEVIĆ

of the deceased.[57] It is possible that this reliquary chest, carefully preserved to the present day, was the original in which the body of Stefan Dečanski was placed after being removed from its tomb. If that is the case, according to scholars who have based their arguments upon the fact that the coffin was only decorated on two sides, it was likely positioned with its longer side to the northeast of the iconostasis and its left side to the south face of the northeast pillar (Figure 3.7).[58]

Establishing the cult of a saint starts with his or her death, which signifies the beginning of a new transcendental existence and requires the writing of an

---

[57] On the paradisiacal symbolism of metal, see Gerhart B. Ladner, *God, Cosmos, and Humankind: The World of Early Christian Symbolism* (Berkeley: University of California Press, 1995), 110, 133. See also Popović, *Srpski valdarski grob*, 108; Jaś Elsner, "Relic, Icon and Architecture: The Material Articulation of the Holy in Early Christian Art," in *Saints and Sacred Matter: The Cult of Relics in Byzantium and Beyond*, ed. Cynthia Hahn and Holger A. Klein (Washington, DC: Dumbarton Oaks Research Library and Collection, 2015), 13–41, 16.

[58] Ćorović-Ljubinković, *Srednjovekovni duborez*, 55; Todić and Čanak-Medić, *Manastir Dečani*, 32.

FIGURE 3.7 Dečani monastery, church of the Christ Pantokrator, Serbia, 14th century, old position of the reliquary, picture taken c.1941
PHOTO: AFTER PETKOVIĆ AND BOŠKOVIĆ, *DEČANI*

appropriate Life as well as offices and hymns.[59] The first Life of Stefan Dečanski was written during the period of the reign of King Stefan Dušan and was

---

59 Leontije Pavlović, *Kultovi lica kod Srba i Makedonaca* [The cult of individuals among Serbs and Macedonians] (Smederevo: Narodni muzej, 1965), 99–109; Popović, "Sveti kralj Stefan Dečanski,"147.

compiled by Danilo's continuer, likely between 1337 and 1340.[60] This Life does not give much information on the translation of the king's body to the reliquary, nor does it give accounts of his saintliness. It takes the form of a historiography rather than a hagiography.[61]

The most comprehensive information on King Dečanski's translation and canonization comes from the writings of Grigorije Camblak at the beginning of the 15th century.[62] In his narrative, which may have originated from living memory or a now lost source, Camblak describes the invention, elevation, and translation of the king's body using standard hagiographic models based on the usual topoi of the saint.[63] Camblak states that seven years after the body of the king was placed in his final grave in Dečani, the king appeared on three occasions in a dream of a sacristan demanding the disinterment of his remains. Only after the same dream was experienced by the *hegumenos* of the monastery did the officiating bishop assemble a council of archpriests as well as of members of the clergy. After the stone was removed from the king's grave, the entire church and surrounding area was filled with a fragrant odor and they discovered the saint's uncorrupted body; all present were convinced of his royal holiness. The body was lifted and translated into a new, specially made reliquary casket (Figure 3.8).[64] Camblak describes the miraculous power of the king's relics in detail. The narrative proceeds by offering testimony of a number of miraculous healings that occurred before the saint's relics.[65]

The posthumous portrait of Saint Stefan Dečanski appears on the south face of the northeast pier, just above the reliquary with the king's body

---

60   Danilov nastavljač, "Kralj Stefan Uroš Treći" [King Stefan Uroš the Third], in *Danilovi nastavljači. Danilov učenik, drugi nastavljači Danilovog zbornika*, ed. Dimitrije Bogdanović et al. (Belgrade: Prosveta, 1989), 27–67; Gordon L. Mak Daniel, "Prilozi za istoriju 'Života kraljeva i arhiepiskopa srpskih' od Danila II" [Contributions to the history of the life of the kings and the archbishop of the Serbs by Danilo II], *Prilozi za književnost jezik istoriju i folklor* 46, 1–4 (1980–1984), 42–52; Popović, "Sveti kralj Stefan Dečanski," 144.

61   Popović, "Sveti kralj Stefan Dečanski," 150. The primary document for information regarding the canonization of Stefan Dečanski and elevation of his body is the charter issued to the monastery of Saints Peter and Paul on the River Lim by King Stefan Dušan in 1434 in which King Dušan mentions God's blessing having been bestowed on the body of his holy father, see Vujošević, "Hrisovulja kralja Stefana," 49, 53.

62   Camblak was responsible for creating the image of King Stefan Dečanski as a martyred king. For the life of Grigorije Camblak, see Damnjan Petrović, "Camblakova literarna delatnost u Srbiji [Camblak's literary activity in Serbia]," in Grigorije Camblak, *Književni rad u Srbiji*, trans. Lazar Mirković et al. (Belgrade: Prosveta, 1989), 9–45, esp. 10–19.

63   Popović, "Sveti kralj Stefan Dečanski," 155.

64   Camblak, "Žitije Stefana Dečanskog," 73.

65   Camblak, "Žitije Stefana Dečanskog," 74–82.

THE BODY OF CHRIST AS RELIC ARCHETYPE 89

FIGURE 3.8   Dečani monastery, church of the Christ Pantokrator, Serbia, 14th century, relics of the holy king Stefan Dečanski
PHOTO: DEČANI MONASTERY (SERBIAN ORTHODOX CHURCH)

beside the iconostasis (Figure 3.9).[66] This example of a posthumous portrait of a saint as material evidence of his cult is unique in Serbian medieval art. The portrait, probably executed soon after the translation of the king's body c.1343, depicts Stefan Dečanski in three-quarter view, holding a model of his foundation.[67] The model does not resemble the existing architectural structure and is shown such that the southern parecclesion dedicated to Saint Nicholas is emphasized.[68] Stefan Dečanski is dressed in royal clothing and bowing

---

66 On the portrait, see Svetozar Radojčić, Portreti srpskih vladara u srednjem veku [Portraits of Serbian rulers in the Middle Ages] (Skoplje: Muzej Južne Srbije u Skoplju, 1934), 45–47; Ivan M. Đorđević, "Predstava Stefana Dečanskog uz oltarsku pregradu u Dečanima" [The representation of Stefan Dečanski near the altar partition in Dečani], Saopštenja 15 (1983), 35–42; Vojvodić, "Portreti vladara," 278–280; Popović, "Sveti kralj Stefan Dečanski," 158; Todić and Čanak-Medić, Manastir Dečani, 34–35; Dragana Pavlović, "Kralj Stefan Uroš III Dečanski" [King Stefan Uroš the Third Dečanski], in Srpsko umetničko nasleđe na Kosovu i Metohiji. Identitet, značaj, ugroženost, ed. Miodrag Marković and Dragan Vojvodić (Belgrade: SANU, Kragujevac: Grafostil, 2017), 382–383.
67 For the dates of the painting in Dečani, see Subotić, "Prilog hronologiji," 111–136.
68 Vladimir Petković was the first to notice this on the model, see Petković and Bošković, Dečani, 23; see also, Đorđević, "Predstava Stefana Dečanskog," 35.

FIGURE 3.9   Dečani monastery, church of the Christ Pantokrator, Serbia, 14th century, the holy king Stefan Dečanski, fresco, south face of the northeast pier
PHOTO: LJUBOMIR MILANOVIĆ

THE BODY OF CHRIST AS RELIC ARCHETYPE   91

slightly toward the bust of Christ who blesses from above (Figure 3.10).[69] Next
to the head of the king an inscription identifies him as "The Holy King, enlightened by God, Stefan Uroš III, the founder of this holy church." Under the model
of the church is a brief inscription highlighting the king's prayers to the Savior:

> Receive, Lord the Pantokrator, this gift and my prayers, of your servant
> Stefan the king, for I, with my Son, King Stefan, offer you a divine church.
> I look upon my corruptible body, standing over my grave, and I fear your
> judgment. I belong to you, Pantokrator, have mercy on me on judgment
> day. (Figure 3.11)[70]

Though the location of the inscribed prayer below the model of the church is
unusual, it is reminiscent of some representations of the Virgin which include
a scroll with an intercessory prayer.[71] The content of the prayer certainly has
parallels in Byzantine as well as in Serbian medieval painting.[72]

Gordana Babić was the first to observe the interesting correspondence
between the posthumous portrait of Stefan Dečanski and the rest of the
painted church program, especially the king's patron saints, Saint Nicholas
and Saint Stephen Protomartyr, the patron saints of the house of Nemanjić
(Figure 3.12). She also identified the portrait as being part of the larger eschatological program represented in the eastern part of the naos where Christ the
Pantokrator is depicted surrounded by the Virgin and John the Baptist in the
form of a Deesis (Figure 3.13).[73]

The location of the portrait next to the iconostasis is the result of the transfer of the royal relics.[74] The stone chancel barrier in Dečani was part of the
general architectural conception of the church and its interior decoration,
dating from 1327 to 1335 (Figure 3.14). Branislav Todić has noted that it was
not designed with the intention of placing icons in its intercolumns; rather, as
was the case in most Byzantine churches, its intercolumns were covered with

---

69 For a detailed description of King Stefan Dečanski's portrait, see Đorđević, "Predstava
    Stefana Dečanskog," 35; Vojvodić, "Portreti vladara," 278.

70 For the original text of the inscription with the king's supplication to Christ, see Subotić,
    "Prilog hronologiji," 124. For a translation of the texts, see Todić and Čanak-Medić,
    Manastir Dečani, 34.

71 Vojvodić, "Portreti vladara," 278.

72 Đorđević, "Predstava Stefana Dečanskog," 40; Vojvodić, "Portreti vladara," 278.

73 Gordana Babić, "O živopisanom ukrasu oltarskih pregrada" [On the painted ornamenta-
    tion of altar screens], *Zbornik za likovne umetnosti* 11 (1975), 3–41, 35, see also Popović,
    Srpski vladarski grob, 111–112, 185.

74 Đorđević, "Predstava Stefana Dečanskog," 37.

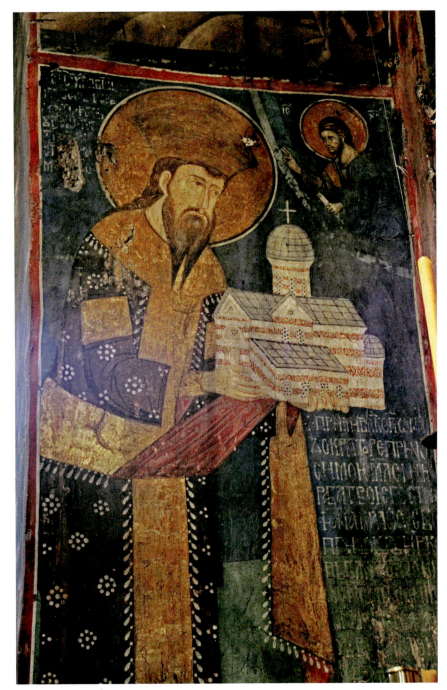

FIGURE 3.10   Dečani monastery, church of the Christ Pantokrator, Serbia, 14th century, the holy king Stefan Dečanski, fresco, south face of the northeast pier, detail
PHOTO: LJUBOMIR MILANOVIĆ

THE BODY OF CHRIST AS RELIC ARCHETYPE 93

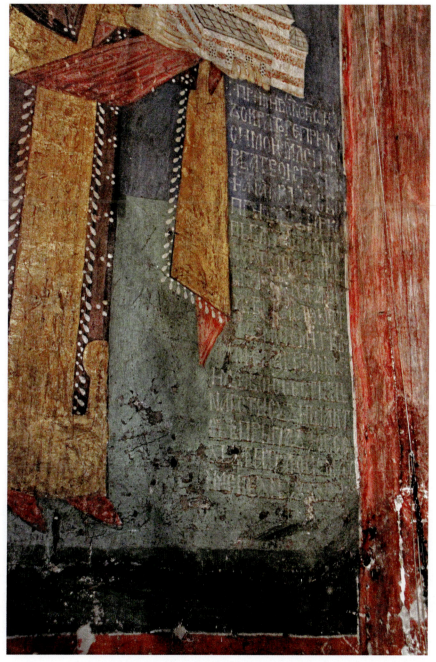

FIGURE 3.11   Dečani monastery, church of the Christ Pantokrator, Serbia, 14th century, holy king Stefan Dečanski, fresco, south face of the northeast pier, detail
PHOTO: LJUBOMIR MILANOVIĆ

FIGURE 3.12   Dečani monastery, church of the Christ Pantokrator, Serbia, 14th century, Saint Stephen Protomartyr, fresco, west wall of the south bay of the naos
PHOTO: LJUBOMIR MILANOVIĆ

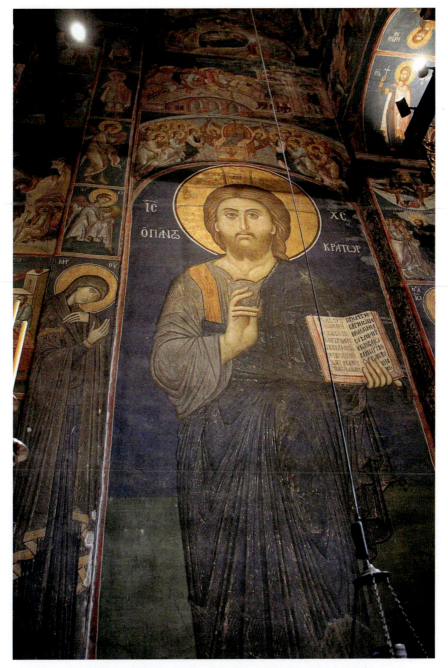

FIGURE 3.13 Dečani monastery, church of the Christ Pantokrator, Serbia, 14th century, Christ Pantokrator from Deesis, fresco, west wall of the south bay of the naos
PHOTO: LJUBOMIR MILANOVIĆ

FIGURE 3.14   Dečani monastery, church of the Christ Pantokrator, Serbia, 14th century, iconostasis, viewed from the back, picture taken c.1941
PHOTO: AFTER PETKOVIĆ AND BOŠKOVIĆ, *DEČANI*

curtains. For Todić, the key reason for the change from curtains to the icons of Saint Nicholas, the Virgin and Child, Christ, and Saint John the Baptist, was the transfer of the relics of King Stefan Dečanski into the altar area in 1343.[75]

The portrait and its inscription has been the subject of much scholarly debate. A majority of scholars have noted that in the written text the saint prays for his salvation and that these words are not what one expects to hear from a saint. They have concluded that observing one's own perishable body, expressing fear of the Last Judgement, or requesting pardon, is contrary to the theological understanding of sainthood during the Middle Ages.[76] This has led many to conclude that the portrait was painted in an early stage of his saintly

---

75   He based his opinion on the absence of traces of grooves or evidence of anything that might have been used for fixing the icons on the iconostases on either the colonnettes or on the upper edges of the parapets. Branislav Todić, "Ikonostas u Dečanima—prvobitni slikani program i njegove poznije izmene" [Iconostasis in Dečani—original painting program and its later changes], *Zograf* 36 (2012), 115–129, 115–116.

76   Popović, "Sveti kralj Stefan Dečanski," 150–158, Todić and Čanak-Medić, *Manastir Dečani*, 34–35; Marjanović-Dušanić, *Sveti kralj*, 360; Todić, "Ikonostas u Dečanima," 116.

THE BODY OF CHRIST AS RELIC ARCHETYPE   97

cult, before it was fully formed, before Dečanski received an office or a real hagiography.[77]

Other scholars, however, have pointed out that the portrait, accompanied by its inscription, underlined the relationship between the founder and Christ. This relationship is expressed, on one hand, by the prayer of Stefan Dečanski and, on the other, by the blessing of Christ. This is the only inscription of this kind found in medieval Serbian wall painting, which reveals much about the beliefs of the founder.[78] Scholars have argued that the portrait indicates that, after Dečanski was canonized, he came to stand directly before Christ as an intercessor, not only for his own soul, but also for that of his son, King Dušan, as well. This portrait therefore represents Stefan Dečanski's future appearance at the Last Judgement.[79]

Prior scholars have not focused on the connection of the body of the saint and the altar, which represents the symbolic tomb of Christ in which His body remained for three days. There are multiple ways by which a saint's body may be recognized as a relic within the Christian tradition.[80] Some saints become holy during their lifetime, and some at the moment of their death.[81] For others, years of miracles and wonders, or the discovery of their uncorrupted bodies are required as proof of holiness.[82] In the case of Dečanski, as we have seen, his body was found to be incorrupt. This means that his body was transfigured with God's grace and its state of incorruptibility was material proof of the saint's full *theosis*. Though the portrait inscription mentions the saint's perishable body, this in fact gestures to his humility.[83] That is to say, the king's

---

77   Popović, "Sveti kralj Stefan Dečanski," 161.
78   Đorđević, "Predstava Stefana Dečanskog," 36. Lazar Mirković has noted that the explanation for the text of the prayer should be sought in the Dečani charter, see Lazar Mirković, "Da li na freskama u niškoj grobnici (kraj IV) veka imamo portrete sahranjenih u njoj?" [Do we have the portraits of those buried in Niš mausoleum (end of 4th century) represented in its frescoes?], *Zbornik Narodnog muzeja* 5 (1967), 227–229.
79   Đorđević, "Predstava Stefana Dečanskog," 42; Vojvodić, "Portreti vladara," 279.
80   Michel Kaplan, "De la dépouille à la relique: formation du culte des saints à Byzance du Vᵉ au XIIᵉ siècle," in *Les reliques. Objets, cultes, symboles: Actes du colloque international de l'Université du Littoral-Côte d'Opale (Boulogne-sur-Mer), 4–6 septembre 1997*, ed. Edina Bozóky and Anne Marie Helvétius (Turnhout: Brepols, 1999), 19–38; Michel Kaplan, "L'ensevelissement des saints: rituels de création des reliques et sanctification à Byzance d'après les sources hagiographiques," in *Mélanges Gilbert Dagron* (Paris: Association des amis du Centre d'histoire et civilisation de Byzance, 2002), 319–332.
81   Katherine Marsengill, *Portraits and Icons: Between Reality and Spirituality in Byzantine Art* (Turnhout: Brepols, 2013), 271–277.
82   Talbot, "The Relics of New Saints," 211–219.
83   Ivan M. Đorđević, "Dve Molitve Stefana Dečanskog pre bitke na Velbuždu i njegov odjek u umetnosti" [Two prayers of Stefan Dečanski before the Battle of Velbuzd and his echo in art], *Zbornik za likovne umetnosti* 15 (1979), 135–150.

body should be viewed as a body sanctified by God, but still connected to the earth while the soul of the saint has already joined God in heaven. While the soul is able to traverse the two worlds, the body is still bound to Earth.[84] The Resurrection will reunite the soul with the body. By mentioning the Last Judgement and his fear of it, Stefan Dečanski was pointing to the final resurrection when both his body and soul would be reunited with Christ.

The juxtaposition between the Dečanski portrait on the northeast pier and the reliquary casket has been seen as mirroring the position of the founder portrait of King Stefan Uroš III on the south wall in relation to his first tomb.[85] Ivan Đorđević has noted that the king's posthumous portrait differs from that on the south wall of the naos by showing the gradual change in facial color between the portrait of the king and the portrait of the saint.[86] This is explained by the words of John of Damascus who said that "The saints, in their lifetime, were filled with the Holy Spirit and when they are no more, His grace abides with their spirits and with their bodies in their tombs, and also with their likeness and sacred icons, not by nature but by grace and divine power ..."[87] For Damascus, the connection between the type and the prototype lies in likeness, meaning that through the type we convey the prototype. Thus both the king's body and his posthumous portrait emanate the grace of God embedded in them. Katherine Marsengill has observed that the sanctification of the soul is expressed in the body and becomes visible through the portrait of the person.[88]

The connection between the saint's body and Christ's body as its prototype is perhaps best illustrated in the story of the stylite Lazaros of Galesion. The occasion described in his Life concerns the removal of his dead body from a pillar. In the words of the saint's biographer, "they had lifted up Lazaros' body on the pillar and let it hang suspended in order to bring it down ... nothing else could be seen among them at the time except for woe and lamentation and inconsolable weeping. Moreover, [the image of] my Jesus was reproduced again at the sight of that sacred body, and it really seemed as if He could be

---

84   Marsengill, *Portraits and Icons*, 275.

85   Todić, "Ikonostas u Dečanima," 118.

86   Đorđević, "Predstava Stefana Dečanskog," 41. On the portrait of Stefan Dečanski on the south wall of the naos and its controversies, see Vojvodić, "Portreti vladara," 265–275, with older bibliography.

87   John of Damascus, *Or. I, De Imaginibus*, PG 94, 1249D. For an English translation see Mary H. Allies, trans., *St. John Damascene on Holy Images* (London: Thomas Baker, 1898), 22.

88   Marsengill, *Portraits and Icons*, 260.

THE BODY OF CHRIST AS RELIC ARCHETYPE   99

seen being taken down from the cross once more."[89] This example clearly shows the perception of onlookers who were able to recognize the prototype in the transfigured body of the holy.

The commemorative portrait of the king, as well as his holy body, were placed in close proximity to the iconostasis which represents the boundary between visible and invisible worlds.[90] It conceals the altar from the viewer, but at the same time, reveals heavenly witnesses represented on the icons of saints as well as of the Virgin Mary and Christ.[91] The figure of King Stefan Dečanski should be seen as another witness, who in the company of other saints, serves as a guide for the faithful to a vision of the Divine Kingdom. As intercessors, saints become gateways for prayers for the salvation of the human race, prayers which will only be fulfilled at the Last Judgement. The bodies of saints become a source of faith and reassurance of resurrection; powerful examples that should be followed.[92] The iconostasis reveals the heavenly realm and makes it spiritually visible, but only to those enlightened by God.[93] As part of the iconostasis, icons are functionally connected to the altar space, the symbolism of which points to the dogma about the redemption of sins.[94] Juxtaposing the portrait of Saint Stefan Dečanksi and his holy body in front of the iconostasis gave the faithful a model to follow, while the inscription on the portrait warns them that nothing is certain until the Last Judgement and resurrection.

---

89   Gregory the Cellarer, *The Life of Lazaros of Mt. Galesion*, Chapter 251. For an English translation, see Gregory the Cellarer, *The Life of Lazaros of Mt. Galesion: An Eleventh-Century Pillar Saint*, intro. and trans. Richard P.H. Greenfield (Washington, DC: Dumbarton Oaks, 2000), 360. Saint Lazaros died in 1053 and his Life was composed soon after by one of his followers, Gregory the Cellarer, see Marsengill, *Portraits and Icons*, 274.

90   Nicholas P. Constas, "Symeon of Thessalonike and the Theology of the Icon Screen," in *Threshold of the Sacred*, ed. Sharon E.J. Gerstel (Washington, DC: Dumbarton Oaks Research Library and Collection, 2006), 163–185. For the iconostasis in Byzantine churches, see Christopher Walter, "The Origin of the Iconostasis," *Eastern Churches Review* 3 (1971), 251–267, 262–263; also Babić, "O živopisanom ukrasu," 14–20.

91   On the theological meaning of the iconostasis, see Pavel Florensky, *Iconostasis*, trans. Donald Sheehan and O. Andrejev (Crestwood, NY: St. Vladimir's Seminary Press, 2000), 62.

92   Wendy Mayer, "Introduction," in *St. John Chrysostom: The Cult of the Saints*, intro. and trans. Wendy Mayer and Bronwen Neil (Crestwood, NY: St. Vladimir's Seminary Press, 2006), 11–35, 30.

93   Slobodan Ćurčić, "Architecture as Icon," in *Architecture as Icon. Perception and Representation of Architecture in Byzantine Art*, ed. Slobodan Ćurčić and Evangelia Hadjitryphonos (New Haven: Yale University Press, 2010), 3–39, 26–29.

94   Babić, "O živopisanom ukrasu," 9.

The displaying of relics before the iconostasis, as is the case in Dečani, should be viewed in light of the symbolic meaning of the chancel barrier, and as a link between type and archetype; between the saintly relics and Christ's body. The iconostasis was the barrier between the earthly (present) and the heavenly (future) realms. Placing the uncorrupted body of the saint next to the heavenly realm emphasized his intercessory role in the Second Coming of Christ. The juxtaposition of the king's body and the icon of Christ aligned with the altar in Dečani provides insight into the relationship between icons and bodily relics more broadly. As demonstrated in this essay, icons and relics are both imbued with holiness and are also evidence of the miracle of the Incarnation, and thus linked to its archetypal form, the body of Christ.

Acknowledgements

This text is part of the research supported by the Ministry of Education, Science, and Technological Development of the Republic of Serbia. I would like to thank to my dear friend Dr. Allan Doyle, Assistant Professor at Parsons School of Design and The New School, New York City, for his close reading of the text, helpful suggestions, and corrections.

CHAPTER 4

From Earth to Heaven: Transcendental Concepts of Architecture in Late Roman and Early Byzantine Art (*c.*300–700)

Cecilia Olovsdotter

This chapter considers the use of architectural motifs as symbolic concepts in Late Roman and Early Byzantine art.[1] Although formally, functionally, and contextually related to built counterparts, the visual constructions dealt with here do not, or only in limited and ambiguous ways, represent 'real' monumental architecture. Late antique art is rich in what may be called architectural imagery, i.e. figural compositions where an architectural structure provides a visually prominent and regularizing element. Arches, portals, pedimented fronts, aedicules, and domes certainly appeared in Greco-Roman art before late antiquity, but much less frequently, and for the most part in funerary works. The significant increase in and formal and contextual diversification of architectural motifs in the visual culture of late antiquity can perhaps chiefly be explained by their suitability for the hieratic and abstracted mode of representation that was developed in this period, i.e., their usefulness in the creation of symbolic art, but they would arguably also have reflected an expanded visual conception of architecture in general, and of certain architectural types and themes as bearers of abstract meaning in particular.[2] Indeed, late antique pictorial or imaged architecture may be considered as graphic illustrations of the ideational superstructures attached to actual or built architecture in this period: physical architecture and imaged architecture were part of the same language

---

1 I am indebted to several institutions for their support of my research on imaged architecture in late antique visual culture, of which this chapter is one result: the Swedish Research Institute in Istanbul; the Swedish Institute of Classical Studies at Rome; the Royal Swedish Academy of Letters, History and Antiquities; the Bank of Sweden Tercentenary Foundation; the Fondazione Famiglia Rausing (Rome); the Enbom Foundation (Stockholm); the Torsten and Ingrid Gihl Foundation (Stockholm); the Lars Hierta Memorial Foundation (Stockholm); and the Royal Society of Arts and Sciences in Gothenburg.

2 Cf. Bandmann's notion that the allegorical or metaphoric meanings attached to certain typologized architectural motifs ("building components") generated abstracted pictorial forms (ergo that imaged architecture encapsulated and conveyed the symbolic meanings associated with its built prototypes); Günter Bandmann, *Early Medieval Architecture as Bearer of Meaning*, trans. Kendall Wallis (New York: Columbia University Press, 2005), 67.

© KONINKLIJKE BRILL NV, LEIDEN, 2023 | DOI:10.1163/9789004537781_006

of forms, constituting mutually reflective articulations of one universal architectural perception. As a visual technique and means of expression essentially unconstrained by the physical laws of tectonics, imaged architecture allowed for near limitless variation, modification, and synthesis of established architectural types and elements. The resulting creations range from the reductively abstract to the imaginatively fantastical, often architectonically illogical and sometimes seemingly nonsensical, yet systematic analysis of them reveals clear and consistent patterns not only in terms of their conceptual construction but also of their contextual application and relevance.[3] Generally speaking, the function and meaning of architectural motifs in late antique art were to define and glorify man in his different roles and fields of action, and to give visual form to prevailing ideas and beliefs about the nature and composition of society, the world, and the cosmos.[4]

---

3 A monographic study of imaged architecture in Late Roman and Early Byzantine visual culture is under preparation by the present author.

4 Although this understanding of the nature and applications of imaged architecture in late antiquity can neither be considered far-fetched nor inconsequential, such meaningful connotations have only fleetingly been touched upon in the literature; indeed the very proliferation and systematic modes of application of architectural motifs in art in this specific period seems largely to have gone unobserved. Any interest shown has typically been of a purely formal nature, either aesthetic (as ornamental frameworks or space-fillers) or archaeological (as representations or even depictions of specific buildings, *viz. a priori* identifiable and genealogically traceable architectural prototypes), but either way essentially devoid of intrinsic meaning. A different, but likewise formal, analysis is offered by Paul Lampl in his brief but seminal article on architectural representations in early medieval Christian art, where it is held that such representations were not inspired by any built or "real" architecture, whether specific or typological, but entirely dictated by "the mind of the late antique artist," thus suggesting a disassociation between architectural forms/types and any symbolic associations tied to them, and also (somewhat astonishingly) that early medieval architects and image makers originated their architectural schemes independently from each other; Paul Lampl, "Schemes of Architectural Representation in Early Medieval Art," *Marsyas* 9 (1961), 6–13, esp. 7–10. More in line with my understanding of imaged architecture as a bearer of contextual meaning is Günter Bandmann's idea that certain primitive architectural forms typified, as visual forms, in antiquity and "received"—*viz.* continued, adapted, and in some cases attributed more definite or new meanings and functions—in Christian late antiquity and the Early Middle Ages as inherently denotative of a "higher content," i.e., specific ideas and associations related to cultural context (history, tradition, religion, social and political circumstances, and concepts); Bandmann, *Early Medieval Architecture*, 15–27, 30, 55, 59–70. For a concise critical survey of the extant literature on architectural motifs in Roman and late antique art, see Cecilia Olovsdotter, "Architecture and the Spheres of the Universe in Late Antique Art," in *Envisioning Worlds in Late Antique Art: New Perspectives on Abstraction*

The most widely employed architectural types—in the archetypal sense—for late antique imaged architecture were monumental portals and gates (notably city gates and triumphal arches), the pedimented fronts of temples and shrines, and the composite arched and prostyle front variously referred to as the arched, Syrian, or (in the late antique context particularly) palatial *fastigium*.[5] The common denominators of these three building types—in simplified terms gate, temple, and palace—were their liminal quality, whether it denoted the passage between exterior and interior spheres and/or the meeting place of human and divine, and that they were inherently designed for ritual or ceremonial purposes. As conceptual forms they had since ancient times been associated with certain occurrences, practices, and concepts, such as boundary, arrival, entry, passage, triumph, the divine house, the house of the dead, the heavenly sphere, the seat of power, elevated status, majesty, apotheosis, etc., and a rich visual record testifies that these associations were further strengthened and sublimated in late antiquity. In imagery, the functions and meanings associated with certain architectural types and structures were habitually articulated through the addition of cosmic (earthly, heavenly, transcendental) symbols, selected and applied according to principles of relevance and synergy of meaning. Together, architecture and symbols provided frameworks that variously specified and universalized the meaning of the main theme and purpose(s) of an image or visual program.[6] The material, contextual, and geographical diffusion of such architectural configurations throughout late antique art, and the consistency with which they were realized, suggest a period-specific collective tendency or 'mindset' to conceptualize the world—phenomena, relationships, temporal sequences, atemporal states and dignities—in terms of structural form (formal type), connectivity, organization, and containment. In what follows I will concentrate on the late antique use of the arch and the pedimented front as means for visualizing transcendence and immortality.

---

and Symbolism in Late-Roman and Early-Byzantine Visual Culture (*c. 300–600*), ed. Cecilia Olovsdotter (Berlin/Boston: De Gruyter, 2019), 138–139, n. 4.

5 For the different denominations of the arched *fastigium*, and its predominantly palatial usage in late antiquity, see nn. 75 and 77.

6 For a presentation of the symbols most frequently combined with imaged architecture in late antiquity, and the principles that guided their selection and distribution on/around it, see Olovsdotter, "Architecture and the Spheres," 150–154.

1 The Arch

The arch was an established and widely employed motif of transition in Roman architecture and art, and in late antiquity it had evidently come to be regarded as a theme with many adaptations. The notions of movement, arrival, entry, and passage with which the arch was traditionally associated provided relevant and effective metaphors for a number of occurrences and acts customarily celebrated through architecture and art. Most prominent of these was victory, a concept absolutely central to Roman power politics, religion, and historiography, around which a whole civilization and cosmology were constructed.[7]

In the two panels of a commemorative ivory diptych commissioned by Probus in connection with his Western consulship in 406 (Figure 4.1)[8] we find a classically Roman example of the arch as a symbol of passage. The arch accompanies the full-figure representation of the consul's appointer, the emperor Honorius (384–423), who poses as if having just entered through it, wearing the costume and attributes of a victorious Roman general and world ruler (Gorgon-adorned cuirass, spear, shield, *victoriola*-surmounted orb). Understood contextually, and following a string of conventional Roman associations, this arch may be read in several interconnected ways, none of which is referable to any historical event or physical place: as a reference to the *adventus* of the victorious emperor through a city gate and/or his passing through a triumphal arch as part of a triumphal procession (*processus triumphalis*); as an allusion to the idea of imperial victory as the beginning of a new prosperous cycle in the history of Rome;[9] and, given that the diptych commemorates a consulship, as a reference to the beginning of a new annual cycle (*novus annus*) through the consul's taking of office on the New Year, the apparatus,

---

7   For useful analyses of the Roman victory concept and its manifestations in all major areas of Roman and late antique society, see Hendrik Simon Versnel, *Triumphus: An Inquiry into the Origin, Development and Meaning of the Roman Triumph* (Leiden: Brill, 1970); J. Rufus Fears, "The Theology of Victory at Rome: Approaches and Problems," in *Aufstieg und Niedergang der Römischen Welt* 2.17:2 (Berlin/New York: De Gruyter, 1981), 736–826; and Michael McCormick, *Eternal Victory: Triumphal Rulership in Late Antiquity, Byzantium, and the Early Mediaeval West* (Cambridge: Cambridge University Press, 1986).

8   Rome or northern Italy, 406; Aosta, Tesoro della Cattedrale. Richard Delbrueck, *Die Consulardiptychen und verwandte Denkmäler* (Berlin/Leipzig: De Gruyter, 1929), no. 1; Wolfgang Fritz Volbach, *Elfenbeinarbeiten der Spätantike und des frühen Mittelalters* (Mainz: Philipp von Zabern, 1976), no. 1; Cecilia Olovsdotter, *The Consular Image: An Iconological Study of the Consular Diptychs* (Oxford: John and Erica Hedges, 2005), esp. 168, plate 14.

9   Cf. Versnel's interpretation of the triumphator; Versnel, *Triumphus*, 356–396.

FIGURE 4.1   Consular diptych of Probus; Rome or northern Italy, 406; Aosta, Tesoro della Cattedrale
PHOTO: DIEGO CESARE, REGIONE AUTONOMA VALLE D'AOSTA, ARCHIVI DELL'ASSESSORATO BENI CULTURALI, TURISMO, SPORT E COMMERCIO DELLA REGIONE AUTONOMA VALLE D'AOSTA—FONDO CATALOGO BENI CULTURALI

procedure, and ideological construct of which were directly modelled on those of the Roman triumph.[10]

10   Versnel, *Triumphus*, 95–98, 129–131, 302f–303, 356–380, 371–373; Sabine G. MacCormack, *Art and Ceremony in Late Antiquity* (Berkeley/London: University of California Press, 1981), 52–55; McCormick, *Eternal Victory*, esp. 84–91; Ernst Künzl, *Der römische Triumph. Siegesfeiern im antiken Rom* (Munich: C.H. Beck, 1988), 106, 129; Jörg Rüpke, *Domi militiae*.

The arch remained a recurrent motif in the consular diptychs, which were an important category of commemorative artwork commissioned and distributed in multiples by the annually appointed consuls (*consules ordinarii*) of Rome and Constantinople from the late 4th century to 542, when Justinian abolished this highest and most ancient of Roman state offices.[11] Although long since emptied of executive power, and consisting only of ceremonial and pecuniary obligations (processions, the giving of games, the public distribution of largesse), the last centuries of the consulate's existence saw its resurgence as the most prestigious position in the Roman civil career (*cursus honorum*),[12] a resurgence very much evidenced by the consular diptychs themselves, which, in adherence to long-established ideals and practices of Roman commemorative art, served to advertize and glorify their honorands' status and the superior merits and virtues by which they had earned it.[13] In some diptychs commissioned by Areobindus (Figure 4.2)[14] and Clementinus (Figure 4.3)[15]

Die religiöse Konstruktion des Krieges in Rom (Stuttgart: F. Steiner, 1990), 231; Stéphane Benoist, *Rome, le prince et la Cité. Pouvoir impérial et cérémonies publiques (1er siècle av.–début du IVe siècle apr. J.-C.)* (Paris: Presses universitaires de France, 2005), 195–308; and Olovsdotter, *The Consular Image*, esp. 184–189. For the period of Honorius specifically, see also Claudianus, *Panegyricus de quarto consulatu Honorii Augusti*, 361–425 (relating Honorius's consular *adventus* into Rome in 404).

11   The motivation behind the suspension of the ordinary consulate by Justinian in 542 was that it competed unacceptably with the imperial status in the public arena; e.g., Christian Courtois, "Exconsul. Observations sur l'histoire du consulat à l'époque byzantine," *Byzantion* 19 (1949), 37–58, esp. 54; Roger S. Bagnall, Alan D.E. Cameron, Seith R. Schwartz, and Klaas A. Worp, *Consuls of the Later Roman Empire* (Atlanta: American Philological Association, 1987), 10–12.

12   For the Late Roman consulate (ordinary, imperial, suffect, honorary, and ex-), see Courtois, "Exconsul;" Rodolphe Guilland, "Études sur l'histoire administrative de l'empire byzantin. Le consul, ο υπατος," *Byzantion* 24 (1954), 545–578; and Bagnall et al., *Consuls of the Later Roman Empire*. As documented through the consular diptychs: Delbrueck, *Die Consulardiptychen*, 3–80; and Olovsdotter, *The Consular Image*, esp. 68–92. For a concise presentation of the Late Roman consulate, see also Elisabetta Ravegnani, *Consoli e dittici consolari nella tarda antichità* (Rome: Arcane, 2006), 21–107.

13   On the characterization, functions, and dissemination of the consular diptychs in the period of their production (*c*.370–541), see Delbrueck, *Die Consulardiptychen*, 3–22; Anthony Cutler, "The Making of Justinian's Diptychs," *Byzantion* 54 (1984), 75–115, esp. 105–108; Olovsdotter, *The Consular Image*, esp. 1–10; and Cecilia Olovsdotter, "Anastasius' I Consuls: Ordinary Consulship and Imperial Power in the Consular Diptychs from Constantinople," *Valör. Konstvetenskapliga studier* 1–2 (2012), 33–47.

14   Constantinople, 506. E.g., Paris, Musée du Moyen-Âge—Cluny, inv. Cl. 13135; Delbrueck, *Die Consulardiptychen*, no. 11; Volbach, *Elfenbeinarbeiten*, no. 10; Olovsdotter, *The Consular Image*, no. 9 C; see also Olovsdotter, "Architecture and the Spheres," 142–143 with fig. 7.4.

15   Constantinople, 513; Liverpool, National Museums Liverpool—World Museum, inv. M10036. Delbreuck, *Die Consulardiptychen*, N 16; Volbach, *Elfenbeinarbeiten*, no. 15; Olovsdotter, *The Consular Image*, no. 10.

FIGURE 4.2
Consular diptych of Areobindus; Constantinople, 506; Paris, Musée national du Moyen Âge—Cluny, inv. Cl. 13135
PHOTO: © RMN-GRAND PALAIS (MUSÉE DE CLUNY—MUSÉE NATIONAL DU MOYEN ÂGE) / THIERRY OLLIVIER

in Constantinople in the first decades of the 6th century, the tectonically abridged and spatially ambiguous arched structures that enclose the consuls' figures cannot be linked to any specific type of building or ceremony but serve as suitably monumental and symbol-laden visual frames for the consuls as they solemnly pose at their ceremonial entry into office on the New Year,[16]

---

16 On the increasingly synthetical 'three-into-one' mode adopted in the consular diptychs, especially in Constantinople, for representing the opening procession (*processus*

FIGURE 4.3   Consular diptych of Clementinus; Constantinople, 513; Liverpool, National Museums Liverpool—World Museum, inv. M10036
PHOTO: COURTESY NATIONAL MUSEUMS LIVERPOOL, WORLD MUSEUM

FROM EARTH TO HEAVEN

thereby 'triumphally' opening a new annual cycle in the history of Rome[17] and 'forever' entering their names in her public annals.[18] The columnar arch framing Areobindus is rather plain and generic, whereas that accompanying Clementinus is elaborated to evoke a triumphal arch, with an inscribed entablature consisting of the consul's *tabula ansata*, and an attic displaying figural reliefs in the form of a cross flanked by the *imagines clipeatae* of the appointing emperor, Anastasius I (491–518), and his empress, Ariadne, in a visual formula signifying the joint and harmonious rulership in Christ of the divine imperial couple.[19] That the arch had become an established visual symbol for the consular status and ceremonial is compellingly demonstrated by two minuscule insets on the perpendicular center-fold of Areobindus's toga, which show a consul standing hieratically in a columnar arch. The concept returns in a more elaborate form in the mid-6th-century 'Christ and Mary' diptych in Berlin

---

      consularis), the giving of/presiding over of games in the circus/hippodrome and amphitheater, and the distribution of largesse—ceremonies which were all (naturally) enacted against monumental architectural backdrops in the city centers of Rome and Constantinople designated for them, see Olovsdotter, *The Consular Image*, 68–71.

17   On the association of consulship with Roman victory and triumph, and the formulation of the consul's public success in terms of victory, see notably Versnel, *Triumphus*, 356–397; McCormick, *Eternal Victory*, 82–83 (discussing the relationship between imperial-dynastic victory and consular victory); and Olovsdotter, *The Consular Image*, 132–148 and esp. 184–198. Traditionally and ideally, a consular appointment was received in reward for a victory or other achievement in war, the idea being that proven victory and successfulness (a god-given quality) could thus be channeled into civil society for the benefit of the state and civil society; Versnel, *Triumphus*, 377–378. For the continuance of the practice of appointing military generals to the consulate in the late antique period, see Bagnall et al., *Consuls of the Later Roman Empire*, 4–6.

18   The *Fasti consulares*, so termed for the two annually appointed consuls whose names headed each year, had since the consulate's institution with the Roman Republic (*c.*509 BCE) served as the official record against which the Romans measured time and registered historical events. On the association of the consulate with the concept of continuity in late antiquity, see, e.g., Josef Engemann, "Ein Missorium des Anastasius. Überlegungen zum ikonographischen Programm der 'Anastasius'-Platte aus dem Sutton Hoo Ship-burial," in *Festschrift für Klaus Wessel zum 70. Geburtstag*, ed. Marcell Restle (Munich: Editio Maris, 1988), 103–115, esp. 111–112; Kim Bowes, "Ivory Lists: Consular Diptychs, Christian Approbation and Polemics of Time in Late Antiquity," *Art History* 24, no. 3 (2001), 338–357, esp. 347–353; and Olovsdotter, *The Consular Image*, 197–202.

19   The concord in Christ between the ruling couple was thought to establish and maintain harmony and unity on all planes of existence; see notably Robert Grigg, "Symphonian aeido tes basileias. An Image of Imperial Harmony on the Base of the Column of Arcadius," *Art Bulletin* 59 (1977), 469–482, esp. 476–478; in the consular context, see Olovsdotter, *The Consular Image*, 149 and 151 esp. and Olovsdotter, "Anastasius' I Consuls," 37–39.

(Figure 4.4),[20] which represents each of the godlike dignitaries—Christ as teacher of God's law (*Christus Doctor*), Mary as Theotokos with the Christ-child on her lap—each presiding like a Roman magistrate in front of a columnar arch complemented, beneath the archivolt and between the column capitals, with a *concha* (scallop shell), a symbol of immortality and divinity occurring widely in art and architecture from the late 3rd century,[21] and closed curtains (*vela*) announcing the sacrosanctity of the couple and screening the mystical sphere to which they belong from the eyes of the viewer. In the spandrels of the arch, the busts of Luna and Sol denote the cosmic and eternal nature of that sphere, and the cosmic and regenerational power of the Mother and Son through whom it might be accessed.[22]

The Romans' associations of the arch with victory and its vital function in the cyclic renewal of the cosmic forces was richly visualized in the Chronography of the year 354,[23] a work in which fantastical architectural frames

---

20   Constantinople, mid-6th century; Berlin, Staatliche Museen, Skulpturensammlung und Museum für Byzantinische Kunst, inv. 564–565. Volbach, *Elfenbeinarbeiten*, no. 137; Danielle Gaborit-Chopin, *Elfenbeinkunst im Mittelalter* (Berlin: Gebr. Mann, 1978), cat. 24; and Robert Cormack and Maria Vassilaki eds., *Byzantium 330–1453. Royal Academy of Arts, London, 25 October 2008–22 March 2009* (London: Royal Academy of Arts, 2008), no. 25.

21   The significance of the *concha* motif in Roman art, notably sepulchral, has plausibly been related to the myth of Aphrodite-Venus's birth from the sea (generation, divinity) and with the passage of the spirits of the dead across the water to the Blessed Isles (apotheosis, immortality); see, e.g., Roger Stuveras, *Le putto dans l'art romain* (Brussels: Latomus, 1969), 153–154; Friedrich Matz, "Stufen der Sepulkralsymbolik in der Kaiserzeit," *Archäologischer Anzeiger* (1971), 102–116, esp. 105–106 (alternatively interpreting the shell *clipeus* on Roman sarcophagi as a symbol for epiphany); Josef Engemann, *Untersuchungen zur Sepulchralsymbolik der späteren römischen Kaiserzeit* (Münster: Aschendorff, 1973), 65–67, 88–89; Donatella Scarpellini, *Stele romane con "imagines clipeatae" in Italia* (Rome: "L'Erma" di Bretschneider, 1987), 89–90; Thelma K. Thomas, *Late Antique Egyptian Funerary Sculpture: Images for this World and the Next* (Princeton, NJ: Princeton University Press, 2000), 79; and Olovsdotter, *The Consular Image*, 144–145, 152–155.

22   A traditional motif category of Roman triumphal art, Sol and Luna (in figural and sign form) continued to appear through the Late Roman and Early Byzantine period, Sol specifically being associated with the emperor in his divine and triumphal aspect, and, reflexively, with Christ; for the latter development, see notably Martin Wallraff, *"Christus verus sol." Sonnenverehrung und Christentum in der Spätantike* (Münster: Aschendorff, 2001). For the personified Sun and Moon in Late Roman and Byzantine Jewish art, see Erwin Ramsdell Goodenough, *Jewish Symbols in the Greco-Roman Period* (Princeton, NJ: Princeton University Press, 1988), 116–127.

23   Rome, 354; Vatican, Biblioteca Apostolica Vaticana, inv. Romanus 1 MS, Barb.lat. 2145. The well-known calendar created by the scribe Filolacus on commission from the Roman Valentinus (as indicated by the dedicatory frontispiece, fol. 1) is only preserved through some 16th- and 17th-century copies, the most complete of which is the Vatican Barberini version (inv. as above) copied for Peiresc in 1620 from the then still extant Carolingian Codex Luxemburgensis; see Henri Stern, *Le calendrier de 354. Étude sur son texte et sur ses*

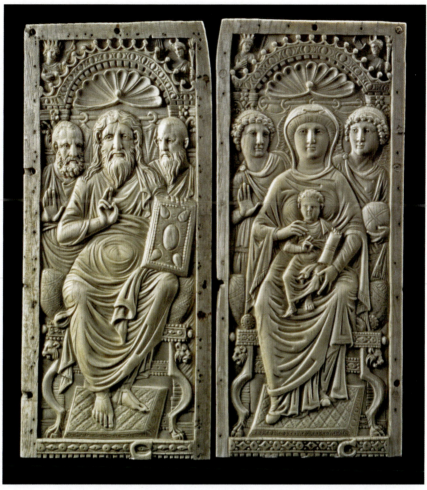

FIGURE 4.4 Christ and Mary diptych; Constantinople, mid-6th century; Berlin, Staatliche Museen, Skulpturensammlung und Museum für Byzantinische Kunst, inv. 564–565
PHOTO: FOTONACHWEIS: STAATLICHE MUSEEN ZU BERLIN, SKULPTURENSAMMLUNG UND MUSEUM FÜR BYZANTINISCHE KUNST / ANTJE VOIGT

constituted a visually prominent ingredient throughout. The composition that framed the list of imperial birthdays, *Natales Caesarum*, in the seventh folio (Figure 4.5) of the calendar was shaped like a triumphal double arch

illustrations (Paris: Imprimerie nationale, 1953), 14–41; and Michele Renee Salzman, *On Roman Time: The Codex-Calendar of 354 and the Rhythms of Urban Life in Late Antiquity* (Berkeley/Los Angeles: University of California Press, 1990), 70–73.

FIGURE 4.5   Chronography of 354, fol. 7 *Natales Caesarum*; Rome, 354; Vatican, Biblioteca Apostolica Vaticana, inv. Romanus 1 MS, Barb.lat. 2154
PHOTO: © BIBLIOTECA APOSTOLICA VATICANA

FROM EARTH TO HEAVEN 113

superimposed by a segmental pediment enclosing an imperial bust; the crowning cornice was rendered as a geometricized version of the star-spangled intrados of a triumphal arch, a scheme designed to evoke the heavenly vault,[24] the destination of all victors.[25] Framed by this heavenly vault, the emperor appeared in godlike state, right hand raised in the gesture of supreme power,[26] and with attributes similar to those of Sol Invictus, the sun god in his triumphal, unconquered aspect, with whom Late Roman emperors associated themselves:[27] the nimbus and the orb of world rulership crowned by the

---

24 E.g., Karl Lehmann, "The Dome of Heaven," *Art Bulletin* 27 (1945), 1–27; Bernhard Schleißheimer, "Kosmas Indikopleustes, ein altchristliches Weltbild" (diss., University of Munich, 1959), 16–24 (on the celestial interpretation of the dome and barrel-vault among early Christian writers); Sigfried Giedion, *Architecture and the Phenomena of Transition* (Cambridge, MA: Harvard University Press, 1971), 150–154; and André Grabar, "L'iconographie du ciel dans l'art chrétien de l'antiquité et du haut Moyen-Âge," *Cahiers archéologiques* 30 (1982), 5–24, esp. 5–16. On the immortal, divine, and eternal symbolism of the star motif (including radiate, spiral, rosette (petalled, acanthus-leafed), diamond-shaped, crossed, etc., variants), see G.W. Elderkin, "Architectural Detail and Antique Sepulchral Art," *American Journal of Archaeology* 39 (1935), 518–525, esp. 523–525; Hélène Danthine, "L'imagerie des trônes vides et des trônes porteurs de symboles dans le Proche-Orient ancien," in *Mélanges syriens offerts à René Dussaud*, vol. 2 (Paris: Librairie Orientaliste Paul Geuthner, 1939), 861; Jürgen Thimme, "Chiusinische Aschenkisten und Sarkophage der hellenistische Zeit," *Studi Etruschi* 23 (1954), 25–147, esp. 60–63; Goodenough, *Jewish Symbols*, 122–123; Bente Kiilerich, "Representing an Emperor: Style and Meaning on the Missorium of Theodosius I," in *El disco de Teodosio*, ed. Martín Almagro-Gorbea, José M. Álvarez Martínez, José M. Blázquez Martínez, and Salvador Rovira (Madrid: Real Academia de la historia, 2000), 273–280, esp. 280; and Olovsdotter, "Architecture and the Spheres," 150–151.
25 On heaven and the apotheotic beliefs of the Roman elites, see notably Simon R.F. Price, "From Noble Funerals to Divine Cult: The Consecration of Roman Emperors," in *Rituals of Royalty: Power and Ceremonial in Traditional Societies*, ed. David Cannadine and Simon R.F. Price (Cambridge: Cambridge University Press, 1987), 56–105; on the perception of heaven as the sphere of immortality in antiquity, see also Goodenough, *Jewish Symbols*, 127–134.
26 On the raised right hand gesture with palm turned outwards and fingers kept together as a gesture of divine or supreme power in Roman art, see notably Richard Brilliant, *Gesture and Rank in Roman Art* (New Haven: Academy, 1963), 96–102, 196.
27 On the solar association of late imperial power and ceremonial, see, e.g., Gaston Halsberghe, *The Cult of Sol Invictus* (Leiden: Brill, 1972); also Salzman, *On Roman Time*, 149–153; Antonio Carile, "Credunt aliud Romana palatia caelum. Die Ideologie der PALATIUM in Konstantinopel, den Neuen Rom," in *Palatia. Kaiserpaläste in Konstantinopel, Ravenna und Trier*, ed. Margarethe König, Eugenia Bolognesi Recchi-Franceschini, and Ellen Riemer (Trier: Rheinisches Landesmuseum, 2003), 27–32, esp. 27 and 30; Stephan Berrens, *Sonnenkult und Kaisertum von den Severen bis zu Constantin I. (193–337 n. Chr.)* (Stuttgart: Steiner, 2004); and Wolfgang Löhr, "Konstantin und Sol Invictus in Rom," *Jahrbuch für Antike und Christentum* 50 (2007), 102–110; in late antique visual culture, see,

phoenix, the latter proclaiming the cosmic regeneration effected by generations of victorious Roman rulers.[28] Imperial victory as such was represented by
two Victoriae standing on the inscribed imposts that supported the heavenly
vault, a scheme evidently inspired by the pairs of Victoriae traditionally orna-
menting the spandrels of triumphal arches. Very similar conceptions appear
in some frontispieces of 6th-century illuminated Christian manuscripts, such
as in folio 129v of the Italian St Augustine Gospels,[29] where the figure of Luke
presides in a shrine composed as a triumphal arch with columned piers ornamented with figural friezes (compare the Arch of Septimius Severus in the
Forum Romanum (203)), a segmental pediment crowned by a star-patterned
archivolt, and the evangelist's tetramorph image (the bust of a winged ox) as
'pedimental sculpture.' The arch-framed canon tables in the Syrian Rabbula

---

e.g., Hans Peter L'Orange, *Studies in the Iconography of Cosmic Kingship in the Ancient World* (Oslo: Aschehoug, 1953) and Petra Matern, *Helios und Sol: Kult und Ikonographie des griechischen und römischen Sonnengottes* (Istanbul: Ege Yayınları, 2002).

28   On the orb as a symbol of world or cosmic rulership (*orbis terrarum, orbis caelestis*) and its application as an insignium in late antique imperial and official art, see, e.g., Josef Deér, "Der Globus der spätrömischen und byzantinischen Kaiser. Symbol oder Insignie?," *Byzantinische Zeitschrift* 54 (1961), 291–318; Tonio Hölscher, *Victoria Romana. Archäologische Untersuchungen zur Geschichte und Wesensart der römischen Siegesgöttin von den Anfängen bis zum Ende des 3. Jhs.n.Chr.* (Mainz: Philipp von Zabern, 1967), 23–46; Klaus Wessel, "Insignien," in *Reallexikon zur byzantinischen Kunst*, 3 (Stuttgart: A. Hiersemann, 1978), 369–498, esp. 403–407; Marcell Restle, "Herrschaftszeichen," *Reallexikon für Antike und Christentum* 14 (1988), 937–966, esp. 946; Olovsdotter, *The Consular Image*, 98–113; also Pascal Arnaud, "L'image du globe dans le monde romain: science, iconographie, symbolisme," *Mélanges de l'École française de Rome. Antiquité* 96, no. 1 (1984), 53–116, esp. 102–111. On the association of the phoenix, ancient Egyptian symbol of death and rebirth, with the Late Roman emperor as eternal victor and with the resurrected Christ, including solar associations, see notably Roel van den Broek, *The Myth of the Phoenix According to Classical and Early Christian Tradition* (Leiden: Brill, 1972), esp. 146–304 and 423–458; also Robin Margaret Jensen, *Understanding Early Christian Art* (New York/London: Routledge, 2000), 159–160; and Maurizio Chelli, *Manuale dei simboli nell'arte. L'era paleocristiana e bizantina* (Rome: EdUP, 2008), 60.

29   Italy, possibly Rome, 6th century; Cambridge, Corpus Christi College Library, MS 286. Francis Wormald, *The Miniatures of the Gospels of St. Augustine, Corpus Christi College ms. 286.* (facs.) (Cambridge: Cambridge University Press, 1954), 3–5, 26 esp., plates II, VII (somewhat irrelevantly deriving the arch from the *porta regia* of the Roman *scae-
nae frons*); André Grabar, *L'età d'oro di Giustiniano. Dalla morte di Teodosio all'Islam.* trans. G. Veronesi (Milan: Feltrinelli, 1966), 212–214 with color plate 239; Kurt Weitzmann, *Late Antique and Early Christian Book Illumination* (New York: Braziller, 1977), 114–115 with plate 42; Dorothy Verkerk, "Biblical Manuscripts in Rome 400–700 and the Ashburnham Pentateuch," in *Imaging the Early Medieval Bible*, ed. John Williams (University Park, PA: Pennsylvania State University Press, 1999), 97–120.

FROM EARTH TO HEAVEN

Gospels[30] follow similar principles, but with more abstracted and imaginative results. Whilst the canon table in, for example, folio 4[31] conforms to what was then becoming a standard 'Eusebian' scheme for framing harmonized sections of the Gospels—four tall and narrow archlets gathered beneath a greater arch profusely ornamented with celestial and paradisaic symbols to indicate the eternal life that awaited those who followed the four paths in one indicated by the Gospels[32]—the arch that encloses two concordant sections from Matthew and John in folio 9 (Figure 4.6) is a modified version of the basic quadripartite scheme, its outer column shafts having been reshaped into arched aedicules enclosing the named evangelists in full figure. The rise of the right archlet is filled by an externally coffered dome, a cosmic motif[33] which in an ecclesiastical context would naturally be associated with the domed spaces and ciboria of the Christian church; the figure of Matthew seated in state beneath this celestial dome as he reads, right hand raised in the formal gesture of speech from his own Gospel, presented a meta-image for the priestly reader-viewer of the folio as he preached the Gospel to his congregation in church. The archivolt of the left archlet encloses a segmental tympanum or lunette conceived

30   Syria, 586; Florence, Biblioteca Medicea Laurenziana, inv. cod. Plut. I, 56.

31   Reproduced in, e.g., Weitzmann, *Book Illumination*, 69–70 with plate 34.

32   Cf. Olovsdotter, "Architecture and the Spheres," 145. For a liturgy-oriented variant of this interpretation, see Savary Gohar Grigoryan, "The Roots of *Tempietto* and its Symbolism in Armenian Gospels," *Iconographica* 13 (2014), 11–24, esp. 21. Other interpretations of the architectural frameworks in late antique canon tables include the tomb *Aedicula* in the church of the Holy Sepulchre in Jerusalem (Carl Nordenfalk, *Die spätantiken Kanontafeln. Kunstgeschichtliche Studien über die eusebianische Evangelien-Konkordanz in den vier ersten Jahrhunderten ihrer Geschichte* (Gothenburg: Isacsons, 1938); Paul A. Underwood, "The Fountain of Life in Manuscripts of the Gospels," *Dumbarton Oaks Papers* 5 (1950), 41–138, esp. 110–118); the Christian church or a church portal (Günter Bandmann, "Beobachtungen zum Etschmiadzin-Evangeliar," in *Tortulae. Studien zu altchristlichen und byzantinischen Monumenten*, ed. Walter Nikolaus Schumacher (Rome: Herder, 1966), 11–29, esp. 16–17 and 23); and (within the Armenian context specifically) a ciborium-like 'dwelling' for the biblical salvation mysteries (Thomas F. Mathews and Avedis K. Sanjian, *Armenian Gospel Iconography: the Tradition of the Glajor Gospel.* (Washington, DC: Dumbarton Oaks Research Library and Collection, 1991), esp. 173–174).

33   Lehmann, "Dome of Heaven;" Louis Hautecoeur, *Mystique et architecture: symbolisme du cercle et de la coupole* (Paris: Picard, 1954); E. Baldwin Smith, *Architectural Symbolism of Imperial Rome and the Middle Ages* (Princeton, NJ: Princeton University Press, 1956), 71–94; Giedion, *Architecture and the Phenomena of Transition*, 79, 150–154 esp.; Bandmann, *Early Medieval Architecture*, 185–186; also Otto Treitinger, *Die oströmische Kaiser- und Reichsidee nach ihrer Gestaltung im höfischen Zeremoniell* (Jena: W. Biedermann, 1938), esp. 57–58; and Olovsdotter, "Architecture and the Spheres," 147–150, 159–160; in the Byzantine context especially, notably Jelena Bogdanović, *The Framing of Sacred Space: The Canopy and the Byzantine Church* (New York: Oxford University Press, 2017).

FIGURE 4.6 Rabbula Gospels, fol. 9v Matthew and John; Syria, 586; Florence, Biblioteca Medicea Laurenziana inv. cod. Plut. I, 56
PHOTO: © FIRENZE, BIBLIOTECA MEDICEA LAURENZIANA, MS PLUT. 1.56, F. 9V. SU CONCESSIONE DEL MIC. È VIETATA OGNI ULTERIORE RIPRODUZIONE CON QUALSIASI MEZZO

FROM EARTH TO HEAVEN

as a *concha*, with its characteristically radiating striation rendered as a minuscule arcade, thus merging the immortality symbolism of the scallop shell[34] with the ceremonial connotations of the arcade (for the ceremonial interpretation of the arcade motif, see further below). A simpler, yet equally significant, version of an arch is found in the frontispiece to the Genesis, folio 2r, of the Ashburnham Pentateuch (Figure 4.7).[35] It is formed of two pairs of coupled colonnettes spanned by a slender archivolt ornamented with a geometricized roses-and-lilies version of the star-spangled vault, and a keystone shaped as the central medallion of a *corona laurea triumphalis*; an inverted, distinctly dome-shaped *concha* is suspended from the crown of the arch, and the intercolumniation is hung with curtains parted to reveal an inscriptional tablet listing the first five books of the Old Testament in Latin and Hebrew. Two paradisaic birds are perched atop the arch's extrados. The scheme could simultaneously be understood as an opening onto the mystery of creation and a triumphal entrance into the sacred history of the world and mankind.

In late antique funerary art, the arch was frequently used as a visual symbol for the passage between life and afterlife, similar to the door motif that often appeared on Roman funerary monuments but more abstract and cosmic in meaning: whereas the door, closed or partially open, essentially referred to the grave context, indicating the earthly passage of the deceased from the world of the living into the liminal station of the tomb (*domus aeterna*, Hades),[36] the arch's openness and celestial-triumphal connotations would have suggested a transcendental passage from one cosmic sphere to another. The arch as a transcendental gateway is visualized with exemplary clarity on the

---

34 See n. 21.

35 Alternatively the Tours Pentateuch; Italy, *c.*600 (in my view the most plausible attribution; other suggestions include North Africa and Spain); Paris, Bibliotheque nationale de France, inv. MS nouv. acq. lat. 2334: Weitzmann, *Book Illumination*, 118–125 with plates 44–47; Verkerk, "Biblical Manuscripts in Rome," esp. 117; Dorothy Verkerk, *Early Medieval Bible Illumination and the Ashburnham Pentateuch* (Cambridge: Cambridge University Press, 2004), 44–45, 54–55.

36 Cf. Britt Haarløv, *The Half-Open Door: A Common Symbolic Motif within Roman Sepulchral Sculpture* (Odense: University Press of Southern Denmark, 1977), esp. 86–87; Glenys Davies, "The Door Motif in Roman Funerary Sculpture," in *Papers in Italian Archaeology, 1. The Lancaster Seminar: Recent Research in Prehistoric, Classical, and Medieval Archaeology*, ed. Hugo McK. Blake, Timothy W. Potter and David B. Whitehouse (Oxford: John and Erica Hedges, 1978), 203–226.; and Verity Platt, "Framing the Dead on Roman Sarcophagi," in *The Frame in Classical Art: A Cultural History*, ed. Verity Platt and Michael Squire (Cambridge: Cambridge University Press, 2017), 353–381, esp. 363–375; also (concerning Roman-Judaic funerary art specifically), Bernard Goldman, *The Sacred Portal* (Detroit: Wayne State University Press, 1966), 101–124.

FIGURE 4.7 Ashburnham Pentateuch, fol. 2r Genesis; Italy (Rome?), 6th century; Paris, Bibliothèque nationale de France, inv. MS nouv. acq. lat. 2334
PHOTO: BIBLIOTHÈQUE NATIONALE DE FRANCE

center-front of a mid-4th-century 'Passion' sarcophagus from the catacombs of Domitilla in Rome.[37] Ornamented with a *concha* (symbol of immortality)

---

37   Rome, *c*.350; Vatican, Musei Vaticani (Museo Pio Cristiano), inv. 31525; see for example Friedrich Wilhelm Deichmann, Giuseppe Bovini and Hugo Brandenburg, *Repertorium der christilich-antiken Sarkophage, 1. Rom und Ostia* (Wiesbaden: Franz Steiner Verlag, 1967), 48–49 cat. 49, Pl. 16, 49; for a good photographic reproduction of the motif see also

FROM EARTH TO HEAVEN 119

beneath the archivolt and the busts of Sol and Luna (symbols of cosmic regeneration) in the spandrels, it encloses a pseudo-scenic visualization of Christian victory over death composed around a large cross (prime symbol of Christian victory) crowned by a triumphal laurel wreath (insignium of the victor)[38] encircling the *Chi-Rho* (Christian victory sign) held in the beaks of two doves (Christian symbol of the resurrected spirit)[39] and an eagle (imperial symbol of apotheosis);[40] flanking the cross on the groundline are two of the Roman

---

https://www.museivaticani.va/content/museivaticani/it/collezioni/musei/museo-pio -cristiano/sarcofagi-_a-colonne/sarcofago-con-scene-della-passione-di-cristo.html [Accessed September 13, 2022].

38 The triumphator's laurel wreath (*corona laurea triumphalis*) and its garland counterpart (*corona longa triumphalis*), both set with a central jewel or medallion, are amply attested in Roman visual culture; e.g., August Friedrich Pauly and Georg Wissowa, *Real-Encyclopädie der Classischen Altertumswissenschaft* (Stuttgart: Metzler, 1893–1978), vol. 13.2 (1927), 1440–1441f s.v. "Lorbeer" (A. Steier); Helmut Kruse, *Studien zur offiziellen Geltung des Kaiserbildes im römischen Reiche* (Paderborn: Ferdinand Schöningh, 1934), 24–48; Andreas Alföldi, "Insignien und Tracht der römischen Kaiser," *Mitteilungen des Deutschen Archäologischen Instituts, Römische Abteilung* 50 (1935), 1–171, esp. 36–39; Theodor Klauser, "Aurum Coronarium," *Mitteilungen des Deutschen Archäologische Instituts, Römische Abteilung* 59 (1944), 129–153; Versnel, *Triumphus*, 56f, 72–77, 378f with n. 4; MacCormack, *Art and Ceremony*, 174, 195, 243–246; McCormick, *Eternal Victory*, 82, 86; Künzl, *Der römische Triumph*, 86–88; Restle, "Herrschaftszeichen," 951; Jutta Rumscheid, *Kranz und Krone. Zu Insignien, Siegespreisen und Ehrenzeichen der römischen Kaiserzeit* (Tübingen: E. Wasmuth Verlag, 2000); and Olovsdotter, *The Consular Image*, esp. 138–142.

39 In Greco-Roman art the dove was, along with other small birds, ususally part of vegetal compositions, typically picking at plants or drinking from cups, and thus associated with fruitfulness and regeneration; transposed into the Christian context it became associated with the Holy Ghost and the human spirit as released from the body (Matthew 3:16; Luke 3:22), but also, as is well known, with peace.

40 In antiquity, the eagle (*aquila*) was an attribute of the high gods Zeus and Jupiter, and subsequently of the Roman emperor as Jupiter's chosen representative on Earth; as a symbol of Jovian and imperial power and warfare, the *aquila* appeared on the ceremonial scepter of the Roman triumphator, consul, emperor, and on Roman legionary standards (*signa*); Pauly and Wissowa, *Real-Encyclopädie*, vol. 1.1 (1894), 375 s.v. "Adler" (E. Oder); Pauly and Wissowa, *Real-Encyclopädie*, vol. 2 A.1 (1921), 1335–1336f s.v. "Signa" (J.W. Kubitschek); Fears, "Theology of Victory," esp. 744; Hans Rupprecht Goette, "Corona spicea, corona civica und Adler. Bemerkungen zu drei römischen Dreifussbasen," *Archäologischer Anzeiger* (1984), 573–589, esp. 586–589; Javier Arce, *Funus imperatorum. Los funerales de los emperadores romanos* (Madrid: Alianza, 1988), 131–140; Olovsdotter, *The Consular Image*, 76–79, 111–114, 155–157. The eagle's transcendental function was also linked to the Roman *consecratio*, the funerary cremation ritual by which, according to Roman belief, the soul of the deceased emperor (and later any members of the elite) was released and conducted to heaven by one or two eagles; MacCormack, *Art and Ceremony*, 99–101, 112; Goette, "Corona spicea," 586 with n. 34. Visual testimonies to the psychopomp eagle are the apotheosis relief on the column base of Antoninus Pius and Faustina in Rome (161 CE; Vatican, Musei Vaticani), the so-called *Consecratio* ivory panel (Rome, c.400; London, British Museum, inv. 1857, 10–13), a number of funerary monuments from the 2nd century CE

FIGURE 4.8   Ravennese sarcophagus, 3rd–4th century; Ravenna, Museo Arcivescovile
PHOTO: AFTER KOLLWITZ AND HERDEJÜRGEN, *DIE SARKOPHAGE*, FIG. 19.1,
CAT. A 49

soldiers guarding Christ's tomb, hunched on boulders suggestive of the rocky site of the Sepulchre and/or Golgotha, the place of the Resurrection. Other funerary versions of the transcendental arch range from minimalistic, sign-like conceptions such as the pair of columnar arches flanking a *tabula ansata* on a 3rd-century Ravennese sarcophagus later reinscribed for the Theodorican courtier Seda (Figure 4.8)[41] and their more elaborated Ravennese counterparts with or without *conchae* and framing Christian transcendence symbols such as the Golgotha cross or the *Agnus Dei*,[42] to the complex and endlessly varied compositions characteristic of Coptic stelae, where arches form part of intricate architectural constellations suffused with Egyptian, Roman, and Christian transcendence symbols. One of many such constellations is witnessed on a stela in Los Angeles (Figure 4.9)[43] displaying a two-registered composition dominated by an arch enclosing a syncretic conflation of the falcon-headed Horus (Egyptian sky god) and the ascending eagle (Roman symbol of triumph and apotheosis); the arch is formed of a looped interlace border (an 'eternal' pattern) and filled in its entirety by an oblong *concha* (symbol of immortality) against which the Horus-eagle stands as if in a niche shrine. In an arched

---

(apotheotic significance), and the consular diptychs from the late 5th century (triumphal significance).

41   Limestone sarcophagus (front); Ravenna, 3rd century; Ravenna, Museo Arcivescovile. E.g. Johannes Kollwitz and Helga Herdejürgen, *Die Sarkophage der westlichen Gebiete des Imperium Romanum*, vol. 2, *Die ravennatischen Sarkophage* (Berlin: Mann, 1979), fig. 19,1–2, cat. A 49–50.

42   A representative range of 5th-century Ravennese sarcophagi featuring tripartite architectural compositions with arches and gabled *aediculae* on their fronts are illustrated in Kollwitz and Herdejürgen, *Die Sarkophage*, plates 11–92.

43   Egypt, 5th to 8th century; Los Angeles, Los Angeles County Museum of Art, inv. 47.8.10.

FIGURE 4.9 Coptic funerary stela; Egypt, 5th–8th century; Los Angeles, Los Angeles County Museum of Art, inv. 47.8.10
PHOTO: MUSEUM ASSOCIATES/LACMA

'celestial' register above the arch is a cross (symbol of Christian victory over death) set against a radiate background (a solar motif) and flanked by a confronted lion and stag (Coptic symbols of power and victory).[44] In this scheme of layered and intertwined symbolisms, the arch presents a gateway to apotheosis, eternity, and victory over death.

The arch as a more universal topos for Christian transcendence, and the immortalized state of Christian apostles and saints, can be exemplified by a late 6th-century silver book-cover plaque from Syria (one of a pair) in the Metropolitan Museum of Art (Figure 4.10).[45] It shows an official-looking Saint Paul standing within a columnar arch with an archivolt conceived as a triumphal laurel wreath—a reference to Paul's triumph over death—and with peacocks (symbols of apotheosis and paradise)[46] perched in the spandrels above the extrados.

The transitional associations of the arch made it well suited for ceremonial representations involving several figures or scenes, as is demonstrated by the many arcades—the arch multiplied—that appear on late antique triumphal monuments, sarcophagi, church ambones, reliquaries, *pyxides*, cups, and other liturgical and devotional objects of an elongated, polygonal, or rounded format. The regularizing and monumentalizing framework provided by an arcade helped lend unity and clarity to complex figure constellations and to emphasize directional, chronological, and hierarchical differentiations. The widespread

---

44   For the symbolic meanings associated with the combination of lion and deer/stag and with the confronted or heraldic scheme with two animals symmetrically flanking a cross in Coptic art, see Linda Evans, "Animals in Coptic Art," *Göttinger Miszellen* 232 (2012), 63–73, esp. 64–66.

45   Embossed with details picked out in gold leaf; Kaper Koraon or Antioch (Syria), 550–600; New York, Metropolitan Museum of Art, inv. 50.5.1 (a pendant plaque, inv. 50.5.2, shows Saint Peter). Margaret English Frazer, "Pair of Book Covers with Peter and Paul," in *Age of Spirituality: Late Antique and Early Christian Art, Third to Seventh Century*, ed. Kurt Weitzmann (New York: The Metropolitan Museum of Art, 1979), 618–619, no. 554; Margaret English Frazer, "Early Byzantine Silver Book Covers," in *Ecclesiastical Silver Plate in Sixth-Century Byzantium: Papers of the Symposium Held May 16–18, 1986, at the Walters Art Gallery, Baltimore, and Dumbarton Oaks, Washington, DC, organized by Susan A. Boyd, Marlia Mundell Mango, and Gary Vikan*, vol. 3, ed. Susan A. Boyd and Marlia Mundell Mango (Washington, DC: Dumbarton Oaks Research Library and Collection, 1992), 71–76, esp. 72–73, fig. 7 (and 4); and Marlia Mundell Mango, *Silver from Early Byzantium: The Kaper Koraon and Related Treasures* (Baltimore, MD: Walters Art Gallery, 1986), 199–205, nos. 44–45 (Paul and Peter).

46   In antiquity the peacock was an attribute of the high goddesses Hera and Juno and the symbol of apotheosis for Roman empresses (equivalent to the emperor's eagle), and in its Christian adaptation a symbol of resurrection, paradise, and eternal beatitude (Augustinus, *De civitate Dei*, 21.4); see, e.g., Dietrich Boschung, *Antike Grabaltäre aus den Nekropolen Roms* (Bern: Stämpfli, 1987), 51; Jensen, *Understanding Early Christian Art*, 159; and Chelli, *Manuale dei simboli*, 77–78.

FIGURE 4.10 Silver plaque with representation of Saint Paul; Syria, 550–600; New York, Metropolitan Museum of Art, inv. 50.5.1
PHOTO: FLETCHER FUND, 1950

use of the arcade, notably in artworks of a ceremonial character and/or context, would doubtless have reflected the functions served by arcades and porticoes as backdrops for ceremonial action—triumphal *adventi* and *rediti*, religious processions, etc.—in the imperial palaces, church basilicas, and urban centers of the period,[47] which were, generally speaking, also the contexts where such art objects were used. An epitomic visual testimony to the arcade's ceremonial connotations is found on the so-called Trier ivory plaque, representing, in dense and complex abbreviation, the *adventus* procession of a relic through a Constantinopolitan cityscape defined by the triple-tiered arcaded portico against and inside which the procession and its numerous spectators appear.[48] Another, more symbolic, example of how the arcade could be used in late antique art is a monumental marble ambo from Hagios Georgios in Thessaloniki (Figure 4.11),[49] where the scheme encloses a representation of the Nativity: the announcing angel, the magi, and the shepherd, each framed by an arch, are rendered in clockwise movement towards Mary Theotokos enthroned at the front-right. Here the arcade takes the form of a niche arcade with *conchae*, suggesting the scene takes place in a transcendental sphere, and its ceremonial character is further emphasized by parted curtains in some of the intercolumniations, a motif associated with sacred

---

47   Cf. Olovsdotter, "Architecture and the Spheres," 145. On the functions of the porticoed street in late antique urban centers and in visual representations, see notably Hendrik W. Dey, *The Afterlife of the Roman City: Architecture and Ceremony in Late Antiquity and the Early Middle Ages* (New York: Cambridge University Press, 2015), 65–126; for the cityscape as backdrop for triumphal and religious processions, see also, e.g., Franz Alto Bauer, *Stadt, Platz und Denkmal in der Spätantike: Untersuchungen zur Ausstattung des öffentlichen Raums in den spätantiken Städten Rom, Konstantinopel und Ephesos* (Mainz: Philipp von Zabern, 1996), 380–388.

48   Probably from a reliquary; Constantinople, 5th to 7th century; Trier, Domschatz. E.g. Volbach, *Elfenbeinarbeiten*, no. 143; Suzanne Spain, "The Translation of Relics Ivory, Trier," *Dumbarton Oaks Papers* 31 (1977), 281–304; Kenneth G. Holum and Gary Vikan, "The Trier Ivory, *Adventus* Ceremonial, and the Relics of St. Stephen," *Dumbarton Oaks Papers* 33 (1979), 113–133; John Wortley, "The Trier Ivory Reconsidered," *Greek, Roman and Byzantine Studies* 21 (1980), 381–394; Laurie J. Wilson, "The Trier Procession Ivory: A New Interpretation," *Byzantion* 54 (1984), 602–614; and Leslie Brubaker, "The Chalke Gate, the Construction of the Past, and the Trier Ivory," *Byzantine and Modern Greek Studies* 23 (1999), 258–285, esp. 270–281 (proposing, unconvincingly I think, a redating of the ivory to the 9th or early 10th century).

49   Constantinople or Thessaloniki, 450–550; Istanbul, İstanbul Arkeoloji Müzeleri, inv. 1090 T. The most thorough analysis of this ambo's iconographic programme is offered by Warland; Rainer Warland, "Der Ambo aus Thessaloniki. Bildprogramm—Rekonstruktion—Datierung," *Jahrbuch des Deutschen Archäologischen Institut* 109 (1994), 371–385.

FIGURE 4.11   Ambo from Hagios Georgios; Thessaloniki, 500–550; Istanbul, İstanbul Arkeoloji Müzeleri, inv. 1090 T
PHOTO: CECILIA OLOVSDOTTER

boundaries and imperial ceremonial, and as such suitable for the representation of divine royalty.[50] A more abstracted version of the arcade design is

---

50   The motif of the curtain or veil (*velum, vela*), closed or open, is common in late antique art, secular as well as sacral (polytheistic, Christian, Judaic), where it serves as a ceremonial, mystical, and variously concealing and revealing or 'unveiling' demarcator between two spheres, in general terms between outer-worldly and inner-otherworldly/sacred. The motif's applications in art seem largely to have corresponded with contemporary uses of curtains in public and religious contexts. On the palatial use of curtains to screen off the sacrosanct imperial person from his subjects, see Treitinger, *Oströmische Kaiser- und Reichsidee*, 55–56; Frank von Unruh, "Unsichtbare Mauern der Kaiserpaläste. Hofzeremonien in Rom und Byzanz," in *Palatia. Kaiserpaläste in Konstantinopel, Ravenna*

FIGURE 4.12   Votive bronze *situla*; Constantinople (?), 6th century; Istanbul, İstanbul Arkeoloji Müzeleri, inv. 852
PHOTO: CECILIA OLOVSDOTTER

found on a 6th-century votive bronze *situla* originating from the late antique church at Kale-e Zerzevan in southeastern Anatolia (Figure 4.12),[51] around the

---

und Trier, ed. Margarethe König, Eugenia Bolognesi Recchi-Franceschini, and Ellen Riemer (Trier: Rheinisches Landesmuseum, 2003), 33–48, esp. 36; J. Michael Featherstone, "*De Cerimoniis* and the Great Palace," in *The Byzantine World*, ed. Paul Stephenson (London/New York: Routledge, 2010), 162–174, esp. 165–166 and 169. For the use of curtains in the Early and Middle Byzantine church, see notably Robert F. Taft, "The Decline of Communion in Byzantium and the Distancing of the Congregation from the Liturgical Action: Cause, Effect, or Neither?," in *Thresholds of the Sacred: Architectural, Art Historical, Liturgical, and Theological Perspectives on Religious Screens, East and West*, ed. Sharon E.J. Gerstel (Washington, DC: Dumbarton Oaks Research Library and Collection, 2006), 27–50, esp. 40–49; on the religious (Judeo-Christian) use of the curtain as a screen for the sacred, a cosmic or mystical veil, and a veil between life and afterlife in art, see notably Goodenough, *Jewish Symbols*, 141, 146, 203–204, 212–214.

51   With tin plating and punched motifs and inscription; Syria (?), 450–550; Istanbul, İstanbul Arkeoloji Müzeleri, inv. 852. Marlia Mundell Mango, Cyril Mango, Angela Care Evans, and

FROM EARTH TO HEAVEN 127

body of which runs a continuous arcade framing jeweled crosses ornamented inside and out with flower-shaped stars (or vice versa) to suggest a heavenly and paradisaic sphere, and a triumphal-wreath motif decorating the archivolts as a reference to victory in its Christian interpretation of triumph over death. As indicated by the accompanying inscription, the vessel was offered to give thanks for the salvation (from illness and death, presumably) of the giver Antipatros and his household.[52]

2   The Pedimented Front

The pedimented front, or columned *fastigium*, was almost as frequent an occurrence as the arch in late antique visual culture. Indeed, the two motifs would often appear together in one and the same composition, as their functions and symbolisms complemented and to some extent overlapped with one another, with the given distinction that the front signified an enclosed space (the space within or beyond) and therefore 'dwelling' or 'state,' not 'passage' or 'movement.' The quintessential visual formula for 'pedimented front' is eminently exemplified by temple representations on Roman coin reverses, and can be described as a reductive, frontally rendered structure raised on a podium—the classic prostyle Roman temple—with columns clustered to the sides to reveal the deity in the *cella*, some simple device on the triangular tympanum and/or as roof acroteria, and the occasional inscription on the entablature.[53] These numismatic temples display few and modest variations, and their distinctive elements would not necessarily have reflected those of their prototypes: for

---

Michael Hughes, "A 6th-Century Mediterranean Bucket from Bromeswell Parish, Suffolk," *Antiquity* 63 (1989), 295–311, esp. 301; Javier Arce, "Un grupo de situlas decoradas del la Antigüedad tardía: función, cronología, significado," *Antiquité tardive* 13 (2005), 141–158, esp. 150 with fig. 15.

52 The Greek inscription along the rim translates as "In fulfillment of a vow and for the salvation of Antipatros and all his house / [May] the Lord protect you."

53 On the non-specific and symbolic character of Late Roman coin types, see Philip V. Hill, "Buildings and Monuments of Rome on Coins of the Early 4th Century, AD 294–313," *Numismatica e antichità classiche* 13 (1984), 215–227; Elisha Ann Dumser, "The AETERNAE MEMORIAE Coinage of Maxentius: An Issue of Symbolic Intent," *Journal of Roman Archaeology* Suppl. 61 (2006), 106–118; and Nathan T. Elkins, *Monuments in Miniature: Architecture on Roman Coinage* (New York: American Numismatic Society, 2015), esp. 131–140. Valuable contributions on architectural representations on Roman coins are also offered by Günter Fuchs, *Architekturdarstellungen auf römischen Münzen der Republik und der frühen Kaiserzeit* (Berlin: De Gruyter, 1969), esp. 47–129; Paul Zanker, "In Search of the Roman Viewer," in *The Interpretation of Architectural Sculpture in Greece and Rome*, ed. Diana Buitron-Oliver (Washington, DC: National Gallery of Art/University Press of New England, 1997), 179–191, esp. 179–183.

FIGURE 4.13   Gold bracelet with representation of a temple to Isis; Egypt (Alexandria?), 4th century; Paris, Bibliothèque nationale de France, inv. Seyrig.1972.1318
PHOTO: BIBLIOTHÈQUE NATIONALE DE FRANCE

the sake of visual clarity (and because the building's identity could be stated by a legend) the number of columns could be reduced, the pedimental sculpture exchanged for some more rudimentary centerpiece—disc, *patera*, wreath, an indeterminate blob or cluster—that might have alluded to some attribute or function of the resident deity, as might the occasional inclusion of acroterial figures, or just the general idea of pedimental/roof sculpture, but, intrinsically always to the pediment's correspondence to the heavenly sphere of the gods.[54] An evocative late antique rendering of the concept is witnessed on an Egyptian openwork gold bracelet with a central motif in the form of a tetrastyle temple to Isis-Fortuna (Figure 4.13).[55] The miniature figure of the goddess, displaying the mixed attributes of Isis and her Roman sister goddess of fortune and prosperity, is frontally enthroned in the central intercolumniation to indicate her dwelling inside the *cella*; a *concha* is attached to the top of her head to signal

---

54 For the celestial interpretation of the pediment and tympanum, see notably Peter Hommel, "Giebel und Himmel," *Istanbuler Mitteilungen* 7 (1957), 11–55.
55 Gold worked in *opus interrasile*; Egypt (Alexandria?), 300–425; Paris, Bibliothèque Nationale de France, inv. Seyrig.1972.1318.

FROM EARTH TO HEAVEN

her divinity, the special symbol of Isis—the horned headdress cradling the sun disc—ornaments the tympanum, and the podium bears the legend '*ΕΥΤΟΚΙΣ*' ('give birth happily'), thus indicating a talismanic function of the bracelet. With its simplicity and clarity of form, this imaged temple front constitutes an exemplary illustration of the structural disposition of the pedimented front as a visual archetype. Integrating the principle of centrality with a triple crossing of the lateral and vertical axes (center-left-right, middle-lower-upper), it provided the optimal framework for the kind of centralized, symmetrical, stratified, and hierarchical image compositions that became the norm in late antiquity.

Like their predecessors on the Roman throne, the Christian rulers of the Late Roman Empire claimed divine status, but an emperor's image enframed by a pedimented front is a rare occurrence in the period's art; the arch and the arched or palatial *fastigium* were clearly regarded as more appropriate architectural types for expressing prevailing conceptions of imperial power—absolute and everlasting victoriousness, legitimacy, authority, and stability[56]—than the simple pedimented and prostyle temple since ancient times associated with resident divinity.[57] The same may be said for the figure of Christ, whose iconography was strongly influenced by imperial (and consular) models in the first centuries of the Christian Empire. One exception to what, judging by the state of the evidence, seems to have been a general pattern could once be found in folios 13 and 14 of the Chronography of 354 (Figure 4.14), where Constantius II *Augustus* and Constantius Gallus *Caesar* posed as imperial consuls between the open curtains of a pedimented aedicule,[58] thereby announcing the solemn opening of a new annual cycle. The divine status attributed to the imperial persons naturally required visualization irrespective

---

56   See further next section.

57   See Boschung's discussion of the symbiosis between temple and cult statue, the house and the deity's "dwelling presence" inside, in Roman visualizations of temples; Dietrich Boschung, "Kultbilder als Vermittler religiöser Vorstellungen," in *Kult und Kommunikation: Medien in Heiligtümern der Antike*, ed. Christian Frevel and Henner von Hesberg (Wiesbaden: Reichert, 2007), 63–87, esp. 69–70 and 82–83.

58   Constantius and Gallus displayed the gem-incrusted imperial variant of the triumphal *ornatus*, which also included the diadem. The triumphal toga costume (*vestis triumphalis*), whether worn by a triumphator, consul, or imperial consul, replicated the star-patterned (cosmic) costume of Jupiter Optimus Maximus in his Capitoline temple in Rome. On the divine origin and cosmic symbolism associated with the triumphal *ornatus*, see, e.g., Versnel, *Triumphus*, 57–58, 77, 83–84, 89–93, 126–131, 302–303; and Künzl, *Der römische Triumph*, 85–129; also Olovsdotter, *The Consular Image*, esp. 71–74.

FIGURE 4.14 Chronography of 354, fol. 13 Constantius II as consul; Rome, 354; Vatican, Biblioteca Apostolica Vaticana, inv. Romanus 1 MS, Barb.lat. 2154
PHOTO: © BIBLIOTECA APOSTOLICA VATICANA

FROM EARTH TO HEAVEN   131

of context, and so they were presented like gods inside their temples,[59] the nimbi (Late Roman solar attribute of imperial divinity) encircling their heads signaling their manifest presence (*di(v)i praesentes*), holding in their left hand the scepter of dominion, and in their extended right an attribute or gift bestowed on their worshippers and subjects—in the case of Constantius II a cascade of coins in sign of his supreme bounty, in the case of Gallus a *victoriola* in sign of his imperial victoriousness. Palatial associations were, however, not lacking: the tympana of these 'imperial cult temples' each enclosed an arched niche conch in what may well have been intended as an abstracted reference to the arched pediment of the palatial *fastigium*, the stylized scallop shell filling the conchs combining with the nimbi to announce the immortal status of the living ruler, while two radiate discs suspended in space above the building indicated the heavenly realm and the solar association of imperial power.

A shrine-like front also appears in some consular diptychs. In the diptych of Boethius, consul of the West in 487 (Figure 4.15),[60] the honorand poses ceremonially in front of a tall and narrow aedicule with an inscribed architrave beneath a triangular tympanum with a triumphal wreath encircling the family monogram of the *gens Boethii* as pedimental sculpture. The structure can be interpreted as a symbolic frame for the consular status, institution, and ceremonial in general, and in particular as a shrine to the *victoria* of the Boethii, i.e., to their accumulated success and prominence in Roman public life and, hence, to their immortality in the collective memory of Rome.[61] The immortal glory of family (*gloria stemmatis, fortuna genitatis*)[62] is fundamentally also what the aedicule framing Flavius Anastasius, consul of the East in 517, in his commemorative diptychs is about (Figure 4.16),[63] even if its placement and

---

59   Compare Stern, *Le calendrier de 354*, 310–311.

60   Brescia, Museo di Santa Giulia. Delbrueck, *Die Consulardiptychen*, no. 7; Volbach, *Elfenbeinarbeiten*, no. 6; Olovsdotter, *The Consular Image*, no. 6.

61   The Boethii belonged to the high aristocracy of Rome and counted several high office holders among their members and ancestors; John Robert Martindale, *The Prosopography of the Later Roman Empire, II. A.D. 395–527* (Cambridge: Cambridge University Press, 1980), 231–233; S.J.B. Barnish, "Transformation and Survival in the Western Senatorial Aristocracy, c. A.D. 400–700," *Papers of the British School at Rome* 56 (1988), 120–155, esp. 125–126; Olovsdotter, *The Consular Image*, 139–140, 177, 204.

62   Cassiodorus, *Variae*, 1.42.1; also Beat Näf, *Senatorisches Standesbewusstsein in spätrömischer Zeit* (Freiburg: Universitätsverlag, 1995), 206–207; and Olovsdotter, *The Consular Image*, esp. 172 and 204.

63   Constantinople, 517; Paris, Bibliothèque Nationale de France, MMA, inv. 55. Delbrueck, *Die Consulardiptychen*, no. 21; Volbach, *Elfenbeinarbeiten*, no. 21; Olovsdotter, *The Consular Image*, no. 11 A.

FIGURE 4.15   Consular diptych of Boethius, Rome or northern Italy 487; Brescia, Museo di Santa Giulia
PHOTO: SU CONCESSIONE DELLA FONDAZIONE BRESCIA MUSEI

function in the panels' compositions can visually and contextually also be associated with the tribunal in the hippodrome or amphitheater from whence the consul presided over his inaugural games (here represented in separate registers below the consul). The aedicule is rendered as a miniature Roman temple with pedimental sculpture and acroteria: the former is constituted by

FIGURE 4.16   Consular diptych of Anastasius; Constantinople, 517; Paris, Bibliothèque nationale de France, MMA, inv. 55
PHOTO: BIBLIOTHÈQUE NATIONALE DE FRANCE

a *concha* that has been subtly shifted downwards from the center of the tympanum to cup around the consul's head, thus blurring the natural boundaries between man and architecture, and between man and effigy; the latter by three imperial *imagines clipeatae* representing the appointing emperor Anastasius I (apex), the empress Ariadne (lower right), and an ex-consul of the Anastasian house (lower left).[64] The emperor's image is supported on a laurel garland or 'long triumphal wreath' (*corona longa triumphalis*)[65] held by two winged and smiling *erotes* and Victoriae standing in dancing strides on the *simae* in a constellation that concisely and efficiently proclaims the transcendent victoriousness, prosperity, and happiness of the emperor and his dynasty.[66] In the Roman tradition, the *imago clipeata* was regarded as an apotheotic portrait form suitable for depicting persons of ancestral and immortal status,[67] and here the dynastic trio and the consul did indeed all belong to the same family, the consul being great-nephew to his imperial namesake.[68]

---

64 Delbrueck, *Die Consulardiptychen*, 124; Alan D.E. Cameron, "The House of Anastasius," *Greek Roman and Byzantine Studies* 19 (1978), 259–276, esp. 263; Olovsdotter, *The Consular Image*, 48–55, 116–117.

65 The garland variant of the *corona laurea triumphalis*; see *supra* n. 38.

66 The *eros*, or putto, is a figure with a long tradition in Greek, Etruscan, and Roman visual culture, where it generally signifies perennial or eternal prosperity and happiness. It is a standard feature of triumphal art, where its function is to illustrate the superior prosperity and happiness brought by imperial victory (*felicitas temporum*, 'happiness of the times'), whereas its role in funerary art is to indicate the regeneration and abundant pleasure that await the dead in the afterlife; see notably Stuveras, *Le putto romain*, 85–107, 138–144, 165–171 esp.; also Franz Cumont, *Recherches sur le symbolisme funéraire des romains* (Paris: Geuthner, 1942), e.g., 7, 46, 340–349, 398–410, 452 and 496–497 with figs. 77, 97 and 104; John Boardman ed., *Lexicon Iconographicum Mythologiae Classicae* III.2 (1986), 683–726 s.v. "Eros/Amor, Cupido," nos. 61–702 (N. Blanc & F. Gury); and Olovsdotter, *The Consular Image*, 129–131 with references.

67 Plinius, *Naturalis historia*, 35.4–11; (typological) Johannes Bolten, *Die Imago Clipeata. Ein Beitrag zur Porträt- und Typengeschichte* (Paderborn: F. Schöningh, 1937); (historical, contextual) Rudolf Winkes, *Clipeata imago. Studien zu einer römischen Bildnisform* (Bonn: R. Habelt, 1969) and Rudolf Winkes, "Pliny's Chapter on Roman Funeral Customs in the Light of Clipeatae Imagines," *American Journal of Archaeology* 83 (1979), 481–484; (funerary) Scarpellini, *Stele romane*; (official) Olovsdotter, *The Consular Image*, 110–112 and 116–117 esp. The *imago clipeata* can be seen as a portait variant of the *clipeus virtutis* ('shield of virtue'), an honorific emblem awarded to Roman citizens for military or civilian excellence under the Republic and early Empire (e.g., Hölscher, *Victoria Romana*, 102–107; and Winkes, *Clipeata imago*, 18–43), and a recurrent motif in imperial and official art until Justinian (e.g., Olovsdotter, *The Consular Image*, esp. 110–111). On the recurrent use of the *imago clipeata* in late antique imaged architecture, see Olovsdotter, "Architecture and the Spheres," 153.

68 Anastasius I favored family members, among which a number were (mostly adopted) nephews, as appointees to the ordinary consulate, and he also appointed himself to it

FROM EARTH TO HEAVEN   135

In Greek as well as in Roman funerary culture, the pedimented front had long been used as a solemn frame for the commemorated dead, notably on stelae, the shape of which—a rectangular, upright block of stone—lent itself well to gabled structures, whether elaborated with reliefs to resemble a real building or kept to its most basic shape, the silhouette of a pedimented facade.[69] A marble stela displayed in the courtyard of the Archaeological Museums in Istanbul (Figure 4.17)[70] is in the best tradition of such sepulchral fronts, carved in the semblance of an aedicular shrine with Ionian columns supporting a triangular pediment beneath which, heads framed by a voussoir arch, the full-figure images of the commemorated couple stand like statues on a podium formed of an inscribed *tabula ansata*.[71] On the pediment are two Gorgon heads flanked by dolphins (apotropaic figures of protection and safe guidance),[72] and in the spandrels between archivolt and architrave are winged *erotes* lifting amphorae (symbolizing regeneration, happiness, and the fulfilment of funerary rites by the living to sustain the dead in afterlife).[73] This imaged temple-tomb or tomb-shrine, like its numerous counterparts from around the Roman Mediterranean, represented the dwelling place of the departed between this

---

three times; Attilio Degrassi, *I fasti consolari dell'impero romano dal 30 avanti Cristo al 613 dopo Cristo* (Rome: Edizioni di Storia e Letteratura, 1952), 285 (index); Carmelo Capizzi, *L'imperatore Anastasio I (491–518). Studio sulla sua vita, la sua opera e la sua personalità* (Rome: Pont. Institutum orientalum studiorum, 1969), 43–44; Cameron, "The House of Anastasius," 261–262; Martindale, *Prosopography*, 82–83, 96–99, 143, 796; Olovsdotter, *The Consular Image*, 79 and 117 esp.; and Olovsdotter, "Anastasius' I Consuls."

69   The stela as a form of funerary monument was gradually discontinued in the 4th century, as the growing Christian community, who practiced inhumation, preferred to be buried in sarcophagi.

70   Byzantium or Constantinople (?), 3rd to early 4th century; Istanbul, İstanbul Arkeoloji Müzeleri (courtyard).

71   The *tabula ansata*, a dovetail-handled tablet, was a widespread form of Roman commemorative and votive plaque, also in late antiquity, and not only in the funerary context.

72   In Rome, as earlier in Greece, the *gorgoneion* or Gorgon head was used as an apotropaic, victory-inducing sign by the army (e.g. Pauly and Wissowa, *Real-Encyclopädie*, VII.2 (1912), 1650f s.v. "Gorgo" (B. Niese)), and it decorated the breastplate of Mars (Ultor), the Roman emperor (see, e.g., Honorius's cuirass in the consular diptych of Probus (fig. 1)), and gladiators. For the apotropaic significance of the Gorgon head in sepulchral art, see, e.g., Cumont, *Recherches sur le symbolisme*, 339; for the dolphin as a conveyor of souls to the Isle of the Blessed in Etrusco-Italic funerary art, see Thimme, "Chiusinische Aschenkisten," 158–159; for Gorgons in Christian art, see James Hall, *Dictionary of Subjects and Symbols in Art* (London: J. Murray, 1979), 105–106 (a symbolic prefiguration of Christ's death and resurrection through the saving of Jonah from the whale); Jensen, *Understanding Early Christian Art*, 159; and Chelli, *Manuale dei simboli*, 58.

73   For the *eros* or putto in Roman funerary art, see note 66.

FIGURE 4.17 Funerary stela of a couple; Byzantium/Constantinople (?), 3rd–4th century; Istanbul, İstanbul Arkeoloji Müzeleri (courtyard)
PHOTO: CECILIA OLOVSDOTTER

FROM EARTH TO HEAVEN 137

FIGURE 4.18 Lead sarcophagus; Roman Syria (mod. Baabda), 3rd century;
Istanbul, İstanbul Arkeoloji Müzeleri, inv. 1149 M
PHOTO: CECILIA OLOVSDOTTER

world and the next, a place where their *manes* or shades continued to dwell to receive the veneration of the living. Another conception of a sepulchral front, reduced to its most elementary and symbolic shape, is found on a cast lead sarcophagus of what is commonly referred to as the Tyre type (Figure 4.18),[74] the abstracted relief ornamentation of which characteristically combines architectural, cosmic, and apotropaic motifs. The tripartite relief composition on the front of this particular sarcophagus consists of a larger 'celestial' unit of rosette-stars set in a coffer-like grid, flanked to the sides by two smaller architectural units enclosing aedicules conceived of two twisted columns joined by twisted raking *simae*. Centered inside each aedicule is an apotropaic Gorgon head, and rosette-stars are arranged above the *simae* and between the column bases. In all its simplicity, the scheme represents the two stages of the precarious journey beyond death: the tomb and heaven.

3   Arch and Pedimented Front Combined

The combination or conflation of an arch with a pedimented front is a fairly frequent occurrence in late antique art, the Syrian, arched, or palatial *fastigium* being the most notable and formalized example of this.[75] From the

---

74   Roman Syria (mod. Baabda, Lebanon), 3rd century (?); Istanbul, İstanbul Arkeoloji Müzeleri, inv. 1149 M.
75   The arched *fastigium* is an achitecural scheme with many denominations, including Syrian *fastigium* or pediment (the motif regularly appears on temples in Roman Syria and Asia from the 1st century onwards), palatial and ceremonial *fastigium*, arched pediment, arcuated entablature, Syrian arch-gable, Syrian entablature, arcuated lintel, *serliana* (from the Italian Renaissance architect Sebastiano Serlio). For a general overview of the

1st century CE, this characteristic tetrastyle scheme with an arcuated, usually wider, central intercolumniation[76] began to appear on religious buildings, imperial monuments, and in the minor arts, from the Roman provinces of Syria and Asia in the East to Italy and Gaul in the West, but it was not until late antiquity, when it became firmly integrated into palatial architecture, that it developed into a more contextually circumscribed and symbolically defined motif. The tetrastyle front that still dominates the inner prostyle court of Diocletian's palatial complex in Split (Spalato) (c.300) set the standard for a scheme that would be reproduced in imperial palaces and church basilicas throughout the empire.[77] Combining an arched portal with a columned *fastigium*, raised like a Roman temple on a stepped podium, and provided with a tribunal in front of the central arch, the palace *fastigium* in Split, and

---

various terms traditionally and currently in use for the motif, see Manuel Parada López de Corselas, "La arquitectura de poder y su recepción: la 'serliana.' ¿Viaje de formas, viaje de contenidos?," in *Ver, viajar y hospedarse en el mundo romano*, ed. Gonzalo Bravo and Raúl González Salinero (Madrid/Salamanca: Signifer Libros, 2012), 561–582, esp. 182–186.

76 Triple-arched varieties also occur, as notably exemplified by the Theodorican *palatium* mosaic in Ravenna; see further n. 77.

77 Besides the *palatium* at Split, the arched *fastigium* was incorporated in the imperial palaces of Ravenna and Constantinople, located within the palace compounds and fronted by peristyle courts. The Ravennese *fastigium* is documented through the well-known PALATIVM mosaic decorating the nave wall of Sant' Apollinare Nuovo (Ostrogothic original c.505, Justinianic modification 547), and the tribunal or ceremonial porch (Delphax) of the Great Palace in Constantinople more lately graphically reconstructed as part of the *Byzantium 1200* project (2003–2010; A. Tayfun Öner; http://www.byzantium1200.com/greatpalace.html reproducing in detail the Split *fastigium* in its current, partially modified, state, and attributing it to the Constantinian palace ('Daphne')). On the forms and functions of the tertrastyle and arched *fastigium* in late antique *palatia*, see, e.g., Bandmann, *Early Medieval Architecture*, 113–115; and Dey, *The Afterlife of a Roman City*, esp. 49–52. The arched *fastigium* was also used as a monumentalizing gateway into or inside imperial church basilicas: in the Constantinian Lateran basilica in Rome it took the form of a statued screen between nave and apse (for visual reconstructions, see Molly Teasdale Smith, "The Lateran Fastigium, a Gift of Constantine the Great," *Rivista di archeologia cristiana* 46 (1970), 149–175, esp. fig. 3; and Sible de Blaauw, "Imperial Connotations in Roman Church Interiors. The Significance and Effect of the Lateran Fastigium," in *Imperial Art as Christian Art—Christian Art as Imperial Art. Expression and Meaning in Art and Architecture from Constantine to Justinian*, ed. J. Rasmus Brandt and Olaf Steen (Rome: Bardi, 2001), 137–146, esp. figs. 1–2); in the Theodosian basilica of Hagia Sophia in Constantinople it served as an imperial *propylaeum* to the basilica from the west (reconstructions based on remains on the site include those of Grabar, *L'età d'oro di Giustiniano*, 82 fig. 87; Wolfgang Müller-Wiener, *Bildlexikon zur Topographie Istanbuls: Byzantion-Konstantinopolis-Istanbul bis zum Beginn des 17. Jahrhunderts* (Tübingen: Verlag Ernst Wasmuth, 1977), 84–86; and Ken R. Dark and Jan Kostenec, *Hagia Sophia Project: 2004–2007 Survey Seasons* (Prague: Univerzita Karlova, 2012) with figs. 1–2, available online at http://ukar.ff.cuni.cz/node/160).

FROM EARTH TO HEAVEN

subsequently Constantinople and Ravenna, served the double function of a monumental entrance to the inner sanctum of the imperial residence and an elevated place from whence the emperor could appear in state before his court and subjects. The double association of the arched pediment with a triumphal arch and a temple[78] made it an eminent vehicle for propagating the divine status and superior victoriousness of the imperial person, and in its imaged form it came to be used as a visualization of imperial power, authority, and dynasty residing in its sacral palatial setting, the *sacrum palatium* or *domus divina*.[79] Thus, famously, the motif has been employed on the silver *missorium* of Theodosius I in Madrid (Figure 4.19), created in celebration of that emperor's 10th anniversary on the Eastern throne in 388.[80] Its relief represents the father of the Theodosian dynasty presiding in godlike majesty beneath the central arch of a palatial *fastigium*, accompanied in the side intercolumniations by his co-emperors at the time—Valentinian II (left), Arcadius (right)—and attended by military guards as he ceremonially confers a codicil of appointment on an official approaching him humbly with veiled hands from below-left, each figure carefully sized and positioned according to his place in the courtly hierarchy. The functions and meanings of this Theodosian palatial *fastigium* are several and intertwined: on a 'real' or physical level it provides a proper palatial setting for a formal act of state (the appointment of an official) whilst affirming Theodosius's primacy within the Roman empire, state, and army; on a

---

78   On the association of the late imperial palace with a temple, the sacrality of the imperial palace, and the cultic status of the residing emperor, see Andreas Alföldi, "Die Ausgestaltung des monarchischen Zeremoniells am römischen Kaiserhof," *Mitteilungen des Deutschen Archäologischen Instituts, Römische Abteilung* 49 (1934), 1–118, esp. 32; Treitinger, *Die oströmische Kaiser- und Reichsidee*, 50–51; Smith, *Architectural Symbolism*, 180–181 esp.; MacCormack, *Art and Ceremony*, 25, 296; Klaus-Peter Matschke, "Sakralität und Priestertum des byzantinischen Kaisers," in *Die Sakralität von Herrschaft. Herrschaftslegitimierung im Wechsel der Zeiten und Räume. Fünfzehn interdisziplinäre Beiträge zu einem weltweiten und epochenübergreifenden Phänomen.* ed. Franz-Reiner Erkens (Berlin: Akademie Verlag, 2002), 143–149; Carile, "Credunt aliud Romana palatia," 27–28; Unruh, "Unsichtbare Mauern," 34, 36–38; and Bandmann, *Early Medieval Architecture*, esp. 130.

79   Jochen Martin, "Das Kaisertum in der Spätantike," in *Usurpationen in der Spätantike. Akten des Kolloquiums "Staatsreich und Staatlichkeit," 6.–10. März 1996, Solothurn/Bern,* ed. François Paschoud and Joachim Szidat (Stuttgart: Franz Steiner Verlag, 1997), 47–62, esp. 48–49; Matschke, "Sakralität und Priestertum des byzantinischen Kaisers," 151–155; on the association of the imperial palace with a temple, see also Treitinger, *Die oströmische Kaiser- und Reichsidee*, 50–51; MacCormack, *Art and Cermony*, 25, 269.

80   Madrid, Real Academia de la Historia; Constantinople (?), 388. The Latin legend inscribed along the rim translates as "Our lord Theodosius, emperor in perpetuity, on the very felicitous day [of the] ten[th year of his reign]."

FIGURE 4.19   Silver *missorium* of Theodosius I; Constantinople (?), 388; Madrid, Real Academia de la Historia
PHOTO: AFTER DELBRUECK, *DIE CONSULARDIPTYCHEN*, PLATE 62

symbolic level it proclaims the victoriousness, order, harmony, and continuity of Theodosian dynastic rule, and—as illustrated on the 'ground' in the exergue, where the Venus-like figure of Tellus reclines luxuriously amidst flowers, grain, and joyfully fluttering *erotes*—its favorable influence on the prosperity and regeneration of the earth (*felicitas temporum*, 'happiness of the times').[81]

---

81   See n. 66. On the related concept of *felicitas imperatoria*, which may be translated as the imperial quality of prosperity- and peace-bringing victoriousness, see notably Erik Wistrand, *Felicitas imperatoria* (Gothenburg: Acta Universitatis Gothoburgensis, 1987).

The arched *fastigium*, with its associations with the divine ruler and his sacred palace, was also considered well suited for framing biblical royalty, as is evocatively demonstrated by the so-called David plates: a set of nine figural silver plates created in Constantinople in the first decades of the 7th century, and narrating the early life of King David, with the combat against Goliath as centerpiece.[82] Illustrated here is the third plate in the sequence (Figure 4.20), showing the young David appearing before King Saul in a scheme very similar to that of Theodosius's *missorium*. As on the other three 'architectural' plates in the set, the image is composed around an abstracted version of a palatial *fastigium*: four columns supporting a centrally arcuated architrave conceived as a *corona longa triumphalis* with a central medallion as keystone. Beneath the arch a nimbate Saul presides in the formal stance and costume of an Early Byzantine emperor as he addresses/blesses David, likewise nimbate, approaching his throne from the left, while a senior dignitary (Samuel?) stands to the right; armed guards flank the group to the sides, and in the 'earthly' compartment of the exergue are motifs of abundance and largesse (a fruit- or grain-filled basket and two coin-sacks standing among growing flowers). The common denominator of the four architectural David plates is their ceremonial theme, each of them picturing a rite of passage performed at the palace of Saul as David gradually progresses towards kingship. The relevance of a 'victor's *fastigium*' for the David cycle, which in a paraphrase on the paradigmatic rise of a Roman emperor to power[83] is centered around the deeply Roman idea of victory, power, and immortality as the rewards of superior virtue, is evident.

---

82   David plate 3, "David before Saul"; Constantinople, 613/629–630; from the second Lambousa treasure, Cyprus; New York, Metropolitan Museum of Art, inv. 17.190.397. See further Kurt Weitzmann ed., *Age of Spirituality, Late Antique and Early Christian Art, Third to Seventh Century* (Catalogue of the exhibition at The Metropolitan Museum of Art, November 19, 1977, through February 12 1978) (New York: The Metropolitan Museum of Art, 1979), 475–483, nos. 425 and 427 esp.; Suzanne Spain Alexander, "Heraclius, Byzantine Imperial Ideology and the David Plates," *Speculum* 52:2 (1977), 217–237; Ruth E. Leader, "The David Plates Revisited: Transforming the Secular in Early Byzantium," *Art Bulletin* 82, no. 3 (2000), 407–427; Ruth E. Leader-Newby, *Silver and Society in Late Antiquity. Functions and Meanings of Silver Plate in the Fourth to Seventh Centuries* (Aldershot: Routledge, 2004), 173–219; Cormack and Vassilaki, *Byzantium 330–1453*, 385, nos. 30–32, 86–87, plate 30–32; and Helen C. Evans and Brandie Ratliff eds., *Byzantium and Islam: Age of Transition (7th–9th Century)* (New York: Metropolitan Museum of Art, 2012), 16–17, no. 6A–F.

83   Control-stamped with the sign of the emperor Heraclius (610–641) in Constantinople, it has plausibly been suggested that the David plates were commissioned by Heraclius or someone of his house to celebrate the Persian victory and recapture of Jerusalem in 628–629; notably Leader, "David Plates Revisited."

FIGURE 4.20   'David' silver plate, (3/9) David before Saul; Constantinople, 613/629–630; New York, Metropolitan Museum of Art, inv. 17.190.397
PHOTO: GIFT OF J. PIERPONT MORGAN, 1917

4   Conclusion

The examples I have considered here represent but a very small fraction of the rich and manifold corpus of late antique and early medieval artworks with architectural motifs that have been preserved, yet they give a clear idea of the conceptual and symbolic qualities that were associated with certain architectural types in late antique culture—in this case the arch and the pedimented front—and how these qualities were consciously, consistently, and creatively brought into play in its art. In the strongly public-minded Late Roman and Early Byzantine society, every man's status and successes were to be promoted and every man's hoped-for attainment of immortality after death affirmed, and a monumental architectural frame conveying notions of transcendence well rooted in belief, tradition, and practice, and furnished with a relevant constellation of articulating symbols, could lend such accomplishments and aspirations a universal, even cosmic, significance—in art as in life. As functional constructions, the arch and the pedimented front were designed to separate, interconnect, and contain; as symbolic motifs, they could be used to distinguish and connect outer and inner spheres, here and beyond, earth and heaven, the physio-temporal and eternal. Their centralized and stratified structures were clearly perceived by the Romans and early Byzantines as optimal tools for visualizing the cosmic order they imagined and aspired toward: the physical and vegetal world below, the human state and the physical manifestation of the divine in the middle, and the superior and otherworldly sphere of heaven or paradise, the gods or Christ—the destination of every man in his quest for immortality—above. The visual systems constructed with and around the arch and the pedimented front were thus simultaneously designed to express the completeness, containment, and permanence of the cosmic order, and to define man's movement within and between its levels or spheres as dictated by the cosmic laws of transition and regeneration.

CHAPTER 5

Representation of the Temple in the Sarajevo Haggadah: Type or Archetype?

Čedomila Marinković

Following the four-year-long Jewish rebellion against the Romans, on the ninth day of the Jewish month of Av in the year 3831 after the Creation, i.e., in the summer of 70 CE, Roman legions under the command of the emperor Titus destroyed the city of Jerusalem and the Second Temple, thus putting an end to the political and religious independence of Jews in their land. This was the turning point in Jewish history: a traumatic event, a national catastrophe that changed the lives of Jews for good, marking the beginning of almost two millennia of Jewish *galut* (diaspora). In the centuries that followed, religious life, once defined by the Temple existence, underwent serious changes too. The practice of sacrifice ceased and was replaced with the study of the Holy Scriptures and performing of *mitzvot* (good deeds). The Temple as a gathering place was replaced with the synagogue. The reconstruction of the (future) Third Temple became an important aspect of messianic expectation and Temple-related imagery soon developed into one of the dominant themes of Jewish art.[1]

As Jews became an often persecuted minority, the cultural strategies used in the approach to Jewish art should be different from those used for Christian art. Jewish figural art was influenced by varying dynamics of acculturation within a non-Jewish environment.[2]

---

1 Helen Rosenau, *Vision of the Temple: The Image of the Temple of Jerusalem in Judaism and Christianity* (London: Oresko Books, 1974); Elisabeth Revel-Neher, *L'arche d'alliance dans l'art juif et chrétien du second au dixième siècles. Le Signe de la Rencontre* (Paris: Association des amis des études archéologiques du monde byzantino-slave et du christianisme oriental, 1984); Vanessa Crosby, "Imagined Architectures and Visual Exegesis: Temple Imagery in the Illuminated Manuscripts of the Iberian Jews," *Journal of the Australian Early Medieval Association* 2 (2006), 43–55; Katrin Kogman-Appel, "The Temple of Jerusalem and the Hebrew Millennium in a Thirteenth-Century Jewish Prayer Book" in *Jerusalem as Narrative Space*, ed. Anette Hoffmann and Gerhard Wolf (Leiden: Brill 2012), 187–208.
2 Living as a minority and adapting to the new conditions of the exile, Jewish religious authorities developed sophisticated strategies of coping with either Christian or Muslim visual culture around them translating outside artistic models into a specific Jewish idiom. See Katrin Kogman-Appel, "Jewish Art and Non-Jewish Culture: The Dynamics of Artistic Borrowing

---

© KONINKLIJKE BRILL NV, LEIDEN, 2023 | DOI:10.1163/9789004537781_007

In this chapter, I address some questions concerning the representation of the Temple in the Sarajevo Haggadah. Is this representation narrative or symbolic, and what layers of meaning does it convey? How original or isolated is it, and are there any differences between the Temple representation in Sephardic and in Ashkenazi visual imagery? What can we deduce from comparing them? And, finally, to keep within the larger framework of this book, is the representation of the Temple in the Sarajevo Haggadah type or archetype?

How to address these questions? Utilizing architecture as an epistemological tool, it is possible to examine the 'rhetoric of architecture,' as recently shown by Robert Ousterhout and Jelena Bogdanović.[3] In his discussion on the topic of Solomon's Temple in Byzantine art, Ousterhout distinguishes between word-driven (or metaphoric) and image-driven (or symbolic) meanings of architectural forms. Bogdanović presents the rhetoric of architecture as codified visual and architectural conventions that frame specific meanings beyond the visible and spatial. Textual referentiality is especially relevant for Jewish studies.

1 Some Methodological Remarks

Jews are the people of the book. First Moses on Mount Horeb, and later all Jews, heard their God instead of seeing him. Jews built their knowledge of the world by listening to God, not by seeing him. This vocative character of Judaism is emphasized by the basic prayers—שְׁמַע יִשְׂרָאֵל (Listen Israel) (Deuteronomy 6:4). The view that pagans *see* their gods and that Jews *hear* him represents a well-known topos in academic discourse.[4]

---

in Medieval Hebrew Manuscript Illumination," *Jewish History* 15 (2001), 188–189; Katrin Kogman-Appel, "Jewish Art and Cultural Exchange: Theoretical Perspectives," *Medieval Encounters* 17 (2011), 1–26.

3 Robert Ousterhout, "New Temples and New Solomons" in *The Old Testament in Byzantium*, ed. Paul Magdalino and Robert Nelson (Washington, DC: Dumbarton Oaks research Library and Collection, 2010), 223–253; Jelena Bogdanović, "The Rhetoric of Architecture in the Byzantine Context: The Case Study of the Holy Sepulchre," *Zograf* 38 (2014), 1–21.

4 Heinrich Graetz, *The Structure of Jewish History and other Essays*, trans. and ed. I. Schorsch (New York: The Jewish Theological Seminary of America, 1975), 68–69; Thorleif Bowman, *Hebrew Thought Compared with Greek* (London: SCM Press, 1960), 113–122; Susan Handelman, *The Slayers of Moses: The Emergence of Rabbinic Interpretation in Modern Literary Theory* (Albany: State University of New York Press, 1982), 33; Kalman Bland, "Medieval Jewish Aesthetics: Maimonides, Body, and Scripture in Profiat Duran," *Journal of the History of Ideas* 54 (1993), 533–559, esp. 535; Lionel Kochan, *Beyond the Graven Image: A Jewish View* (New York: New York University Press, 1997).

The second divine commandment defines the whole attitude of Jews towards art.[5] Jewish traditional education, unlike its Christian counterpart, avoids the use of visual language as a didactic resource and establishes a clear hierarchy by which the written text has been and remains the supreme source of knowledge and truth. Despite this fundamental standpoint, the visual arts have been present in Jewish life since biblical times. The Bible gives us plenty of information about the visual arts, especially architecture. It describes the construction of Noah's Ark (Genesis 6: 14–16) and the building of the Tower of Babel (Genesis 11: 3–4). After the Exodus from Egypt, in five chapters and more than 125 verses, the מִשְׁכָּן (the Tabernacle, Exodus 26: 1–30) is described, with even the name of its builder specified (Exodus 31: 1–6). The Bible also describes the shape and decoration of the Ark of the Covenant (Exodus 25: 10–40), and the garments of the *kohen hagadol* (high priest) (Exodus 28: 4–42) as well as the building of the First Temple, Solomon's Temple (1 Kings, 6: 1–38).

During the Middle Ages, the Jewish relationship with the visual changed, as can be seen from the numerous testimonies of applied art, illuminated manuscripts, and the remaining synagogal architecture. It is certain that, from that period on, visual arts became an integral part of Jewish life that was particularly strong in certain periods and in specific communities. From the 12th century onwards, the Jewish relationship with the visual is particularly elaborate. The visions of sages like Maimonides, Rashi, Rabbi Solomon ben Meir, Judah Halevi, Abraham Ibn Ezra, and Rabbi Jacob ben Reuben represent the starting point for a lively discussion on this subject.[6] Polemicists encouraged an attack on Christian images.[7] Kabbalists enriched the debate with theological complexities and iconographic symbolism.[8] Talmudists watched that nobody transgressed the boundary between permissible and prohibited visual idolatry. But as Bland recently showed, no matter how many pictures were produced, none of these thinkers and undoubtedly great authorities advocated either an aniconic or iconoclastic attitude.[9] Their affirmative

---

5 "Thou shalt not make yourself a carved image, nor any image of what is in heaven above, or on earth beneath or in the water under the earth," (Exodus 20:4).

6 Kalman Bland, *The Artless Jew: Medieval and Modern Affirmation and Denial of the Visual* (Princeton: Princeton University Press, 2001), 109–141.

7 *Sefer ha Brit* by Jozeph Kimhi was written in 1170. It served to help the Jews in their frequent polemics with Christians. *Sefer Josef Ha Mequane* by Joseph ben Nathan provided general guidelines for Jews on how to deal with the Christian dogma. See Katrin Kogman-Appel, "Coping with Christian Pictorial Sources: What Did Jewish Miniaturists Not Paint?" *Speculum* 75, no. 4 (2000), 819.

8 Michael A. Batterman, "The Emergence of the Spanish Illuminated Haggadah Manuscripts," (PhD diss., Northwestern University, Illinois, 2000).

9 Bland, *The Artless Jew*, 141.

attitude towards visual arts confirms the artistic practice of Jewish communities in the Middle Ages. Decorated synagogues rose up across Europe and pilgrims were amazed by architectural monuments they encountered during their travels.[10] Illuminations adorned Bibles, *haggadot* (illustrated books for Pesach), *mahzorim* (prayer books), and *ketubot* (marriage contracts); tombstones were carved with symbols; *judaica* such as *menorot* (ritual candelabras), *keter torahs* (Torah crowns), *rimonim* (finials adorning the Torah scrolls), and *yadaim* (Jewish ritual pointers) were made in metal; and talismans and amulets were decorated, as well as textiles like *meils* (Torah mantles) and *parohets* (curtains that cover the Torah Ark), pottery dishes for Shabbat and Pesach, glass *kiddush* cups (wine goblets used for the Sabbath), clothes and jewelry. Works of visual art were omnipresent in medieval Jewish culture.

Within this culture, the Bible definitely sets the boundaries of what idolatry is but does not see all works of art as a threat. Bland humorously observes, "in the context of medieval Jewish culture, the Bible is not understood as an iconoclastic manifesto."[11] Regardless, opinion on Jewish 'artlessness'—the prejudice accepted and widespread in the mid-19th century in Protestant Germany, in which the Jewish aniconism opposed pagan visuality—has remained until the present time the dominant belief among scholars and, above all, in non-academic circles, regardless of whether they are distinctly anti-Semitic or even philo-Semitic.[12]

---

10   Rabbi Benjamin of Tudela left an account in 1176 of the most important works of art of Spain, southern France, Italy, Greece, Asia Minor and Africa. Among them are the descriptions of Constantinople's monumental architecture. See Rabbi Benjamin of Tudela, *The Itinerary of Benjamin of Tudela*, critical text, translations and commentaries by Marcus N. Adler (New York: Feldheim, 1907). This document is available as an electronic book within the Gutenberg project: http://www.gutenberg.org/files/14981/.

11   Bland, *The Artless Jew*, 140. On medieval halachic legislation concerning visual arts, see ibid., 152.

12   This topic was extensively and provocatively addressed by Michael A. Batterman, "Genesis in Vienna: The Sarajevo Haggadah and the Invention of Jewish Art," in *Image: Manuscripts, Artists, Audiences: Essays in Honor of Sandra Hindman*, ed. David S. Areford and Nina Rowe (London: Ashgate, 2004), 309–327, 316. See Kochan, *Beyond the Graven Image*; Richard I. Cohen, *Jewish Icons: Art and Society in Modern Europe* (Berkeley/Los Angeles: University of California Press, 1998), 3; Anthony Julius, *Idolizing Pictures: Idolatry, Iconoclasm and Jewish Art* (London: Thames & Hudson 2000); Margaret Olin, *The Nation Without Art: Examining Modern Discourses on Jewish Art* (Lincoln: University of Nebraska Press, 2001). Ruth Mellinkoff's standpoint on this issue is particularly indicative. According to her, the images that appear in medieval Jewish manuscripts "were taken from the stereotypical anti-Jewish image as the Jews lacked the tradition of representing human figures," and that "patrons, despite the obvious negativity of the featured characters, and great prices they had to pay for the paintings, accepted these manuscripts because they were accustomed to *watching* without *seeing*." Ruth Mellinkoff, *Outcasts:*

Unlike in Christian art, where the connection with the Second Temple was more metaphoric, expressed through words, ceremonies, and relics,[13] in Jewish art it was mimetic, referring directly to the outer appearance of the Temple, the basic features of which were known mainly from literary sources[14] and various illustrations on coins and in frescoes, mosaics, manuscripts, and applied arts.

But how was the Temple depicted in these representations?

Usually, the Second Temple imagery depicts an imposing tetra-style structure with architectural motifs (bases, capitals) typical of pagan (Roman or Greek) temples of those times,[15] with huge doors and triangular gable. Sometimes there is a large curtain tied in a knot hanging over the central part of the door.

If we examine these representations, we are faced with some striking questions. Of the whole Temple why is only the facade represented? And why is the main portal so exaggerated in size? As Ousterhout recently emphasized, it was important that the interior of the Temple was off limits for the great majority of the public, and most ceremonies took place outside the temple, in front of the facade where the main altar stood.[16] Also, the symbolic significance of the entrance door points towards the logical answer about the importance of the Temple facade.

Since medieval art is anti-illusionist in its character, there were certain basic principles of architectural schematization that are valid for the representation of the architecture. In the mind of the medieval beholder, these principles certainly would not affect the idea of the 'reality' of the type of building understood as a sensible model or pattern of the building as it actually was. As I have argued elsewhere, the principles of elimination of volume of the building (*eliminatio angoli*), enlargement of certain features (*augmentatio*), reduction in number or alternation of shape (*reductio numeri, reductio formae*) or

---

Signs of Otherness in Northern European Art of the Late Middle Ages (Berkeley: University of California Press, 1994), 84.

13   See Ousterhout, "New Temples and New Solomons," 223–253, esp. 252.

14   Josephus Flavius, "Jewish Wars," in *Internet Sacred Texts Archive*, http://sacred-texts .com/jud/josephus/war-5.htm; Josephus Flavius, "Antiquities of the Jews," in *Internet Sacred Texts Archive*, http://sacred-texts.com/jud/josephus/ant-15.htm (accessed January 10, 2017). *Mishnah Middot* 4:7, https://www.sefaria.org/topics/second-temple?tab=sources (accessed August 3, 2022).

15   The Herodian Temple, *stricto senso*, was stylistically a Hellenistic structure. See Michael Avi-Yonah, "The Facade of Herod's Temple: An Attempted Reconstruction," in *Religions in Antiquity: Essays in Memory of Erwin Ramsdell Goodenough*, ed. Jacob Neusner (Leiden: Brill, 1968), 326–335.

16   Ousterhout, "New Temples," 227.

FIGURE 5.1 Representation of the Jerusalem Temple on the silver tetradrachm of Bar Kochba, undated issue, year 134/5 CE. Obverse: representation of the Temple with the rising star
PHOTO: PUBLIC DOMAIN CLASSICAL NUMISMATIC GROUP, INC. HTTP://WWW.CNGCOINS.COM [ACCESSED JUNE 16, 2022]

replacement of some elements (*inversio*)[17] were very often applied in architectural representations of the medieval period, in both Christian and Jewish art.

These illustrative formulae can be revealed in Jewish fine arts starting from the schematic model, originally on the silver tetradrachm coins from the period of the second Jewish revolt under Simon Bar Kochba (132–135 CE) (Figure 5.1), through the fresco decoration of synagogues in Dura-Europos

---

17 Čedomila Marinković, "Principles of the Representation of the Founder's (ktetor's) Architecture," in *Serbia and Byzantium: Proceedings of the International Conference Held on 15 December 2008 at the University of Cologne*, ed. Mabi Angar and Claudia Sode (Frankfurt: PL Academic Research, 2013), 57–73, esp. 67–72.

(Figure 5.2), catacombs of Rome and Bet Shearim and objects of applied art, to the splendid mosaic floors of numerous synagogues built in the Galilee region between the 4th and 6th centuries like on the floor mosaic in Hammat Tiberias (Figure 5.3).

To such representations of the Temple an obvious messianic, symbolic meaning was added through representation of the Ark of the Covenant.[18] The Tabernacle and the Ark are displayed in the same way: placed between the two central columns of the Temple facade just as the statue of a Roman god stood in pagan temples, a frontal view of a box with rounded tips that form the wings of the cherubim is represented. They were made "according to the pattern that was shown to you on the mountain."[19] The sanctuary and the recipients are symbolic representations of Creation and a mystical dwelling place of God's presence—*Shekhinah*.[20]

Katrin Kogman-Appel posits that early Christendom did not develop any art prior to approximately 200 CE and that early Christian art grew out of the Jewish religion.[21] Therefore, the attitude of early Christians to the image and to figural art may quite naturally have been similar to that of the Jews.[22] From the 5th century on, signs of Christian image worship increased and became firmly established and accepted around the last decades of the 6th century. Somewhere around c.550, Jews ceased to commission, create, or use figural art.[23] For almost seven centuries after that, Jews employed only aniconic

---

18 One of the greatest mysteries of the Bible is the disappearance of the Ark of the Covenant. The Ark is mentioned as being placed in the First Temple (1 Kings: 8 3–8) but does not appear in the dedication ceremony of the Second Temple (Ezra 3). See Theodore E. Ehrlich, "The Disappearance of the Ark of the Covenant," *Jewish Bible Quarterly* 40, no. 3 (2012), 174–178.

19 Exodus, 25:40.

20 Few subjects in Judaism are as central as the notion of God's presence, 'dwelling' in the Holy Temple in Jerusalem. See Mordechai Cohen, "Interpreting the Resting of the *Shekhinah*: Exegetical Implications of the Theological Debate among Maimonides, Nahmanides and Sefe Ha-Hinnukh," in *The Temple of Jerusalem: From Moses to Messiah*, ed. Steven Fine (Leiden: Brill, 2011), 237–275.

21 Katrin Kogman-Appel, "Christianity, Idolatry, and the Question of Jewish Figural Painting in the Middle Ages," *Speculum* (2009), 75–107, 87. Floor mosaics produced in the land of Israel from the 3rd to 6th centuries CE do not differ much from the visual language of church and synagogues, for example, the Temple representation on the mosaic floor of the synagogue in Sepphoris. If there were no menorahs and the Hebrew and Aramaic inscriptions, the mosaic could be mistaken for a church mosaic. See Steven Fine, "Art and Liturgical Context of the Sepphoris Synagogue," in *Galilee through Centuries: Confluences of Cultures*, ed. Eric M. Meyers (Winona Lake, IN: Eisenbrauns, 1999), 232.

22 Fine, "Art and Liturgical Context of the Sepphoris Synagogue," 232.

23 It was most probably the development of the Christian worship of icons that led to the abandonment of figural art among Jews around that time. See Kogman-Appel, "Jewish Figural Painting," 83.

FIGURE 5.2 Synagogue, Dura-Europos, 3rd century. Torah Shrine
PHOTO: © ALAMY

FIGURE 5.3   Hammat Tiberias 4–5th century synagogue. Detail of the mosaic floor depicting the holy Ark surrounded by two large candelabra and other ceremonial objects
PHOTO: ZEV RADOVAN/BIBLE LAND PICTURES © ALAMY

models of decoration.[24] Jewish figurative art eventually reappeared around the year 1290, in the decoration of illuminated manuscripts. This change was due to an altered Jewish perception of Christianity.[25]

24   Katrin Kogman-Appel, *Jewish Book Art Between Islam and Christianity: The Decoration of Hebrew Bibles in Medieval Spain* (Leiden: Brill, 2004).
25   Rashi (Rabbi Solomon ben Isaac, 12th century) was the first to observe such a change, stating that contemporary gentiles are not "skilled in idolatry '*beki 'in*'" as Talmud referred to. The transition from "not skilled" to "not adherent" is the first sign of this shift in perception. At the same time, the Christian attitude toward Jews changed too. During the first half of the 13th century, Christian theologians became increasingly interested in Jewish postbiblical law, i.e., Talmud. Contemporary Jews—as opposed to biblical Jews—had developed anti-Christian attitudes, which is believed to be rooted in Talmud. This development led to a series of public trials, like the two Paris Talmud trials (1240 and 1269), the Barcelona trial (1263), and the burning of rabbinical texts in 1242 in Paris. Ultimately, these events led to a cultural paradox—at a time of the lowest possible mutual relationship, Jewish-Christian cultural exchange was at a peak. See more in Kogman-Appel, "Jewish Figural Painting," 92.

The first examples of Hebrew illuminated manuscripts appeared around the same time in southern Germany.[26] Later, during the first decades of the 14th century, Jews in Spain also began to use figurative art in religious books. The shift in the Jewish perception of Christians was an influential factor in the development of Jewish figurative art, and it enabled borrowings of Christian motifs, models, and symbols, thus leading to the creation of Jewish medieval illuminated haggadot, the prayer book for Pesach Seder.[27]

Representations of the Temple are not common in haggadot, but we have some important exceptions from Ashkenaz and Sfarad. In the Jewish post-Temple art tradition, both literary and visual, Jerusalem and the Temple represent the focus of messianic hopes. These two are often combined into one because it was thought that the reconstruction of Jerusalem means the starting

---

26   It is believed that the oldest illuminated haggadah—the Birds' Head Haggadah (Israel Museum Jerusalem, MS 180/57)—was created in the region of Mainz in Germany around the year 1300. See Michael M. Epstein, *The Medieval Haggadah, Art: Narrative, Religious Imagination* (New Haven: Yale University Press, 2011), 5 (with an extensive overview of the older literature). Katrin Kogman-Appel, however, moves this dating and considers that the year 1290 can be taken as the year of creation of the illuminated haggadah, quoting British Library MS. Or 2737 as a first Illuminated haggadah. Cf. Katrin Kogman-Appel, *Illuminated Haggadot from Medieval Spain* (University Park: Pennsylvania State University Press, 2006), 81; Kogman-Appel, "Jewish Figural Painting," 76. On the Ashkenazi school of haggadot, see Bezalel Narkiss, *Hebrew Illuminated Manuscripts* (Jerusalem: Leon Amiel 1969), 42–56; Katrin Kogman-Appel, *Die zweite Nürnberger und die Jehuda Haggada: Jüdische Illuminatoren zwischen Tradition und Fortschritt* (Frankfurt: Peter Lang 1999); Katrin Kogman-Appel, "Sephardic Ideas in Ashkenaz—Visualizing the Temple in Medieval Regensburg," *Simon Dubnow Institute Yearbook* 8 (2009), 245–277; Sarit Shalev-Eyni, *Jews among Christians: Hebrew Book Illumination from Lake Constance* (Turnhout: Brepols, 2010).

27   Jewish medieval book art has been linked to the development of urban Christian lay workshops in the 13th century. Early Medieval Christian scriptoria were exclusively monastic and therefore inaccessible to Jews. Only in secular workshops, the byproduct of urban development, could Jews acquire painting techniques, purchase, or borrow model books and commission manuscript decoration. In the following decades it became increasingly customary for wealthy Jews of Germany and northern France to have their Bibles, prayer books and other texts adorned with figurative miniatures. There is no evidence that there was any kind of figurative Jewish art prior to 1290. During the early part of the 14th century, a new tradition of illuminating haggadot became widespread in Spain also. Most of the surviving haggadot originated in Catalonia where some wealthy communities existed. Their status declined during the second half of that century but remained fairly decent till the pogroms of 1391. The sumptuous Spanish haggadot, mostly commissioned by the wealthy members of the community, open with a cycle of full-page miniatures preceding the text. Iconographical cycles usually include scenes from Exodus relating to the exile from Egypt. See Batterman, "Spanish Illuminated Haggadah."

point of the Temple rebuilding. In the Middle Ages, those hopes were associated with Passover, the feast that celebrates liberation from slavery in Egypt.

2 Temple Representation in the Sarajevo Haggadah

Probably the best-known and certainly the most original of all Sephardic haggadot is the Codex 4436 known as the Sarajevo Haggadah, today kept in the National Museum of Bosnia and Herzegovina in Sarajevo.[28] It contains the most extensive cycle of all Sephardic haggadot, with 34 pages full of illuminations. A good deal of recent scholarship has been devoted to the imagery and iconographic program of the Sarajevo Haggadah, but none of it has addressed representation of the Temple.[29]

Compared to other Sephardic haggadot, the usual iconographic program of the introductory cycle of the Sarajevo Haggadah was extended, with the inclusion of the representation of the Temple towards the very end of the opening illustrations (Figure 5.4). This illustration continues the biblical Exodus cycle and is followed by the ritual Pesach scenes and representation of the synagogue. For the 'designers' of the Sarajevo Haggadah, the Passover salvation does not end with the Exodus from Egypt—as is the case in most of the haggadot—but with the return of the chosen people to Israel and the building of the Temple. However, the Temple represented in the Sarajevo Haggadah does not indicate the ancient Temple of Jerusalem but a future, eschatological Third Temple, further stressed by the caption located below בֵּית הַמִּקְדָּשׁ יִבָּנֶה בִּמְהֵרָה וְאָמֵן (temple to be built soon, in our time).[30]

---

28 Library of the National Museum of Bosnia and Herzegovina in Sarajevo, C 4436.

29 Cecil Roth, *The Sarajevo Haggadah and its Significance in the History of Art* (Belgrade: Jugoslavija 1973); Herbert Broderick, "Observation on the Creation Cycle of the Sarajevo Haggadah," *Zeitschrift für Kunstgeschichte* 47 (1984), 320–332; Shulamit Laderman and Katrin Kogman-Appel, "The Sarajevo Haggadah: The Concept of Creatio Ex-Nihilo and the Hermeneutical School Behind It," *Studies in Iconography* 25 (2004), 89–127; Kogman-Appel, *Illuminated Haggadot*, 99–109.

30 בֵּית הַמִּקְדָּשׁ יִבָּנֶה בִּמְהֵרָה וְאָמֵן (trans. *beit ha migdaš i bane bimera veamem*). Tractate Taanit, chapter IV, ends with a similar statement: "This is the temple that will be built in our time." See http://www.jewishvirtuallibrary.org/jsource/Talmud/taanit4.html (accessed August 14, 2013). According to some scholars, this addition to the usual haggadah cycle has parallels in Christian Psalters that have Christ's Second Coming as the closing scenes. See Sarit Shalev-Eyni, "Jerusalem and the Temple in Hebrew Illuminated Manuscripts: Jewish Thought and Christian Influence," in *L'interculturalita dell'ebraismo*, ed. Mauro Perani (Ravenna: Longo, 2004), 175.

FIGURE 5.4 Representation of the Temple in the Sarajevo Haggadah (14th century CE), National Museum of Bosnia and Herzegovina
PHOTO: © JEWISH COMMUNITY OF BOSNIA AND HERZEGOVINA

The Temple of the Sarajevo Haggadah is represented using an architectural structure that resembles a fortified city, with the Temple and the Ark of the Covenant within. Two gates with large arched openings and gabled roofs on both sides and crenellated walls that connect them with visually accented masonry work push to the limits of the depicted zone, not leaving any unpainted space. Under the central arch, flanked by two tall, roofed structures with open, oversized doors, one can see the facade of the Temple: two golden pillars with capitals and distinct lintels around a huge door and, inside, the most sacred part of the Temple, *kodesh haKodashim* (Holy of Holies), wide open. Inside, represented on the blue background *luhot a brit*, are the Table of (easily legible) Commandments and the wings of the two cherubim above.

While in Jewish art in late antiquity (3rd–6th century) the messianic Temple is symbolically represented as the Ark of the Covenant, during the medieval period the patrons and the artists preferred to express messianic hope through the representation of the Temple utensils. This kind of representation is common in the decoration of Sephardic Bibles, and gave rise to the conclusion that—in the absence of the actual Temple in Jerusalem—an illuminated Bible was considered a 'small temple.' That is why, from the 14th century on in Spain, it became common to call the Bible the *mikdashyah*—shrine, Temple of the Lord.[31]

Basically, representations of the Temple from the Sarajevo Haggadah render the appearance of the western facade of the Temple, as reconstructed by Schwartz and Peleg, seen from the (opened) Nikanor Gate (Figure 5.5). In the center there is a Temple facade of unusual height, with crenellation on the roof. Underneath there are five openings.[32] The main entrance has a semi-circular arch in the form of a seashell and a huge door opening carved in marble and flanked with two golden columns with elaborated bases and Corinthian capitals. The texture of the Temple is realistically suggested with meticulously painted masonry work.[33] Besides that, the Nikanor Gate is flanked by a pair of

---

31 Joseph Gutmann, "Masora Figurata in the Mikdashyah: The Messianic Solomonic Temple in a 14th-Century Spanish Hebrew Bible Manuscript" in *8th International Congress of Masoretic Studies Chicago 1988*, ed. E.J. Revell (Missoula: Scholars Press, 1990), 71–77; Kogman-Appel, *Jewish Book Art*.

32 Although these openings do not exist on the Schwartz and Peleg ideal reconstruction, we know from written sources that there were many chambers in the main building and that their openings were necessary for lighting and ventilation. Joshua Schwartz and Yehoshua Peleg, "Notes on the Virtual Reconstruction of the Herodian Period Temple and Courtyards," in *The Temple of Jerusalem: From Moses to Messiah*, ed. Steven Fine (Leiden: Brill, 2011), 69–89.

33 From Josephus we know that the "Temple was built of hard, white stones, each of which was 25 cubits in length."

FIGURE 5.5 Tentative reconstruction of the Herodian Temple facade
DRAWING: SCHWARTZ AND PELEG, "NOTES ON THE VIRTUAL RECONSTRUCTION OF THE HERODIAN PERIOD TEMPLE AND COURTYARDS," 81, ILLUSTRATION 7. COURTESY OF PROF. JOSHUA SCHWARTZ AND YEHOSHUA PELEG

two-storey towers with huge doors.[34] All the above-mentioned architectural elements—bases and capitals of the flanking columns, semi-arch above the entrance, and rows of stone in the facade—produce some degree of physical reality which is not shared by other late antique or medieval Jewish representations of the Temple. Comparing it to the Schwartz and Peleg ideal model of the Temple, the Sarajevo Haggadah's Temple representation displays only a few discrepancies: openings on the main buildings and towers flanking the Nikanor Gate are either non-existent, in the case of the former, or fewer, in the case of latter.[35] Roofs are not represented as flat as they are in the reconstruction,[36] and the function of the two buildings adjacent to the main

---

34   I here refer to Michael Avi-Yonah's reconstruction of the Courtyards of the Second Temple and especially the Nikanor Gate. See Michael Avi-Yonah, *Pictorial Guide to the Model of Ancient Jerusalem at the Time of the Second Temple* (Jerusalem: Palphot, 2003), 24–25.

35   Omissions of this kind are not rare in representations of architecture in medieval art. See Čedomila Marinković, *Slika podignute crkve* [Image of the completed church] (Belgrade: PB Press, 2007), 45–49.

36   Although the roof in the ideal reconstruction is represented as flat, there is certainly doubt about it. In many other existing examples, roofs are represented schematically. Marinković, *Slika podignute crkve*, 45–49.

facade is not clear. Even the golden and yellowish colors of the pillars and facade are based on textual sources.[37]

This representation of the Temple is not simply schematic and stereotypical but is a multi-layered architectural symbol. It is very hard to make any comparison with the structure of the Herodian Temple that once existed on the Temple Mount because nobody really knows what the Second Temple looked like. Although today there are several hundreds of reconstructions of it, many of them are no more than religious imaginings.[38] There is no archaeological evidence of the Herodian Temple, and there are only three reliable written sources that one can base the reconstruction upon. The major written sources for the description of Herodian Temple appear in two sections in Flavius Josephus' *Jewish Wars* and in *Antiquities of the Jews*, written some 20 years later.[39] The other significant description in written sources is found in *Mishnah Middot*, chapters 1–5.[40] Altogether they provide a very scant source of information about the outer appearance of the Temple, especially its facade. Recently, Schwartz and Peleg suggested a new, scientifically based, reconstruction of the Temple.[41] Comparing this reconstruction to the Sarajevo Haggadah's Temple representation, one can find some striking similarities. Even at the time of the preparation of the Sarajevo Haggadah, the archaeological material for the reconstruction of the Herodian Temple in Jerusalem was lacking. How then was this representation conceived? Was it made based on model books, memory, or written sources, on the basis of the word-driven (or metaphorical) meaning, or was it based on image-driven (or symbolic) meaning?

There is no clear consensus on the provenance of the overall cycle of the Sarajevo Haggadah. Scholars have pointed to similar visual models—French,

---

37   Josephus tells us that the exterior of the building was covered with massive plates of gold. But there was "one gate ... which was of Corinthian brass." Josephus Flavius, "Jewish Wars" 5, 3.

38   The best-known and most widespread is the famous Michael Avi-Yonah reconstruction that was made in 1962–1966 for the Holyland Hotel in Jerusalem and was later moved to the Israeli Museum in 2005–2006. See Maya Balakirtsky-Katz, "Avi Yonah's Model of Second Temple Jerusalem and the Development of Israeli Visual Culture," in *The Temple of Jerusalem: From Moses to Messiah*, ed. Steven Fine (Leiden: Brill, 2011), 349–365.

39   Josephus's literary work was already widespread in Christian Europe in late antiquity. Karen M. Kletter, "The Christian Reception of Josephus in Late Antiquity and the Middle Ages," in *A Companion to Josephus*, ed. Honora Howell Chapman and Zuleika Rodgers (Chichester: John Wiley & Sons, 2015).

40   Hugues Vincent, "Le temple hérodien d'après la Mišnah," *Revue Biblique* 61, 5–35, 398–418.

41   Schwartz and Peleg, "Notes on the Virtual Reconstruction," 69–89.

REPRESENTATION OF THE TEMPLE IN THE SARAJEVO HAGGADAH 159

Spanish or even Byzantine.[42] For the time being, and in accordance with the most recent research by Kogman-Appel, the conclusion is that the artist of the Sarajevo Haggadah developed "numerous original schemes ... and the result was an almost fully independent cycle."[43]

In order to understand more clearly the specific architectural representation in the Sephardic Sarajevo Haggadah, we shall consider one Ashkenazi haggadah which dates from about the period of our consideration. It is the Birds' Head Haggadah, illuminated probably in Mainz around the year 1300, which is now kept in the Israel Museum in Jerusalem (MS 180–57).[44] This manuscript consists of 47 folia, of which only two are full pages of illuminations, while the rest are distributed as marginal illustrations within the text or as *bas de page* on 33 pages. On the closing miniature on fol. 47 r, instead of the representation of the Jerusalem Temple as in the Sarajevo Haggadah, we have one with the Renewed Jerusalem. Here, the standard topos of architectural representation is used for Jerusalem, that is to say, the heavenly city is represented in terms of a splendid Gothic structure: a pair of two-storey towers with crenellation flank the gabled gate, decorated with a trefoil Gothic frame. The Temple and the city are descending together from the heavens, while four people stand below, raising their hands and pointing to them in veneration. The texture of the roof and the construction method are particularly pronounced. The right-side label clearly identifies the city as Jerusalem.

Given the context of the haggadah text in which it occurs, as presented here, Jerusalem bears the same messianic idea as the Temple in the Sarajevo Haggadah. However, these two representations are completely different. Why does the change in visualization of the same messianic ideas occur in the

---

42   There were attempts to connect certain iconographical features of the Sarajevo Haggadah introductory cycle with the St. Louis Psalter (Paris, Bibilotheque nationale de France, MS Latin 10525, made between 1253 and 1270), Vienna Bible moralisée (Vienna, Österreichische Nationalbibliothek, 2554 from around 1220) as well as with Byzantine Octateuch manuscripts, for example, the one that is kept in the Vatican (Biblioteca Apostolica, cod. Gr. 746, fol. 194 v). For more, see Kogman-Appel, *Illuminated Haggadot*, 9–109, and Kurt Weitzmann and Massimo Barnabo, *The Byzantine Octateuchs* (Princeton: Princeton University Press, 1999), fig. 711. However, this Byzantine influence was recently questioned by Lowden. See John Lowden, "Illustrated Octateuch Manuscripts: A Byzantine Phenomenon" in *The Old Testament in Byzantium*, ed. Paul Magdalino and Robert Nelson (Cambridge, MA: Harvard University Press, 2010), 107–153.

43   Kogman-Appel, *Illuminated Haggadot*, 107.

44   Moshe Spitzer, ed., *The Bird's Head Haggadah of the Bezalel National Art Museum in Jerusalem* (Jerusalem: Tarshis Books, 1965–1967), 2:15–19; Meyer Schapiro, "The Bird's Head Haggada: An Illustrated Hebrew Manuscript of ca. 1300," in *Late Antique, Early Christian and Medieaval Art, selected papers* (New York: George Braziller, 1993), 380–388.

Ashkenazi haggadah, and what is the meaning that is suggested by this architectural representation?

Sarit Shalev-Eyni argues, most plausibly, that this imagery was inspired by the Christian perception of the Heavenly Jerusalem as referred to in the book of Revelation.[45] Ashkenazi messianic expectation had an explicit apocalyptic character going back to late antiquity.[46] According to this, the Third Temple will descend miraculously from the heavens upon the city of Jerusalem. This is based on the Redemption Midrashim (*midrashei ge'ulah*), a group of early medieval texts based on late antique apocalyptic texts.[47]

In contrast, these ideas didn't flourish in Spain, where, under the strong influence of Maimonides, the messianic attitude was more naturalistic. Maimonides elaborated the description and comments on the Temple and its implements. In both the *Mishneh Torah* and the *Commentary on Mishneh*, Maimonides wrote at length about the Temple.[48] Manuscripts of the latter even contain the plan of the sanctuary, meant to function as instructive information, not as a decoration. There were even Maimonides's sketches for the future Temple.[49]

There is good reason to assume that the choice of a particular compositional scheme for the representation of the Temple both in the Sarajevo Haggadah and the Birds' Head Haggadah had much to do with the beliefs and the messianic concepts of those who designed it. Both Spanish and German Jewish art of illuminated manuscripts were informed to various degrees by Christian visual culture. The artists of haggadot adopted the Christian pictorial method and gave it a different meaning. Ashkenazi imagery depended less on Christian sources, whilst the art of Sephardic haggadot exhibits various ways of interaction with Christian art.[50]

---

45   Sarit Shalev-Eyni, "Jerusalem and the Temple," 173–191.

46   One of the very first examples one can find is in Enoch 90:29.

47   This idea that the Third Temple "will descend fully formed from heaven" was further adopted by Rashi in his commentary to the Sukkat Treatise of Babylonian Talmud (41a). Quotation is after Sarit Shalev-Eyni, "Jerusalem and the Temple," 177.

48   Maimonides declared that the Third Temple "will be built by the human hands of Messiah" (Code of Law, Sefer Mishpatim, 11:1) and "if he did and succeeded and built the Temple, he is certainly Messiah." Sarit Shalev-Eyni, "Jerusalem and the Temple," 178.

49   Oxford, Bodleian library, MS Poc. 295. Maimonides "Commentary to the Mishnah," fol. 295r., produced in Spain or Egypt in the second half of the 12th century; for a good photographic reproduction of the sketches see also https://hebrew.bodleian.ox.ac.uk /catalog/manuscript_430 [Accessed June 12, 2022]. See Kogman-Appel, "Jewish Book Art," 75–82.

50   Kogman-Appel, "Jewish Figural Painting," 77.

However, the Renewed Jerusalem, illustrated in the Birds' Head Haggadah as descending from the heavens, is almost a replica of the Christian Gothic type of the Heavenly Jerusalem whilst, on the other hand, in Sephardic art, which in general depended more on Christian models, nothing of that kind was ever represented. In the history of Jewish art, similar models existed only prior to the 6th century and it is highly speculative whether the designer of our haggadah could have known any of this.[51] Furthermore, if one seeks Byzantine influence, it was very unlikely for the 'designer' of the Sarajevo Haggadah, not only because there is no documentation of cultural relations between 14th-century Barcelona and Byzantium but particularly considering the views of Rabbi Eliezer ben Nathan (d. 1170), who stated that, due to their icon worship and the whole Eastern visual culture, Byzantines, among all other Christians, were "faithful idolaters."[52]

Despite different social circumstances, philosophical and theological schools, and artistic influences, topoi of architectural representations move from one area to another, changing cultures, and even crossing the very well-maintained religious boundaries. The topoi carried their narrative potential and established their own autonomous visual language, a *lingua franca* of architectural representation basically understandable to a medieval audience either Jewish, Christian, or Byzantine.

Representation of the Temple from the Sarajevo Haggadah, being a specific addition to its iconographic program, wasn't made after any known visual model, either Christian or Jewish, Eastern or Western. Referring above all and to a great extent to the Temple, a very physical reality—as described in written sources—the (as yet) unknown but unusually creative and insightful artist of the Sarajevo Haggadah wished above all to convey the real appearance of the Temple of Jerusalem in terms of the expectation of the approaching messianic era. This messianism, however, was not the mystic, apocalyptic one promoted by the Tosafists but the realistic and naturalistic approach to messianism that was developed by Sephardic philosophers during the lifetime of Maimonides.

---

51 Almost all the examples from Israeli synagogues were rediscovered either at the beginning or at the end of the 20th century: Dura-Europos and Hammat Tiberias in 1920, El Kirbeh in 1990 and Sepphoris in 1993.

52 This statement refers to Byzantine icon worship, saying that "In Russia and the lands of Greece they are certainly skilled (in idolatry) as they put (objects of) idolatry on all their gates, doors, houses and walls of the houses." Jews of that period were thus aware of the cultural difference between Latin and Greek Christendom regarding icon worship. For them, all Christians were idolaters but Byzantines were so to speak 'faithful idolaters' whereas Western Christians had become negligent. Kogman-Appel, "Jewish Figural Painting," 95.

In the present state of research, it appears that the representation of the Temple in the Sarajevo Haggadah is a unique representation and rare example of *creatio ex nihilo* (to borrow the expression from Kogman-Appel and Laderman's famous study[53]) of an artist who basically relayed his own creativity. This proves that the rhetoric of the architecture as a universal epistemological method that combines word-driven (or metaphorical) and image-driven (or symbolic) meaning produced architectural forms that were not only very powerful carriers of messages but at the same time also a very important form of mnemonic image—in this case of the Temple in Jerusalem. As such, the representation of the Temple from the Sarajevo Haggadah, with its recognizable form and acquired familiar meaning, is pointing beyond itself, to the archetype of Temple representation in Jewish art and basis of the reconstruction of the (future) Third Temple itself.

Acknowledgements

The text is dedicated to Prof. Ivana Marcikić with my warmest gratitude for her insightful suggestions.

---

53   Kogman-Appel and Laderman, "The Sarajevo Haggadah," 89–128.

CHAPTER 6

Type and Archetype: Echoing Architectural Forms of the Church of Nea Moni

Marina Mihaljević

The subject of this paper, the church of Nea Moni situated on the Aegean island of Chios, was built by Emperor Constantine IX Monomachos (1042–1055). By virtue of its exquisite mosaic decoration and imposing architecture, it certainly represents one of the finest Byzantine churches (Figure 6.1).[1] The church of Nea Moni includes a simple square naos surmounted by a large dome over the octagonal transitional zone comprised of eight tall squinches (Figure 6.2). The lower square and the upper octaconch zones were masterfully connected by the insertion of double colonnettes, which accorded the notable impression of circularity to the naos of the church (Figure 6.3). Therefore, it is not surprising that a later local tradition mentions the church as an imitation of the centrally planned mausoleum of Constantine the Great in the complex of the Constantinopolitan church of the Holy Apostles.[2]

In its exterior appearance, the design of the church is overwhelmingly dominated by a large dome (Figure 6.4).[3] Besides its substantial size, the dome originally exhibited yet another significant aspect, namely, the corners of its drum incorporated two-tiered marble colonnettes, doubled in their lower zone in a manner reflecting the arrangement in the interior of the church (Figure 6.5). The drum design with double colonnettes was also prominently featured in

---

1 Doula Mouriki, *The Mosaics of Nea Moni on Chios*, vols. 1–2 (Athens: The Commercial Bank of Greece, 1985) and Charalambos Bouras, *Nea Moni on Chios: History and Architecture* (Athens: The Commercial Bank of Greece, 1982) remain seminal studies on the church of Nea Moni. For new results on its building history, see Sotiris Voyadjis, "The Katholikon of Nea Moni in Chios Unveiled," *Jahrbuch der Österreichischen Byzantinistik* 59 (2009), 229–242.

2 As recorded by the 19th century, the church was a copy of the "plan of Holy Apostles the small, that is, the smaller Church of the Holy Apostles." For a broader interpretation, see Bouras, *Nea Moni on Chios*, 139–145.

3 Nea Moni's dome was inaccurately rebuilt after being destroyed in the 1881 earthquake. Fortunately, two photographs of the dome taken after the earthquake but before the rebuilding have facilitated a reconstruction of its original appearance.

© KONINKLIJKE BRILL NV, LEIDEN, 2023 | DOI:10.1163/9789004537781_008

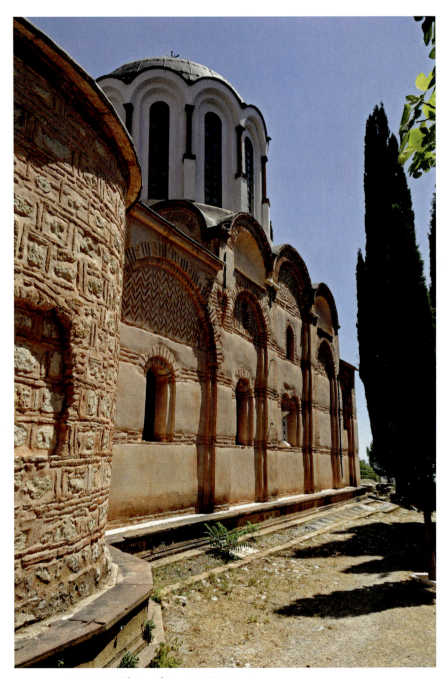

FIGURE 6.1   Nea Moni, Chios, 11th century. Exterior view
PHOTO: MARINA MIHALJEVIĆ

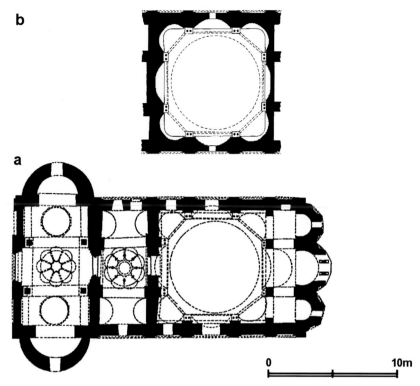

FIGURE 6.2 Nea Moni, Chios, 11th century. Plan
DRAWING: MARINA MIHALJEVIĆ

later replicas of the church of Nea Moni: the church of Panagia Krina at Vavily and Hagioi Apostoloi at Pyrgi on the island of Chios.[4]

Due to its novel structural solution, which has been considered to be a pre-model for a distinct—standard—Middle Byzantine structural type, the so-called Greek octagon, the typological approach was predominant in studies of Nea Moni's architecture.[5] In the scholarly search for the origins of the domed

---

4 The dome of the church at Pyrgi still preserves the circle of double colonnettes between the dome windows. The paired colonnettes are also clearly visible on the fresco model of the church in the narthex of Panagia Krina. Bouras, *Nea Moni on Chios*, 109, figs. 91–94. Also Charalambos Bouras, *Chios* (Athens: National Bank of Greece, 1974), 30ff.

5 For the standard Middle Byzantine plan types and their evolution, see Richard Krautheimer, *Early Christian and Byzantine Architecture*, 4th ed. (New Haven/London: Yale University Press, 1986), 354–369. The churches of the so-called Greek octagon type are first known from the Greek mainland, and later on revived in several churches on the island of Chios: Charalambos Bouras, "Twelfth and Thirteenth Century Variations of the Single Domed

FIGURE 6.3 Nea Moni, Chios, 11th century. Reconstruction of the interior
DRAWING: MARINA MIHALJEVIĆ AFTER ANASTASIOS ORLANDOS (IN BOURAS, *NEA MONI*, FIGS. 57 AND 78)

octagon and the subsequent Greek octagon type, the presence of Nea Moni's double colonnettes has played a surprisingly significant role. Specifically, the paired colonnettes have been compared with similar stylistic elements evident in Armenian architecture in order to support the argument for the Armenian provenance of this structural type.[6]

Octagon Plan," *Deltion tēs Christianikēs Archailogikēs Hetaireias* 9 (1977–1979), 21–32. In fact, when applied here, the term domed octagon is somewhat misleading since in reality the church's upper part possesses an octaconch arrangement. Bouras, *Nea Moni on Chios*, 133–138, refutes earlier theories about the derivation of Nea Moni's structural type from the plan of Hosios Loukas ('mainland complex/cross-domed octagon') and stresses the uniqueness of Nea Moni's upper octaconch arrangement.

6 Thomas F. Mathews, "Observations on the Church of Panagia Kamariotissa on Heybeliada (Chalke), Istanbul," *Dumbarton Oaks Papers* 27 (1973), 126–127. The idea of the Armenian origin of the domed octagon has long been present in studies of Byzantine architecture: Gabriel Millet, *L'École grecque dans l'architecture byzantine* (Paris: E. Leroux, 1916), 105–118; Eustathios Stikas, *L'église byzantine de Christianou en Triphylie (Pélponnèse) et les autres édifices de même*

FIGURE 6.4 Nea Moni, Chios, 11th century. Reconstruction of the west elevation
DRAWING: MARINA MIHALJEVIĆ (AFTER BOURAS, *NEA MONI*, FIGS. 104 AND 115)

Apart from the aforementioned discussion, the double colonnettes and the mirroring of the interior design elements on the exterior of the church have escaped further attention. A scholarly approach based upon typological and stylistic concerns thus set the stage for the potential narrative significance of church's architecture being overlooked.[7] Recently, Nea Moni's marble

---

    type (Paris: Boccard, 1951), 34ff; Bouras, *Nea Moni on Chios*, 151, disregards the relationship of Nea Moni's features with similar double and triple dome colonnettes that are common stylistic traits in Armenian architecture, and rejects the idea that this can be an extra argument for the proposed Armenian origin of the Nea Moni's architecture.

7 See the seminal introductory study on the transfer of meaning in architecture: Richard Krautheimer, "Introduction to an 'Iconography of Medieval Architecture'," *Journal of the Warburg and Courtauld Institutes* 5 (1942), 1–33. See also Günter Bandmann, *Early Medieval Architecture as Bearer of Meaning*, trans. Kendall Wallis (New York: Columbia University

FIGURE 6.5 Nea Moni, Chios, 11th century. Reconstruction of the dome
DRAWING: MARINA MIHALJEVIĆ AFTER BOURAS, *NEA MONI*,
FIGS. 89–90 AND 107

colonnettes were considered within the context of the rhetoric of Byzantine architecture and related to the church of the Holy Sepulchre in Jerusalem.[8] This chapter revisits the occurrence of these architectural elements with the addition of several notes regarding the architectural references to the Holy Sepulchre in Middle Byzantine architecture, and additionally explores their eventual repercussions for re-examining and establishing a more nuanced view of 'type' in Byzantine architecture.

Indeed, the interest of Nea Moni's builders in the centrally planned or, to rephrase it, 'circular' naos is not unusual within the context of Middle

---

Press, 2005). For recent comments on Krautheimer's study, see Robert Ousterhout, "New Temples and New Solomons," in *Old Testament in Byzantium*, ed. Paul Magdalino and Robert Nelson (Washington, DC: Dumbarton Oaks Research Library and Collection, 2010), 228–229.

8 Jelena Bogdanović, "The Rhetoric of Architecture in the Byzantine Context: The Case Study of the Holy Sepulchre," *Zograf* 38 (2014), 1–21, defines rhetoric of architecture as "codified visual and architectural conventions as a series of transpositions that frame specific meanings other than and beyond visible and spatial."

TYPE AND ARCHETYPE 169

Byzantine architecture.[9] In addition to Nea Moni, several other Middle Byzantine examples demonstrate the same concern. For instance, one of the most evocative earlier examples is the church discovered at the site of Küçükyalı (Maltepe) in Istanbul on the Asia Minor shore of the Bosporus.[10] The church includes a finely planned narthex and an elaborate sanctuary on its west and east ends, which is more or less typical of Middle Byzantine churches (Figure 6.6). Its naos, however, presents an unusual interior arrangement: a regular octagon inscribed within a square external outline.

In the region of the Balkans, the church of the Theotokos Eleousa (1080), situated in the village of Veljusa, North Macedonia, presents yet another illustrative example. It is a small, intricately planned building with a narthex and an attached southern chapel (Figure 6.7b).[11] Its founder, Bishop Manuel, was presumably buried in the domed narthex of the church.[12] The church's naos is centrally planned and features an expanded cruciform arrangement with a central domed unit and four terminating conchs. The southern *parekklesion* is a miniature replica of the main church with a somewhat simplified central plan and a similar exterior treatment. The three domes of the Eleousa church exhibit a distinct exterior design. As was the case with Nea Moni's dome, their polygonal drums are accentuated by stepped masonry around the windows and engaged double colonnettes at the angles between the facets (Figure 6.8).

The dome of the only quatrefoil church in the capital, the Panagia Mouchliotissa (Theotokos Panagiotissa), possibly erected during the 11th or

---

9   Marina Mihaljević, "Constantinopolitan Architecture of the Komnenian Era (1080–1180) and its Impact in the Balkans," (PhD diss., Princeton University, 2010), 28–33, for the broader context of Middle Byzantine architecture.

10   The site was identified and often discussed as recent archaeological excavations uncovered the church building built above a large substructure, previously regarded as the Palace of Bryas, built by Emperor Theophilos before 843. See Alessandra Ricci, "The Road from Baghdad to Byzantium and the Case of the Bryas Palace," in *Byzantium in the Ninth Century: Dead or Alive?* ed. Leslie Brubaker (Farnham, Surrey, UK: Ashgate, 1997), 131–149. Alessandra Ricci, "Reinterpretation of the 'Palace of Bryas': A study in Byzantine Architecture, History and Historiography" (PhD diss., Princeton University, 2008), 175–178, suggests identification of the church as the *katholikon* of the monastery of Satyros, built by Ignatios, patriarch of Constantinople, between 867 and 877, during his second appointment to the patriarchal throne.

11   Mihaljević, *Constantinopolitan Architecture*, 66–73, for detailed analyses of Veljusa's architecture with earlier bibliography. See also Slobodan Ćurčić, "Architectural Significance of the Subsidiary Chapels in Middle Byzantine Churches," *Journal of the Society of Architectural Historians* 36, no. 3 (1977), 97–99, for the satellite arrangement of the subsidiary chapels.

12   Petar Miljković-Pepek, *Veljusa* (Skopje: Folozofski fakultet, 1981), 86.

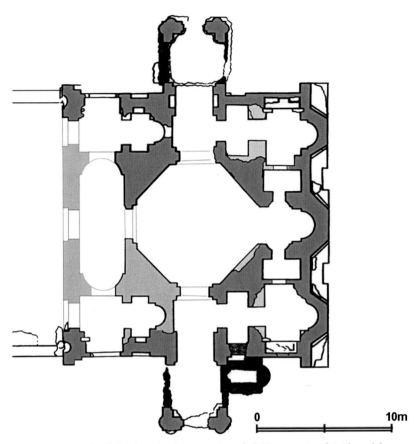

FIGURE 6.6 Küçükyalı (Maltepe), 9th century, Istanbul (Constantinople). Plan of the church
DRAWING: MARINA MIHALJEVIĆ AFTER RICCI, "REINTERPRETATION OF THE 'PALACE OF BRYAS'"

even 10th century, exhibits a similar feature (Figure 6.7a).[13] The drum of its dome preserves a sequence of external blind arches, which presumably

---

13 Recently several scholars have challenged the 13th century dating of the church. Charalambos Bouras, "Hē Architektonikē tēs Panagias ton Mouchliou stēn Kōnstantinoupoli," [The architecture of Panagia Mouchliou in Constantinople], *Deltion tēs Christianikēs Archailogikēs Hetaireias* 4, no. 26 (2005), 35–50, proposed the early 11th century for the construction of the church. Vitalien Laurent, *Les corpus des sceaux de l'empire byzantine*, vol. 5, 2 (Paris: Centre national de la recherche scientifique, 1965), 94–96, points to the evidence that the church and the monastery of the Panagiotissa was in existence as early as the 11th or even the 10th century. See also Paul Magdalino, *Constantinople médiévale: Études sur l'évolution des structures urbaines* (Paris: Boccard 1996), 97–98.

TYPE AND ARCHETYPE 171

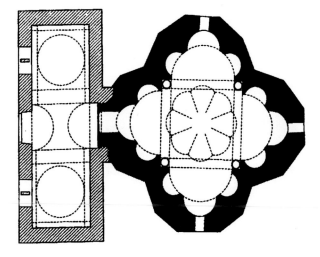

FIGURE 6.7A Panagia Mouchliotissa (Theotokos Panagiotissa), Istanbul (Constantinople), 10th–11th century
DRAWING: MARINA MIHALJEVIĆ AFTER BOURAS, "HĒ ARCHITEKTONIKĒ TĒS PANAGIAS TON MOUCHLIOU STĒN KŌNSTANTINOUPOLI" [THE ARCHITECTURE OF PANAGIA MOUCHLIOU IN CONSTANTINOPLE], FIGS. 8 AND 43

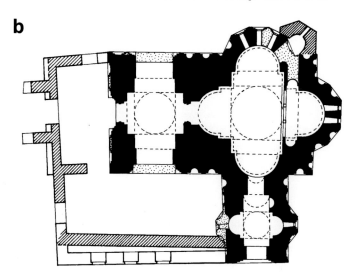

FIGURE 6.7B Theotokos Eleousa, Veljusa, 11th century. Plan
DRAWING: MARINA MIHALJEVIĆ

FIGURE 6.8 Theotokos Eleousa, Veljusa, 11th century. Domes
PHOTO: MARINA MIHALJEVIĆ

indicate the original presence of paired colonnettes (Figure 6.9).[14] It is remarkable for this study that all three mentioned Middle Byzantine examples—Nea Moni, Mouchliotissa and Veljusa—combine two common features: circular naoi and double colonnettes on their domes.[15]

Yet the supremacy of Nea Moni's dome over the exterior of the church is rather exceptional. Its great dimensions, both its width and its height, created an impression of a monumental canopy surmounting the church. Moreover, the insistent correspondence between Nea Moni's interior and exterior designs, both featuring the use of paired colonnettes, seems to have no parallel in Byzantine architecture. In light of this, it is reasonable to ask whether there

---

14 Bouras, "Panagias ton Mouchliou," 43, fig. 9, with further analysis of the church's architecture and the reconstruction of its original plan. Similar design with the double colonnettes appears on the main dome of the *katholikon* of the Athonite monastery of Vatopedi, dated to the very end of the 10th century. Stavros V. Mamaloukos, *To Katholiko tēs monēs Vatopediou, Historia kai arhitektonikē* [The katholikon of the Vatopedi monastery, history and architecture] (Athens: Ethniko Metsovio Polytechneio, Tmēma Architektonōn, Spoudastērio Historias tēs Architektonikēs, 2001) ascribes the architecture of the Vatopedi church to the Constantinopolitan sphere of influence.

15 Mihaljević, *Constantinopolitan Architecture*, 66–73, provides a broader discussion of the similarities between Veljusa, Mouchliotissa, and Nea Moni.

FIGURE 6.9 Panagia Mouchliotissa (Theotokos Panagiotissa), Istanbul (Constantinople), 10th–11th century. Dome
PHOTO: MARINA MIHALJEVIĆ

was any particular reason, other than the general concerns of Byzantine architecture, that could have inspired the highlighted design of Nea Moni's dome.

Several scholars have noted that the mosaic program of the church of Nea Moni has pronounced imperial connotations.[16] The portrayal of King Solomon as a bearded man in the representation of the Anastasis bears a resemblance to Emperor Constantine IX, the *ktetor* of the church.[17] In a manner known from Byzantine culture, the emperor was thus celebrated as the New Solomon.[18] In modern scholarship, Constantine IX has been credited with the reconstruction of the church of the Holy Sepulchre, which makes this praise more pertinent as it recalls the emperor's pious endeavors at the principal Christian shrine.[19]

Extending the message communicated by the mosaic decoration, the unusual architectural conception of the church of Nea Moni could possibly also be intended to honor the emperor as the New Solomon, by underscoring his building accomplishments.[20] The emperor's reputation as a great builder,

---

16 Mouriki, *The Mosaics of Nea Moni*, 137–138; Henry Maguire, "The Mosaics of Nea Moni: An Imperial Reading," *Dumbarton Oaks Papers* 46, 207–213; Ousterhout, "New Temples," 249–250; Robert Ousterhout, "Originality in Byzantine Architecture: The Case of Nea Moni," *The Journal of the Society of Architectural Historians* 51, no. 1 (1992), 59.

17 Anna Karzonis, *Anastasis: The Making of an Image* (Princeton: Princeton University Press, 1986), 216; Mouriki, *The Mosaics of Nea Moni*, 137–138. In the 11th century, a similar image was represented in the apse of the Anastasis Rotunda. See Alan Borg, "The Lost Mosaic of the Holy Sepulchre, Jerusalem," in *The Vanishing Past: Studies in Medieval Art, Liturgy and Metrology Presented to Christopher Hohler*, ed. Alan Borg and Andrew Martindale (Oxford: British Archaeological Reports, International Series 111, 1981), 7–12.

18 Robert Ousterhout, "New Temples," 226, points to Eusebius's address to Paulinus, Bishop of Tyre, in the dedicatory speech at the cathedral of Tyre, as the first mention of the later common Byzantine topos. For a broader discussion, see Claudia Rapp, "Old Testament Models for Emperors in Early Byzantium," in *Old Testament in Byzantium*, ed. Paul Magdalino and Robert Nelson (Washington, DC: Dumbarton Oaks Research Library and Collection, 2010), 175–198.

19 Based on the record of local tradition made by William of Tyre in c.1165, the reconstruction of the Holy Sepulchre has usually been assigned to Emperor Constantine IX Monomachos. Recently, Martin Biddle, *The Tomb of Christ* (Stroud: Sutton Publishing, 1999), 74–88, esp. 77–81, suggested the patronage of Michael IV the Paphlagonian (1034–1041). It is certain that the rebuilding started soon after the demolition of the church in 1009. After 1012, several subsequent Byzantine rulers were involved in its reconstruction. Biddle's remarks leave the possibility that the scope of Monomachos's involvement in the reconstruction of the church should be re-examined, and notes that his works were "at most second phase of an operation which began 1012." In both cases, it is interesting to examine whether the architectural conception of the church of Nea Moni may be germane to revealing the emperor's relationship with the holy shrine.

20 Bouras, *Nea Moni on Chios*, 23–24. The emperor's major Constantinopolitan foundation was the monastery of St. George in Mangana with the sumptuous *katholikon* and surrounding buildings. According to Psellus, the monastery was built with great

TYPE AND ARCHETYPE

as much as his probable engagement in Jerusalem, supports the idea that the model for his new foundation of Nea Moni was the church of the Holy Sepulchre. Yet the question remains: what architectural devices were used in an effort to achieve such a likeness?

With respect to their architecture, the two churches, Nea Moni and the church of the Holy Sepulchre, differ significantly.[21] The perplexing nature of medieval architectural copies and the modes of reiterations of the specific architectural forms have received much scholarly attention.[22] Krautheimer's seminal study on this topic introduces a number of medieval buildings built to resemble the Holy Sepulchre.[23] These buildings bear various degrees of similarity with the physical appearance of the Holy Sepulchre and present different approaches to achieving the desired likeness. Nevertheless, the centrality of the interior has been one of their recurring features.[24] Bearing this in mind,

---

expenditure due to the constant enlargements and changes of plan: Michael Psellus, *Fourteen Byzantine Rulers: The Chronographia of Michael Psellus*, trans. Edgar R.A. Sewter (London: Penguin Books, 1966), 6.55: 182; 6.185: 250–251. For further information regarding the contents and operation of Monomachos's foundation in Mangana, see Nicolas Oikonomides, "St. George of Mangana, Maria Skleraina, and the 'Malyj Sion' of Novgorod," *Dumbarton Oaks Papers* 34–35 (1980–1981), 239–246. For archaeological remains, see Robert Demangel and Ernest Mamboury, *Le quartier des Manganes et la première region de Constantinople* (Paris: Boccard, 1939), 23–36, pls. IV–V.

21 Robert Ousterhout, "Rebuilding the Temple: Constantine Monomachus and the Holy Sepulchre," *Journal of the Society of Architectural Historians* 48 (1989), 66–78, for a review of the Holy Sepulchre's construction phases.

22 Krautheimer, "Introduction," 1–33.

23 The earliest known replica of the Holy Sepulchre, the church of St. Michael in Fulda, was erected in the 9th century. Subsequent architectural studies expanded the scope of Krautheimer's study by including wider topographical, artistic, and functional aspects of medieval copies. See Robert Ousterhout, "The Church of Santo Stefano: A 'Jerusalem' in Bologna," *Gesta* 20, no. 2 (1981), 311–321. The question of religious ideas associated with the construction of the architectural replicas of the Holy Sepulchre in medieval Europe was also further explored by Robert Ousterhout, "Loca Sancta and the Architectural Response to Pilgrimage," in *Blessings of Pilgrimage*, ed. Robert Ousterhout (Urbana, Chicago, IL: University of Illinois Press, 1990), 108–137. Recently, Kathryn Blair Moore, *The Architecture of the Christian Holy Land: Reception from Late Antiquity through the Renaissance* (Cambridge: Cambridge University Press, 2017), examined architectural replicas of the Holy Sepulchre within a broader context of interrelationships between Christians, Jews, and Muslims.

24 Ousterhout, "Loca Sancta," 110–111, specifically mentions a central round, or polygonal, core, with or without the outer ambulatory present in a great number of medieval copies of the church. Two Byzantine examples, both with uncertain identification, were mentioned as being erected in the form of the Holy Sepulchre. The substructure found below the church of Hagios Menas, identified as the martyrium of Karpos and Papylos (4th century), and the building known as the Balaban Ağa Mescidi, recognized as the

the manifest effort to centralize Nea Moni's interior is noteworthy. The double colonnettes appear to be an important architectural device in the attempt to achieve this. Their introduction in the interior of the square naos not only provided a means of connecting the two disjointed architectural registers—the lower square and the upper octaconch—but they effectively took a primary role in space articulation by making the square base of the lower zone secondary in comparison to the central octagonal arrangement above it.[25] Still, we may wonder whether the choice of paired colonnettes has a particular significance in the design of the church.

In modern architecture theory, Anthony Vidler recognizes the so-called 'third' typology of architecture, which proposes that an architectural element—type—selected for replication or reinterpretation, cannot be divorced from its original meaning, which remains its diachronic constitutive element.[26] For our consideration, it is important to note that, due to its general remoteness and the political situation in the 11th century, the Byzantines were mostly unable to visit the holy shrine. In large part, the understanding of the Holy Sepulchre's physical appearance relied exclusively on written descriptions and circulated visual representations.[27] Effectively, the modeling of Nea Moni's dome was presumably conducted without any insight into the factual appearance of the church of the Holy Sepulchre.

One may assume that the written records, recounting a range of devotional practices and describing their sensory aspects, were certainly a very powerful

---

Theotokos tou Kouratoros (5th century), both have central arrangements. The former was probably a rotunda with a surrounding C-shaped ambulatory and a wide altar space, whereas the latter was set as a hexagonal building with six stepped rectangular exedras incorporated within the depth of its perimeter walls. See Wolfgang Müller-Wiener, *Bildlexikon zur Topographie Istanbuls* (Tübingen: Verlag Ernst Wasmuth, 1977), 98–99; 186–187; Thomas F. Mathews, *The Byzantine Churches of Istanbul: A Photographic Survey* (University Park, PA: Pennsylvania State University Press, 1976), 25–27, 206–208, for a review of scholarly research, plans, and earlier bibliography.

25 Ousterhout, "Originality in Byzantine Architecture," 48–60, interprets the incongruities of Nea Moni's structural system as a result of the alteration of the plan from the initial cross-in-square to domed octagon.

26 Anthony Vidler, "The Third Typology," *Oppositions* 7 (Winter 1977), reprinted in *Architecture Theory Since 1968*, ed. K. Michael Hays (Cambridge, MA/London, GB: MIT Press, 1998), 284–294.

27 The written records are collected and translated in John Wilkinson, *Jerusalem Pilgrims Before the Crusades* (Jerusalem: Ariel Publishing House, 1977). For visual sources, see Biddle, *The Tomb of Christ*, 20–28, with systematic and comprehensive review of the visual records of the Aedicula of Christ and the surrounding rotunda. See also Gary Vikan, *Early Byzantine Pilgrimage Art*, rev. ed. (Washington, DC: Dumbarton Oaks Byzantine Collection, 2011).

TYPE AND ARCHETYPE

medium in transferring pilgrimage experience.[28] Art representations known from various devotional objects might have considerably supplemented the texts and played a crucial role in visualizing the physical settings of the holy sites. This is especially valid if we take into account the relative consistency in their constituent iconographic schemes. Therefore, it is quite possible that the visual representations of the Holy Sepulchre could have played a significant role in providing a model for the design of the church of Nea Moni.

Indeed, the correspondence between the design of Nea Moni's dome and the architectural representation in the famous Munich Ascension ivory (c.400) has been noted.[29] In short, the Sepulchre is depicted there as a cubical structure with a circular aedicula outlined by a ring of double columns, strikingly similar to Nea Moni's dome (Figure 6.10). This correspondence has been strictly rejected by researchers of the church and evaluated as irrelevant due to the significant chronological separation.[30] If, however, we take into account the relative frequency and dissemination of this design, and consider Vidler's precept on meaning in architectural type, it is worth reconsidering whether this parallel may in fact hold a certain significance despite the difference in the dates of their creation.

As scholars have already noted, in Byzantine art the church of the Holy Sepulchre and the Aedicula of Christ were often conflated.[31] The columns, present in both structures, were instrumental in merging their representations into a single exchangeable image. Even with such an ambiguity, the Munich ivory stands in contrast to more specific early pilgrimage representations and textual descriptions, which do not indicate the presence of double columns

---

28 Moore, *The Architecture of the Christian Holy Land*, 6–8, for the importance of pilgrimage records. For the religious experience of pilgrimage sites, see Jonathan Sumption, *Pilgrimage: an Image of Mediaeval Religion* (Totowa, NJ: Rowman and Littlefield, 1976), 89–94; John Wilkinson, "Early Christian Pilgrimage," in *Egeria's Travels*, ed. John Wilkinson (Warminster: Aris & Phillips, 1999), 4–34. For the sensory aspects of religious experience, see Béatrice Caseau, "The Senses in Religion: Liturgy, Devotion, and Deprivation," in *A Cultural History of the Senses in the Middle Ages*, ed. Richard G. Newhauser (Oxford: Bloomsbury Academic, 2014), 89–110; Emma J. Wells, "Overview: The Medieval Senses," *The Oxford Handbook of Later Medieval Archaeology in Britain*, ed. Christopher Gerrard and Alejandra Gutiérrez (Oxford: Oxford University Press, 2018), 681–696.

29 Bayerisches Nationalmuseum, Munich (Inv. No. MA 157). See Robin Margaret Jensen, *Understanding Early Christian Art* (New York/London: Routledge, 2000), 156–166; Herbert L. Kessler, "Narrative Representations," in *The Age of Spirituality: Late Antique and Early Christian Art, Third to Seventh Century*, ed. Kurt Weitzman (New York: Metropolitan Museum of Art, 1979), 454–455.

30 Bouras, *Nea Moni on Chios*, 151.

31 Robert Ousterhout, "The Temple, the Sepulchre, and the Martyrion of the Savior," *Gesta* 29, no. 1 (1990), 44–53, esp. 48.

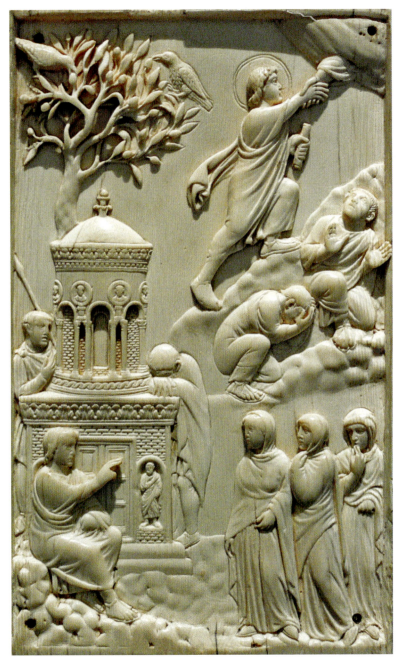

FIGURE 6.10   The Tomb and the Ascension of Christ, ivory, c.400, Bayerisches
Nationalmuseum, Munich, Inv. Nr. MA 157
PHOTO: ANDREAS PRAEFCKE. WIKIMEDIA COMMONS, HTTPS://
EN.WIKIPEDIA.ORG/WIKI/FILE:REIDERSCHE_TAFEL_C_400
_AD.JPG [ACCESSED JULY 9, 2022]

either on the aedicula or in the rotunda of the Holy Sepulchre.[32] Nevertheless, the tradition of representing the double columns within the context of the Holy Sepulchre has a long legacy in Christian art.[33] The 14th-century Vatican manuscript with a representation of The Descent of the Holy Fire prominently features a canopy with paired columns over the Tomb of Christ.[34] This practice goes beyond the Middle Ages, when the paired columns appear relatively often in visual representations of the Holy Sepulchre.[35]

Now, if we consider the symbolic references pertinent for the formation of the particular visual identity of the church of the Holy Sepulchre, we find that its textual association with the Temple may have played a significant role. From its erection in the 4th century, Christian writers, primarily Eusebius, commonly promoted a symbolic association between the church of the Holy Sepulchre and the Temple.[36] It is not surprising, then, that this intangible–ideological

---

32   John Wilkinson, "The Tomb of Christ: An Outline of Its Structural History," *Journal of the Council for British Research in the Levant* 4, no. 1 (1972), 83–97; Biddle, *The Tomb of Christ*, 65–73, 81–88, with extensive discussion of the original appearance and Byzantine phases of the Aedicula of Christ.

33   Biddle, *The Tomb of Christ*, 85, mentions the possibility that the double columns were incorporated in the hexagonal ciborium over the tomb chamber during the 11th century, however, without any substantiating record.

34   The Descent of the Holy Fire, illuminated manuscript, 14th century, Biblioteca Vaticana, cod. Urb.lat.1362, f. 1v.; for a good photographic reproduction of the folio see https://digi .vatlib.it/view/MSS_Urb.lat.1362 [Accessed September 21, 2022].

35   Biddle, *The Tomb of Christ*, 29–52, for a review and discussion of representations of the aedicula from the 12th century to the present day. Biddle points to the wide dissemination and reworking due to the introduction of printing, which recommends scrutiny in the evaluation of independent evidential value. Some of these representations also include the depiction of the church. For example, several preserved wooden models of the church of the Holy Sepulchre that can be disassembled to reveal a model of the aedicula were produced in late 17th or early 18th century for the Franciscan monasteries in the Holy Land as souvenirs for rich pilgrims or presentable gifts. They often display the paired columns both in the apse of the Crusader's church and at the drum of the dome surmounting the aedicula. Depending on the quality of the model, the former are often rendered as the two-tiered columns. See Michele Piccirillo, *La Nuova Gerusalemme, Artigianato Palestinese al servizio dei Luoghi Santi* (Bergamo: Edizioni Custodia di Terra Santa, 2007); Biddle, *The Tomb of Christ*, 42–44, figs. 44–45.

36   Kathleen E. McVey, "Spirit Embodied: The Emergence of Symbolic Interpretations of Early Christian and Byzantine Architecture," in *Architecture as Icon*, ed. Slobodan Ćurčić and Evangelia Hadjitryphonos (New Haven: Yale University Press, 2010), 45–50, provides a detailed discussion of Eusebius's speech delivered on the occasion of the dedication of the church at Tyre in 315 CE. His evocations of the Temple were used as an efficient rhetorical device in authorizing the status of holiness to the church building. Ousterhout, "The Temple," 44–46, 49–50, emphasizes Eusebius's desire to link Christianity with the idea of the fulfillment of the Old Testament prophecy. This symbolic parallel possibly found its reflection in the correspondence between the Holy Sepulchre's liturgical service and the

concord finds physical expression in the art representations of the church. In its formative stage, thus, the visual identity of the church of the Holy Sepulchre was heavily informed by the imagery associated with the Temple, presumably coming from early Jewish representations.[37] Within a group of surviving early Jewish examples, there are several representations of the Temple that display paired columns as an important architectural aspect. For instance, an early representation of the Temple on the tetradrachm of Bar Kochba (undated issue, year 3–134/5 CE) prominently features four double columns adorning its porch (Figure 6.11).[38] Similarly, the famous architectural representation of the Temple on the tympanon of the Torah Shrine in the synagogue of Dura-Europos shows two paired columns flanking the representation of the inner Ark (Figure 6.12). One can find an identical feature at the synagogue at Capernaum, where two paired columns adorn the frames of the southern windows.[39] It is important to note that the Temple had already been destroyed before the creation of the mentioned early Jewish examples, so these images bear witness to a collective memory record, which influenced and shaped subsequent iconography of the Temple. In view of this, one can rightfully ask whether the established identity in the Jewish visual records may have influenced the physical appearance of the original aedicula.

Portable objects, pilgrimage souvenirs—flasks, lamps, and the like—appear to have played manifold devotional roles, as they effectively acquired and transmitted the blessings of the original sacred sites.[40] In the same manner, the Holy Land buildings themselves carried a similar devotional weight as they

---

service in the Temple. See also Ousterhout, "New Temples," 223–253, for appropriation of ideas related to the Temple in Byzantine architecture.

37 This correspondence effectively resulted in interchangeable images, where both the Holy Sepulchre and the Temple were represented as large structures on columns sheltering a smaller one, i.e., the Aedicula of Christ and the Ark of the Covenant respectively. Robert Ousterhout, "The Temple," 47–48. See Helen Rosenau, *Vision of the Temple: The Image of the Temple of Jerusalem in Judaism and Christianity* (London: Oresko Books, 1979), 20–21, for a comprehensive review of visual representations dating from the Bar Kochba revolt of 132–135 CE to contemporary religious architecture.

38 Bar Kochba Revolt coinage was issued by the Judean rebel state, headed by Simon Bar Kochba, during the Bar Kochba revolt against the Roman Empire of 132–135 CE.

39 Robert Ousterhout, "The Temple," fig. 7, 48–49, notes that the Capernaum columns are spiraled. This is often both in representations of the rotunda and the aedicula, due to the tradition stating that the spiral columns of the shrine of Saint Peter in Rome originated from the Temple of Jerusalem.

40 Vikan, *Early Byzantine Pilgrimage Art*; Cynthia Hahn, "Loca Sancta Souvenirs: Sealing the Pilgrim's Experience," in *Blessings of Pilgrimage*, ed. Robert Ousterhout (Urbana, Chicago, IL: University of Illinois Press, 1990), 85–96.

TYPE AND ARCHETYPE 181

FIGURE 6.11   Tetradrachm of Bar Kochba, undated issue, year 134/5 CE. Obverse: representation of the Temple with the rising star
PHOTO: PUBLIC DOMAIN CLASSICAL NUMISMATIC GROUP, INC. HTTP://WWW.CNGCOINS.COM [ACCESSED JUNE 9, 2022]

were venerated as witnesses to holy persons and events.[41] It is thus apparent that the visual representations empowered with the credibility of the authentic records of the holy events represented the true image of the holy buildings in the human imagination.[42] In view of this, it is not difficult to imagine that

41   Moore, *The Architecture of the Christian Holy Land*, 21–52, for a mechanism in symbolization; the Holy Land buildings as substitutes for the missing principal relics—the bodies of Christ and the Virgin Mary. See also Ousterhout, "Loca Sancta," 108–137, for a parallel function of portable objects and architecture.
42   Slobodan Ćurčić, "Architecture as Icon," in *Architecture as Icon*, ed. Slobodan Ćurčić (New Haven: Yale University Press, 2010), 9–26, parallels the role of architectural representations with the images of saints depicted on icons as primary objects of religious veneration and conduits to the heavenly domains.

FIGURE 6.12   Synagogue, Dura-Europos, 3rd century. Torah Shrine
PHOTO: © ALAMY

TYPE AND ARCHETYPE

the shapes of the buildings that recalled the image of the Holy Sepulchre were also informed by the iconographic elements perpetuated in art representations. Apparently, the physical appearance of these replicas was not exclusively adjusted to some form of the factual knowledge of the inaccessible church but frequently to the mental image promoted by long-lasting 'authentic' art (and architectural) conceptions.[43]

Therefore, there is a possibility that the unusual design of the church of Nea Moni stems from the circulating visual ideas that had been reassigned to the church of the Holy Sepulchre from the older representational tradition related to the Temple. In the particular case of Nea Moni, such an association affirms that the ideological — imperial narrative recognized in its mosaic decoration also informed the architecture of the church. Much in the same vein as Nea Moni's fresco decoration, the architectural features of the church were shaped to convey the image of the devout emperor by highlighting his building enterprises, and presumably acclaiming his connection with Jerusalem's holy sites.

It may also be reasonable to compare the emperor's achievements with the replicas of the Holy Sepulchre known from the Christian West. In scholarly discussions about the various motivations for the erection of these copies, the response to a pilgrimage is particularly pronounced.[44] The recreation of *loca sancta* comes either as a means of memorialization and recreation of the visit to and impact of the holy place, or an enhancement to a pilgrimage site. In addition, the funerary function of such replicas is also very frequent. Both of the mentioned examples, the churches in Veljusa and Mouchliotissa, were erected to shelter the tombs of their founders, which parallels Western examples and justifies the connection of their features—double colonnettes and the circular plan—to the church of the Holy Sepulchre.[45] Among the reasons stated for the erection of Holy Sepulchre replicas in the medieval West, the closest in motivation to our example in Nea Moni are perhaps the round

---

43 Bogdanović, "The Rhetoric of Architecture," 11–21, on the examples of famous Byzantine descriptions of the Holy Sepulchre written by Patriarch Photios (9th c.) and Abbot Daniel (12th c.) acknowledges the practice of *ars memoriae*, and proposes its critical role both in forming the collective memory of the buildings and in their actual architectural reconstructions.

44 Geneviève Bresc-Bautier, "La dévotion au Saint-Sépulcre de Jérusalem en Occident: imitations, invocation, donations," *Cahiers de Saint-Michel de Cuxa* 38 (2007), 95–106. See also Ousterhout, "Loca Sancta," 108–137.

45 Miljković-Pepek, *Veljusa*, 86, for Veljusa; Semavi Eyice, "Les églises byzantines à plan central d'Istanbul," *Corso di cultura sulle'arte ravennate e byzantina* 26 (1979), 115–149, for Mouchliotissa.

churches erected by various knightly orders as a signal of their intention to protect and maintain the holy sites.[46]

Notwithstanding the different motivation for the erection of the church of Nea Moni, a comparison with the devotional practices related to the Western copies of the Sepulchre is not irrelevant. In addition, the mentioned particularity of interior and exterior design is important.[47] The dome, as an exterior, public statement, not only manifestly recaptures the form of the Aedicula of Christ but also, as in many Western replicas intended for or linked to a previous pilgrimage, Nea Moni's interior could evoke in visitors to the church the 'true experience' of the sacred site as an involved participant. In securing the potency of religious experience, the church's interior created a physical setting for the visitor's active attendance, thus emphasizing the primary architectural intention and reinforcing the desired ideological message. In this case, the validity of architectural settings assured that the builder of Nea Moni was legitimately lauded as the New Solomon.[48]

It has been noted that in such instances, the messages expressed by art and architecture were fostered by an appropriate laudatory text. Because there is no such text in the case of Nea Moni, the question remains as to whether the concord of art and architectural settings of the church communicated the idea of the Holy Sepulchre to contemporaries in a comprehensible manner. Judging by the dissemination and diversity of the above-mentioned examples, the answer is affirmative.

The same pattern can be recognized in architecture of Byzantine neighbors. For instance, if we return to Armenian architecture, mentioned at the beginning of this article, we will find an especially relevant contemporaneous example. The church of Surb Prkitch in Ani (Holy Savior) was erected in 1035 by Prince Ablgharib Pahlavid to house a relic of the True Cross.[49] Accordingly, its design was clearly appropriated to evoke the Holy Sepulchre.

---

46   Robert Ousterhout, "Loca Sancta," 116–117.

47   Ćurčić, "Architecture as Icon," 23–26, interprets the duality in the Byzantine understanding of the architecture of the church building, where the beauty of the exterior allows for its visual perception, in contrast to the beauty of the interior, which can only be comprehended spiritually.

48   Jaś Elsner, "The Rhetoric of Buildings in the De Aedificiis of Procopius," in *Art and Text in Byzantium*, ed. Liz James (Cambridge: Cambridge University Press, 2007), 33–57, esp. 39–49, for Procopius's use of architectural descriptions as imperial panegyric. In his rhetoric, the buildings stand for and effectively endorse the virtues of the emperor.

49   Armen Kazaryan, İsmail Yavuz Özkaya, and Alin Pontioğlu, "The Church of Surb Prkich in Ani (1035). Part 1: History and Historiography—Architectural Plan—Excavations of 2012 and Starting of Conservation," *Journal of the International Association of Research in History of Art* 0143 (15 November 2016), https://www.riha-journal.org/articles/2016

TYPE AND ARCHETYPE

The interior of the church is arranged as an octaconch with a large main apse (Figure 6.13). Its exterior is almost round, rendered as a nineteen-sided polygon. It is surmounted by an enormous, only slightly narrower, dome. Both exterior registers, the base and the drum of the dome, are decorated by arcades resting on paired colonnettes (Figure 6.14).[50] Moreover, the interior is articulated by a row of non-structural columns placed in contact with the walls between the apsidioles.

In terms of any of the common criteria of architectural typology, the two churches, Nea Moni and the church of the Holy Savior, are apparently very different. Their plans, their architectural style, and their intended functions significantly differ. If, however, we observe their architecture from a conceptual, rather than typological, perspective, the proximity of architectural ideas is striking. Both churches display an inclination toward the centrality of the interior, their domes are remarkably large, and the columns and colonnettes are conspicuously present in the exterior and within the interior. In view of this, it is striking that the previously mentioned, much smaller, Constantinopolitan church of Mouchliotissa also incorporates all these elements: a central plan, double colonnettes on the exterior of the dome, and the interior columns placed in contact with the walls.[51] All these elements, manifestly present in our examples, the churches of Nea Moni and Surb Prkitch, suggest that the church of Mouchliotissa (Theotokos Panaiotissa) was originally erected with the intention to replicate the church of the Holy Sepulchre. Moreover, I would argue that in all their aspects—the significant size of the dome, and the comparably structured interior with exposed columns—the churches of Nea Moni and Surb Prkitch were actually inspired by the patterns known from the circulating representations of the church of the Holy Sepulchre. Their architecture, in effect, faithfully recollects the image of the huge domed and columned church of the Holy Sepulchre nesting the similarly shaped Aedicula of Christ that was already established in pilgrimage art (Figure 6.15).

It is clear that the architectural features of Nea Moni and other mentioned churches reveal Byzantine architects to be capable of formally conceptualizing and embedding architectural forms with highly sophisticated theological and ontological ideas. The repeated conceptual similarity in all these instances,

---

/0143-kazaryan-ozkaya-pontioglu. Due to the possession of such an important devotional object, the church became an important pilgrimage site.

50   From this, we may maintain the fact that doubled colonnettes are a common stylistic feature in Armenian architecture. Yet our further analyses will open the question of their conceptual derivation, and the possible meaning in their architectural appropriation.

51   *Supra*, n. 15. Today, only two of the columns, hidden by a modern iconostasis, are preserved in the church.

FIGURE 6.13   Surb Prkitch, Ani, 11th century. Exterior, from the south
PHOTO: MARINA MIHALJEVIĆ

FIGURE 6.14　Surb Prkitch, Ani, 11th century. Interior from the southeast
PHOTO: MARINA MIHALJEVIĆ

FIGURE 6.15   Pilgrim's ampulla no. 18, reverse
PHOTO: © DUMBARTON OAKS, BYZANTINE COLLECTION, WASHINGTON, DC

despite their geographic, stylistic, and structural characteristics, certainly brings to mind the idea of 'type.' If we acknowledge the potent role of architecture in the perpetuation of *memoriae* by its physical presence as well, our examples radically change the perception of type in Byzantine architecture as the synchronic, codified assembly of particular physical characteristics. Notwithstanding their differences, our examples appear to be representatives of a distinct 'genre,' one that cannot be delineated by chronological or geographical boundaries but is rather conceptualized around the meaningful content assigned to the elements of Byzantine architecture.

CHAPTER 7

In Search of Archetype: Five-Domed Churches in Middle and Later Byzantine Architecture

Ida Sinkević

Five-domed churches are a small but distinct group of edifices that were built in Byzantium from at least the 6th century.[1] They are found across the empire and its borderlands, in the capital city of Constantinople as well as in remote places in Greece, Italy, Russia, Serbia, and Armenia. Although only a few have been preserved, they have been studied extensively by scholars. Significant differences in their structural and compositional features, however, have provoked a wide range of methodological approaches. A number of scholars have recognized five-domed churches as a separate architectural type, and some have even attempted to establish formal and structural criteria for their typological identification and evolution.[2] Conversely, several scholars have pointed out notable variations in the disposition of the domes, as well as in the planning and spatial articulation of these churches, concluding that they should be studied as a part of general architectural and structural trends from a distinct

---

1 This study is a revised and expanded version of the paper presented at the 23rd International Byzantine Studies Conference (Belgrade, Serbia, August 2016) in the session on Type and Archetype in Byzantine Cultural Landscape. It builds upon my previous research published in Ida Sinkević, *The Church of St. Panteleimon at Nerezi: Architecture, Programme, Patronage* (Wiesbaden: Reichert, 2000) and Ida Sinkević, "Formation of Sacred Space in Later Byzantine Five-Domed Churches: A Hierotopic Approach," in *Hierotopy. The Creation of Sacred Spaces in Byzantium and Medieval Russia*, ed. Alexei Lidov (Moscow: Indrik, 2006), 260–276. I am grateful to Professor Jelena Bogdanović, the co-chair of the session, for inviting me to participate and to Professor Diane Cole Ahl for her insightful comments and editorial remarks.

2 See Evangelia Hadžitrifonos, "Pristup tipologiji petokupolnih crkava u vizantijskoj arhitekturi" [Approaches to typology of five-domed churches in Byzantine architecture], *Saopštenja* 22/23 (1990–1991), 41–76; Stefanos Sinos, *Die Klosterkirche der Kosmosoteira in Bera (Vira)* (Munich: Beck, 1985), 211–222; Horst Hallensleben, "Untersuchungen zur Genesis und Typologie des 'Mystratypus'," *Marburger Jahrbuch für Kunstwissenschaft* 18 (1969), 105–118; and Slobodan Nenadović, *Bogorodica Ljeviška: njen postanak i njeno mesto u arhitekturi Milutinovog vremena* [The Mother of God Ljeviška: The origin and place in the architecture of Milutin's time] (Belgrade: Narodna knjiga, 1963), 119–135.

© KONINKLIJKE BRILL NV, LEIDEN, 2023 | DOI:10.1163/9789004537781_009

period and/or location. Thus the latter group has subordinated the presence of domes to the overall architectural planning of edifices.[3]

This essay aims at approaching five-domed churches from a different perspective. Rather than seeing them as a complex organism of different formal elements, an important point that earlier scholars have capably addressed, I will examine five-domed churches through the lens of a Byzantine beholder. In so doing, I will focus on the five-domed churches from the Middle and Late Byzantine periods that feature four domed compartments symmetrically placed around the cruciform core of the church.[4] Similar in shape, size, and exterior decoration, these subsidiary domes are in most instances the result of the initial planning of a church and not an afterthought.[5]

Five-domed churches are visually striking. With all five domes projecting upwards and outwards in balance, symmetry, and harmony, these edifices are significantly different from other Byzantine churches. This distinction hardly went unnoticed by contemporary Byzantine beholders; it seems almost certain that they were already perceived as an individual type at that time. Moreover, their multi-dome configuration likely suggested a symbolic meaning too, since conceptual and metaphorical interpretations permeated Byzantine culture. Firstly, five-domed churches evoked the idea of heaven on earth to the faithful. They perpetuated the notion recorded in the writings of the early Christian bishop and scholar Eusebius of Caesarea (c.260–340) that Christian worship in an earthly church echoes the angelic worship in the heavenly temple.[6] In addition, the presence of many domes could be associated with multiple churches and ultimately connected to the Heavenly Jerusalem, the capital of the eternal

---

3   For a discussion and bibliography, see Slobodan Ćurčić, *Architecture of the Balkans from Diocletian to Süleyman the Magnificent* (New Haven/London: Yale University Press, 2010), 273–275, 409–410, 645–646, 662–666.

4   Five-domed churches from earlier periods are mostly destroyed and known only from literary sources that are often ambiguous in discussing specific architectural features. Many of these monuments, such as Justinian's church of the Holy Apostles in Constantinople, dated to the 6th century, appear to have exhibited subsidiary domes on the arms of the cross; see Richard Krautheimer, *Early Christian and Byzantine Architecture* (4th ed. revised by Richard Krautheimer and Slobodan Ćurčić) (New York: Yale University Press, 1986), 241–244. However, the exact number of domes is somewhat problematic; see Ćurčić, *Architecture of the Balkans*, 200–201. For a discussion about typology of these early monuments, see Hadžitrifonos, "Pristup tipologiji petokupolnih crkava," 42–45.

5   The intentionality of planning, uniformity of shape, size, and decoration, as well as their symmetrical disposition in relation to the central dome, separates five-domed churches from other multi-domed edifices.

6   Eusebius, *Ecclesiastical History*, vol. 2, trans. J.E.L. Oulton, Loeb Classical Library 265 (Cambridge, MA, 2000 [1932 edition]), 10.4.21–26; see also Allan Doig, *Liturgy and Architecture: From Early Church to Middle Ages* (Burlington, VT: Ashgate, 2008).

IN SEARCH OF ARCHETYPE   191

Messianic Kingdom. As the eschatological city with a multitude of churches and a place of perpetual liturgy, the Heavenly Jerusalem appears to be illustrated as a five-domed church in the frontispiece miniature of the 12th-century Homilies of James Kokkinobaphos, Vat. gr. 1162, fol. 2v (Figure 7.1).[7] Could a concept, an association with Jerusalem, rather than a physical and/or material object, represent a model, an archetype, for the five-domed church?

A more formal definition, generally accepted in architectural theory, maintains that each architectural type exhibits not only common characteristics but also has a common model—an archetype—from which copies are made.[8] Following that pattern, Middle Byzantine five-domed churches were believed to have been related to the famous, albeit now lost, five-domed church, the Nea Ekklesia, the New Church. Built in c.880 in close proximity to the imperial palace in Constantinople, commissioned by the Byzantine emperor Basil I (867–886), and glorified in texts, the Nea Ekklesia showcased a novel architectural structure.[9] According to a lengthy description of the church preserved in an *ekphrasis*, the *Vita Basilii* (c.950),[10] the Nea was a five-domed edifice with a roof that "gleams with gold and is resplendent with beautiful images as with stars, while on the outside it is adorned with brass that resembles gold."[11]

---

7   For a discussion of the manuscript, see Alexei Lidov, "Heavenly Jerusalem: the Byzantine Approach," in *Jewish Art* 23/24, 1997/98, 341–353. The literature on the significance and symbolic implication of the Holy City of Jerusalem is vast. Among more recent publications, see Maria Cristina Carile, *The Vision of the Palace of the Byzantine Emperors as a Heavenly Jerusalem* (Spoleto: Fondazione Centro italiano di studi sull'alto Medioevo, 2012); J. Goudeau, M. Verhoeven, and W. Weijers, eds., *Imagined and Real Jerusalem in Art and Architecture* (Leiden: Brill, 2014); Jelena Erdeljan, *Chosen Places. Constructing New Jerusalems in Slavia Orthodoxa* (Leiden: Brill, 2017).

8   For a discussion and definition of terms (type, archetype, prototype, typology, etc.), I have relied mostly on Paul-Alan Johnson, *The Theory of Architecture: Concepts, Themes, and Practices* (New York: Van Nostrand Reinhold, 1994), 288–292. Definitions, however, vary throughout history. See Jelena Bogdanović, "Rethinking the Dionysian Legacy in Medieval Architecture: East and West," in Filip Ivanović, ed., *Dionysius the Areopagite: Between Orthodoxy and Heresy* (Newcastle Upon Tyne: Cambridge Scholars, 2011), 109–134; Rafael Moneo, "On Typology," *Oppositions* 13 (1978), 23–45; Anthony Vidler, "The Idea of Type: The Transformation of the Academic Ideal: 1750–1830," *Oppositions* 8 (1977), 95–115.

9   Ćurčić, *Architecture of the Balkans*, 273–275; Robert Ousterhout, *Master Builders in Byzantium* (Princeton: Princeton University Press, 1999), 36–37; and Paul Magdalino, "Observations on the Nea Ekklesia of Basil I," JÖB 37 (1987), 51–63.

10   The text was believed to have been written by Constantine VII; see *Theophanes Continuatus*, ed. Immanuel Bekker (Bonn: Weber, 1838), 211–355, esp. 325–327; trans. in Cyril Mango, *The Art of the Byzantine Empire 312–1453: Sources and Documents* (Engelwood Cliffs, NJ: Prentice-Hall, 1972), 192–193.

11   Mango, *The Art of the Byzantine Empire*, 194. For later medieval descriptions, see George P. Majeska, *Russian Travelers to Constantinople in the Fourteenth and Fifteenth*

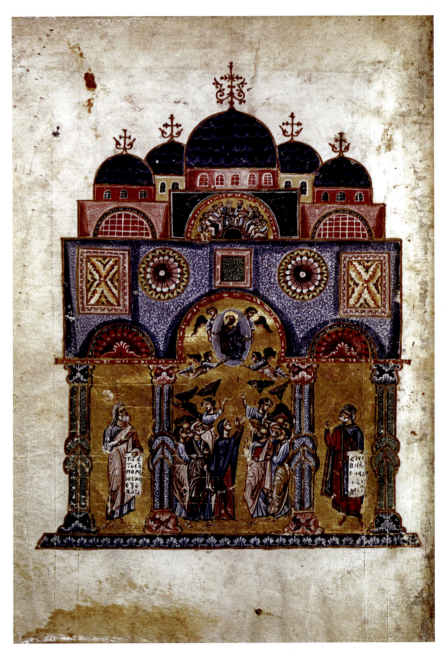

FIGURE 7.1 Homilies of James Kokkinobaphos, Vat. gr. 1162, fol. 2v, 12th century
PHOTO: © UNIVERSAL HISTORY ARCHIVE/UIG/BRIDGEMAN IMAGES

IN SEARCH OF ARCHETYPE   193

Each of the domed chapels had a separate dedication: to Christ, the Archangel Gabriel, the Prophet Elijah, the Virgin and Saint Nicholas. Multiple dedications recall multiple churches and ultimately a resonant archetypal memory of the Heavenly Jerusalem.

The original appearance of the lost church is recorded in a few summary drawings; its five-domed composition has been compared to another early post-iconoclastic church in the capital, the North Church of Constantine Lips also known as the Fenari Isa Camii (10th century).[12] It has also been suggested that the Nea featured a cross-domed plan, although the presence of such planning is ambiguous in the textual evidence.[13] The church of Constantine Lips, which was also five-domed and may have been influenced by the Nea, was a two-storied, cross-in-square building with four lateral domes crowning the upper-level chapels and symmetrically disposed around the central dome.[14] In addition to influencing the churches of the capital, the Nea has also been identified as a model for a new type of five-domed church that appeared on the periphery of the empire. Paul Magdalino's seminal study on the meaning and significance of this church argues convincingly that the Nea was singled out for its imperial connotations.[15] As a foundation of Basil I, its consecration ceremony was appropriated to honor him. Moreover, the selection of relics kept in the church revealed Basil's wish to be associated both with the first Christian emperor, Constantine I, and with the Old Testament King Solomon. Furthermore, Magdalino brought to our attention the importance of the number five in the symbolic interpretation of the monument. The five dedications of the five domes might have been introduced to underscore the idea of ecclesiastic pentarchy: the ecclesiastic and political ambitions to unify the five patriarchates of the church after the Iconoclasm. As stated by Magdalino, "its

---

     Centuries (Washington, DC: Dumbarton Oaks Research Library and Collection, 1984), 37, 247; and Anthony of Novgorod, in Sofija Khitrovo, *Itinéraires russes en Orient* (Geneva: Fick, 1889), 98–102.

12   For a discussion and bibliography, see Ćurčić, *Architecture of the Balkans*, 273–275.

13   A reconstruction of the Nea as a 'cross-domed' type church with four, symmetrically placed corner domed compartments had been proposed by Ćurčić in 1980 and repeated in his monumental study on the architecture of the Balkans. See Slobodan Ćurčić, "Architectural Reconsideration of the Nea Ekklesia," *Byzantine Studies Conference Abstracts* 6 (1980), 11–12; and Ćurčić, *Architecture of the Balkans*, 274–275; 854–55, n. 37. For a more tentative reconstruction and a brief but useful discussion about Byzantine texts as a source for understanding buildings (with bibliography), see Ousterhout, *Master Builders*, 35–37 (especially n. 47).

14   Ćurčić, *Architecture of the Balkans*, 274–275.

15   Magdalino, "Observations on the Nea Ekklesia," 51–63.

five gleaming domes were a visible expression of the ecumenical concord that the council of 879 was called to restore."[16]

All of these concepts seemingly contributed to the perception and the reception of this monument throughout the empire and its borderland. The Nea was considered an icon of imperial power which was copied and repeated in a variety of ways in provincial settings. It may also have served as a model for Middle Byzantine five-domed churches as discussed above. However, if we define archetype as "the original pattern from which copies are made," as has been done in contemporary theory of architecture, the Nea would hardly pass the test.[17] This is apparent when we consider, for example, the two most prominent Middle Byzantine five-domed churches which reflect close associations with the capital due to their imperial patronage, the church of the Virgin Kosmosoteira in Pherrai (1152) in Western Thrace, founded by Isaak Komnenos (Figure 7.2), and the church of St. Panteleimon at Nerezi (1164) in North Macedonia, commissioned by Alexios Angelos Komnenos (Figure 7.3).[18] Both churches are in a provincial location, both were commissioned by a member of the imperial family, both are five-domed, and both are the main church or *katholikon* of their respective monasteries. However, with regard to their size, architectural planning, decoration, and spatial articulation, the two churches are significantly different. To start with, the church at Pherrai, measuring 18.5 × 23.5 meters, is much larger than Nerezi (9.5 × 16 meters). The large size and the system of proportions of the Pherrai church reveal Constantinopolitan building practices of the time. A close architectural relationship between the church at Pherrai and the buildings of the capital is also seen, for example, in the scalloping shape of the interior of the domes, in the use of brick, and in the large, high-shouldered triple windows.[19] Quite the opposite of Pherrai, while also exhibiting five domes, Nerezi is small and reveals an archaic planning formula with full walls separating western chapels from the naos (Figure 7.4).[20]

The five-domed churches from the later Byzantine periods have even less in common with the Nea. The planning and spatial articulation of the interior of these churches represent a striking departure from the Middle Byzantine monuments, as will be discussed later in this paper. Their outside

---

16   Magdalino, "Observations on the Nea Ekklesia," 57.

17   Johnson, *The Theory of Architecture*, 288–292.

18   For Nerezi, see Sinkević, *The Church of St. Panteleimon at Nerezi*. For Kosmosoteira, see Sinos, *Die Klosterkirche der Kosmosoteira in Bera (Vira)* and Ousterhout, *Master Builders*, 122–126.

19   Discussed by Ćurčić, *Architecture of the Balkans*, 408–409.

20   For a discussion of the architectural features of Nerezi, see Sinkević, *The Church of St. Panteleimon at Nerezi*, especially pp. 11–16.

FIGURE 7.2 Church of the Virgin Kosmosoteira, Pherrai, 1152, southwest view
PHOTO: HTTPS://COMMONS.WIKIMEDIA.ORG/WIKI/FILE:MONASTERY
_OF_PANAGIA_KOSMOSOTIRA,_FERRES,_EVROS.JPG [ACCESSED JUNE 6, 2022]

FIGURE 7.3 Church of St. Panteleimon, Nerezi, 1164, south view
PHOTO: IDA SINKEVIĆ

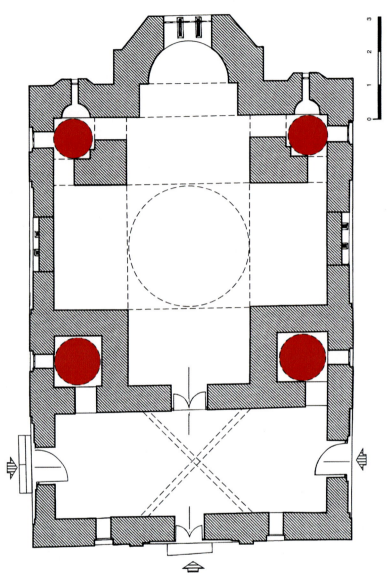

FIGURE 7.4 Church of St. Panteleimon, Nerezi, 1164, floor plan
DRAWING: IDA SINKEVIĆ

IN SEARCH OF ARCHETYPE

appearance, such as the verticality of the composition of exterior forms exhibited in the 14th-century church of the Dormition of the Virgin, the *katholikon* of the Gračanica monastery and the sense of squeezed domes apparent in the 14th-century church of the Virgin of Ljeviška, Prizren (see Figure 7.7),[21] reflects a complex set of circumstances that includes the individual desires of the patron, limitations imposed by the topography of the site itself, and a variety of functional concerns. Moreover, the connection with the capital is also tenuous since, despite the popularity of the Nea, very few imperial churches in Constantinople were in fact five-domed.[22]

In my view, the establishment of a common denominator that brings these five-domed churches into a coherent group goes beyond any systematic examination of individual formal, aesthetic, and structural elements. Rather it requires an investigation into the ways in which the domes were perceived by a contemporary beholder. When Byzantines looked at the dome(s), they were unlikely to have thought of structural elements, pendentives, systems of proportions, laws of statics, or any other formal and/or structural concerns. Symbolically, however, a dome was more than a 'pile of bricks,' as it recalled the image of Christ, the ruler, the judge, and/or benefactor of all mankind, as well as a plethora of dogmatic messages embellishing the domical vault. The synergistic effect of the physical shape of the dome and its metaphysical content perpetually evoked the cosmic dimension and reverberated with spiritual messages. Thus, rather than providing an artificial division between form and content, I propose to examine the relationship between architectural articulation and painted decoration of domes in five-domed churches.

Over a decade ago, in an article that surveyed the decoration of five-domed churches, I looked into the role of the five domes in the formation of sacred space in Middle and Late Byzantine churches.[23] My investigation focused on the selection of images displayed in subsidiary domes and their relationship to the program of the central dome. I concluded that the repertory of images

---

21 Both Gračanica monastery and the church of the Virgin of Ljeviška are located in the disputed territory of Kosovo. Kosovo unilaterally declared independence from Serbia in 2008, but international recognition of Kosovo has been mixed and the international community continues to be divided on the issue. The Republic of Serbia continues to view Kosovo (which it refers to as Kosovo and Metohija) as part of its territory, but it has no de facto rule in the province, which is protected by the United Nations peacekeeping force (UNMIK).

22 Ousterhout, *Master Builders*, 26–38, draws the same conclusion regarding cross-in-square churches, which were commonly associated with imperial patronage. Yet there were many other church types commissioned by members of the royal family.

23 See Sinkević, "Formation of Sacred Space in Later Byzantine Five-Domed Churches," 260–276.

FIGURE 7.5 Church of St. Panteleimon, Nerezi, 1164, southeast dome, fresco, Ancient of Days
PHOTO: IDA SINKEVIĆ

in subsidiary domes expands and/or repeats those in the central dome, that domical vaults of five-domed churches display a very similar program to those seen in single and other multi-domed churches, and that the uppermost level of five-domed churches displays a significant programmatic connection to the central dome, thus expanding the uppermost horizontal stratum of the church.

Traditionally, the program of subsidiary domes has been studied only in relation to the images below. This vertical connection, while important, fostered the idea of spatial segregation. However, the fusion of carefully planned, symmetrically articulated, and stylistically unified features of the exterior of domes suggests that a parallel synthesis likely occurred in their interior decoration as well. Embraced in this carefully designed harmony of a painted image and its architectural setting, the Byzantine beholder was comforted and led into the world of sacred messages. This is evident in both Nerezi and Pherrai. The subsidiary domes at Nerezi display four images of Christ: as Emmanuel; as the Ancient of Days (Figure 7.5); as Priest (Figure 7.6); and as a mature man. Images of angels are represented in all four drums. The central dome has been repainted but, judging by iconographic practices of the time, likely exhibited Christ Pantokrator.[24] The images of Christ in subsidiary domes at Nerezi are

---

24   Sinkević, *The Church of St. Panteleimon at Nerezi*, 39–44.

IN SEARCH OF ARCHETYPE 199

FIGURE 7.6 Church of St. Panteleimon, Nerezi, 1164, southwest dome, fresco, Christ Priest
PHOTO: IDA SINKEVIĆ

symbolic of the Incarnation (Emmanuel); the terrestrial life of Christ, which embodies His suffering (mature man, Pantokrator); His victory over death (as the Ancient of Days); and His priesthood. The image of Christ Priest emphasizes Christ's role as the one who established the sacrament of the Eucharist, who officiates as heavenly priest, and whose actions are recreated in the terrestrial rite. The symbolic meaning of these images is also recollected in the secret prayer recited by a priest while the choir sings the *Cherubikon*, a hymn commonly sung at the Great Entrance during the Eucharistic liturgy. It reads:

> Nevertheless, through Thine unspeakable and boundless love for mankind, Thou didst become man, yet without change or alteration, and as Ruler of All didst become our High Priest, and didst commit to us the ministry of this liturgical and bloodless sacrifice. For Thou alone, O Lord our God, rulest over those in Heaven and on earth; who are borne on the throne of the Cherubim.[25]

---

25 C.E. Hammond, *Liturgies Eastern and Western*, ed. F.E. Brightman, 2 vols. (Oxford, 1965), 377, 15–25; translated in *The Orthodox Liturgy*, 107–108; cited in Sinkević, *The Church of St. Panteleimon at Nerezi*, 42.

The prayer recollects the terrestrial life of Christ, referring to the main stages of His life, and includes the importance of His function as a priest in the economy of human salvation. Thus it expresses in text the same messages that are visually connected through the images in the domical vaults at Nerezi.

Similar messages are also displayed in the domes at Pherrai, with the Pantokrator in the central dome, archangels hovering over the eastern chapels and the Virgin and a mature Christ topping the western domes. And so in both the Nerezi and Pherrai churches the images of the subsidiary domes closely connect to the program of the central dome.[26] Despite the architectural differences noted above, these two churches display similar selections of images in their domical vaults. It is also important to note that the selection of images and the messages of the program in the subsidiary domes of Nerezi and Pherrai compare closely to the iconography of central domes of 11th- and 12th-century churches in other regions of the empire, such as Macedonia, Cyprus, and Russia.[27] For example, in the 11th-century Virgin of Eleousa at Veljusa near Strumica (North Macedonia), a small, domed quatrefoil church with a domed narthex and a domed subsidiary chapel, the central dome reveals the image of the Pantokrator surrounded by the Virgin and archangels, as seen in the domes at Pherrai. Its subsidiary domes feature images of Emmanuel and the Ancient of Days as at Nerezi.[28]

A very similar iconographic arrangement to that of Nerezi is seen later in the early 14th-century church of the Virgin of Ljeviška (1306/1307) in Kosovo.[29] The Virgin of Ljeviška is a transitional monument which both iconographically and architecturally provides a link between the Middle Byzantine and Palaeologan periods (Figure 7.7). It is also one of the earliest five-domed churches in which the program has been preserved in both the central and subsidiary domes. The decoration of the central dome at Ljeviška displays the image of the Pantokrator surrounded by angels; prophets are depicted in the drum and evangelists in the pendentives. In the summit of

---

26 Sinkević, "Formation of Sacred Space," 265–267.

27 For a discussion about programs in the domes, see Sinkević, "Formation of Sacred Space," 265–267. See also Nikolaos Gkioles, *O Byzantinos Troulos kai to eikonografiko tou programma* [On the Byzantine dome and the iconography of its program] (Athens: Ekdoseis Kardamitsa, 1990); and Annemarie Weyl Carr, "The Thirteenth-Century Murals of Lysi," in *A Byzantine Masterpiece Recovered: the Thirteenth-Century Murals of Lysi, Cyprus*, ed. Annemarie Weyl Carr and Laurence J. Morrocco (Austin: University of Texas Press, 1991), 15–113; and Tania Velmans, "Quelques programmes iconographiques de coupoles chypriotes du XIIᵉ au XVᵉ siècle," *Cahiers archéologiques* 32 (1984), 137–162.

28 Petar Miljković-Pepek, *Veljusa* (Skopje: Filozofski fakultet, 1981), 192–196, 204–206.

29 Draga Panić and Gordana Babić, *Bogorodica Ljeviška* [The Mother of God Ljeviška] (Belgrade: Srpska književna zadruga, 1975).

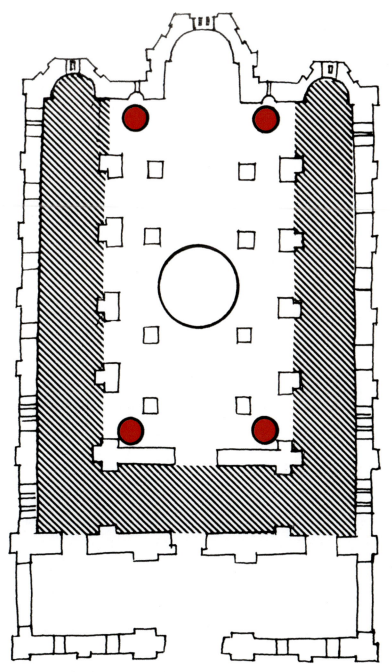

FIGURE 7.7   Church of the Virgin of Ljeviška, 1306/1307, floor plan
DRAWING: AFTER ĆURČIĆ, *GRAČANICA: KING MILUTIN'S CHURCH*, FIG. 101D

the subsidiary domes, one finds four medallions of Christ—as Emmanuel, the Ancient of Days, Christ Priest, and an image of the mature Christ that resembles the Pantokrator—thus recalling the iconography of subsidiary domes seen in the Middle Byzantine church of Nerezi. As discussed earlier, the images of Christ in the subsidiary domes are connected to the central dome in that they expand upon the meaning and significance of the centrally located Pantokrator. The connection between the central and subsidiary domes of the church of the Virgin of Ljeviška is further strengthened by the portrayal of prophets in the side domes. They extend a procession represented in the drum of the central dome.[30]

Architecturally, the church of the Virgin at Ljeviška displays subsidiary domes squeezed between the arms of the cross of the naos, as seen in Middle Byzantine churches (figs. 4, 7).[31] Departing from earlier tradition, at Ljeviška one observes the development of additional spaces that envelop the cruciform core of the church. Known as narthexes, ambulatory wings, and *peristöon*, these additional spaces became an integral component of five-domed churches in Palaeologan times.[32] However, during this period, the subsidiary domes in five-domed churches migrated to the outermost compartments of the edifice, as seen in the church of the Holy Apostles in Thessaloniki (1310–1314) and at Gračanica (1318–1321).[33] In the Palaeologan period, the auxiliary domes at the outermost compartment of the edifice are associated with three types of church plan. They are seen in churches with additional components enveloping the naos, such as at Gračanica (Figure 7.8), in churches of tri-conchal plan mostly located on Mount Athos and in Serbia, such as Manasija, and in several churches at Mystras that display a basilican plan in the lower part of the building and cross-in-square on the upper story, as seen in Aphendiko (*c*.1310) and Pantanassa (consecrated in 1428).[34]

---

30   Sinkević, "Formation of Sacred Space in Later Byzantine Five-Domed Churches," 268.

31   For a discussion, see Slobodan Ćurčić, *Gračanica. Istorija i arhitektura* [Gračanica. History and architecture] (Belgrade: Cicero, 1999), 95–129; also available in English, Slobodan Ćurčić, *Gračanica: King Milutin's Church and Its Place in Late Byzantine Architecture* (University Park, PA: Pennsylvania State University Press, 1979), 70–90. See also Nenadović, *Bogorodica Ljeviška*.

32   For the genesis of late Byzantine architecture see Ćurčić, *Gračanica: King Milutin's Church*, 70–90. For a discussion of terminology, see Evangelia Hadjitryphonos, "Peristöon or Ambulatory in Byzantine Church Architecture," *Saopstenja* 34 (2002), 131–145.

33   For Holy Apostles, see Marcus Rautman, "The Church of Holy Apostles in Thessaloniki: A Study in Early Palaeologan Architecture," (PhD diss., Indiana University, Bloomington, IN, 1984), 20–27; see also Ćurčić, *Gračanica: King Milutin's Church*, 85–90, figs. 9–11, 101.

34   For Gračanica, see Ćurčić, *Gračanica: King Milutin's Church*, 31–70; for the five-domed churches of tri-conchal plan, see Vojislav Korać and Marica Šuput, *Arhitektura vizantijskog*

IN SEARCH OF ARCHETYPE 203

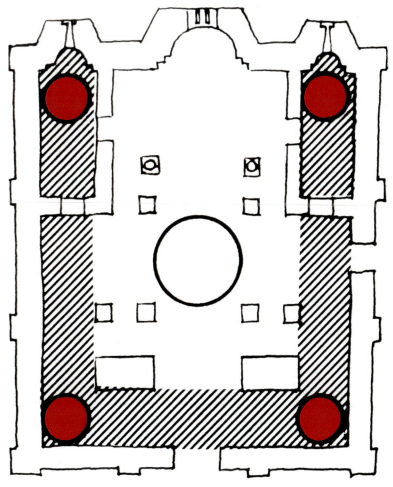

FIGURE 7.8 Church of the Mother of God, Gračanica monastery, 1321, floor plan
DRAWING: AFTER ĆURČIĆ, *GRAČANICA: KING MILUTIN'S CHURCH*, FIG. 101F

In all three types of church, subsidiary domes are placed far away from the central dome and pulled to the extreme corners of the building, quite unlike their Middle Byzantine predecessors which exhibit a close structural relationship between side domes and the central dome. Indeed, in five-domed churches that resemble the plan of Gračanica, the domes are completely disassociated

sveta [Architecture of the Byzantine world] (Belgrade: Vizantološki institut, SANU, 1998), 357–399; for Mystras, see Hallensleben, "Untersuchungen zur Genesis und Typologie des 'Mistratipus'," 105–118. See also Sinkević, "Formation of Sacred Space in Later Byzantine Five-Domed Chruches," 268–270.

from the naos, since they cover the chapels on the east side and the narthex on the west.[35]

However, the 12th-century repertory of images, with the Pantokrator almost invariably represented in the central dome and images of the Virgin, Christ, and angels in subsidiary domes, has commonly been retained in these later monuments. For example, the images of Christ, seen in western subsidiary domes of the Holy Apostles, and the appearance of archangels, the Ancient of Days, Emmanuel, and the Virgin in the 14th-century Ravanica Monastery in Serbia recall similar selections of images at Nerezi, Pherrai and the church of the Virgin of Ljeviška.[36] Thus, despite their physical distance, the programmatic unity of a select repertory of images encircled in medallions in five-domed churches reserved exclusively for domical vaults was retained in the Palaeologan period.

At this time, a new theme was introduced in the central dome: the Divine Liturgy. And with this introduction, the liturgical tendencies evident in many 12th-century domes were fully realized. Following the concept that the terrestrial rite is but a mirror image of the rite performed in the heavenly sphere, the Divine Liturgy is the celestial equivalent of the liturgical procession of the Great Entry.[37] Christ is shown as heavenly priest celebrating the liturgy with a host of His heavenly associates, the angels who approach Him in procession, as the deacons approach the minister in the terrestrial rite. They are sometimes dressed in imperial garb as seen in the early rendition of the theme in the *katholikon* of the Panagia Olympiotissa Monastery in Elassona, Greece (14th century), or shown wearing the robes of deacons, and carrying a large variety of liturgical vessels and implements, such as candles, fans, and Eucharistic bread and wine, as seen at Gračanica (Figure 7.9).[38] The presence of the altar

---

35   For a discussion, see Ćurčić, *Gračanica: King Milutin's Church*, 70–80.

36   For Holy Apostles, see Christine Stephan, *Ein byzantinisches Bildensemble: Die Mosaiken und Fresken der Apostolkirche zu Thessaloniki* (Worms: Wernersche Verlagsgesellschaft, 1986) and Andreas Xyngopoulos, "Les fresques de l'église des Sts. Apôtres à Thessalonique," in *Art et société a byzance sous les Paléologues: Actes du Colloque de Venise, Septembre 1968* (Venice: Institut hellénique d'études byzantines et post-byzantines, 1971), 83–89. For Ravanica, see Vojislav J. Djurić, "Ravanički živopis i liturgija" [The murals and liturgy of Ravanica], in *Manastir Ravanica—spomenica o šestoj stogodišnjici*, ed. Branislav Živkovic (Belgrade: Izdanje Manastira Ravanice, 1981), 60–75.

37   On the Divine Liturgy, see Ashton L. Townsley, "Eucharistic Doctrine and the Liturgy in Late Byzantine Painting," *Oriens christianus* 58 (1974), 58–61 and Ioan D. Stefanescu, *L'illustration des liturgies dans l'art de Byzance et de l'Orient* (Brussels: Institut de philologie et d'histoire orientales, 1932).

38   Efthalia C. Constantinides, *The Wall Paintings of the Panagia Olympiotissa*, 2 vols. (Athens: Canadian Institute of Archeology in Athens, 1992), vol. 2, plates 6–13. Branislav Todić,

FIGURE 7.9 Church of the Mother of God, Gračanica monastery, 1321, central dome, interior view
PHOTO: COURTESY BLAGO FUND, INC.

signifies Christ's ministry as well as His sacrifice. Sacrificial aspects are particularly emphasized at Gračanica by the presence of two altars, one of which displays Christ as Eucharistic host. Like the deacons in the terrestrial rite, the angels are approaching the altar in a ceremonial motion. While specific iconographic elements vary from one church to another, the parallelism between terrestrial and celestial liturgies remains a standard feature.

The presence of the Divine Liturgy in the dome alludes to Christ's incarnation and explains the secrets of mystical re-enactment of His sacrifice in the

Gračanica. Slikarstvo [Gračanica, Painting] (Pristina: Muzej u Prištini, 1999), 138–140; figs. 6–25.

liturgy. Thus the concepts of incarnation, salvation, divine and human nature, and the priesthood of Christ, implied in the images displayed traditionally in subsidiary domes, are encompassed in the new scene surrounding the image of the Pantokrator in the central dome. As a result, the space of the subsidiary domes was opened for iconographic innovations.

For example, at Gračanica and in St. George church at Staro Nagoričino (North Macedonia) we see the images of the evangelists in the summit of subsidiary domes (Figures 7.10 and 7.11). The evangelists, like the other images seen in the domes, testify to Christ's incarnation as they were witnesses of His epiphany, His life, and His salvific mission. Iconographically, they were no strangers to the decoration of domical vaults. We see them already, in their symbolic guise, in Early Byzantine churches, such as the Mausoleum of Galla Placidia (c.430–450) and in the Archbishop's Chapel (Cappella Arcivescovile, 494–519) in Ravenna. In later Byzantine monuments, the images of evangelists are allocated to pendentives, supporting the heavenly realm of the church, that is to say its central dome, both physically and symbolically. However, in single-domed churches, they appear sporadically in the central dome, as seen, for example, in the late 10th- to early 11th-century church of the Metamorphosis at Koropi in Greece. Therefore, the presence of evangelists in subsidiary domes is by no means surprising, since they harmonize thematically with the concepts presented in the central dome.

This programmatic unity of the uppermost level of five-domed churches was seemingly intended to overcome architectural barriers and emphasize the omnipresence of Christ throughout the entire space of the edifice. It appears that at least conceptually, if not physically, to the mind of Byzantine beholders, the church evoked a unified sphere, a huge domed interior with the image of Christ in its center, His various functions in concentric circles, and evangelists at the corners, as seen at Gračanica. Revealed in a diagram-like manner, such a composition is apparent in the preface miniature of the Gospel Book, MS E.D. Clarke 10, f. 2v from the Bodleian Library, Oxford (Figure 7.12).

The emphasis upon placing side domes at the outermost corners of the buildings, seen in both Middle Byzantine and Palaeologan five-domed churches, may be explained as a formal and structural concern. After all, especially in Palaeologan architecture, the domed compartments are small and high, and the domes themselves are remote. The images within these domes are often obscured by light and very difficult to see. Essentially, their accessibility is predicated mostly on the faith of the beholder. However, very few, if any, compositional elements in Byzantium, architectural or decorative, express purely formal and aesthetic concerns. Rather, the placement of subsidiary domes at the outermost corners of the building, along with a clearly expressed

FIGURE 7.10 Church of the Mother of God, Gračanica monastery, 1321, fresco, Evangelist John, southeast dome

PHOTO: COURTESY BLAGO FUND, INC.

FIGURE 7.11   Church of the Mother of God, Gračanica monastery, 1321, fresco, Evangelist Luke, northeast dome
PHOTO: COURTESY BLAGO FUND, INC.

programmatic unity of the images in the domes, suggests that the five domes are not to be viewed as five isolated segments of heaven but as a single unit, for there is only one celestial sphere and it is not fragmented. Thus, rather than copying one or any specific edifice as a model, the five-domed churches reflect the prototype of a dome, domical vault, or a heavenly canopy.[39]

---

39   The connotations of canopy as an architectural type are explored in this volume by Jelena Bogdanović. See also Jelena Bogdanović, *The Framing of Sacred Space: The Canopy and the Byzantine Church* (New York, 2017).

IN SEARCH OF ARCHETYPE 209

FIGURE 7.12   Gospel Book, MS E.D. Clarke 10, f. 2v, 11th century, Oxford, Bodleian Library
PHOTO: © BODLEIAN LIBRARY OXFORD

CHAPTER 8

The Canopy as 'Primitive Hut' in Byzantine Architecture

Jelena Bogdanović

One of the central 'type and archetype' concepts in architectural theory and practice is the primitive hut, the first, essential, and original architectural unit. The primitive hut, as both an intellectual exercise and a design principle in architecture, has been utilized when addressing the fundamental relationship between architecture and nature, for devising architectural typology, and for organizing architectural knowledge.[1] It continues to be discussed in architectural practice. First outlined by Vitruvius, a Roman architect and engineer in the 1st century BCE, the paradigm of the ancient wooden hut has, since its inception, been both a historical and a theoretical principle.[2] Most likely influenced by ancient Greek philosophers who reasoned about the arts of humankind, Vitruvius presented the 'hut,' within the context of the origin and invention of architecture, as the first building, a model for architecture that could be passed on through generations, a model deeply rooted in nature and its primordial first principles (earth, air, fire, and water).[3] These first principles—attributed to the Pythagoreans and summarized by Empedocles and Aristotle—defined a holistic system to explain and utilize the properties of both animate and inanimate objects and a variety of phenomena in the Aristotelian universe which included both the terrestrial and celestial domains.[4] Vitruvius applied this philosophical system to architecture, and in particular to building materials, masonry, and building types, as well as their fitting properties.[5] He

---

1   On the role of type in ideation design practices, see Joori Suh, "An Interactive Generative Abstraction System for the Archetype-Based Pre-Ideation Process (IGATY)," *Design Science* 3, e9 (2017), 1–30, with extensive bibliographical references on scholarship about type and archetype.

2   Vitruvius, *Ten Books on Architecture*, trans. Ingrid D. Rowland, commentary and illustrations Thomas Noble Howe, with additional commentary by Ingrid D. Rowland and Michael J. Dewar (Cambridge/New York: Cambridge University Press, 1999), bk. 2, chaps. 1–2.

3   Vitruvius, *Ten Books on Architecture*, bk. 2, chap. 2.

4   Vitruvius, *Ten Books on Architecture*, bk. 2, chap. 2, with additional commentaries by Rowland and Dewar on pp. 173–178.

5   Vitruvius, *Ten Books on Architecture*, bk. 2, chap. 2, discusses the composition of the building materials and ratios of first elements within them, as well as the presence or absence of the elements, and explains physical properties such as hardness, moistness, or temperature.

© KONINKLIJKE BRILL NV, LEIDEN, 2023 | DOI:10.1163/9789004537781_010

THE CANOPY AS 'PRIMITIVE HUT' IN BYZANTINE ARCHITECTURE 211

then expanded upon related properties of an architectural construction at a given locale topographically, environmentally, and culturally. Vitruvius's hut, therefore, elevated the role of architecture beyond shelter to that of a powerful mediator between humankind and nature. The hut simultaneously framed a theoretical investigation on the purpose of architecture as a discipline.

Scholarship on the primitive hut usually picks up on Vitruvius's text and its reception in the rationalist philosophy of the Enlightenment.[6] The primitive hut was theorized by Marc-Antoine Laugier in the 18th century as a rational and honest expression of structure. He argued for the primitive hut, which he calls the 'rustic hut,' as a means for moving away from representational qualities and superfluous stylistic features in architecture. Laugier's critical *Essai sur l'architecture*, in its second edition in 1755, presented the much reproduced and discussed allegorical engraving of the Vitruvian hut.[7] This edition of the essay also initiated positivistic studies of typology in architecture that reflect the rational order of nature. The frontispiece of Laugier's text, illustrated by Charles Eisen, effectively summarized the idea of the hut in architecture. In a bucolic, Arcadian setting, architecture, depicted as a young woman, leans against the broken pieces of a stylized Hellenistic pediment and Ionic capital. Inspired by her creative muse, here represented by a childish putto, she points to the wooden hut as the essence of architecture that grows in harmony with nature (Figure. 8.1). At the time Laugier wrote his radical piece, he was disgruntled by the failures of Baroque and Neoclassical architecture because, he argued, they focused on architectural surface and its representation. His return to the notion of the primitive hut was a revolutionary call to go back to the origins and essence of architecture. The origin of each architectural element was in nature; the architectural structures comprised of such elements ultimately resulted from nature and its ordering.[8] Hence the primitive hut came to be understood not necessarily as a historical example—a specific building open to empirical and archaeological scrutiny—but rather as a quasi-natural

---

6 Marc-Antoine Laugier, *An Essay on Architecture* (Los Angeles: Hennessey and Ingalls, [2009] 1977), translation of the original text Marc-Antoine Laugier, *Essai sur l'architecture* (Paris: Duchesne, 1755). Among critical texts on type and typology in theory of architecture as related to the idea of the hut are the 1962 essay by Argan reproduced in Gulio Carlo Argan, "On the Typology of Architecture," in *Theorizing a New Agenda for Architecture*, ed. Kate Nesbitt (New York: Princeton Architectural Press, 1996), 242–246; Anthony Vidler, "The Third Typology," *Oppositions* 7 (1977), 13–16; Leandro Madrazo Agudin, "The Concept of Type in Architecture: An Inquiry into the Nature of Architectural Form," (PhD diss., Zurich ETH, 1995). See also Richard Weston, *100 Ideas that Changed Architecture* (London: Lawrence King Publishers, [2015] 2011), sv. "hut" on p. 79; "type" on p. 175; Paul-Alan Johnson, *The Theory of Architecture: Concepts, Themes, and Practices* (New York: Van Nostrand Reinhold, 1994), 288–295.

7 Laugier, *Essai sur l'architecture*.

8 Vidler, *The Third Typology*, 13–16; Madrazo, "The Concept of Type," 36, 81–82, 172–176.

FIGURE 8.1 Primitive hut, engraving, Charles Eisen, frontispiece of Marc-Antoine Laugier, *Essai sur l'architecture*, 2nd ed., 1755
PHOTO: PUBLIC DOMAIN IMAGE FROM DOME, DIGITIZED CONTENT FROM THE MIT LIBRARIES' COLLECTIONS, DOME.MIT.EDU [ACCESSED JUNE 3, 2022]

THE CANOPY AS 'PRIMITIVE HUT' IN BYZANTINE ARCHITECTURE 213

structure made of four tree trunks growing to a roughly rectangular plan, with logs for lintels and branches for an elementary pitched roof. The hut conveys the generic idea of architecture as the first human-made shelter and basic spatial unit, which can be creatively recreated as an architectural principle of a functional and formally sound structure.

In the 19th century, Quatremère's threefold model of the hut, tent, and cave further elaborated on Vitruvius's wooden hut as a sensible model, or a prototype, and a fundamental principle inherent to both natural forms and art forms derived from nature.[9] Quatremère's elaboration of the architectural type based on the hut, tent, and cave pointed to a diverse cultural understanding of architecture closely associated with climate, location, and economy, while additionally offering itself to typological studies in architecture.[10] Type, more an idea than a physical model, became a creative theme, conceptual space, and a process in architectural design. As such, it allowed for a broader understanding of typology in architectural design. Architects and architectural theorists Anthony Vidler and Leandro Madrazo subsequently even proposed a search for "progressive forms" of community generated by its built environment.[11]

Yet the majority of scholars rarely consider architectural type—particularly the origins and reception of Vitruvius's concept in architectural thought in religious contexts. An exception to this is Joseph Rykwert, who does so in meaningful and much-needed detail. He traces the primitive hut back to the Old Testament narrative of the paradisiac house in his seminal text *On Adam's House in Paradise*.[12] In the process, he highlights how intentionality and

9   Madrazo, "The Concept of Type," 179–202; Werner Oechslin, "Premises for the Resumption of the Discussion of Typology," *Assemblage* 1 (1986), 36–53.

10   Madrazo, "The Concept of Type," 179–202; Oechslin, "Premises," 36–53; Jonathan Noble, "The Architectural Typology of Antoine Chrysostome Quatremère de Quincy (1755–1849)," *Edinburgh Architectural Research* 27 (2000), 145–159.

11   Vidler, *The Third Typology*, 13–16, on p. 13 calls this paradigm in the work of Le Corbusier the "second typology." See also Madrazo, "The Concept of Type," 316–323 and Leandro Madrazo, "Durand and the Science of Architecture," *Journal of Architectural Education* 48, no. 1 (1994), 12–24, where he highlights the relevance of typological methods for epistemology of architecture.

12   Joseph Rykwert, *On Adam's House in Paradise: The Idea of the Primitive Hut in Architectural History* (New York: Museum of Modern Art, 1972). See also Michael W. Meister and Joseph Rykwert, "Afterword: Adam's House and Hermit's Huts: A Conversation" in Ananda K. Coomaraswamy, Michael W. Meister, and Indira Gandhi National Centre for the Arts, *Ananda K. Coomaraswamy: Essays in Early Indian Architecture* (New Delhi: Indira Gandhi National Centre for the Arts, 1992), 125–131, where Rykwert further elaborates on the hut as a principle for justification of design and conceptual form-giving element in architecture. I thank Tracy Miller for calling my attention to this text.

metaphor are inherent in architecture. In his summary of Gothic church architecture, he describes it as a kind of primitive hut with origins in a rustic form of roofing and tree symbols of the Cross as the tree of life and the Tree of Jesse.[13] In my opinion, Rykwert rightly refocuses his discussion of the hut within the performative contexts of religious traditions. He highlights the strong relationships between the hut and the world, as well as between the hut and the body, which are repeatedly reinforced in Judeo-Christian ritual processions and services.[14] Rykwert uses Psalm 117 (118): 26–27 to sum up the essence of the procession related to Tabernacle celebrations in synagogues and the Temple service: "Blessed is he who comes in the name of the Lord; we blessed you from the house of the Lord. God is the Lord, and He revealed Himself to us; Appoint a feast for yourselves, decked with branches, Even to the horns of the altar." This very psalm is still sung daily in Byzantine-rite churches at the Orthros, the last night service.[15] In the Byzantine-rite church, the psalm abounds with architectural references that identify the Tabernacle (tent) with the Temple, and the Temple with salvation in paradise and in the body of the omnipresent Christ:

> The Lord is my strength and song, and is become my salvation. The voice of rejoicing and salvation *is* in the tabernacles (tents) of the righteous ... Open to me the gates of righteousness; I will go into them ... This gate of the Lord into which the righteous shall enter ... the stone which the builders refused is become the head stone of the corner ... Blessed is he who comes in the name of the Lord ...
>
> PS 118 (117): 14–26

Such a strong ontological argument that presupposes the existence of God eventually refocuses the question of nature as discussed in Vitruvius's primitive hut to the justification of architecture through nature as absolute and divine.

Even though the medieval copies of Vitruvius's texts are well attested to, it is generally assumed that medieval architects did not engage with the idea of the hut.[16] However, scholars of medieval literature did address and

---

13   Rykwert, *On Adam's House*, 100–101.
14   Rykwert, *On Adam's House*, 141–192.
15   Rykwert, *On Adam's House*, 183–184.
16   Carol Herselle Krinsky, "Seventy-Eight Vitruvius Manuscripts," *Journal of the Warburg and Courtauld Institutes* 30 (1967), 36–70, discusses 78 Vitruvius texts recovered in western Europe and dated to between the 8th and 15th centuries.

reaffirm the reception of Vitruvius during the Middle Ages.[17] Ann Raftery Meyer convincingly pointed to close references between Vitruvius's discussion on the signified and signifier in architecture and Bede's (*c.*673–735) exegesis of biblical architecture of the Tabernacle and Temple by rereading his texts *De tabernaculo* (*c.*721–725) and *De templo* (*c.*729–731) which highlight analogies between divine creation and human artistry.[18] She and a few other scholars further implied that the 6th-century Hagia Sophia in Constantinople is the most cited architectural example, which confirms the medieval notion that the Tabernacle-Temple typifies the Christian church. This is additionally attested to in the legendary account that the Byzantine emperor Justinian exclaimed upon the construction of the church: "Solomon, I have outdone thee!"[19] Yet the role of the primitive hut in the medieval domain is generally left out of major architectural debates. Without going into a detailed examination of whether this results from our limited understanding of medieval primary sources on the role of type in architecture, or from the strong positivistic scholarship that prevailed over time and, in the search for the indisputable laws in architecture, restricted the scholarly methods used in studies of medieval architecture, or even from the difficulties in elaborating on architecture in medieval times with regard to which our knowledge of architectural practices and training remains severely limited, it is worth acknowledging a few points. Namely, the two most critical references to the importance of the primitive hut for medieval architects are related to the relatively open definition of the primitive hut, which spans the range between sensible model and abstract concept, as well as to the controversial use of the notion of the primitive hut in polemical texts and design practices.

---

17   On the medieval reception of Vitruvius, see Kenneth J. Conant, "The After-Life of Vitruvius in the Middle Ages," *Journal of the Society of Architectural Historians* 27, no. 1 (1968), 33–38; Nadine Schibille, "Astronomical and Optical Principles in the Architecture of Hagia Sophia in Constantinople," *Science in Context* 22, no. 1 (2009), 27–46; Wim Verbaal, "The Vitruvian Middle Ages and Beyond," *Arethusa* 49/2 (2016), 215–225, with older bibliography.

18   Ann Raftery Meyer, *Medieval Allegory and the Building of the New Jerusalem* (Woodbridge: Boydell and Brewer, 2003), 14–17. For original texts by Bede, see Bede, *Bedae Venerabilis opera. Paris II: Pera exegetica*, 2A: *De Tabernaculo. De Templo. In Ezram et Neemiam*, ed. David Hurst (Turnhout: Brepols, 1969).

19   Meyer, *Medieval Allegory and the Building of the New Jerusalem*, 15–16. See also Robert Ousterhout, "New Temples and New Solomons: The Rhetoric of Byzantine Architecture," in *The Old Testament in Byzantium*, ed. Paul Magdalino and Robert Nelson (Washington, DC: Dumbarton Oaks Research Library and Collection, 2010), 223–253; Jelena Bogdanović, *The Framing of Sacred Space: The Canopy and the Byzantine Church* (New York: Oxford University Press, 2017), 267–273, with older references.

The frontispiece of Laugier's text proved how effectively the primitive hut and its visual representation communicates the meaning of architecture among scholars, practitioners, and architectural enthusiasts, widely and across different times and geographies. Yet beyond its relatively simple geometry and rationalized formal elements paradigmatically illustrated there, the primitive hut is a deeply philosophical construct, and is constantly both specific and vague. It is specific in its definition as an enclosed three-dimensional space and a comprehensible image of a generic human dwelling. At the same time, it remains vague. Ancient Greek philosophy places it somewhere between a sensible model (prototype) and a principle inherent to natural and art forms in Aristotelian terms. Platonic philosophy, on the other hand, places it as an abstract idea or form as it appeared to the divine mind prior to creation, i.e., the ideal principle (archetype).[20]

Then again, archetype and type are found in the writings of early Christian philosophers such as Dionysius the Areopagite and Irenaeus, bishop of Lyons. Dionysius actually defined the terms and concepts of the type and archetype as we use them today. In his *Celestial Hierarchy*, focusing on angelic hierarchy, Dionysius the Areopagite, whose preserved writings can be dated to the 6th century at the latest, introduces the type (τύπος) and archetype (ἀρχέτυπον).[21] In this construct, type is a model, a pattern, while archetype is the original type from which physical replicas are made. The type and archetype explained in *Celestial Hierarchy*, I would argue, provide a sophisticated tool for understanding both idea (εἶδος, ἰδέα) and form (εἰκών, σχῆμα, μόρφωσις) in architecture. Type emerges as a balanced understanding of a model invested with

---

20 Quatremère employs both an Aristotelian and a Platonic approach. Madrazo, "The Concept of Type," 179–202 emphasizes Plato's influences above all. Erwin Panofsky, *Idea: A Concept in Art Theory*, trans. Joseph J.S. Peake (New York/London: Harper & Row, 1968), 33–43, 191–201, considers both Platonic and Aristotelian approaches towards idea as a theoretical concept in medieval art. Because medieval architects do not build houses derived from natural phenomena, but rather from the divinely inspired images architects carry within themselves, as suggested by those following the thinking of Aristotle, Augustine, and Saint Thomas Aquinas. Panofsky subsequently proposed the seemingly non-existent ties between cause and effect in architectural production and suggested the lack of architectural theory in the medieval context. I thank Ida Sinkević for discussing Panofsky's work with me.

21 Dionysius Areopagita, *Corpus Dionysiacum*, 2 vols. ed. Beate Regina Suchla, Günter Heil, and Adolf M. Ritter (Berlin: De Gruyter, 1990–1991) [including *De coelesti hierarchia* (*Celestial Hierarchy*), henceforth CH], CH II. See also n. 6 above and Introduction to this volume. On the dating of the texts attributed to Dionysius the Areopagite and about the author's identity, see Ronald F. Hathaway, *Hierarchy and the Definition of Order in the Letters of Pseudo-Dionysius: A Study in the Form and Meaning of the Pseudo-Dionysian Writings* (The Hague: Martinus Nijhoff, 1969), 31–36.

THE CANOPY AS 'PRIMITIVE HUT' IN BYZANTINE ARCHITECTURE 217

both sensible and ideal properties.[22] The idea and form, in the context of the type and archetype that Dionysius postulated, could have been contemplated through material entities: "*Holy contemplations can therefore be derived from all things* [emphasis mine], and the above-names incongruous similitudes can be fashioned from material things to symbolize that which is intelligible and intellectual, since the intellectual has in another manner what has been attributed differently to the perceptible."[23]

If we apply the concept of type and archetype to canopies, which generically stood for the essence of sacred architecture in the Byzantine context,[24] Dionysius the Areopagite's reason for creating material types for the typeless archetypes explains how the canopy of Byzantine architecture can be related to the sacred:

> But if one looks at *the truth of the matter* [emphasis mine], the sacred wisdom of scripture becomes evident, for, when the heavenly intelligences are represented with forms, great providential care is taken to offer no insult to the divine powers, as one might say, and we ourselves are spared a passionate dependence upon images which have something lowly and the vulgar about them. Now, *there are two reasons for creating types for the typeless, for giving shape to what is actually without shape* [emphasis mine]. First, we lack the ability to be directly raised up to conceptual contemplations. We need our own upliftings that come naturally to us and which can raise before us the permitted forms of the marvelous and unformed sights. Second, it is most fitting to the mysterious passages of scripture that the sacred and hidden truth about the celestial intelligences be concealed through the inexpressible and the sacred and be inaccessible to the *hoi polloi*. Not everyone is sacred, and, as scripture says, knowledge is not for everyone.[25]

Materiality emerges as a critical feature of the type in order to communicate the truth. Yet the divide between the immaterial archetype and material type within architecture would remain pervasive. This dichotomy between the immaterial and material aspects of architecture, embodied in the primitive

---

22   I touched upon this theme of the relationship between type and archetype in Jelena Bogdanović, "Rethinking the Dionysian Legacy in Medieval Architecture: East and West," in *Dionysius the Areopagite: Between Orthodoxy and Heresy*, ed. Filip Ivanović (Newcastle Upon Tyne: Cambridge Scholars, 2011), 109–134.

23   CH II.

24   Bogdanović, *The Framing of Sacred Space*, esp. 295–299.

25   CH 140A–B.

hut, additionally points to the divide between the noetic and iconic features of architecture. Dionysius the Areopagite explains: "*Using matter, one may be lifted up to the immaterial archetypes* [emphasis mine]. Of course, one must be careful to use the similarities as dissimilarities, as discussed, to avoid one-to-one correspondences, to make the appropriate adjustments as one remembers the great divide between the intelligible and the perceptible."[26]

Irenaeus, in his work *Against Heresies* (*c*.180), enriched the ontological concept of the type when he directly associated the Ark, as the essential biblical architectural creation, with a type of the body of Christ and elaborated the two-fold and coeval nature of a type as being simultaneously physical and spiritual.[27] Irenaeus broadened a hypothesis on the architectural type of the Ark, usually represented as a chest or canopy in visual arts,[28] as being closely knit with the idea of the heavenly Temple, "received by way of type, as it was shown to Moses on the Mount [of Sinai]."[29]

In the 8th century, in his *Ecclesiastical History and Mystical Contemplation*, Germanus, the patriarch of Constantinople (d. 733), additionally promoted a strongly interconnected relationship between the church, the Temple, the Tabernacle (from Latin *tabernaculum*, meaning tent or hut), the Ark, and the church altar ciborium. The latter was interpolated with the Christian meanings of the Tomb of Christ, whereas a canopy as the generic type for all these holy structures remained simultaneously architecturally and ontologically connected to the body of Christ and the Christian community:

> *The church is the temple of God* [emphasis mine] (cf. 1 Cor. 3:10–17; 2 Cor. 6:16), a holy place, a house of prayer (cf. Isa. 56:7; Matt. 21:13; Mark 11:17; Luke 19:46), the assembly of the people, the body of Christ (cf. 1 Cor. 3:10–17, 12:27; Col. 1:24; Eph. 2:19–22).
>
> The church is an earthly heaven, where the heavenly God dwells and walks about (2 Cor. 6:16; Lev. 16:12; Deut. 23:5). *It represents the crucifixion, the burial and the resurrection of Christ* [emphasis mine]. It is glorified more than *the tent of witness* [tabernacle] of Moses, in which are the mercy seat and the Holy of Holies (cf. Exod. 25–27). It is prefigured by the patriarchs, foretold by the prophets, founded by the apostles (cf. Eph. 2:19), adorned by the hierarchs, and fulfilled by the martyrs....

---

26   CH 144B–C.

27   Irenaeus, *Against Heresies* in *Five Books of S. Irenaeus: Bishop of Lyons, Against Heresies* (Charlton, SC: Nabu Public Domain Reprints, 2010; originally published by Oxford in 1872), 558–559.

28   Bogdanović, *The Framing of Sacred Space*, 19–20, with further bibliographical references.

29   Irenaeus, *Against Heresies*, 361–362.

The ciborium [canopy] *represents here the place where Christ was cruci-fied* [emphasis mine]; for the place where He was buried was nearby and raised on a base. *It is placed in the church to represent the crucifixion, burial, and resurrection of Christ* [emphasis mine].

It similarly corresponds to the Ark of the Covenant of the Lord [emphasis mine], which is called the Holy of Holies and His holy place. Next to it God commanded that two Cherubim of hammered work be placed on either side (cf. Exod. 25:18)—for KIB is the ark, and OURIN is the effulgence, or the light, of God.[30]

In the 13th century, theorist of canon law William Durandus (*c.*1230–1296), in his architectural treatise *The Symbolism of Churches and Church Ornaments* (1286), connected architectural symbolism directly back to Dionysius's work, and more specifically connected type and its derivative archetype and antitype with architectural typology inclusive of its physical aspects.[31]

The canopy as an architectural type in the Byzantine context remained inseparable from its divinely inspired archetype. I concur with Perl, who demonstrated that, in both philosophical Neoplatonic and religious Judeo-Christian contexts, the archetype stood equally for the idea and the form of the divine mind prior to creation.[32] Open to noetic contemplation, the archetype nevertheless remains relatively independent, often different from, though not mutually exclusive of, the antitype, which is foreshadowed and identified by the type. In the Christian context, therefore, Old Testament concepts and forms of the Tabernacle and the Holy of Holies of the Jewish Temple become the type of the Christian sanctuary.[33] As I have already demonstrated, this hypothesis has crucial consequences, because it defines the Christian church not as an antitype of a synagogue or pagan basilica but in continuity with the Jewish Temple

---

30 Saint Germanus of Constantinople, *On the Divine Liturgy*, ed. Paul Meyendorff (Crestwood, NY, 1984), 57–59.

31 William Durandus, *The Symbolism of Churches and Church Ornaments: A Translation of the First Book of the* Rationale Divinorum Officiorum (New York: Charles Scribner's Sons, 1893), chap. 6. Inductive argument, lxiv–lxvi. On the importance of Durandus's treatise on architecture, see "William Durandus from *The Symbolism of Churches and Church Ornaments* (1286)," in *Architectural Theory*, vol. 1., *An Anthology from Vitruvius to 1870*, ed. Harry Francis Mallgrave (Malden, MA/Oxford: Blackwell Publishing, 2006), 24–25. See also my discussion in Bogdanović, *Rethinking the Dionysian Legacy*, 109–134, esp. 125–126.

32 Eric D. Perl, *Theophany: The Neoplatonic Philosophy of Dionysius the Areopagite* (Albany: State University of New York Press, 2007), 5.

33 Margaret Barker, *The Great High Priest: The Temple Roots of Christian Theology* (London and New York: T&T Clark/Continuum, 2003) also investigates the roots of Christian sanctuary in the Temple tradition.

as its prototype.[34] Moreover, in such a context, the archetype is not a specific building, a historical example one can identify in the physical world, but rather an intellectual concept and design principle, which strongly resonates with the notion of the primitive hut in architecture, as established by Vitruvius and his intellectual followers.

Though the term 'hut' did not itself remain apparent in the scantly preserved and relevant writings of Byzantine authors, the basic architectural idea of the 'hut-canopy' was pervasive in depictions of the Ark and the Temple as models for Byzantine architecture and its humanistic value, where the role of the human body and thought remained inseparable from architecture. This can be effectively illustrated by the numerous images of the Presentation of Christ in the Temple, including the famous 11th-century golden mosaic from the Hosios Loukas monastery (Figure 8.2), where the Temple takes the shape of a four-columned hut, with three depicted columns and the fourth being Christ, and assumes its new role as 'being-place' within the Christian context.[35] The paradoxical two fold and coeval nature of Christ as being both human and divine is further complicated by Byzantine interest in the role of Mary, the Mother of God.

The 14th-century icon from the monastery of Hilandar on Mount Athos points to one of the countless images of the Temple as depicted in Byzantine and Byzantine-inspired religious icons (Figure 8.3).[36] The icon shows the Presentation of the Mother of God in the Temple, also known in Byzantine scholarship as the Entry of the Ever Virgin Mary and Most Holy Mother of God-Theotokos into the Temple, and in Slavic studies as *Vavedenije* (The Entry). The image of the Temple in this icon strongly resembles the widely recognized hut from the famous frontispiece from Laugier's book (cf. Figure 8.1). Against the golden background that conventionally represents the sacred, the wooden hut-like canopy rests on four slender columns with quasi-Corinthian capitals, upon which four arches support a wooden pyramidal roof. The somewhat surprising but recurring depiction of the Temple as a humble hut reveals the visual language of the Eastern Christians, where the hut-like canopy simultaneously stands for the generic depiction of the Temple, the Ark, and

---

34   Bogdanović, "Rethinking the Dionysian Legacy," 109–134, esp. 125–126, supported by arguments from Durandus's treatise.

35   I discuss the canopies in Hosios Loukas in greater detail in Jelena Bogdanović, "Framing Glorious Spaces in the Monastery of Hosios Loukas," in *Perceptions of the Body and Sacred Space in Late Antiquity and Byzantium*, ed. Jelena Bogdanović (New York/London: Routledge, 2018), 166–189.

36   On the icon, see Dimitrije Bogdanović et al., *Chilandar* (Belgrade: Monastery of Chilandar in cooperation with Jugoslovenska revija, 1997), 86.

THE CANOPY AS 'PRIMITIVE HUT' IN BYZANTINE ARCHITECTURE 221

FIGURE 8.2 Presentation of Christ in the Temple, mosaic, *katholikon* of the Hosios Loukas monastery, Greece, 11th century
PHOTO: PUBLIC DOMAIN IMAGE BY HANS A. ROSBACH FROM WIKIMEDIA COMMONS HTTPS://COMMONS.WIKIMEDIA.ORG/WIKI/FILE:HOSIOS_LOUKAS_KATHOLIKON_(NAVE,_NORTH-WEST_SQUINCH)_-_PRESENTATION_02.JPG [ACCESSED JUNE 3, 2022]

the church sanctuary.[37] The purple-red curtain that partially covers the pyramidal roof of the canopy recalls the Tabernacle and the desert tent made of cloth, as recorded in the biblical passages.[38] At the same time, the curtain suggests the Lord's cloak and Christ Himself, the garments of salvation from the Vision of Isaiah (cf. Isa. 61:10).[39] Additionally, I agree with the suggestion that the curtain, stretching between the roofs of the canopy and the partially visible architectural structure, indicates that the scene is taking place inside the Temple.[40] Therefore, the image effectively highlights the potential of a canopy as a structure to balance the coexistence of the interior and exterior space. It also evokes interiority as a sense of inner being, presence, and life, and exteriority as life in the material world.

37   Bogdanović, *The Framing of Sacred Space*, 295–299.
38   On the cloth for the biblical tent made of blue, purple, and scarlet threads, see Exodus 26.
39   Alfredo Tradigo, *Icons and Saints of the Eastern Orthodox Church* (Los Angeles: J. Paul Getty Museum, 2006), 98–100.
40   Tradigo, *Icons and Saints of the Eastern Orthodox Church*, 98–100.

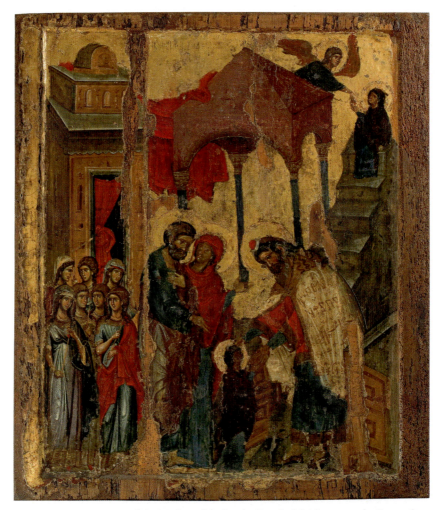

FIGURE 8.3 Presentation of the Mother of God in the Temple (also known as the Entry of the Ever Virgin Mary and Most Holy Mother of God Theotokos into the Temple; *Vavedenije*), icon, Hilandar, Mt. Athos, 14th century
PHOTO: COURTESY OF THE FOUNDATION OF THE HOLY MONASTERY HILANDAR

The icon from Hilandar follows a recognizable iconographic convention for the Presentation of the Mother of God in the Temple which is attested to in the 2nd-century account of the Protoevangelion (Infancy Gospel) of James, which problematized her role in the paradoxical coexistence of the Savior's human and divine natures.[41] This scene of the Presentation of the Mother

---

41   Following the 2nd-century narratives from the Protoevangelion of James, patristic writings of the 4th and 5th centuries elaborated the spiritual importance of the life of Mary,

of God in the Temple had been visualized in the Christian East by the late 10th century.[42] The Hilandar icon shows the child Mary brought by her parents, Joachim and Anna, to the high priest Zacharias. Standing at the open doors of the Temple sanctuary, the high priest is welcoming Mary to the most sacred space. Two additional scenes frame this central event of the Presentation. On the left-hand side, the red curtain of the doors of a towering building is tied in the middle and pushed aside, as the seven maidens, following Mary, have just come in. Seven daughters of Zion adorned by seven virtues accompany Mary and offer her as a sacrifice to God. On the right-hand side behind Zacharias, the Virgin's future life in the Temple is depicted. Mary is sitting on top of a stepped platform in the inner sanctum, the upper room and heart of the Temple. Fed with the bread of contemplation by an angel, the Virgin receives the divine nourishment.

The repeating pattern of the canopy highlights important features of the primitive hut in the Christian context. With all its architectural elements, the canopy on the icon represents the Temple and also resembles a canopy, the actual piece of church furnishing found in Byzantine-rite churches. In the

---

Mother of God. Tradigo, *Icons and Saints*, 98–100; Bissera V. Pentcheva, *Icons and Power: The Mother of God in Byzantium* (University Park, PA: Pennsylvania State University Press, [2014] 2006), chap. 1. The Patristic writings on Mary are immense. For a condensed overview in English, see Jaroslav Pelikan, *The Christian Tradition: A History of the Development of Doctrine*, vol. 1 of *The Emergence of the Catholic Tradition (100–600)* (Chicago: University of Chicago Press, [1991] 1975), 241–242, 259–265, 270–271, 276–277, 289, and 314. On the Marian feasts, see Martin Jugie, "La première fête mariale en Orient et en Occident, l'avent primitif," *Échos d'Orient* 22 (1923), 129–152. On the visual representations of the Life of the Virgin the most exhaustive study is offered by Jacqueline Lafontaine-Dosogne, "Iconography of the Cycle of the Virgin," in *Kariye Djami*, 4 vols., ed. P.A. Underwood (London: Routledge, 1966), vol. 4, 163–193, 197–241; Jacqueline Lafontaine-Dosogne, *Iconographie de l'enfance de la Vierge dans l'Empire byzantin et en Occident*, vol. 1 (Bruxelles: Académie Royale de Belgique, 1992). On the visual representations of Mary according to the Apocrypha, see David R. Cartlidge and J.K. Elliott, *Art of Christian Legend: Visual Representations of the New Testament Apocrypha* (London/New York: Routledge, 2001), 21–46. Among Byzantine hymnographers highlighting the Entry of the Virgin into Temple in their texts are works by Tarasius of Constantinople or George (Gennadius) Scholarius. Tarasius of Constantinople, *In ss. Dei Matrem in Templum Deductam* [On the Entry of the Theotokos in the Temple] in *Patrologia Graeca* (167 vols.), ed. J.-P. Migne (Paris, 1857–1866) [henceforth PG], 98, 1481–1496; George (Gennadius) Scholarius, *In festum ingressus beatae Virginis Mariae in templum* [On the Feast of the Entry of the Virgin Mary in the Temple], in *Bibliotheca Hagiographica Graeca*, ed. François Halkin (Brussels: Société des Bollanistes, 1957), 1147. See also Jaakko Olkinuora, *Byzantine Hymnography for the Feast of the Entrance of the Theotokos* (Helsinki: Picaset Oy, 2015).

42   The apocryphal Protoevangelion of James referring to the Entry/Presentation of the Virgin received its visual counterparts as early as the late 10th century, judging by the image of the Presentation of the Virgin in the *Menologion of Basil II* gr. 1613, fol. 198, illuminated in Constantinople between 976 and 1025. Pentcheva, *Icons and Power*, 138–140.

foreground, in the center of the icon, the arms and bodies of Mary's parents and the high priest Zacharias form yet another canopy, a 'living' canopy. The man-made sanctuary canopy simultaneously frames the altar table and foreshadows the 'living' canopy, the one over the small figure of Mary surrounded by the towering figures of her parents and the high priest.[43] The two canopies are depicted with similar size and form, and balance not only the composition of the icon, but also its content and meaning. The 'living' canopy draws attention to Mary as the source of life, as the most sacred vessel, chosen by God to be His Mother.[44] The altar ciborium simultaneously emphasizes Christian beliefs in the girl's ultimate destiny and her role in the salvation of humankind. For those who accepted the Byzantine doctrine of the Incarnation, the Virgin and the Temple were identified with one another, since "Mary lives inside the

---

43   Though we cannot observe an altar table in the icon from Hilandar, other images depicting the Presentation of the Virgin often show tables covered in red cloths, providing a powerful and suggestive imagery of altar tables. Thus, even when an altar table is not depicted, the repetitive and conventional imagery of the same subject influenced the beholders to connect the canopy from the Presentation of the Virgin with the familiar images of altar canopies.

44   Mary as a living Temple and the living Ark was explained in numerous sources known to the Byzantines: Protoevangelion of James; Tarasius of Constantinople, *In ss. Dei Matrem in Templum Deductam* [On the Entry of the Theotokos in the Temple], 1481–1496; Saint Germanus of Constantinople, *In Praesentationem ss. Deipare* [Homily on the Presentation] PG 98, 290–320; George (Gennadios) Scholarios, *In festum ingressus beatae Virginis Mariae in templum* [On the Feast of the Entry of the Virgin Mary in the Temple], 1147; Acts of the Third Ecumenical Council, in Giovanni Domenico Mansi, *Sacrorum conciliorum nova et amplissima collectio*, vols. 4, 5, 6 and 9 (Paris, Leipzig, 1901–1927) [hereafter *Mansi*], vol. 4, 580E, 1253A/C, 1256B; Epiphanius of Cyprus, *In laudes S. Mariae deiparae* (*dubia*) [In Praise of Mary, the Mother of God], PG 43, 488CD, 492B/D, 496D; Andrew of Crete, *In nativitatem B. Mariae* [On the Nativity of the Supremely Holy Theotokos], PG 97, 868C, *Canon in B. Annae conceptionem* [Canon on the Blessed Anne's Conceiving], PG 97, 1316AB. References to Christ building His temple, i.e., His body from His mother's flesh in: Acts of the Third Ecumenical Council, *Mansi*, vol. 4, 613A, 624D, 633D, 656A, *Mansi*, vol. 5, 24C, 40C, 292BC, 305B; Acts of the Fourth Ecumenical Council, *Mansi*, vol. 6, 669B, 736B; Acts of the Fifth Ecumenical Council, *Mansi*, vol. 9, 584E; Cyril of Alexandria, *Festal Letters, 1–12*, ed. John J. O'Keefe, trans. Philip R. Amadon (Washington, DC: The Catholic University of America Press, 2009), letters v.7:90–91 and viii.6:69–76; Andrew of Crete, *In nativitatem B. Mariae ii/iv*, PG 97:883A, 868B; Patriarch Photios, *Epistulae*, 3 vols., ed. B. Laourdas and L.G. Westerink (Leipzig: Teubner, 1983–1985), iii, 35 (epistle 284:1303–1308). These references to primary sources are compiled from works by Doula Mouriki, "The Octateuch Miniatures of the Byzantine Manuscripts of Cosmas Indicopleustes" (PhD diss., Princeton University, 1970), 124; Maria Evangelatou, "The Illustration of the Ninth-Century Byzantine Marginal Psalters: Layers of Meaning and Their Sources" (PhD diss., University of London, 2002), n. 706; and Michel van Esbroeck, "The Virgin as the True Ark of the Covenant," in *Images of the Mother of God*, ed. Maria Vassilaki (Aldershot: Ashgate, 2005), 63–68.

sanctuary just as Jesus will live inside her body; Christ's divinity thus is entirely hidden within his humanity."[45] Together, the two canopies in the icon integrate the events of the entry of the Mother of God into the Temple. The upper room of the inner sanctuary where she receives the divine nourishment of heavenly bread, furthermore, foreshadows the liturgical and Eucharistic events witnessed in the actual church during liturgical rites.[46] The suggestive realism of the 'living' canopy, based on the evocative depiction of the human encounter between Mary, her parents, and the high priest, as well as the realism of the man-made canopy depicted as an altar canopy, complement the devotional and liturgical response of the Byzantines and those embracing their tradition.

The presence of Mary, the Mother of God, as represented twice in relation to the canopy, suggests a spatio-temporal reality and the essence of a Byzantine church that grows in harmony with the divine plan, or to put it in Vitruvius's terms, in harmony with nature as an absolute order of life. This multilayered Marian concept of 'Ark-Virgin-Church' highlights the highly developed architectural and ontological construct of the Byzantine canopy as a 'primitive hut' in the person of Mary. The ontological complexity is achieved via the early Christian construct of the Ark and Christ, as already elaborated by Irenaeus in the 2nd century, and by the inauguration of the feast of the Presentation of the Virgin in the Temple in the 6th century[47] that celebrated her dedication to God and her future vocation as a living Temple, the living Ark, and Mother of the incarnate Lord.[48]

The canopy as a design and building module invested with biblical, Christological, or Marian meanings was widely used in Byzantine architecture. In my research of canopies examined from archaeological and architectural

---

45   Tradigo, *Icons and Saints*, 98.

46   The upper room is emphasized by the fact that the Virgin is seated on the stepped base of the inner sanctum, occasionally also sheltered by a canopy.

47   On November 21, 543, Byzantine emperor Justinian I instituted the public celebration of the Marian feast of the Presentation of the Virgin in the Temple. The feast day later spread to Constantinople, presumably at some point in the 7th or 8th century, and later on throughout the Byzantine Empire. Tradigo, *Icons and Saints*, 98.

48   The typological association of the Virgin and the Tabernacle is illustrated by an image of the *Smyrna Octateuch*, fol. 81v, in which the Virgin and Child are enclosed within a double frame decorated with pearls and stones and in a shell-like niche. Mouriki, "Octateuch Miniatures," 124; Elisabeth Revel-Neher, "On the Hypothetical Models of the Byzantine Iconography of the Ark of the Covenant," in *Byzantine East, Latin West: Art Historical Studies in Honor of Kurt Weitzmann*, ed. Doula Mouriki et al. (Princeton: Department of Art and Archaeology, Princeton University, 1995), 405–414. On the related liturgical references, see *Festal Menaion*, ed. Mother Mary and Bishop Kallistos Ware (South Canan, PA: St. Tikhon's Seminary Press, 1998), 51–52.

perspectives, a particular focus was placed on canopies as liturgical furnishings and the basic structural units of the Byzantine church—a four-columned structural core with a dome and vaulted bays.[49] The relationship between the 'ideal structures' understood as 'primitive huts' of different sizes and scales and how they achieved different forms and were materialized in Byzantine churches, I argue, allow us to discuss canopies as basic units for the definition of various Byzantine architectural 'types.'[50] Inaugurated by the Hagia Sophia as a huge canopy set as a central core of the basilica, the plasticity and monumentality of the canopied Byzantine-rite church has been reaffirmed in numerous examples of centrally planned canopied churches, as well as various types of cross-inscribed and cross-in-square churches. All are essentially composed around the central domical canopied core within a nine-square grid, as can be shown in the example of 14th-century Byzantine-rite church of the Matejič monastery (Figures 8.4, 8.5, and 8.6).

While I have demonstrated how numerous Byzantine churches were built by utilizing the canopy as an architectural *parti*, an overall design principle, it seems appropriate to highlight once again the inseparable performativity of the canopy as a hut experienced within liturgical rites.[51] In her analysis of nature and the sacred in the Byzantine context, Veronica della Dora explains effectively how liturgy "did not speak of things, but *from* things."[52] Indeed, the beginning of the liturgical day in the Byzantine-rite church opens with the Orthodox vesper services and a hymn composed by King David. The psalm by King David—which is chanted while the priest stands outside the closed Royal Doors, the central sanctuary doors of the templon screen, named as such because it potentially carried related associations with the Temple architecture[53] celebrates divine creation: "Bless the Lord, O my soul. O Lord my God ... Who coverest thyself with light as with a garment; who stretchest out

---

49   Bogdanović, *The Framing of Sacred Space*, 264–294.

50   Bogdanović, *The Framing of Sacred Space*, 251–263.

51   Bogdanović, "The Domed Canopy in Byzantine Church Design," *Sacred Architecture Journal* 37 (Spring 2020), 11–15, also online https://www.sacredarchitecture.org/articles/the_domed_canopy_in_byzantine_church_design; Bogdanović, *The Framing of Sacred Space*, 264–294.

52   Veronica della Dora, *Landscape, Nature, and the Sacred in Byzantium* (Cambridge: Cambridge University Press, 2016), 88.

53   Bogdanović, *The Framing of Sacred Space*, 216–229, with references to Cyril Mango, "On the History of the Templon and the Martyrion of St. Artemios at Constantinople," *Zograf* 10 (1979), 40–43, Christopher Walter, "New Look at the Byzantine Sanctuary Barrier," *Revue des études byzantines* 51 (1993), 203–228; Vasileios Marinis, *Architecture and Ritual in the Churches of Constantinople. Ninth to Fifteenth Centuries* (Cambridge: Cambridge University Press, 2014), 41.

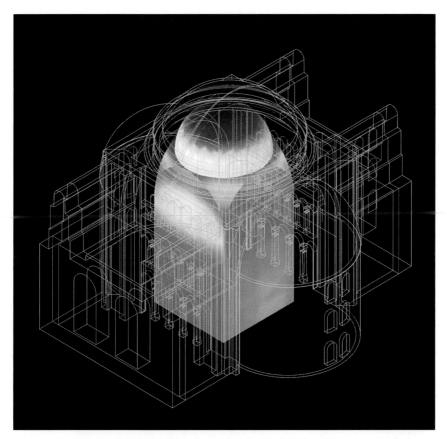

FIGURE 8.4 Hagia Sophia, Constantinople, modern Istanbul, Turkey, 6th century, analysis showing light penetration in the central canopy
DRAWING: ALEX BLUM CREATED BY USING RHINOCEROS, AUTODESK REVIT, AND PHOTOSHOP

the heavens like a *curtain* (*tent*) [emphasis mine]; Who layeth the beams of his chambers in the waters: who maketh the clouds his chariot: who walketh upon the wings of the wind: Who maketh his angels spirits (winds, *pneumata-πνεύματα*) [emphasis mine]; his ministers a flaming fire: Who laid the foundations of the earth, that it should not be removed for ever" (Ps 104 (103):1–5). Veronica della Dora rightly highlights that, "as the psalm reverberates within the church's walls, pillars become trees, domes a starry heaven, the floor the earth."[54] I would further add that the psalm simultaneously reaffirms the church as a primitive hut, with strong reference to Vitruvius's hut as visualized in the

54 Della Dora, *Landscape, Nature, and the Sacred*, 88.

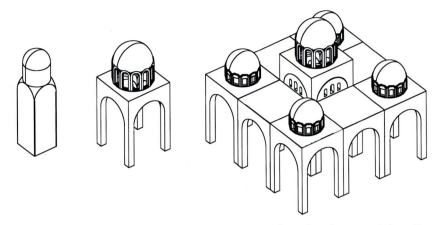

FIGURE 8.5 Process from volume to canopy to nine-square design based on canopied *parti* in Byzantine churches
DRAWING: ALEX BLUM CREATED BY USING AUTODESK REVIT AND ADOBE ILLUSTRATOR

FIGURE 8.6 Five-domed *katholikon* of the Matejič monastery, Skopska Crna Gora, Northern Macedonia, 14th century
PHOTO: IVAN DRPIĆ

Byzantine imagery of the Ark, the Tabernacle (tent-hut), the Temple, and the church, and even stretches forward towards the depiction of Laugier's hut. The psalm echoes within the Stoic philosophical system, upon which rests the intellectual reasoning of Vitruvius's hut as simultaneously a micro- and a macrocosmic creation, being rooted in nature and its primordial elements—earth, air, fire and water.[55] Stoic philosophy established active elements around fire and air "which together constituted the divine *pneuma*, the life force that bound together the entire world and existed in eternity."[56] Bissera Pentcheva has already demonstrated how the divine *pneuma* in the Byzantine-rite church is the creative force and vital spirit of the church that fills matter so that the inert (church) becomes alive.[57] She broadened the meaning of *pneuma* in particular, with an emphasis on the wind-like movement of the incense and the sound of the hymns of liturgical performance in the activated space of the church building itself.[58] Curiously enough, in a few illustrated medieval copies of Vitruvius's text, including the oldest preserved 9th-century British Museum Harley 2767, the illustrations most often show the wind diagram.[59] Windblown leaves and vegetal motifs of the capitals of the columns of the Byzantine

---

55 See above, n. 3. On the role of fire, water, earth, and air in the creation of sacred space, see also edited volumes by Alexei Lidov: Lidov, ed. *Hierotopy of Light and Fire in the Culture of the Byzantine World* [Iyerotopiya ognya i sveta v kul'ture vizantiyskogo mira] (Moscow: Theoria, 2017); Lidov, ed. *Holy Water in the Hierotopy and Iconography of the Christian World* [Svyataya Voda v iyerotopii i ikonografii khristianskogo mira] (Moscow: Theoria, 2017); Lidov, ed. *The Hierotopy of Holy Mountains in Christian Culture* [Iyerotopiya svyatoy gory v khristianskoy kul'ture] (Moscow: Theoria, 2019); Lidov, ed. *Air and Heavens in the Hierotopy and Iconography of the Christian World* [Vozdukh i nebesa v iyerotopii i ikonografii khristianskogo mira] (Moscow: Theoria, 2019).

56 Vitruvius, *Ten Books on Architecture*, bk. 2, chap. 2, with additional commentaries by Rowland and Dewar on Stoic philosophy in Vitruvius's text on p. 178. On the role of Stoic philosophy and the *pneuma* in Byzantium see, for example, Troels Engberg-Pederson, "A Stoic Understanding of the Pneuma and Resurrection in 1 Corinthians 15," and Troels Engberg-Pederson, "The Bodily Pneuma in Paul," in *Cosmology and the Self in the Apostle Paul: The Material Spirit* (New York: Oxford University Press, 2010), 8–74. Katerina Ierodiakonou, "The Greek Concept of *Sympatheia* and Its Byzantine Appropriation in Michael Psellos," in *The Occult Sciences in Byzantium*, ed. Paul Magdalino and Maria Mavroudi (Geneva: La Pomme d'Or, 2007), 97–117, esp. 100–103.

57 Bissera Pentcheva, *Hagia Sophia: Sound, Space, and Spirit in Byzantium* (University Park, PA: Pennsylvania State University Press, 2017) and Bissera Pentcheva, *Sensual Icon: Space, Ritual, and Senses in Byzantium* (University Park, PA: Pennsylvania State University Press, 2013), 45–48.

58 Pentcheva, *Hagia Sophia: Sound, Space, and Spirit in Byzantium* and Pentcheva, *Sensual Icon: Space, Ritual, and Senses in Byzantium*.

59 Krinsky, *Seventy-Eight Vitruvius Manuscripts*, 36–70, esp. 41.

FIGURE 8.7   'Windblown' capital with acanthus leaves, Hagios Demetrios, Thessaloniki, Greece, 5th century
PHOTO: NEBOJŠA STANKOVIĆ

churches activated by *pneuma* (Figure 8.7),[60] in my opinion, only reinforce the complexity of the Byzantine church as a material, sensible manifestation of the primitive hut and the adaptation of Vitruvius's reasoning on architecture within a Christian context.

∙ ∙ ∙

In conclusion, I would like to propose that the Byzantine 'primitive hut' decipherable in the form and idea of a canopied *parti*, as a basic spatial and symbolic unit of the Byzantine-rite church, undeniably rests on a robust intellectual concept. The formal appearance of the canopy as the 'hut' in the Byzantine context is related to the process of mimesis and transposition of meanings as a catalyst that informs the generative design process rather than

---

60   Eugene W. Kleinbauer, "The Iconography and the Date of the Mosaics of the Rotunda of Hagios Geiorgios, Thessaloniki," *Viator* 3 (1972) 27–108, discusses early use of windblown capitals in a variety of Early Christian and Byzantine churches on pp. 104–106.

a dogmatic formula or a direct structural model that would eventually simplify and replace the complexities of the design process. It also positions the canopy as a theoretical house, relevant for architectural taxonomy. Simultaneously, the canopy in Byzantine architecture is strongly relatable to the primitive hut as postulated by Vitruvius and enriched with Judeo-Christian philosophies, and much less with the hut theorized by the architectural scholars of the Enlightenment, who recurrently mistook the hut for a dogma of rational and structural purity in architecture that can be positively affirmed by archaeological evidence from classical Greek temples.[61] The canopy, a generic and generative architectural form which can be effectively reconstructed in people's imagination and creatively recreated both as an ideal, universal building, and a historical object, played a major role in Byzantine-rite churches.[62] Not only did the canopied bay constitute the major building module of the Byzantine church, but, when executed on different scales, it most closely related the form and meaning of the architectonics of the altar canopy (ciborium) and church core, as evidenced in Byzantine religious texts, images, and buildings. Echoing Vitruvius's primitive hut, when compared to rational, positivist architectural theory based on Laugier's and Quatremère's elaboration of it, the origins of the Byzantine canopy—both the hut and the tent—cannot be found in nature and natural phenomena, however, but in nature as absolute, in divine creation. Yet both the Byzantine canopy and the primitive hut of Laugier promote the pursuit of the truth in the matter by giving type (shape) to the typeless (shapeless) archetype, which is the basis of the tectonics in architecture between its physical and metaphysical realms.[63] Moreover, the Byzantine canopy as primitive hut instigates consideration of Byzantine architectural typology within a more plastic (tectonic) approach, beyond two-dimensional representations such as floor plans, cross-sections, and elevations. Confirmed

---

61 See excellent discussion of the role of the Greco-Roman concept of the hut as postulated by Vitruvius and used in theories of architecture around the 1750s in Barry Bergdoll, *European Architecture 1750–1890* (Oxford: Oxford University Press, 2000), 10–12 and Christopher Drew Armstrong, "French Architectural Thought and the Idea of Greece," in *A Companion to Greek Architecture*, ed. Margaret Melanie Miles (Chichester, West Sussex: John Wiley and Sons, 2016), 487–506.

62 Bogdanović, *The Framing of Sacred Space*, 264–294; Rykwert, *On Adam's House*, 183–184; Tim Adams, "Benoît Goetz: A French Reader of Rykwert's on Adam's House in Paradise," *Interstices: A Journal of Architecture and Related Arts* 10 (2009), 87–96.

63 Robert Maulden, "Tectonics in Architecture: From Physical to the Meta-Physical," (MArch thesis, MIT, 1986); Kenneth Frampton, *Studies in Tectonic Culture: The Poetics of Construction in Nineteenth and Twentieth Century Architecture* (Cambridge, MA: MIT Press, 1995).

by texts, visual and spatial models, and specific architectural solutions, both the primitive hut of Vitruvius, Laugier, and Quatremère, on the one hand, and the canopy of the Byzantines, on the other, reaffirm an intellectual approach towards architecture. By recognizing conceptual design thinking and by acknowledging the role of the primitive hut in Byzantine architectural design, it is possible to build a long overdue bridge between ancient and early modern architectural theories.

Conclusion: Highlighted Themes, Explanatory Terms, and Critical Mechanisms

Jelena Bogdanović, Ida Sinkević, Marina Mihaljević, and Čedomila Marinković

The essays in this volume demonstrate that typology in visual arts and architecture is a vital topic in late antique and Byzantine studies. Starting with the premise that pictorial arts and architecture constitute two distinct artistic forms, the volume as a whole reveals that a dialogue between type and archetype goes well beyond issues of formalism and representational themes. By addressing fundamental questions about the role and meaning of type and its ultimate source, this project presents a nuanced study of the applicability of typology as a systematic and systemic classification of types in what we today recognize as the separate artistic endeavors of architecture and visual arts in the Mediterranean culture.

In the opening essay, Jelena Anđelković Grašar considers questions of type and archetype in the creation of the empress imagery of the late antique Balkans. Anna Adashinskaya delves into typological investigations of imagery in religious icons of the Byzantines and their referentiality in the medieval context of the Balkans and southern Mediterranean. Ljubomir Milanović clarifies the typological relationship between relics and icons. Cecilia Olovsdotter argues for the relevance of actual architectural accomplishments for the development of visual architectural types in late antique and Early Byzantine visual arts. Čedomila Marinković looks at an independent line of development in Jewish visual art by examining the typological concepts relevant to the pictorial representation of the Temple in the Sarajevo Haggadah. Marina Mihaljević, Ida Sinkević, and Jelena Bogdanović focus on Byzantine ecclesiastical architecture and through selected case studies propose a revised approach to type and archetype in Byzantine architecture. Previous research on architecture has too often relied heavily on iconographical methods in the visual arts and in the process undermined the complexities of architecture as a separate artistic expression. In their essays, Mihaljević, Sinkević, and Bogdanović highlight the importance of diagrammatic reasoning in architecture as a theoretical model and its relevance for architectural practice. At the same time, they point to the congruence of typological and diagrammatic principles in architecture, whereby the conceptual and formal aspects of types are distinct but intricately intertwined rather than separated. Specifically, post-18th-century theories

© KONINKLIJKE BRILL NV, LEIDEN, 2023 | DOI:10.1163/9789004537781_011

of typology posit that even if the diagram connects it also essentially separates two modes of thinking in architecture: conceptual (typal) and formal (typological).[1] By extension, abstraction achieved by using diagrams is recurrently seen as a precondition for the separation of mimetic formal elements from conceptual features in the production of architecture, for the disengagement of historicism from architectural practice, and for distinguishing history from theory. This volume addresses this overarching premise by highlighting that type remains inseparable from its conceptual and formal aspects. This book emphasizes not the dichotomy between typal and typological thought but rather the major relevance of pairing type and archetype, which is pertinent to contemporaneous late antique and Byzantine intellectual thought.

As Marinković additionally enriches the discourse on abstraction in both visual arts and architecture, she clarifies how in medieval Jewish and Christian art the representation of architecture in pictorial terms was never naturalistic or realistic. The digression of painted architecture from the appearance of the real building, and their general, almost diagrammatic similarities could be the consequence of various factors. Among them are the painter's lack of skill, adherence to certain cultural or stylistic choices, the main stylistic trends of the epoch, and the technical manner of artistically conveying the model. In each case, these aspects point to the ways in which the type was communicated rather than to its essence, to the archetype.

Especially important is the mode of transfer between the archetype and type, between the ultimate model and its actual realization in type. In late antique and Byzantine art and architecture, the copy of the archetype was not understood mimetically: only the basic idea of archetype was adopted—sometimes reduced to the sign, frequently not even including many morphological elements. Moreover, the archetype was never transmitted *in toto* but only partially.

Working independently around inconsistent typological terminology and its applicability in the context of the material culture of the late antique and Christian Balkans, the contributors ultimately agree on definitions of these critical terms as follows: The type is a model, a pattern; archetype its essence, the foremost, original type. Prototype is a generic and generative, sensible model; stereotype its fixed but oversimplified version; antitype its future, dynamic counterpart. Such definitions, consistent with more recent definitions of these terms, are engaged with the contemporaneous intellectual reasoning.

---

1 Sam Jacoby, "Typal and Typological Reasoning: A Diagrammatic Practice of Architecture," *The Journal of Architecture* 20, no. 6 (2015), 938–961.

CONCLUSION   235

As we additionally show in this book, they are consistent with investigations of specific case studies and their culturally conditioned referentiality to type and archetype constructs.

Thematically speaking, the essays examine type and archetype within holy and royal imagery,[2] as well as between the buildable and unbuildable.[3] Several recurrent topics emerge as especially relevant for understanding typology in the late antique and Byzantine Mediterranean. The sociopolitical historical framework and modern constructs of center and periphery transpire to be relevant for a more nuanced understanding of typology in both the visual arts and architecture, and its relevance for historical and theoretical studies.[4] Typology thus presented complicates the evolutionist narratives that group surviving artistic and architectural accomplishments based on similarity of formal features and assign them a chronological sequence in the evolution of the type and larger developments in the arts and architecture. The ontological difference between the image and its space, and related questions of mechanisms of describing and accessing the transcendental are likewise highlighted in this volume, contributing to both image and architectural theories.[5]

The broad spectrum of themes presented in the essays also expands the boundaries of the conventional understanding of type and archetype and proposes new methods for assessing, analyzing, and explaining the complex relationships between the type as pattern, action, or model and its initiator and ultimate source and essence, the archetype. In her essay, Anđelković Grašar clarifies the complex mechanisms of the construction of the ideal image of the empress in late antique society and its ultimate source in the non-material world. Adashinskaya explains how the fame of the miracle-working icon known as the Hodegetria, associated with the Constantinopolitan monastery Hodegon, generated many replicas, which were venerated in a way similar to their prototype. She elucidates the indexicality and referentiality of specific types of icons of the Mother of God in the medieval Balkans, whereby the church dedication to the 'icon' essentially refers to transposition of the meaning of the icon as participatory presence of the holy person depicted, rather than the image itself. The Hodegetria icon should be understood not only as

---

2   See chapters by Anđelković Grašar, Adashinskaya, Milanović, Olovsdotter, Mihaljević, and Sinkević in the present volume.
3   See chapters by Adashinskaya, Milanović, Olovsdotter, Marinković, Mihaljević, Sinkević, and Bogdanović in the present volume.
4   Sociohistorical contexts are especially highlighted in the essays by Anđelković Grašar, Adashinskaya, Milanović, Mihaljević, and Sinkević in the present volume.
5   Ontological themes related to the type-and-archetype constructs are prominent in the texts by Adashinskaya, Milanović, Marinković, Mihaljević, and Bogdanović in the present volume.

miracle-working object or proactive template, but also as a concept, as a reference to certain qualities of its ultimate source, the Theotokos, Mother of God. Visuality and beauty remain critical aspects of such type and archetype relationships in iconographical studies, but physical likeness as a guiding principle, beyond its role for organizing our knowledge about the sacred, should be reconsidered.

Similarly, we propose studies of late antique and Byzantine architectural typology within a more plastic (tectonic) approach, beyond the two-dimensional representations of the floor plans, cross-sections, and elevations that are currently seen as critical for reproducibility and referentiality in architecture. Mihaljević demonstrates how the type-and-archetype relationship is not limited to the actual reliance on and replication of a specific physical model. In her study of the architectural forms of the church of Nea Moni in Greece, she looks at physical features, or rather distinct architectural patterns, such as the double colonnettes, and argues that by its actual form this feature contributed to the molding of the church interior into a centralized structure to evoke the Holy Sepulchre in Jerusalem as its architectural prototype, one that over time became identified as the archetypical building in medieval Christendom. Indeed, the physical model is not necessary, although it is often included in the scholarly definitions and use of archetype. Sinkević shows that five-domed churches may be related to the image of the Heavenly Jerusalem because many domes reflect many churches. Yet Sinkević further elucidates that their symmetrical disposition and synergic relationship between exterior articulation and interior decoration actually reveal an architecturally segregated but conceptually unified domical space that finds its origin in a canopied primitive hut, the perennial structure of Byzantine architecture, as discussed in Bogdanović's paper.

The representations of specific architectural elements, such as the arch and the pediment, while potent in their individual symbolic meanings, can be better understood when contextualized in the broader conceptual paradigms of life, death, cosmic cycles, and spirituality, as Olovsdotter argues in her text. The geometric, almost abstract, forms of the arch and pediment also relate to an architectural type that can generate more elaborate architectural forms. This topic of geometry and form as relevant for identification of architectural type is also touched upon in the essays by Mihaljević and Bogdanović, who look at the simple three-dimensional geometry of rounded spaces and four-columned canopies and their potential to designate type and prototype (fully defined physical models) in Byzantine religious architecture. Even when the elements of real architecture are clearly represented and their archetypal significance is culturally well defined, as Olovsdotter details through the

CONCLUSION   237

examples of late antique and early Christian monumental architecture—
portals and gates, notably city gates and triumphal arches, the pedimented
fronts of temples and shrines, and the composite arched fronts of the gates,
temples, and palaces—these elements repeatedly relate to well-known examples of specific architectural accomplishments and clearly established conceptual relationships with their prototypes.

The image drawn from memory, a mnemonic reconstruction, or, specifically, a construction of the third Temple based on archetypal associations
drawn from both literature and imagination, is discussed by Marinković in her
chapter on the visual representations of the Temple of Jerusalem. She details
her analysis based on the unique iconography of the Temple in the Sarajevo
Haggadah and suggests that, despite being unique in its pictorial appearance,
it nonetheless points to the archetypical Temple of Jerusalem. Indeed, the
return to the archetype can be defined not only by the physical likeness, but
also, and even more so, by performative aspects of the image and its func-
tionality, as Adashinskaya similarly discusses in her analysis of what it meant
to replicate the icon of the Virgin (Mother of God) by using specific church
dedications.

Archetype can be recalled through arrangement, the installation in which
the relationship between the body of a saint and the body of Christ is acknowl-
edged in the complex relationship of conceptual, architectural, and artistic
means, as Milanović elaborates. The connection can be drawn through the
positioning of the remains-relics of the saint vis-à-vis his or her portrait. The
templon screen which, when bearing icons, literally becomes the iconostasis,
the wall separating the sanctuary from the church space populated by the
faithful, thus successfully maintains the close connection between the body,
image, and burial of the saint and the body of Christ conceptualized through
the performative liturgical services at the altar in the sanctuary space, just
behind the iconostasis. Therefore, while the relationship between the type
and archetype is known through literature and theological writings, Milanović
effectively elucidates how it was creatively realized and visualized. Images and
objects and their location are contextualized and specified through the entire
installation of the iconostasis, coffin, and iconic images; their salvific messages
further enhanced by rituals performed within the space of the church.

The origins of late antique and Byzantine types should not be searched for
in the natural world, however, but in nature as absolute, in divine creation,
confirming the ontological difference between the type and its archetype.
Bogdanović hypothesizes in her essay that the four-columned canopy can
be studied as a kind of 'primitive hut' in Byzantine architectural typology.
She clarifies that in its own definition and meaning the concept of 'primitive

hut' remains vague: ancient Greek philosophers place it somewhere between a sensible model (prototype) and a principle inherent to natural and art forms in Aristotelian terms, while Platonists see it as an abstract idea or form as it appeared to the divine mind prior to creation, i.e., the ideal principle (archetype).[6] Indeed, in his *Celestial Hierarchy*, focusing on angelic hierarchy, Dionysius the Areopagite, proponent of critical philosophical reasoning on typology in the wider Mediterranean cultural context, introduces the terminology we use today in typological studies. The type (τύπος) is a model, a pattern, and archetype (ἀρχέτυπον) is the original type from which the physical replicas are made, but he does not imply that archetype is material or physical in nature. This is perhaps the reason for the occasionally interchangeable use of archetype and prototype (sensible model) in many current discussions of typology in the visual arts and architecture.[7] Moreover, the reasoning on ontological difference between the type and its archetype aligns with classical philosophical thought on authority and universality. This thinking points to the major difference between late antique and Byzantine architectural theory and that devised by the late 18th century which undermined claims on universality and positioned them as critical for disengagement with history and historicism and equally important for the establishment of restrictively defined epistemological argument in architectural theory.[8]

In this volume, the contributors agree that within the late antique and Byzantine cultural landscape, inclusive of its material culture and aesthetic phenomena, Dionysius the Areopagite's reasoning led toward the creation of material types for the essentially typeless, shapeless, immaterial archetypes,

---

6 See the chapter by Bogdanović in this volume, where she further highlights the role of both Aristotelian and Platonic thinking in addressing typology in the Byzantine context.

7 The interchangeable use of prototype and archetype for representations that aim to convey universal ideas, the rejection of ontological aspects of typology immanent in Plato's philosophy, and the overall development of positivistic studies that reject sensible models as impediments for rational procedures of taxonomy are prominent in Kant's work. See, for example, James J. DiCenso, "The Concept of Urbild in Kant's Philosophy of Religion," *Kant-Studien* 104, no. 1 (2013), 100–132. On ontological difference, that between being and beings, see the critical work by Martin Heidegger, *Being and Time*, trans. John Macquarrie and Edward Robinson (London: SCM Press, 1962). Significantly, the establishment of typology in art and architecture as a scholarly method coincides with the Enlightenment period and its intellectual framework, as articulated by Erwin Panofsky, the major proponent of iconographical studies. See Panofsky's analysis of archetype as the idea created by God in the works of medieval philosophers in Erwin Panofsky, *Idea: A Concept in Art Theory*, trans. Joseph J.S. Peake (New York/London: Harper & Row, 1968), 33–43, 191–201.

8 Jacoby, "Typal and Typological Reasoning," 938–961, summarizes relevant aspects of reasoning about type within post-18th-century architectural theory.

CONCLUSION   239

which can be accessed and contemplated through material types. With no
direct physical references, communicative tools for facilitating the meanings
of the type-and-archetype constructs range from texts and diagrams to evocative imagery and nonverbal and nonfigurative participatory experiences, as
detailed in the essays presented here. Such an implied dichotomy between the
immaterial and material aspects of the visual arts and architecture additionally points to the divide between the noetic and iconic features of arts and
architecture. Dionysius the Areopagite even verbalized this construct by saying that "Using matter, one may be lifted up to the immaterial archetypes."[9]
In their essays, the contributors independently point to an important divide
between intelligible and perceptible aspects of the type-and-archetype constructs, which opens up pathways for theorizing late antique and Byzantine art
and architecture. As argued by Sam Jacoby when discussing architecture and
typological tools, the persistence of such constructs over a prolonged period
of time gives them almost "ahistorical" qualities and allows for the abstraction
of a series of material accomplishments deriving from them.[10] In this book,
we show that the material evidence of select examples, set against the intellectual and creative thoughts of the period and communicative tools for facilitating the meanings of type and archetype, confirms the great importance of
type-and-archetype constructs and their applicability for theoretical discourse
about both architecture and visual arts in late antiquity and Byzantium.
Consequently, as Jacoby also emphasizes when discussing "primitive ideas" as
being critical for theory and practice in architecture, such type-and-archetype
constructs "allow for typological analysis and a judgement of individual forms
against a theoretical possibility of a form (type)."[11] In our work, the possibility for simultaneous theoretical and historical analysis of form as well as
distinguishing aspects of cultural synthesis of the historical and conceptual
knowledge derived from type-and-archetype constructs emerges as especially
relevant.

   This book ultimately argues that the late antique and Byzantine cultural
landscape is rooted in highly conceptual approaches to its rich visual and
material culture whereby the material and immaterial aspects of its type-and-
archetype constructs are inseparable. Such holistic type-and-archetype

---

9   Dionysius Areopagita, *Corpus Dionysiacum*, 2 vols. ed. Beate Regina Suchla, Günter Heil,
     and Adolf M. Ritter (Berlin: De Gruyter, 1990–1991) [including *De coelesti hierarchia*
     (*Celestial Hierarchy*) hereafter CH], CH 144B–C.
10   Jacoby, "Typal and Typological Reasoning," 938–961.
11   Jacoby, "Typal and Typological Reasoning," 938–961, citation on 946.

constructs reveal comprehensive philosophical questions about their meanings, referentiality, and temporality. Rather than drawing on unsustainable socio-political, historicist, and evolutionist narratives based on formalism and typology, the book advocates for revised systemic studies and a fuller understanding of individual artistic forms and their theoretical possibilities. Above all, this book highlights the relevance of pairing type and archetype in refining architecture and image theories.

Bibliography

Primary Sources

Actes de Lavra. Vol. 3, *de 1329 à 1500.* Ed. P. Lemerle, A. Guillou, N. Svoronos, and D. Papachryssanthou. Paris: Lethielleux, 1979.

Actes de Vatopédi. Vol. 1, *des origines à 1329.* Ed. J. Bompaire, J. Lefort, V. Kravari, and Ch. Giros. Paris: Lethielleux, 2001.

Actes de Xénophon. Ed. D. Papachryssanthou. Paris: Lethielleux, 1986.

Agathias. *The Histories.* In *Corpus fontium historiae Byzantinae* 2A, trans. and ed. Joseph D. Frendo. Berlin: De Gruyter, 1975.

Akropolites, Georgios. *Annales.* Ed. I. Bekker. Bonn: E. Weber, 1837.

Allies, Mary H., trans., *St. John Damascene on Holy Images.* London: Thomas Baker, 1898.

Andrew of Crete. *Canon in B. Annae conceptionem.* In *Patrologia Graeca (PG)* 97, ed. J.-P. Migne, 1305–1316. Paris: Imprimerie Catholique, 1857.

Andrew of Crete. *In nativitatem B. Mariae.* In *Patrologia Graeca (PG)* 97, ed. J.-P. Migne, 809–880. Paris: Imprimerie Catholique, 1857.

Andrew of Crete. *Magnus canon.* In *Patrologia Graeca (PG)* 97, ed. J.-P. Migne, 806–1386. Paris: Imprimerie Catholique, 1857.

Basil the Great, Saint. *On the Holy Spirit.* Crestwood, NY: St. Vladimir's Seminary Press, 1980.

Bede. *Bedae Venerabilis opera. Pars II, Opera exegetica.* 2A, *De Tabernaculo. De Templo. In Ezram et Neemiam.* Ed. David Hurst. Turnhout: Brepols, 1969.

Bekker, Immanuel, ed. *Georgius Phrantzes, Joannes Cananus, Joannes Anagnostes.* Bonn: E. Weber, 1838.

Benjamin of Tudela, Rabbi. *The Itinerary of Benjamin of Tudela.* Critical text, translations and commentaries by Marcus N. Adler. New York: Feldheim, 1907.

Boissonade, Jean François, ed. *Anecdota Græca e codicibus regiis descripsit annotatione illustravit,* vol. 2. Paris: Ex Regio Typographeo, 1830.

Byzantine Monastic Foundation Documents: A Complete Translation of the Surviving Founders' Typika and Testaments. Ed. John Thomas and Angela Constantinides Hero. Vols. 1–5. Washington, DC: Dumbarton Oaks Research Library and Collection, 2000.

Community Council of Kouklia. *The Official Site of the Kouklia Village.* http://www .kouklia.org.cy/churches_odigitria.shtm. Accessed June 14, 2017.

Corpus Christianorum. Continuatio Mediaevalis 133. Turnholt: Brepols, 1996.

Cyril of Alexandria. *Festal Letters, 1–12.* Ed. John J. O'Keefe, trans. Philip R. Amadon. Washington, DC: The Catholic University of America Press, 2009.

Dančić, Ðuro, ed. *Životi kraljeva i arhiepiskopa srpskih napisao arhiepiskop Danilo i drugi* [The lives of kings and archbishops, written by Archbishop Danilo and the others]. Zagreb: Svetozar Galec, 1866.

242 BIBLIOGRAPHY

Danilo, Arhiepiskop. *Životi kraljeva i arhiepiskopa srpskih* [Lives of Serbian kings and archbishops]. Trans. Lazar Mirković. Belgrade: Srpska književna zadruga, 1935.

Danilov nastavljač. "Kralj Stefan Uroš Treći" [King Stefan Uroš the Third]. In *Danilovi nastavljači. Danilov učenik, drugi nastavljači Danilovog zbornika*, ed. Dimitrije Bogdanović et al. Belgrade: Prosveta, 1989.

De Vita Imp. Constantini. In "Eusebii Pamphili Caesareae Palaestinae Episcopi," *Opera omnia quaeexistant*, Tomus II, Paris: Migne, 1837.

Delehaye, Hippolyte. *Deux typica byzantins de l'époque des Paléologues.* Brussels: M. Lamertin, 1921.

Dionysius Areopagita. *Corpus Dionysiacum.* 2 vols. Ed. Beate Regina Suchla, Günter Heil, and Adolf M. Ritter. Berlin: De Gruyter, 1990–1991.

Dmitrievsky, Alexei. *Opisanie liturgicheskih rukopisej, hranjashhihsja v bibliotekah Pravoslavnogo Vostoka* [Description of the liturgical manuscripts kept in the libraries of the Orient]. Vol. 1, *Typika.* Kiev: Tipogrsfija Korchak-Novitskago, 1895.

Domentijan. *Životi Sv. Save i Sv. Simeona* [The Lives of St. Sava and St. Simeon]. Trans. Lazar Mirković. Belgrade: Srpska književna zadruga, 1938.

Epiphanius of Cyprus. *In laudes S. Mariae deiparae (dubia).* In *Patrologia Graeca (PG)* 43, ed. J.-P. Migne, 485–501. Paris: Imprimerie Catholique, 1864.

Eusebius. *Ecclesiastical History.* Vol. 2. Trans. J.E.L. Oulton. Loeb Classical Library 265. Cambridge, MA: Harvard University Press, 2000 [1932 edition].

Evagrius. *The Ecclesiastical History of Evagrius.* Ed. Joseph Bidez and Léon Parmentier. London: Methuen, 1898, repr. Amsterdam: Hakkert, 1964.

Festal Menaion. Ed. Mother Mary and Bishop Kallistos Ware. South Canan, PA: St. Tikhon's Seminary Press, 1998.

Gautier, Paul. "Le typikon de la Théotokos Évergétis." *Revue des études byzantines* 40 (1982): 5–101.

Gautier, Paul. "Le typikon de la Théotokos Kécharitôménè." *Revue des études byzantines* 43 (1985): 109–111.

George (Gennadius) Scholarius. *In festum ingressus beatae Virginis Mariae in templum.* In *Bibliotheca Hagiographica Graeca*, ed. François Halkin. Brussels: Société des Bollanistes, 1957.

George Pachymeres. *De Michaele et Andronico Palaeologis libri tredecim.* Ed. Immanuel Bekker, *Corpus Scriptorum Historiae Byzantina.* Bonn: E. Webber, 1835.

George Pachymeres. *Relations historiques.* Ed. A. Failler and V. Laurent. Vol. 1. Paris: Belles Lettres, 1984.

Germanus of Constantinople, Saint. *In Praesentationem ss. Deipare.* In *Patrologia Graeca (PG)* 98, ed. J.-P. Migne, 290–320. Paris: Imprimerie Catholique, 1865.

Germanus of Constantinople, Saint. *On the Divine Liturgy.* Trans. Paul Meyendorff. Crestwood, NY: St. Vladimir's Seminary Press, 1999 [1984].

BIBLIOGRAPHY   243

Geromeri: Testament of Neilos Erichiotes for the Monastery of the Mother of God Hodegetria in Geromeri. Trans. George Dennis. In *Byzantine Monastic Foundation Documents: A Complete Translation of the Surviving Founders' Typika and Testaments*, ed. John Thomas and Angela Constantinides Hero, 1396–1403. Washington, DC: Dumbarton Oaks Research Library, 2000.

Gregoras, Nikephoros. *Historia byzantine*. Ed. L. Schopen. Vol. 1. Bonn: E. Weber, 1829.

Gregory the Cellarer. *The Life of Lazaros of Mt. Galesion: An Eleventh-Century Pillar Saint*. Intro. and trans. Richard P.H. Greenfield. Washington, DC: Dumbarton Oaks, 2000.

Grigorije Camblak. *Književni rad u Srbiji* [Literary work in Serbia]. Trans. Lazar Mirković. Belgrade: Prosveta, 1989.

Halkin, François. "Un ermite des Balkans au XIVe siècle. La vie grecque inédite de St. Romylos." *Byzantion* 31 (1961): 111–147.

Holy Monastery of Giromeri. *Internet Page of the Holy Monastery of Giromeri on the Internet. The monastery today* [Σελίδα της Ιεράς Μονής Γηρομερίου στο Διαδίκτυο. Η μονή σήμερα]. https://www.monigiromeriou.gr/el/shmera.htm. Accessed June 13, 2017.

Horna, Konstantin, ed. "Die Epigramme des Theodoros Balsamon." *Wiener Studien* 25 (1903): 181–183.

Ioannis Malalae. "Chronographia." In *Corpus Fontium Byzantinae* 35, ed. Ioannes Thurn. Berlin: Walter de Gruyter, 2000.

Irenaeus. *Against Heresies* in *Five Books of S. Irenaeus: Bishop of Lyons, Against Heresies*. Charlton, SC: Nabu Public Domain Reprints, 2010 [originally published by Oxford in 1872].

Jerusalem Pilgrimage, 1099–1185. Trans. John Wilkinson, Joyce Hill, and William Francis Ryan. London: Hakluyt Society, 1988.

John of Damascus. *Three Treatises on the Divine Images*. Trans. Andrew Louth. Crestwood, NY: St. Vladimir's Seminary Press, 2003.

John of Ephesus. *Iohannis Ephesini Historiae Ecclesiasticae Pars Tertia*. Ed. Ernest Walter Brooks, *Corpus scriptorum Christianorum Orientalium* 106, Scr. Syr. 54–55. Louvain: L. Durbecq, 1935–36, repr. 1952.

Josephus Flavius. "Antiquities of the Jews." In *Internet Sacred Texts Archive*, http://sacred-texts.com/jud/josephus/ant-15.htm. Accessed January 10, 2017.

Josephus Flavius. "Jewish Wars." In *Internet Sacred Texts Archive*, http://sacred-texts.com/jud/josephus/war-5.htm. Accessed January 4, 2017.

Khitrovo, Sofija. *Itinéraires russes en Orient*. Geneva: Fick, 1889.

Konstantin Mihajlović iz Ostrovice. *Janičarove uspomene ili turska hronika* [Janissary's memories or Turkish chronicle]. Belgrade: Prosveta, 1986.

244　　　　　　　　　　　　　　　　　　　　　　　　　　　　　　　　　BIBLIOGRAPHY

Lactantius. *De mortibus persecutorum*. In *Corpus Scriptorum Ecclesiasticorum Latinorum*, vol. 19, ed. Samuel Brandt and Georgius Laubmann. Prague/Vienna/Leipzig: F. Tempsky; G Freytag, 1890.

Majeska, George P. *Russian Travelers to Constantinople in the Fourteenth and Fifteenth Centuries*. Washington, DC: Dumbarton Oaks Research Library and Collection, 1984.

Mango, Cyril, and Roger Scott, trans. *The Chronicle of Theophanes Confessor: Byzantine and Near Eastern History* AD *284–813*. Oxford: Clarendon Press, 1997.

Mansi, Giovanni Domenico, ed. *Sacrorum conciliorum nova et amplissima collection*. Vols. 4, 5, 6, and 9. Paris, Leipzig, 1901–1927.

Miklosich, Franz, and Joseph Müller, eds. *Acta et diplomata Graeca medii aevi: sacra et profana, collecta et edita*. Vol. 1. Vienna: Carolus Gerold, 1860.

Millet, Gabriel. "Inscriptions byzantines de Mistra." *Bulletin de correspondence hellénique* 23 (1899): 97–156.

Mishnah Middot 4:7. https://www.sefaria.org/topics/second-temple?tab=sources. Accessed 3 August 3, 2022.

Mišić, Siniša. "Hrisovulja kralja Stefana Dušana Hilandaru kojom prilaže vlastelina Rudla" [The chrysobull by King Stefana Dušana to Hilandar, by which he endows the nobleman Rudle]. *Stari Srpski arhiv* 9 (2010): 75–86.

Papadopoulos-Kerameus, Afanasios, ed. "Vosem' grecheskih opisanij svjatyh mest XIV, XV i XVI vv." [Eight Greek descriptions of the holy places of the 14th, 15th and 16th centuries]. *Pravoslavnyj palestinskij sbornik* 56 (1903): 1–291.

Papadopoulos-Kerameus, Afanasios, and Gabriil Destunis. "Kratkij rasskaz o svjatyh mestah Ierusalima i o Strastjah Gospoda nashego Iisusa Hrista i o drugih bezymjannogo, napisannyj v 1253/4 g." [A short narration about the holy places of Jerusalem and about the Passions of our Lord Jesus Christ and about other things, anonymous, written in 1253/4]. *Pravoslavnyj palestinskij sbornik* 40 (1895): 1–30.

Patriarch Photios. *Epistulae*. 3 vols. Ed. B. Laourdas and L.G. Westerink. Leipzig: Teubner, 1983–85.

Paulinus of Nola. *The Poems of St. Paulinus of Nola*. Trans. P.G. Walsh. New York: Newman Press, 1975.

Petit, Louis. "Le monastère de Notre-Dame de Pitié en Macédoine." *Izvestiya Russkogo arheologicheskogo instituta v Konstantinopole* 6 (1900): 1–153.

Petit, Louis. "Typikon du monastère de la Kosmosotira près d'Aenos (1152)." *Izvestiya Russkogo arheologicheskogo instituta v Konstantinopole* 13 (1908): 17–77.

Predelli, Riccardo, and Bosmin Pietro, eds. *I libri commemoriali della Republica di Venezia: Regestri*. Vol. 5. Venice: A spese della Società, 1901.

Prochorov, Gelian, ed. "'Hozhdenie' igumena Daniila" [The 'pilgrimage' of the Hegoumenos Daniil]. In *Pamjatniki literatury Drevnej Rusi*. XII *vek* (Moscow: Chudozhestvennaya Literatura, 1980), 25–114 (Published at Elektronnye publikacii

BIBLIOGRAPHY 245

Instituta russkoj literatury, http://lib.pushkinskijdom.ru/Default.aspx?tabid=4934#. Accessed 16 June 2021).

Procopius. *Buildings*. Trans. Henry Bronson Dewing and Glanville Downey. Loeb Classical Library, vol. 7. Cambridge, MA: Harvard University Press, 1979.

Prokofiev, Nikolai, ed. *Kniga hozhenij. Zapiski russkih puteshestvennikov* XI–XV *vv.* [The book of pilgrimages. Narrations of the Russian travelers in the 14th to 15th centuries]. Moscow: Sovetskaya Rossiya, 1984.

Prokopije iz Cezareje [Procopius]. *Tajna istorija* [Historia arcana]. Trans. Albin Vilhar, ed. Radivoj Radić. Belgrade: Dereta, 2004.

Psellus, Michael. *Fourteen Byzantine Rulers: The Chronographia of Michael Psellus.* Trans. Edgar R.A. Sewter. London: Penguin Books, 1966.

Schreiner, Peter. *Die Byzantinischen Kleinchroniken*. Corpus Fontium Historiae Byzantinae XII/1, vol. 1. Vienna: Österreichische Akademie der Wissenschaften, 1975.

Schreiner, Peter. *Die Byzantinischen Kleinchroniken*. Corpus Fontium Historiae Byzantinae XII/2, vol. 2. Vienna: Österreichische Akademie der Wissenschaften, 1977.

Sexti Aurelii Victoris. *Liber de Caesatibus, praecedunt Origo gentis Romanae et Liber de viris illustribus urbis Romae, subsequitur Epitome de Caesaribus*, ed. F. Pichlmayr. Leipzig: B.G. Teubneri, 1911.

St. Jerome: Letters and Selected Works. A Select Library of Nicene and Post-Nicene Fathers of the Christian Church. 2nd series, vol. 6. Trans. W.H. Fremantle, G. Lewis and W.G. Martley, ed. Philip Schaff and Henry Wace. New York: The Christian Literature Company, 1893.

Synaxarium Ecclesiae Constantinopolitanae e Codice Sirmondiano Nunc Berolinensi. Ed. Hippolyte Delehaye. Brussels: Socios Bollandianos, 1902.

Syrku, Polichronij, ed. *Monaha Grigorija zhitije prepodobnogo Romila* [The Life of venerable Romyl by Monk Gregory]. St. Petersburg: Tipografija Imperatorskoj Akademii Nauk, 1900.

Tarasius of Constantinople. *In* SS. *Dei Matrem in Templum Deductam*. In *Patrologia Graeca* (PG) 98, ed. J.-P. Migne, 1481–1496. Paris: Imprimerie Catholique, 1865.

Theophanes Continuatus. Ed. Immanuel Bekker (Bonn: Weber, 1838), 211–355, trans. Cyril Mango, in *The Art of the Byzantine Empire 312–1453: Sources and Documents*, 192–193. Engelwood Cliffs, NJ: Prentice-Hall, 1972.

Tractate Taanit. http://www.jewishvirtuallibrary.org/jsource/Talmud/taanit4.html. Accessed August 14, 2013.

Vitruvius. *Ten Books on Architecture*. Trans. Ingrid D. Rowland, commentary and illustrations Thomas Noble Howe, with additional commentary by Ingrid D. Rowland and Micheal J. Dewar. Cambridge and New York: Cambridge University Press, 1999.

William Durandus. *The Symbolism of Churches and Church Ornaments: A Translation of the First Book of the* Rationale Divinorum Officiorum. New York: Charles Scribner's Sons, 1893 [also "William Durandus from *The Symbolism of Churches and Church Ornaments* (1286)" in *Architectural Theory*, vol. 1., *An Anthology from Vitruvius to 1870*, ed. Harry Francis Mallgrave (Malden, MA/Oxford: Blackwell Publishing, 2006), 24–25].

Secondary Literature

Abou-El-Haj, Barbara. *The Medieval Cult of Saints: Formations and Transformations.* Cambridge: Cambridge University Press, 1994.

Adams, Tim. "Benoît Goetz: A French Reader of Rykwert's on Adam's House in Paradise." *Interstices: A Journal of Architecture and Related Arts* 10 (2009): 87–96.

Adams, William Y. "Archaeological Classification: Theory Versus Practice." *Antiquity* 62 (1988): 40–56.

Adams, William Y., and Ernest W. Adams. *Archaeological Typology and Practical Reality: A Dialectical Approach to Artifact Classification and Sorting.* Cambridge: Cambridge University Press, 2007.

Alexander, Suzanne Spain. "Heraclius, Byzantine Imperial Ideology and the David Plates." *Speculum* 52, no. 2 (1977): 217–237.

Alföldi, Andreas. "Die Ausgestaltung des monarchischen Zeremoniells am römischen Kaiserhof." *Mitteilungen des Deutschen Archäologischen Instituts, Römische Abteilung* 49 (1934): 1–118.

Alföldi, Andreas. "Insignien und Tracht der römischen Kaiser." *Mitteilungen des Deutschen Archäologischen Instituts, Römische Abteilung* 50 (1935): 1–171.

Alföldi, Maria R. *Die constantinische Goldprägung: Untersuchungen zu ihrer Bedeutung für Kaiserpolitik und Hofkunst.* Mainz: Philipp von Zabern, 1963.

Alföldi-Rosenbaum, Elisabeth. "Portrait Bust of a Young Lady of the Time of Justinian." *Metropolitan Museum Journal* 1 (1968): 19–40.

Allen, Pauline. "Contemporary Portrayals of the Byzantine Empress Theodora (of AD 527–48)." In *Stereotypes of Women in Power: Historical Perspectives and Revisionist Views*, ed. Barbara Garlick, Suzanne Dixon, and Pauline Allen, 93–104. New York/London: Greenwood Press, 1992.

Anagnostakes, Elias. "Apo tēn eikona tēs monachēs Euphrosynēs ston bio tōn Hosiōn tou Megalou Spēlaiou: Ē istoria mias kataskeuēs" [From the image of nun Euphrosyne to the Life of the saints of Megale Spelaion: The history of one foundation]. In *Monachismos stēn Peloponnēso, 4os–15os ai.*, ed. Boula Konti, 171–189. Athens: Institute for Byzantine Research, 2004.

Anđelković Grašar, Jelena. *Femina Antica Balcanica*. Belgrade: Arheološki institut, Evoluta, 2020.

Anđelković Grašar, Jelena. "Image as a Way of Self-Representation, Association and Type Creation for Late Antique Women in the Central Balkans." In *Vivere Militare Est: From Populus to Emperors—Living on the Frontier*, vol. 1, ed. Snežana Golubović and Nemanja Mrđić, 333–364. Belgrade: Institute of Archaeology, 2018.

Anđelković Grašar, Jelena, and Emilija Nikolić. "Stereotypes as Prototypes in the Perception of Women: A Few Remarks from History and Folk Tradition." *Archaeology and Science* 13 (2018): 89–107.

Angelidi, Christine. "Un texte patriographique et édifiant: Le 'Discours narratif' sur les Hodègoi." *Revue des études byzantines* 52 (1994): 113–149.

Angelidi, Christine, and Titos Papamastorakis. "Picturing the Spiritual Protector: From Blachernitissa to Hodegetria." In *Images of the Mother of God: Perceptions of the Theotokos in Byzantium*, ed. Maria Vassilaki, 209–223. Aldershot: Ashgate, 2005.

Angelidi, Christine, and Titos Papamastorakis. "The Veneration of the Virgin Hodegetria and the Hodegon Monastery." In *Mother of God: Representations of the Virgin in Byzantine Art*, ed. Maria Vassilaki, 373–387. Athens: Benaki Museum, 2000.

Angelova, Diliana. "The Ivories of Ariadne and Ideas about Female Imperial Authority in Rome and Early Byzantium." *Gesta* 43, no. 1 (2004): 1–15.

Angelova, Diliana. *Sacred Founders: Women, Men, and Gods in the Discourse of Imperial Founding, Rome through Early Byzantium*. Berkeley: University of California Press, 2015.

Angenendt, Arnold. "Corpus incorruptum: Eine Leitidee der mittelalterlichen Reliquienverehrung." *Saeculum* 42 (1991): 320–346.

Angenendt, Arnold. *Heilige und Reliquien. Die Geschichte ihres Kultes vom frühen Christentum bis zur Gegenwart*. Munich: Nikol, 1997.

Angenendt, Arnold. "Relics and Their Veneration." In *Treasures of Heaven: Saints, Relics, and Devotion in Medieval Europe*, ed. Martina Bagnoli et al., 19–29. New Haven: Yale University Press, 2011.

Angenendt, Arnold. "Zur Ehre der Altäre erhoben: Zugleich ein Beitrag zur Reliquienverehrung." *Römishe Quartalschrift für christliche Altertumskunde* 89 (1994): 221–244.

Arce, Javier. *Funus imperatorum. Los funerales de los emperadores romanos*. Madrid: Alianza, 1988.

Arce, Javier. "Un grupo de situlas decoradas del la Antigüedad tardía: función, cronología, significado." *Antiquité tardive* 13 (2005): 141–158.

Argan, Gulio Carlo. "On the Typology of Architecture." In *Theorizing a New Agenda for Architecture*, ed. Kate Nesbitt, 242–246. New York: Princeton Architectural Press, 1996.

Armstrong, Christopher Drew. "French Architectural Thought and the Idea of Greece." In *A Companion to Greek Architecture*, ed. Margaret Melanie Miles, 487–506. Chichester, West Sussex: John Wiley and Sons, 2016.

Arnaud, Pascal. "L'image du globe dans le monde romain: science, iconographie, symbolisme." *Mélanges de l'École française de Rome. Antiquité* 96, no. 1 (1984): 53–116.

Athanasiadou-Bentoure, Despoina, and Georgos Bentoures. *Kimōlos: Ho topos. Hoi ekklēsies. Hosia Methodia* [Kimolos: The Place. The Churches. Holy Methodia]. Kimolos: Dēmos Kimōlos, 2013.

Avi-Yonah, Michael. "The Facade of Herod's Temple: An Attempted Reconstruction." In *Religions in Antiquity: Essays in Memory of Erwin Ramsdell Goodenough*, ed. Jacob Neusner, 326–335. Leiden: Brill, 1968.

Avi-Yonah, Michael. *Pictorial Guide to the Model of Ancient Jerusalem at the Time of the Second Temple*. Jerusalem: Palphot, 2003.

Babić, Gordana. "O živopisanom ukrasu oltarskih pregrada" [On the painted ornamentation of altar screens]. *Zbornik za likovne umetnosti* 11 (1975): 3–41.

Babić, Gordana. "Les images byzantines et leurs degres de signification: l'exemple de l'Hodigitria." In *Byzance et les images: Cycle de conferences organise au musee du Louvre par le Service culturel du 5 octobre au 7 decembre 1992*, ed. A. Guillou and J. Durand, 189–222. Paris: Musée du Louvre, 1994.

Bacci, Michele. *Il pennello dell'Evangelista*. Pisa: GISEM, 1994.

Bacci, Michele. "The Legacy of the Hodegetria: Holy Icons and Legends between East and West." In *Images of the Mother of God: Perceptions of the Theotokos in Byzantium*, ed. Maria Vassilaki, 321–336. Aldershot: Ashgate, 2005.

Bacci, Michele. *The Many Faces of Christ: Portraying the Holy in the East and West, 300–1300*. London: Reaktion Books, 2014.

Bacci, Michele. "With the Paintbrush of the Evangelist Luke." In *Mother of God: Representations of the Virgin in Byzantine Art*, ed. Maria Vassilaki, 79–89. Athens: Benaki Museum, 2000.

Baert, Barbara. *A Heritage of Holy Wood: The Legend of the True Cross in Text and Image*. Leiden: Brill, 2004.

Bagnall, Roger S., Alan D.E. Cameron, Seith R. Schwartz, and Klaas A. Worp. *Consuls of the Later Roman Empire*. Atlanta: American Philological Association, 1987.

Bagnoli, Martina, et al., eds. *Treasures of Heaven. Saints, Relics, and Devotion in Medieval Europe*. New Haven: Yale University Press, 2011.

Balakirtsky-Katz, Maya. "Avi Yonah's Model of Second Temple Jerusalem and the Development of Israeli Visual Culture." In *The Temple of Jerusalem: From Moses to Messiah*, ed. Steven Fine, 349–365. Leiden: Brill, 2011.

Bandmann, Günter. "Beobachtungen zum Etschmiadzin-Evangeliar." In *Tortulae. Studien zu altchristlichen und byzantinischen Monumenten*, ed. Walter Nikolaus Schumacher, 11–29. Rome: Herder, 1966.

BIBLIOGRAPHY 249

Bandmann, Günter. *Early Medieval Architecture as Bearer of Meaning*, trans. Kendall Wallis. New York: Columbia University Press, 2005.

Barber, Charles. *Contesting the Logic of Painting: Art and Understanding in Eleventh-Century Byzantium*. Leiden: Brill, 2007.

Barber, Charles. *Figure and Likeness: On the Limits of Representation in Byzantine Iconoclasm*. Princeton: Princeton University Press, 2002.

Barker, Margaret. *The Great High Priest: The Temple Roots of Christian Theology*. London/New York: T&T Clark/Continuum, 2003.

Barnes, Timothy D. *The New Empire of Diocletian and Constantine*. London: Harvard University Press, 1982.

Barnish, S.J.B. "Transformation and Survival in the Western Senatorial Aristocracy, c. A.D. 400–700." *Papers of the British School at Rome* 56 (1988): 120–155.

Batterman, Michael A. "The Emergence of the Spanish Illuminated Haggadah Manuscripts." PhD dissertation, Northwestern University, Illinois, 2000.

Batterman, Michael A. "Genesis in Vienna: The Sarajevo Haggadah and the Invention of Jewish Art." In *Image: Manuscripts, Artists, Audiences: Essays in Honor of Sandra Hindman*, ed. David S. Areford and Nina Rowe, 309–327. London: Ashgate, 2004.

Baudinet, Marie-José. "La relation iconique à Byzance au IXe siècle d'après les Antir-rhétiques de Nicéphore le Patriarche: un destin de l'aristotélisme." *Etudes philosophiques* 1 (1978): 85–106.

Bauer, Franz Alto. *Stadt, Platz und Denkmal in der Spätantike: Untersuchungen zur Ausstattung des öffentlichen Raums in den spätantiken Städten Rom, Konstantinopel und Ephesos*. Mainz: Philipp von Zabern, 1996.

Bellinger, Alfred R. *Catalogue of the Byzantine Coins in the Dumbarton Oaks Collection and in the Whittemore Collection*. Vol. 1, *Anastasius I to Maurice (491–602)*. Washington, DC: Dumbarton Oaks, 1966.

Belting, Hans. *Likeness and Presence: A History of the Image Before the Era of Art*. 2nd ed. Chicago: Chicago University Press, 1996.

Benoist, Stéphane. *Rome, le prince et la Cité. Pouvoir impérial et cérémonies publiques (1er siècle av.–début du IVe siècle apr. J.-C.)*. Paris: Presses universitaires de France, 2005.

Bergdoll, Barry. *European Architecture 1750–1890*. Oxford: Oxford University Press, 2000.

Berrens, Stephan. *Sonnenkult und Kaisertum von den Severen bis zu Constantin I. (193–337 n. Chr.)*. Stuttgart: Steiner, 2004.

Biddle, Martin. *The Tomb of Christ*. Stroud: Sutton Publishing, 1999.

Birtašević, Marija. "Jedan vizantijski žižak iz arheološke zbirke Muzeja grada Beograda" [An early Byzantine oil lamp from the archaeological collection of the Belgrade City Museum]. *Godišnjak Muzeja grada Beograda* 2 (1955): 43–46.

Bland, Kalman. *The Artless Jew: Medieval and Modern Affirmation and Denial of the Visual*. Princeton: Princeton University Press, 2001.

Bland, Kalman. "*Medieval Jewish Aesthetics: Maimonides, Body, and Scripture in Profiat Duran.*" *Journal of the History of Ideas* 54, no. 4 (1993): 533–559.

Bogdanović, Dimitrije, et al. *Chilandar*. Belgrade: Monastery of Chilandar in cooperation with Jugoslovenska revija, 1997.

Bogdanović, Dimitrije, Vojislav J. Djurić, and Dejan Medaković. *Manastir Hilandar* [Hilandar monastery]. Belgrade: Jugoslovenska revija, 1997.

Bogdanović, Jelena. "Byzantine Constantinople: Architecture." In *Routledge Handbook of Istanbul*, ed. Kate Fleet (forthcoming).

Bogdanović, Jelena. "Framing Glorious Spaces in the Monastery of Hosios Loukas." In *Perceptions of the Body and Sacred Space in Late Antiquity and Byzantium*, ed. Jelena Bogdanović, 166–189. New York/London: Routledge, 2018.

Bogdanović, Jelena. *The Framing of Sacred Space: The Canopy and the Byzantine Church.* New York: Oxford University Press, 2017.

Bogdanović, Jelena. "The Original Tomb of St Simeon and its Significance for the Architectural History of Hilandar Monastery." *Hilandarski zbornik* 12 (2008): 35–56.

Bogdanović, Jelena. "The Performativity of Shrines in a Byzantine Church: The Shrine of St. Demetrios Performativity in Byzantium and Medieval Russia." In *Spatial Icons: Performativity in Byzantium and Medieval Russia*, ed. Alexei Lidov, 275–301. Moscow: Indrik, 2011.

Bogdanović, Jelena. "Rethinking the Dionysian Legacy in Medieval Architecture: East and West." In *Dionysius the Areopagite: Between Orthodoxy and Heresy*, ed. Filip Ivanović, 109–134. Newcastle Upon Tyne: Cambridge Scholars, 2011.

Bogdanović, Jelena. "The Rhetoric of Architecture in the Byzantine context: The Case Study of the Holy Sepulchre." *Zograf* 38 (2014): 1–21.

Bolten, Johannes. *Die Imago Clipeata. Ein Beitrag zur Porträt- und Typengeschichte*. Paderborn: F. Schöningh, 1937.

Borboudakis, Manuel. "Oi toichographies tēs Panaias tou Merōna kai mia synkekrimenē tasē tēs krētikēs zōgraphikēs" [The murals of Panagia Meronas and one specific tendency in Cretan painting]. In *Pepragmena E' Diethnous Krētologikou Synedriou*, 396–412. Herakleion: Hetairia Krētikōn Historikōn Meletōn, 1986.

Borg, Alan. "The Lost Mosaic of the Holy Sepulchre, Jerusalem." In *The Vanishing Past: Studies in Medieval Art, Liturgy and Metrology Presented to Christopher Hohler*, ed. Alan Borg and Andrew Martindale, 7–12. Oxford: British Archaeological Reports, International Series 111, 1981.

Boschung, Dietrich. *Antike Grabaltäre aus den Nekropolen Roms*. Bern: Stämpfli, 1987.

Boschung, Dietrich. "Kultbilder als Vermittler religiöser Vorstellungen." In *Kult und Kommunikation: Medien in Heiligtümern der Antike*, ed. Christian Frevel and Henner von Hesberg, 63–87. Wiesbaden: Reichert, 2007.

Bošković, Aleksandar. *Kratak uvod u antropologiju* [A brief introduction to anthropology]. Zagreb: Naklada Jesenski i Turk, 2010.

BIBLIOGRAPHY 251

Boss, Sarah Jane. *Empress and Handmaid: On Nature and Gender in the Cult of the Virgin Mary*. London: Cassel, 2000.

Bouras, Charalambos. *Chios*. Athens: National Bank of Greece, 1974.

Bouras, Charalambos. "Hē Architektonikē tēs Panagias ton Mouchliou stēn Kōnstantinoupoli" [The architecture of Panagia Mouchliou in Constantinople], *Deltion tēs Christianikēs Archailogikēs Hetaireias* 4, no. 26 (2005): 35–50.

Bouras, Charalambos. *Nea Moni on Chios: History and Architecture*. Athens: The Commercial Bank of Greece, 1982.

Bouras, Charalambos. "Twelfth and Thirteenth Century Variations of the Single Domed Octagon Plan." *Deltion tēs Christianikēs Archailogikēs Hetaireias* 9 (1977–79): 21–32.

Bowes, Kim. "Ivory Lists: Consular Diptychs, Christian Approbation and Polemics of Time in Late Antiquity." *Art History* 24/3 (2001): 338–357.

Bowman, Thorleif. *Hebrew Thought Compared with Greek*. London: SCM Press, 1960.

Bozóky, Edina, and Anne-Marie Helvétius, eds. *Les reliques: objets, cultes, symboles: actes du colloque international de l'Université du Littoral-Côte d'Opale, Boulogne-sur-Mer, 4–6 septembre 1997*. Turnhout: Brepols, 1999.

Brayer, Edith, Paul Lemerle, and Vitalien Laurent. "Le Vaticanus latinus 4789: histoire et alliances des Cantacuzènes aux XIVe–XVe Siècles." *Revue des études byzantines* 9 (1951): 47–105.

Bresc-Bautier, Geneviève. "La dévotion au Saint-Sépulcre de Jérusalem en Occident: imitations, invocation, donations." *Cahiers de Saint-Michel de Cuxa* 38 (2007): 95–106.

Bresc-Bautier, Geneviève. "Les imitations du Saint-Sepulcre de Jerusalem (IXe–XVe siècles): archéologie d'une devotion." *Revue d'histoire de la spiritualite* 50 (1974): 319–342.

Brilliant, Richard. *Gesture and Rank in Roman Art*. New Haven: Academy, 1963.

Broderick, Herbert. "Observation on the Creation Cycle of the Sarajevo Haggadah." *Zeitschrift zu Kunstgeschichte* 47, no. 3 (1984): 320–332.

Broek, Roel van den. *The Myth of the Phoenix According to Classical and Early Christian Tradition*. Leiden: Brill, 1972.

Brown, Peter. *The Cult of the Saints: Its Rise and Function in Latin Christianity*. Chicago: University of Chicago Press, 1981.

Brubaker, Leslie. "The Chalke Gate, the Construction of the Past, and the Trier Ivory." *Byzantine and Modern Greek Studies* 23 (1999): 258–285.

Brubaker, Leslie. "Memories of Helena: Patterns in Imperial Female Matronage in the Fourth and Fifth Centuries." In *Women, Men and Eunuchs: Gender in Byzantium*, ed. Liz James, 52–75. London/New York: Routledge, 1997.

Brubaker, Leslie. "Sex, Lies and Textuality: The Sacred History of Prokopios and the Rhetoric of Gender in Sixth-Century Byzantium." In *Gender in the Early Medieval*

World: East and West, 300–900, ed. Leslie Brubaker and Julia M.H. Smith, 83–101. Cambridge: Cambridge University Press, 2004.

Brubaker, Leslie, and Helen Tobler. "The Gender of Money: Byzantine Empresses on Coins." In *Gender & History* 12, no. 3 (2000): 572–594.

Bruun, Patrick M. "Constantine and Licinius A.D. 313–337." In *The Imperial Roman Coinage* 7, ed. Carol Humphrey, Vivian Sutherland, and Robert A. Carson. London: Spink and Son Ltd., 1966.

Buchwald, Hans. "The Concept of Style in Byzantine Architecture." In *Form, Style and Meaning in Byzantine Church Architecture*. Aldershot: Ashgate, 1999.

Bulgakov, Sergius. *Relics and Miracles: Two Theological Essays*. Trans. Boris Jakim. Grand Rapids, Michigan: William B. Eerdmans Publishing Company, 2011.

Butler, Alban. *The Lives of the Fathers, Martyrs, and Other Principal Saints*. Vol. 1. Dublin: H. Coyne, 1833.

Bynum, Caroline W. *The Resurrection of the Body in Western Christianity, 200–1336*. New York: Columbia University Press, 1995.

Calza, Raissa. *Iconografia romana imperiale da Carausio a Giuliano (287–363 d. C.)*. Rome: L'Erma di Bretschneider, 1972.

Cameron, Alan D.E. "The house of Anastasius." *Greek Roman and Byzantine Studies* 19 (1978): 259–276.

Cameron, Averil. "The Artistic Patronage of Justin II." *Byzantion* 50 (1980): 62–84.

Cameron, Averil. "The Empress Sophia." *Byzantion* 45 (1975): 5–21.

Cameron, Averil, and Judith Herrin. *Constantinople in the Early Eighth Century: The Parastaseis Syntomoi Chronikai*. Leiden: Brill, 1984.

Čanak-Medić, Milka. *Manastir Dečani. Saborna crkva. Arhitektura* [Monastery Dečani. Cathedral church. Architecture]. Belgrade: Republički zavod za zaštitu spomenkika kulture, 2007.

Capizzi, Carmelo. *L'imperatore Anastasio I (491–518). Studio sulla sua vita, la sua opera e la sua personalità*. Rome: Pont. Institutum orientalum studiorum, 1969.

Carile, Antonio. "Credunt aliud Romana palatia caelum. Die Ideologie der PALATIUM in Konstantinopel, den Neuen Rom." In *Palatia. Kaiserpaläste in Konstantinopel, Ravenna und Trier*, ed. Margarethe König, Eugenia Bolognesi Recchi-Franceschini, and Ellen Riemer, 27–32. Trier: Rheinisches Landesmuseum, 2003.

Carile, Maria Cristina. *The Vision of the Palace of the Byzantine Emperors as a Heavenly Jerusalem*. Spoleto: Fondazione Centro italiano di studi sull'alto Medioevo, 2012.

Carile, Maria Cristina, and Eelco Nagelsmit. "Iconography, Iconology." In *Encyclopedia of the Bible and Its Reception*, vol. 12, ed. Constance Furey, Steven Linn McKenzie, Thomas Chr. Römer, Jens Schröter, Barry Dov Walfish, and Eric Ziolkowski, 778–783. Berlin: De Gruyter, 2016.

BIBLIOGRAPHY

Carr, Annmarie Weyl. "Court Culture and Cult Icons in Middle Byzantine Constantinople." In *Byzantine Court Culture from 829 to 1204*, ed. Henry Maguire, 81–99. Washington, DC: Dumbarton Oaks Research Library, 1997.

Carr, Annmarie Weyl. "Reflections on the Life of an Icon: the Eleousa of Kikkos." *Epetērida Kentrou Meletōn Ieras Monēs Kykkou* 6 (2004): 103–162.

Carr, Annemarie Weyl. "The Thirteenth-Century Murals of Lysi." In *A Byzantine Masterpiece Recovered: the Thirteenth-Century Murals of Lysi, Cyprus*, ed. Annemarie Weyl Carr and Laurence. J. Morrocco, 15–113. Austin: University of Texas Press, 1991.

Carroll, Michael P. *The Cult of the Virgin Mary: Psychological Origins*. Princeton: Princeton University Press, 1992.

Cartlidge, David R., and J.K. Elliott. *Art of Christian Legend: Visual Representations of the New Testament Apocrypha*. London/New York: Routledge, 2001.

Caseau, Béatrice. "The Senses in Religion: Liturgy, Devotion, and Deprivation." In *A Cultural History of the Senses in the Middle Ages*, ed. Richard G. Newhauser, 89–110. Oxford: Bloomsbury Academic, 2014.

Cermanović-Kuzmanović, Aleksandrina. "Jedna kameja iz Ćuprije" [A cameo from Ćuprija]. *Zbornik filozofskog fakulteta* 7, no. 1 (1963): 119–125.

Chatzidakis, Manolis. *Mystras: The Medieval City and the Castle*. Athens: Ekdotike Athenes, 1981.

Chatzidakis, Manuel, and Manuel Borboudakis, *Eikonēs tēs krētikēs technē: apo ton Chandaka ōs tēn Moscha kai tēn Hagia Patroupolē* [Icons of the Cretan School from Candia to Moscow and St. Petersburg]. Exhibition catalogue (Herakleion: Vikelea Dimotiki vivliothiki, 2004 [1993]).

Chelli, Maurizio. *Manuale dei simboli nell'arte. L'era paleocristiana e bizantina*. Rome: EdUP, 2008.

Cohen, Mordechai. "Interpreting the Resting of the *Shekhinah*: Exegetical Implications of the Theological Debate among Maimonides, Nahmanides and Sefe Ha-Hinnukh." In *The Temple of Jerusalem: From Moses to Messiah*, ed. Steven Fine, 237–275. Leiden: Brill, 2011.

Cohen, Richard I. *Jewish Icons: Art and Society in Modern Europe*. Berkeley/Los Angeles: University of California Press, 1998.

Conant, Kenneth J. "The After-Life of Vitruvius in the Middle Ages." *Journal of the Society of Architectural Historians* 27, no. 1 (1968): 33–38.

Constantinides, Efthalia C. *The Wall Paintings of the Panagia Olympiotissa*. 2 vols. Athens: Canadian Institute of Archeology in Athens, 1992.

Constas, Maximos. "Dionysius the Areopagite and the New Testament." In *The Oxford Handbook of Dionysius the Areopagite*, ed. Mark Edwards, Dimitrios Pallis, and Georgios Steiris, 48–63. New York: Oxford University Press, 2022.

Constas, P. Nicholas. "Symeon of Thessalonike and the Theology of the Icon Screen." In *Threshold of the Sacred*, ed. Sharon E.J. Gerstel, 163–185. Washington, DC: Dumbarton Oaks Research Library and Collection, 2006.

Coon, Lynda L. *Sacred Fictions: Holy Women and Hagiography in Late Antiquity.* Philadelphia: University of Pennsylvania Press, 1997.

Cormack, Robert, and Maria Vassilaki, eds. *Byzantium 330–1453. Royal Academy of Arts, London, 25 October 2008–22 March 2009.* London: Royal Academy of Arts, 2008.

Ćorović, Vladimir. "Prilog proučavanju načina sahranjivanja i podizanja nadgrobnih spomenika u našim krajevima u srednjem veku" [Contribution to the study of the method of burial and erecting of gravestones in our region in the Middle Ages]. *Naše starine* 3 (1956): 127–147.

Ćorović-Ljubinković, Mirjana. *Srednjovekovni duborez u istočnim oblastima Jugoslavije* [Medieval woodcut sculpture in the eastern regions of Yugoslavia]. Belgrade: Arheološki institut-posebna izdanja 5, 1965.

Courtois, Christian. "Exconsul. Observations sur l'histoire du consulat à l'époque byzantine." *Byzantion* 19 (1949): 37–58.

Cox Miller, Patricia. "Figuring Relics: A Poetics of Enshrinement." In *Saints and Sacred Matter: The Cult of Relics in Byzantium and Beyond*, ed. Cynthia Hahn and Holger A. Klein, 99–109. Washington, DC: Dumbarton Oaks Research Library and Collection, 2015.

Crosby, Vanessa. "Imagined Architectures and Visual Exegesis: Temple Imagery in the Illuminated Manuscripts of the Iberian Jews." *Journal of the Australian Early Medieval Association* 2 (2006): 43–55.

Cumont, Franz. *Recherches sur le symbolisme funéraire des romains.* Paris: Geuthner, 1942.

Ćurčić, Slobodan. "Architectural Reconsideration of the Nea Ekklesia." *Byzantine Studies Conference Abstracts* 6 (1980): 11–12.

Ćurčić, Slobodan. "Architectural Significance of the Subsidiary Chapels in Middle Byzantine Churches." *Journal of the Society of Architectural Historians* 36, no. 3 (1977): 94–110.

Ćurčić, Slobodan. "Architecture as Icon." In *Architecture as Icon: Perception and Representation of Architecture in Byzantine Art*, ed. Slobodan Ćurčić and Evangelia Hadjitryphonos, 3–39. New Haven: Yale University Press, 2010.

Ćurčić, Slobodan. *Architecture of the Balkans from Diocletian to Süleyman the Magnificent.* New Haven/London: Yale University Press, 2010.

Ćurčić, Slobodan. *Gračanica. Istorija i arhitektura* [Gračanica. History and architecture]. Belgrade: Cicero, 1999.

Ćurčić, Slobodan. *Gračanica: King Milutin's Church and Its Place in Late Byzantine Architecture.* University Park, PA: Pennsylvania State University Press, 1979.

Cutler, Anthony. "The Making of Justinian's Diptychs." *Byzantion* 54 (1984): 75–115.

BIBLIOGRAPHY

Dalgıç, Örgü, and Thomas F. Mathews. "A New Interpretation of the Church of Peribleptos and Its Place in Middle Byzantine Architecture." In *The First International Sevgi Gönül Byzantine Studies Symposium, Istanbul 2007*, 424–431. Istanbul: Vehbi Koç Vakfı, 2010.

Danielou, Jean. *From Shadows to Reality: Studies in Biblical Typology of the Fathers.* Westminster: Newman Press, 1960.

Danthine, Hélène. "L'imagerie des trônes vides et des trônes porteurs de symboles dans le Proche-Orient ancient." In *Mélanges syriens offerts à René Dussaud*, vol. 2, 857–866. Paris: Librairie Orientaliste Paul Geuthner, 1939.

Dark, Ken R., and Jan Kostenec. *Hagia Sophia Project: 2004–2007 Survey Seasons.* Prague: Univerzita Karlova, 2012. http://ukar.ff.cuni.cz/node/160.

Darrouzès, Jean. "Notes pour servir à l'histoire de Chypre (deuxième article)." *Kypriakai Spoudai* 20 (1956): 31–63.

Darrouzès, Jean. "Notes pour servir à l'histoire de Chypre (premier article)." *Kypriakai Spoudai* 17 (1953): 89–90.

Darrouzès, Jean. *Les regestes des actes du Patriarcat de Constantinople.* Vol. 1, fasc. 5, *Les regestes de 1310 à 1376.* Paris: Institut français d'études byzantines, 1977.

Darrouzès, Jean. "Sainte-Sophie de Thessalonique d'après un rituel." *Revue des études byzantines* 34 (1976): 45–78.

Davies, Glenys. "The Door Motif in Roman Funerary Sculpture." In *Papers in Italian Archaeology, 1. The Lancaster Seminar: Recent Research in Prehistoric, Classical, and Medieval Archaeology*, ed. Hugo McK. Blake, Timothy W. Potter, and David B. Whitehouse, 203–226. Oxford: John and Erica Hedges, 1978.

De Blaauw, Sible. "Imperial Connotations in Roman Church Interiors. The Significance and Effect of the Lateran *Fastigium*." In *Imperial Art as Christian Art—Christian Art as Imperial Art. Expression and Meaning in Art and Architecture from Constantine to Justinian*, ed. J. Rasmus Brandt and Olaf Steen, 137–146. Rome: Bardi, 2001.

Deér, Josef. "Der Globus der spätrömischen und byzantinischen Kaisers. Symbol oder Insignie?" *Byzantinische Zeitschrift* 54 (1961): 291–318.

Deér, Josef. *The Dynastic Porphyry Tombs of the Norman Period in Sicily.* Cambridge: Harvard University Press, 1959.

Degrassi, Attilio. *I fasti consolari dell'impero romano dal 30 avanti Cristo al 613 dopo Cristo.* Rome: Edizioni di Storia e Letteratura, 1952.

Deichmann, Friedrich Wilhelm, Giuseppe Bovini and Hugo Brandenburg. *Repertorium der christlich-antiken Sarkophage, 1. Rom und Ostia.* Wiesbaden: Franz Steiner Verlag, 1967.

Delbrueck, Richard. *Die Consulardiptychen und verwandte Denkmäler.* Berlin/Leipzig: De Gruyter, 1929.

Delbrueck, Richard. *Spätantike Kaiserportäts.* Berlin: De Gruyter, 1933.

Delehaye, Hippolyte. *The Legends of the Saints.* London: Longman, 1907.

della Dora, Veronica. *Landscape, Nature, and the Sacred in Byzantium*. Cambridge: Cambridge University Press, 2016.

Demangel, Robert, and Ernest Mamboury. *Le quartier des Manganes et la première region de Constantinople*. Paris: Boccard, 1939.

Demus, Otto. "The Ideal Iconographic Scheme of the Cross-in-Square Church." In *Byzantine Mosaic Decoration: Aspects of Monumental Art in Byzantium*, 14–16. Boston: Boston Book & Art Shop, 1955.

der Parthog, Gwynneth. *Medieval Cyprus: A Guide to the Byzantine and Latin Monuments*. Lefkosia: Moufflon Publications, 2006.

Dey, Hendrik W. *The Afterlife of the Roman City: Architecture and Ceremony in Late Antiquity and the Early Middle Ages*. New York: Cambridge University Press, 2015.

DiCenso, James J. "The Concept of Urbild in Kant's Philosophy of Religion." *Kant-Studien* 104, no. 1 (2013): 100–132.

Dietl, Albert. "Sabine Schrenk, Typos und Antitypos in der frühchristlichen Kunst (Jahrbuch für Antike und Christentum, Erg.-Bd.21), Münster 1995." *Journal für Kunstgeschichte* 2, no. 2 (1998): 121–125.

Dittelbach, Thomas. "La chiesa inferiore." In *La Cappella Palatina a Palermo*, ed. Beat Brenk, 283–293. Modena: Panini Editore, 2010.

Djordjević, Ivan M. "Dve Molitve Stefana Dečanskog pre bitke na Velbuždu i njegov odjek u umetnosti" [Two prayers of Stefan Dečansky before the Battle of Velbuzd and his echo in art]. *Zbornik za likovne umetnosti* 15 (1979): 135–150.

Djordjević, Ivan M. "Predstava Stefana Dečanskog uz oltarsku pregradu u Dečanima" [The representation of Stefan Dečanski near the altar partition in Dečani]. *Saopštenja* 15 (1983): 35–42.

Djurić, Vojislav J. "Ravanički živopis i liturgija" [The murals and liturgy of Ravanica]. In *Manastir Ravanica—spomenica o šestoj stogodišnjici*, ed. Branislav Živković, 60–75. Belgrade: Izdanje Manastira Ravanice, 1981.

Djurić, Vojislav. "Sveti pokroviteli arhiepiskopa Danila II i njegovih zadužbina" [Holy Patrons of the Archbishop Danilo II and his foundations]. In *Arhiepiskop Danilo II i njegovo doba*, ed. Vojislav Djurić, 281–294. Belgrade: SANU, 1991.

Doig, Allan. *Liturgy and Architecture: From Early Church to Middle Ages*. Burlington, VT: Ashgate, 2008.

Donati, Angela, and Giovanni Gentili, eds. *Constantino il Grande. La civiltà antica al bivio tra Occidente e Oriente*. Milan: Silvana Editoriale, 2005.

Drandakis, Nikolaos. *Byzantines toichografies tēs Mesa Manēs* [Byzantine murals of Inner Mani]. Athens: Archaiologiki Etaireia, 1995.

Drijvers, Jan Willem. "Flavia Maxima Fausta: Some Remarks." *Historia* 41, no. 4 (1992): 500–506.

Drijvers, Jan Willem. "Helena Augusta: Cross and Myth. Some New Reflections." In *Millennium 8. Yearbook on the Culture and History of the First Millennium C.E.*, ed. Wolfram Brandes, 125–174. Berlin: De Gruyter Mouton, 2011.

Drijvers, Jan Willem. "Helena Augusta: Exemplary Christian Empress." *Studia Patristica* 24 (1993): 85–90.

Drijvers, Jan Willem. *Helena Augusta: The Mother of Constantine the Great, and the Legend of her Finding of the True Cross*. Leiden: Brill, 1992.

Dufraigne, Pierre. *Adventus Augusti, Adventus Christi: recherche sur l'exploitation idéologique et littéraire d'un cérémonial dans l'Antiquité tardive*. Paris: Institut d'études augustiniennes, 1994.

Dumser, Elisha Ann. "The AETERNAE MEMORIAE Coinage of Maxentius: An Issue of Symbolic Intent." *Journal of Roman Archaeology* Suppl. 61 (2006): 106–118.

Ehrlich, Theodore E. "The Disappearance of the Ark of the Covenant." *Jewish Bible Quarterly* 40, no. 3 (2012): 174–178.

Elderkin, G.W. "Architectural Detail and Antique Sepulchral Art." *American Journal of Archaeology* 39 (1935): 518–525.

Elkins, Nathan T. *Monuments in Miniature: Architecture on Roman Coinage*. New York: American Numismatic Society, 2015.

Elsner, Jaś. "Iconoclasm as Discourse: From Antiquity to Byzantium." *The Art Bulletin* 94, no. 3 (2012): 368–394.

Elsner, Jaś. "Relic, Icon and Architecture: The Material Articulation of the Holy in Early Christian Art." In *Saints and Sacred Matter: The Cult of Relics in Byzantium and Beyond*, ed. Cynthia Hahn and Holger A. Klein, 13–41. Washington, DC: Dumbarton Oaks Research Library and Collection, 2015.

Elsner, Jaś. "The Rhetoric of Buildings in the De Aedificiis of Procopius." In *Art and Text in Byzantium*, ed. Liz James, 33–57. Cambridge: Cambridge University Press, 2007.

Emmanuel, Melita. "Die Fresken der Muttergottes-Hodegetria-Kirche in Spelies auf der Insel Euboia (1311). Bemerkungen zu Ikonographie und Stil." *Byzantinische Zeitschrift* 83, no. 2 (1990): 451–467.

Engberg-Pederson, Troels. *Cosmology and the Self in the Apostle Paul: The Material Spirit*. New York: Oxford University Press, 2010.

Engemann, Josef. "Ein Missorium des Anastasius. Überlegungen zum ikonographischen Programm der 'Anastasius'-Platte aus dem Sutton Hoo Ship-burial." In *Festschrift für Klaus Wessel zum 70. Geburtstag*, ed. Marcell Restle, 103–115. Munich: Editio Maris, 1988.

Engemann, Josef. *Untersuchungen zur Sepulchralsymbolik der späteren römischen Kaiserzeit*. Münster: Aschendorff, 1973.

Epstein, Michael M. *The Medieval Haggadah: Art, Narrative, Religious Imagination*. New Haven: Yale University Press, 2011.

Erdeljan, Jelena. *Chosen Places: Constructing New Jerusalems in Slavia Orthodoxa*. Leiden: Brill, 2017.

Esbroeck, Michel van. "The Virgin as the True Ark of the Covenant." In *Images of the Mother of God: Perceptions of the Theotokos in Byzantium*, ed. Maria Vassilaki, 63–68. Aldershot: Ashgate, 2005.

Etzeoglou, Rhodoniki. "The Cult of the Virgin Zoodochos Pege at Mistra." In *Images of the Mother of God: Perceptions of the Theotokos in Byzantium*, ed. Maria Vassilaki, 239–250. Aldershot: Ashgate, 2005.

Etzeoglou, Rhodoniki. *O naos tēs Odēgētrias tou Brontochiou ston Mystra. Oi toichographies tou nisthēka* [The Church of the Hodegetria of Vrontochion in Mystras. The murals of the narthex]. Athens: Akademia Athenon, 2013.

Etzeoglou, Rhodoniki. "Quelques remarques sur les portraits figurés dans les églises de Mistra." *Jahrbuch der Österreichischen Byzantinistik* 32, no. 5 (1982): 514–515.

Evangelatou, Maria. "The Illustration of the Ninth-Century Byzantine Marginal Psalters: Layers of Meaning and Their Sources." PhD diss., University of London, 2002.

Evans, Helen C., ed. *Byzantium: Faith and Power (1261–1557)*. New York: Metropolitan Museum of Art; New Haven: Yale University Press, 2004.

Evans, Helen C., and Brandie Ratliff, eds. *Byzantium and Islam: Age of Transition (7th–9th Century)*. New York: Metropolitan Museum of Art, 2012.

Evans, Linda. "Animals in Coptic Art." *Göttinger Miszellen* 232 (2012): 63–73.

Evgenidou, Despoina, ed. *The City of Mystras. Mystras, August 2001–January 2002*. Exhibition Catalogue. Athens: Hellenic Ministry of Culture, 2001.

Eyice, Semavi. "Contributions à l'histoire de l'art byzantin: quatre edifices inédits ou mal connus." *Cahiers archéologiques* 10 (1959): 245–250.

Eyice, Semavi. "Les églises byzantines à plan central d'Istanbul." *Corso di cultura sull'arte ravennate e byzantina* 26 (1979): 115–149.

Failler, Albert. "Une donation des époux Sanianoi au monastère des Hodègoi." *Revue des études byzantines* 34 (1976): 111–117.

Fairbairn, Patrick. *Typology of Scripture: Two Volumes in One*. Grand Rapids, MI: Kregel Publications, 1960.

Fears, J. Rufus. "The Theology of Victory at Rome: Approaches and Problems." In *Aufstieg und Niedergang der Römischen Welt* 2.17:2, 736–826. Berlin/New York: De Gruyter, 1981.

Featherstone, J. Michael. "*De Cerimoniis* and the Great Palace." In *The Byzantine World*, ed. Paul Stephenson, 162–174. London/New York: Routledge, 2010.

Feist, Sabine. "The Impact of Late Antique Churches on the Ecclesiastical Architecture during the Transitional Period: The Case Study of St. Irene in Constantinople." In *Transforming Sacred Spaces: New Approaches to Byzantine Ecclesiastical Architecture from the Transitional Period*, ed. Sabine Feist, 129–145. Wiesbaden: Reichert Verlag, 2020.

Fine, Steven. "Art and Liturgical Context of the Sepphoris Synagogue." In *Galilee through Centuries: Confluences of Cultures*, ed. Eric M. Meyers, 227–237. Winona Lake, IN: Eisenbrauns, 1999.

BIBLIOGRAPHY

Finucane, Ronald C. "Sacred Corpse, Profane Carrion: Social Ideals and Death Rituals in the Later Middle Ages." In *Mirrors of Mortality: Studies in the Social History of Death*, ed. Joachim Whaley, 40–60. London: Europa, 1981.

Fisher, Elizabeth A. "Life of the Patriarch Nicephoros I of Constantinople." In *Byzantine Defenders of Images: Eight Saints' Lives in English Translation*, ed. Alice-Mary Talbot, 25–143. Washington: Dumbarton Oaks Papers, 1998.

Florensky, Pavel. *Iconostasis*. Trans. Donald Sheehan and O. Andrejev. Crestwood, NY: St. Vladimir's Seminary Press, 2000.

Frampton, Kenneth. *Studies in Tectonic Culture: The Poetics of Construction in Nineteenth and Twentieth Century Architecture*. Cambridge, MA: MIT Press, 1995.

Frazer, Margaret English. "Early Byzantine Silver Book Covers." In *Ecclesiastical Silver Plate in Sixth-Century Byzantium: Papers of the Symposium Held May 16–18, 1986, at the Walters Art Gallery, Baltimore, and Dumbarton Oaks, Washington DC, organized by Susan A. Boyd, Marlia Mundell Mango, and Gary Vikan*, vol. 3, ed. Susan A. Boyd and Marlia Mundell Mango, 71–76. Washington DC: Dumbarton Oaks Reserarch Library and Collection, 1992.

Frazer, Margaret English. "Pair of Book Covers with Peter and Paul." In *Age of Spirituality: Late Antique and Early Christian Art, Third to Seventh century*, ed. Kurt Weitzmann, 618–619. New York: The Metropolitan Museum of Art, 1979.

Frolow, Andrey. *La relique de la Vraie Croix. Recherches sur le développement d'un culte*. Paris: Institut français d'études byzantines, 1961.

Fuchs, Günter. *Architekturdarstellungen auf römischen Münzen der Republik und der frühen Kaiserzeit*. Berlin: De Gruyter, 1969.

Gaborit-Chopin, Danielle. *Elfenbeinkunst im Mittelalter*. Berlin: Gebr. Mann, 1978.

Garland, Lynda. *Byzantine Empresses: Women and Power in Byzantium, AD 527–1204*. London: Routledge, 1999.

Gavrilović, Anđela. "Zidno slikarstvo crkve Bogorodice Odigitrije u Peći" [Wall paintings of the Church of the Virgin Hodegetria in Peć]. PhD diss., University of Belgrade, Faculty of Philosophy, Art History Department, 2012. http://doiserbia .nb.rs/phd/fulltext/BG20130419GAVRILOVIC.pdf.

Gerola, Giuseppe. *Monumenti Veneti dell'isola di Creta*. Vol. 4. Venice: Istituto Veneto di Scienze, 1932.

Giedion, Sigfried. *Architecture and the Phenomena of Transition*. Cambridge, MA: Harvard University Press, 1971.

Gittings, Elizabeth A. "Civic Life: Women as Embodiments of Civic Life." In *Byzantine Women and Their World*, ed. Ioli Kalavrezou, 35–42. New Haven: Yale University Press, 2003.

Gkioles, Nikolaos. *O Byzantinos Troulos kai to eikonografiko tou programma* [On the Byzantine dome and the iconography of its program]. Athens: Ekdoseis Kardamitsa, 1990.

Gnecchi, Francesco. *I medaglioni romani* I. Milan: Vlrico Hoepli, editore libraio della real casa, 1912.

Goette, Hans Rupprecht. "Corona spicea, corona civica und Adler. Bemerkungen zu drei römischen Dreifussbasen." *Archäologischer Anzeiger* (1984): 573–589.

Goldman, Bernard. *The Sacred Portal.* Detroit: Wayne State University Press, 1966.

Goodenough, Erwin Ramsdell. *Jewish Symbols in the Greco-Roman Period.* Princeton, NJ: Princeton University Press, 1988.

Goppelt, Leonhard. *Typos: The Typological Interpretation of the Old Testament in the New.* Grand Rapids, MI: Wm.B. Eerdmans Publishing, 1982.

Goudeau, J., M. Verhoeven, and W. Weijers, eds. *Imagined and Real Jerusalem in Art and Architecture.* Leiden: Brill, 2014.

Grabar, André. *L'età d'oro di Giustiniano. Dalla morte di Teodosio all'Islam.* Trans. G. Veronesi. Milan: Feltrinelli, 1966.

Grabar, André. "L'iconographie du ciel dans l'art chrétien de l'antiquité et du haut Moyen-Age." *Cahiers archéologiques* 30 (1982): 5–24.

Grabar, André. *Martyrium. Recherches sur le culte des reliques et l'art Chrétien antique.* Paris: Collège de France, 1946.

Grabowski, Francis A. *Plato, Metaphysics and the Forms.* London: Continuum, 2008.

Graetz, Heinrich. *The Structure of Jewish History and Other Essays.* Trans. and ed. I. Schorsch. New York: The Jewish Theological Seminary of America, 1975.

Grigg, Robert. "Symphonian aeido tes basileias. An Image of Imperial Harmony on the Base of the Column of Arcadius." *Art Bulletin* 59 (1977): 469–482.

Grigoryan, Savary Gohar. "The Roots of *Tempietto* and Its Symbolism in Armenian Gospels." *Iconographica* 13 (2014): 11–24.

Grumel, Venance. "Le mois de Marie des Byzantins." *Échos d'Orient* 31 (1932): 257–269.

Gugolj, Branka, and Danijela Tešić-Radovanović. "A Lamp from the Belgrade City Museum with a Representation of ss. Constantine and Helen." In *Symbols and Models in the Mediterranean: Perceiving through Culture*, ed. Aneilya Barnes and Mariarosaria Salerno, 124–135. Newcastle upon Tyne: Cambridge Scholars Publishing, 2017.

Guilland, Rodolphe. "Études sur l'histoire administrative de l'empire byzantin. Le consul, ο υπατος." *Byzantion* 24 (1954): 545–578.

Guillou, André. *Les Archives de Saint-Jean-Prodrome sur le mont Mènécée.* Paris: Presses universitaires de France, 1955.

Gutmann, Joseph. "Masora Figurata in the Mikdashyah: The Messianic Solomonic Temple in a 14th-Century Spanish Hebrew Bible Manuscript." In *8th International Congress of Masoretic Studies Chicago 1988*, ed. E.J. Revell, 71–77. Missoula: Scholars Press, 1990.

Haarløv, Britt. *The Half-Open Door: A Common Symbolic Motif within Roman Sepulchral Sculpture.* Odense: University Press of Southern Denmark, 1977.

BIBLIOGRAPHY

Haberstumpf, Walter. "Dinasti italiani in levante. I Tocco duchi di Leucade: regesti (secoli XIV–XVII)." *Studi veneziani* NS 45 (2003): 165–211.

Hackel, Sergei, ed. *The Byzantine Saint*. Crestwood, NY: St. Vladimir's Seminary Press, 2001.

Hackett, John. *A History of the Orthodox Church of Cyprus*. London: Methuen and Co., 1901.

Hadjitryphonos, Evangelia. "Peristöon or Ambulatory in Byzantine Church Architecture." *Saopštenja* 34 (2002): 131–145.

Hadžitrifonos, Evangelia. "Pristup tipologiji petokupolnih crkava u vizantijskoj arhitekturi" [Approaches to typology of five-domed churches in Byzantine architecture]. *Saopštenja* 22/23 (1990–1991): 41–76.

Hahn, Cynthia. "Loca Sancta Souvenirs: Sealing the Pilgrim's Experience." In *Blessings of Pilgrimage*, ed. Robert Ousterhout, 85–96. Urbana, Chicago, IL: University of Illinois Press, 1990.

Hahn, Cynthia, and Holger A. Klein, eds. *Saints and Sacred Matter: The Cult of Relics in Byzantium and Beyond*. Washington, DC: Dumbarton Oaks Research Library and Collection, 2015.

Hall, James. *Dictionary of Subjects and Symbols in Art*. London: J. Murray, 1979.

Hallensleben, Horst. "Untersuchungen zur Genesis und Typologie des 'Mistratipus'." *Marburger Jahrbuch für Kunstwissenschaft* 18 (1969): 105–118.

Halsberghe, Gaston. *The Cult of Sol Invictus*. Leiden: Brill, 1972.

Hammond, C.E. *Liturgies Eastern and Western*. Ed. F.E. Brightman, 2 vols. Oxford: Clarendon Press, 1965.

Handelman, Susan. *The Slayers of Moses: The Emergence of Rabbinic Interpretation in Modern Literary Theory*. Albany: State University of New York Press, 1982.

Hasenmueller, Christine. "Panofsky, Iconography, and Semiotics." *The Journal of Aesthetics and Art Criticism* 36, no. 3 (1978): 289–301.

Hathaway, Ronald F. *Hierarchy and the Definition of Order in the Letters of Pseudo-Dionysius: A Study in the Form and Meaning of the Pseudo-Dionysian Writings*. The Hague: Martinus Nijhoff, 1969.

Hautecoeur, Louis. *Mystique et architecture: symbolisme du cercle et de la coupole*. Paris: Picard, 1954.

Heidegger, Martin. *Being and Time*. Trans. John Macquarrie and Edward Robinson. London: SCM Press, 1962.

Herrin, Judith. "The Imperial Feminine in Byzantium." *Past & Present* 169 (2000): 3–35.

Herrin, Judith. *Women in Purple: Rulers of Medieval Byzantium*. Princeton, New Jersey: Princeton University Press, 2001.

Herrmann-Mascard, Nicole. *Les reliques des saints. Formation coutumière d'un droit*. Paris: Klincksieck, 1975.

Hill, Philip V. "Buildings and Monuments of Rome on Coins of the Early Fourth Century, AD 294–313." *Numismatica e Antichità Classiche* 13 (1984): 215–227.

Hölscher, Tonio. *Victoria Romana. Archäologische Untersuchungen zur Geschichte und Wesensart der römischen Siegesgöttin von den Anfängen bis zum Ende des 3. Jhs.n.Chr.*, Mainz: Philipp von Zabern, 1967.

Holum, Kenneth G. *Theodosian Empresses: Women and Imperial Domination in Late Antiquity.* Berkeley, Los Angeles: University of California Press, 1982.

Holum, Kenneth G., and Gary Vikan. "The Trier Ivory, *Adventus* Ceremonial, and the Relics of St. Stephen." *Dumbarton Oaks Papers* 33 (1979): 113–133.

Holtzmann, Walther. "Die ältesten Urkunden des Klosters S. Maria del Patir." *Byzantinische Zeitschrift* 26 (1926): 328–351.

Hommel, Peter. "Giebel und Himmel." *Istanbuler Mitteilungen* 7 (1957): 11–55.

Howard-Johnston, James, and Paul Antony Hayward, eds. *The Cult of the Saints in Late Antiquity and the Middle Ages: Essays on the Contribution of Peter Brown.* Oxford: Oxford University Press, 1999.

Ierodiakonou, Katerina. "The Greek Concept of *Sympatheia and Its Byzantine Appropriation in Michael Psellos.*" In *The Occult Sciences in Byzantium*, ed. Paul Magdalino and Maria Mavroudi, 97–117. Geneva: La Pomme d'Or, 2007.

Ivanović, Filip. "Images of Invisible Beauty in the Aesthetic Cosmology of Dionysius the Areopagite." In *Perceptions of the Body and Sacred Space in Late Antiquity and Byzantium*, ed. Jelena Bogdanović, 11–21. Abingdon: Routledge, 2018.

Ivić, Pavle, and Milica Grković. *Dečanske hrisovulje* [Charters from Dečani]. Novi Sad: Institut za lingvistiku, 1976.

Jacoby, Sam. "Typal and Typological Reasoning: A Diagrammatic Practice of Architecture." *The Journal of Architecture* 20, no. 6 (2015): 938–961.

James, Liz. *Empresses and Power in Early Byzantium.* London: Leicester University Press, 2001.

Jensen, Robin Margaret. *Understanding Early Christian Art.* New York/London: Routledge, 2000.

Johnson, Mark. "Acceptance and Adaptation of Byzantine Architectural Types in the 'Byzantine Commonwealth'." In *The Oxford Handbook of Byzantine Art and Architecture*, ed. Ellen C. Schwartz, 373–388. New York: Oxford University Press, 2021.

Johnson, Paul-Alan. *The Theory of Architecture: Concepts, Themes, and Practices.* New York: Van Nostrand Reinhold, 1994.

Jones, Natalie A., Helen Ross, Timothy Lynam, Pascal Perez, and Anne Leitch. "Mental Models: An Interdisciplinary Synthesis of Theory and Methods." *Ecology and Society* 16, no. 1: 46, 2011. URL: http://www.ecologyandsociety.org/vol16/iss1/art46/.

Jovanović, Aleksandar. *Tlo Srbije: zavičaj rimskih careva* [Serbia: Homeland of the Roman Emperors]. Belgrade: Princip-Bonart Press, 2006.

BIBLIOGRAPHY 263

Jugie, Martin. "La première fête mariale en Orient et en Occident, l'avent primitif." *Échos d'Orient* 22 (1923): 129–152.

Julius, Anthony. *Idolizing Pictures: Idolatry, Iconoclasm and Jewish Art*. London: Thames & Hudson, 2000.

Jung, Carl G. *Analytical Psychology: Its Theory and Practice: The Tavistock Lectures*. New York: Pantheon, 1968.

Jung, Carl G. "Approaching the Unconscious." In *Man and His Symbols*, ed. Carl G. Jung, 18–103. Garden City, NY: Doubleday, 1964.

Jung, Carl G. *Collected Works of C.G. Jung*. Vol. 6, *Psychological Types*. Trans. R.F.C. Hull. Princeton: Princeton University Press, [1921] 1976.

Jung, Carl G. "Psychological Aspects of the Mother Type." In *Collected Works of C.G. Jung*, vol. 9:1, *The Archetypes and the Collective Unconscious*. Trans. R.F.C. Hull, 75–110. London: Routledge and Kegan Paul, 1981.

Kalavrezou, Ioli. "Images of the Mother: When the Virgin Mary Became Meter Theou." *Dumbarton Oaks Papers* 44 (1990): 165–172.

Kalligas, Haris. "The Church of Haghia Sophia at Monemvasia: Its Date and Dedication." *Deltion tēs Christianikēs Archailogikēs Hetaireias* 9 (1977–1979): 217–222.

Kalligas, Haris. *Monemvasia: Byzantine City State*. London: Routledge, 2010.

Kalopissi-Verti, Sophia. "Mistra: A Fortified Late Byzantine Settlement." In *Heaven and Earth*. Vol. 2, *Cities and Countryside in Byzantine Greece*, ed. Jenny Albani and Eugenia Chalkia, 224–239. Athens: Hellenic Ministry of Culture, 2013.

Kaplan, Michel. "De la dépouille à la relique: formation du culte des saints à Byzance du Vᵉ au XIIᵉ siècle." In *Les reliques. Objets, cultes, symboles: Actes du colloque international de l'Université du Littoral-Côte d'Opale (Boulogne-sur-Mer), 4–6 septembre 1997*, ed. Edina Bozóky and Anne-Marie Helvétius, 19–38. Turnhout: Brepols, 1999.

Kaplan, Michel. "L'ensevelissement des saints: rituels de création des reliques et sanctification à Byzance d'après les sources hagiographiques." In *Mélanges Gilbert Dagron*, 319–332. Paris: Association des amis du Centre d'histoire et civilisation de Byzance, 2002.

Karydes, Spyros. *Ē Odēgētria Agraphōn Kerkyras. Psēphides apo tē makraiōnē istoria tēs* [The Hodegetria of Agraphoi in Kerkyra. Pieces of its long history]. Kerkyra/Corfu, 2011.

Karydes, Spyros. "Syllogikes Chorēgies stēn Kerkyra kata tēn Prōimē Latinokratia. Epigrafika Tekmēria" [Collective sponsorship in Corfu during the Early Latin rule. Epigraphic evidence]. *Byzantina Symmeikta* 26 (2016): 167–172.

Karzonis, Anna. *Anastasis: The Making of an Image*. Princeton: Princeton University Press, 1986.

Katramis, Nikolaos. *Philologika analekta ek Zakynthou* [Philological collection from Zakynthos]. Zakynthos, 1880.

Kazaryan, Armen, İsmail Yavuz Özkaya, and Alin Pontioğlu. "The Church of Surb Prkich in Ani (1035). Part 1: History and Historiography—Architectural Plan—Excavations of 2012 and Starting of Conservation." *Journal of the International Association of Research in History of Art* 0143 (15 Nov. 2016). http://www.riha-journal.org/articles /2016/0143-kazaryan-özkaya-pontioğlu.

Kazhdan, Alexander, and Henry Maguire. "Byzantine Hagiographical Texts as Sources on Art." *Dumbarton Oaks Papers* 45 (1991): 1–22.

Kent, John P.C. *Roman Coins*. New York: Abrams, 1978.

Kessler, Herbert L. "Narrative Representations." In *The Age of Spirituality: Late Antique and Early Christian Art, Third to Seventh Century*, ed. Kurt Weitzman, 454–455. New York: Metropolitan Museum of Art, 1979.

Kiilerich, Bente. "Representing an Emperor: Style and Meaning on the Missorium of Theodosius I." In *El disco de Teodosio*, ed. Martín Almagro-Gorbea, José M. Álvarez Martínez, José M. Blázquez Martínez, and Salvador Rovira, 273–280. Madrid: Real Academia de la historia, 2000.

Kim, Kwang-ki, and Tim Berard. "Typification in Society and Social Science: The Continuing Relevance of Schutz's Social Phenomenology." *Human Studies* 32, no. 3 (2009): 263–289.

Kitzinger, Ernst. "The Mosaics of the Cappella Palatina in Palermo: An Essay on the Choice and Arrangement of Subjects." *Art Bulletin* 31, no. 4 (1949): 269–292.

Klauser, Theodor. "Aurum Coronarium." *Mitteilungen des Deutschen Archäologische Instituts, Römische Abteilung* 59 (1944): 129–153.

Kleinbauer, Eugene W. "The Iconography and the Date of the Mosaics of the Rotunda of Hagios Geiorgios, Thessaloniki." *Viator* 3 (1972): 27–108.

Kletter, Karen M. "The Christian Reception of Josephus in Late Antiquity and the Middle Ages." In *A Companion to Josephus*, ed. Honora Howell Chapman and Zuleika Rodgers, 368–381. Chichester: John Wiley & Sons, 2015.

Kochan, Lionel. *Beyond the Graven Image: A Jewish View*. New York: New York University Press, 1997.

Koder, Johannes. *Negroponte: Untersuchungen zur Topographie und Siedlungsgeschichte der Insel Euboia während der Zeit der Venezianerherrschaft*. Vienna: Österreichische Akademie der Wissenschaften, 1973.

Kogman-Appel, Katrin. "Christianity, Idolatry, and the Question of Jewish Figural Painting in the Middle Ages." *Speculum* 84 (2009): 75–107.

Kogman-Appel, Katrin. "Coping with Christian Pictorial Sources: What Did Jewish Miniaturists Not Paint?" *Speculum* 75, no. 4 (2000): 816–858.

Kogman-Appel, Katrin. *Die zweite Nürnbergerund die Jehuda Haggada. Jüdische Illuminatoren zwischen Tradition und Fortschrift*. Frankfurt: Peter Lang, 1999.

Kogman-Appel, Katrin. *Illuminated Haggadot from Medieval Spain*. University Park: Pennsylvania State University Press, 2006.

BIBLIOGRAPHY 265

Kogman-Appel, Katrin. "Jewish Art and Cultural Exchange: Theoretical Perspectives." *Medieval Encounters* 17 (2011): 1–26.

Kogman-Appel, Katrin. "Jewish Art and Non-Jewish Culture: The Dynamics of Artistic Borrowing in Medieval Hebrew Manuscript Illumination." *Jewish History* 15 (2001): 187–234.

Kogman-Appel, Katrin. *Jewish Book Art Between Islam and Christianity: The Decoration of Hebrew Bibles in Medieval Spain.* Leiden: Brill, 2004.

Kogman-Appel, Katrin. "Sephardic Ideas in Ashkenaz—Visualizing the Temple in Medieval Regensburg." *Simon Dubnow Institute Yearbook* 8 (2009): 245–277.

Kogman-Appel, Katrin. "The Temple of Jerusalem and the Hebrew Millennium in a Thirteenth-Century Jewish Prayer Book." In *Jerusalem as Narrative Space*, ed. Anette Hoffmann and Gerhard Wolf, 187–208. Leiden: Brill, 2012.

Kogman-Appel, Katrin, and Shulamit Laderman. "The Sarajevo Haggadah: The Concept of Creatio Ex-Nihilo and the Hermeneutical School Behind It." *Studies in Iconography* 25 (2004): 89–127.

Kollwitz, Johannes, and Helga Herdejürgen. *Die Sarkophage der westlichen Gebiete des Imperium Romanum.* Vol. 2, *Die ravennatischen Sarkophage.* Berlin: Mann, 1979.

Kominis, Athanasios. "Paolo di Monembasia." *Byzantion* 29/30 (1959–1960): 231–248.

Kondakov, Nikodim P. *Iconographia Bogomateri.* Vol. 1. St. Petersburg: Typography of the Imperial Academy of Sciences, 1914.

Kondić, Vladimir, and Vladislav Popović. *Caričin Grad, utvrđeno naselje u vizantijskom Iliriku* [Caričin Grad, fortified settlement in the Byzantine Illyricum]. Belgrade: Srpska akademija nauka i umetnosti, 1977.

Korać, Dušan. "Kanonizacija Stefana Dečanskog i promene na vladarskim portretima u Dečanima" [Stefan Dečanski's canonization and changes in the ruling portraits in Dečani]. In *Dečani i vizantijska umetnost sredinom XIV veka: međunarodni naučni skup povodom 650 godina manastira Dečana*, ed. Vojislav J. Đurić, 287–295. Belgrade: Srpska akademija nauka i umetnosti, 1989.

Korać, Vojislav, and Marica Šuput. *Arhitektura vizantijskog sveta* [Architecture of the Byzantine world]. Belgrade: Vizantološki institut, SANU, 1998.

Krautheimer, Richard. "The Carolingian Revival of Early Christian Architecture." *Art Bulletin* 24, no. 1 (1942): 1–38.

Krautheimer, Richard (with Slobodan Ćurčić). *Early Christian and Byzantine Architecture.* 4th ed. New Haven/London: Yale University Press, 1986.

Krautheimer, Richard. "Introduction to an 'Iconography of Mediaeval Architecture'." *Journal of the Warburg and Courtauld Institutes* 5 (1942): 1–33; reprinted in *Studies in Early Christian, Medieval and Renaissance Art* (1969): 115–150.

Krautheimer, Richard. *Rome: Profile of a City, 312–1308.* Princeton, NJ: Princeton University Press, 1980.

Krinsky, Carol Herselle. "Seventy-Eight Vitruvius Manuscripts." *Journal of the Warburg and Courtauld Institutes* 30 (1967): 36–70.

Kruger, Derek. "The Religion on Relics in Late Antiquity and Byzantium." In *Treasures of Heaven: Saints, Relics, and Devotion in Medieval Europe*, ed. Martina Bagnoli et al., 5–17. New Haven: Yale University Press, 2011.

Krunić, Slavica. *Antičke svetiljke iz Muzeja grada Beograda* [Ancient lamps from the Belgrade City Museum]. Belgrade: Muzej grada Beograda, 2011.

Kruse, Helmut. *Studien zur offiziellen Geltung des Kaiserbildes im römischen Reiche*. Paderborn: Ferdinand Schöningh, 1934.

Kühnel, Gustav. *Wall Painting of the Latin Kingdom of Jerusalem*. Berlin: Mann Verlag, 1988.

Künzl, Ernst. *Der römische Triumph. Siegesfeiern im antiken Rom*. Munich: C.H. Beck, 1988.

Kuzmanović Novović, Ivana. "Portreti cara Konstantina i članova njegove porodice na gliptici u Srbiji" [Portraits of Emperor Constantine and members of his family on glyptic in Serbia]. In *Niš i Vizantija* 7, ed. Miša Rakocija, 77–86. Niš: Kulturni centar Niša, 2009.

Łabuda, Piotr. "Typological Usage of the Old Testament in the New Testament." *The Person and the Challenges* 1, no. 2 (2011): 167–182.

Ladner, Gerhart B. *God, Cosmos, and Humankind: the World of Early Christian Symbolism*. Berkeley: University of California Press, 1995.

Lafontaine-Dosogne, Jacqueline. *Iconographie de l'enfance de la Vierge dans l'Empire byzantin et en Occident*. Vol. 1. Bruxelles: Académie Royale de Belgique, 1992.

Lafontaine-Dosogne, Jacqueline. "Iconography of the Cycle of the Virgin." In *Kariye Djami*, 4 vols., ed. Paul A. Underwood, vol. 4, 163–93, 197–241. London: Routledge, 1966.

Lampl, Paul. "Schemes of Architectural Representation in Early Medieval Art." *Marsyas* 9 (1961): 6–13.

Lampros, Spyridon. "Lakedaimónioi vivliográfoi kaí ktítores kodíkon katá toús mésous aiónas kaí epí tourkokratías" [Lacedaemonian bibliographers and commissioners of codices during the Middle Ages and Turkish domination]. *Neos Hellēnomnēmōn* 4, no. 2 (1907): 152–187.

Lampros, Spyridon. "Treis paradoxographikai diēseis" [Three mirabilia narrations about Peloponnesos]. *Neos Hellēnomnēmōn* 4, no. 2 (1907): 129–151.

Langford, Julie. *Maternal Megalomania: Julia Domna and the Imperial Politics of Motherhood*. Baltimore: Johns Hopkins University Press, 2013.

Laugier, Marc-Antoine. *An Essay on Architecture*. Los Angeles: Hennessey and Ingalls [2009] 1977. [Translation of the original text Marc-Antoine Laugier, *Essai sur l'architecture*. Paris: Duchesne, 1755].

Laurent, Vitalien. *Les corpus des sceaux de l'empire byzantine*. Vol. 5, 2. Paris: Centre national de la recherche scientifique, 1965.

Laurent, Vitalien. *Les regestes des actes du Patriarcat de Constantinople*. Vol. 1, fasc. 4, *Les Regestes de 1208 à 1309*. Paris: Institut français d'études byzantines, 1971.

Leader, Ruth E. "The David Plates Revisited: Transforming the Secular in Early Byzantium." *Art Bulletin* 82, no. 3 (2000): 407–427.

Leader-Newby, Ruth E. *Silver and Society in Late Antiquity: Functions and Meanings of Silver Plate in the Fourth to Seventh Centuries*. Aldershot: Routledge, 2004.

Leeming, David Adams, and Jake Page. *Goddess: Myths of the Female Divine*. Oxford: Oxford University Press, 1996.

Legner, Anton. *Reliquien in Kunst und Kult: zwischen Antike und Aufklärung*. Darmstadt: Wissenschaftliche Buchgesellschaft, 1995.

Lehmann, Karl. "The Dome of Heaven." *Art Bulletin* 27 (1945): 1–27.

Lemerle, Paul. "La Chronique improprement dite de Monemvasie: le contexte historique et légendaire." *Revue des études byzantines* 21 (1963): 5–49.

Lenski, Noel. "The Reign of Constantine." In *The Cambridge Companion to the Age of Constantine*, ed. Noel Lenski, 59–90. New York: Cambridge University Press, 2012.

Lidov, Alexei, ed. *Air and Heavens in the Hierotopy and Iconography of the Christian World* [Vozdukh i nebesa v iyerotopii i ikonografii khristanskogo mira]. Moscow: Theoria, 2019.

Lidov, Alexei. "The Flying Hodegetria: The Miraculous Icon as Bearer of Sacred Space." In *The Miraculous Image in the Late Middle Ages and Renaissance*, ed. Erik Thunø and Gerhard Wolf, 286–288, 291–321. Rome: "L'Erma" di Bretschneider, 2004.

Lidov, Alexei. "Heavenly Jerusalem: The Byzantine Approach." *Jewish Art* 23/24 (1997/98): 341–353.

Lidov, Alexei, ed. *The Hierotopy of Holy Mountains in Christian Culture* [Iyerotopiya svyatoy gory v khristanskoy kul'ture]. Moscow: Theoria, 2019.

Lidov, Alexei, ed. *Hierotopy of Light and Fire in the Culture of the Byzantine World* [Iyerotopiya ognya i sveta v kul'ture vizantiyskogo mira]. Moscow: Theoria, 2017.

Lidov, Alexei, ed. *Holy Water in the Hierotopy and Iconography of the Christian World* [Svyataya Voda v iyerotopii i ikonografii khristanskogo mira]. Moscow: Theoria, 2017.

Lidov, Alexei, ed. *Vostochnokhristianskie relikvii* [Eastern Christian relics]. Moscow: Progress-traditsiia, 2003.

Lidova, Maria. "The Earliest Images of Maria Regina in Rome and the Byzantine Imperial Iconography." In *Niš i Vizantija* 8, ed. Miša Rakocija, 231–243. Niš: Kulturni centar Niša, 2010.

Limberis, Vasiliki. *Divine Heiress: The Virgin Mary and the Making of Christian Constantinople*. London: Routledge, 2002.

Löhr, Wolfgang. "Konstantin und Sol Invictus in Rom." *Jahrbuch für Antike und Christentum* 50 (2007): 102–110.

L'Orange, Hans Peter. *Studies in the Iconography of Cosmic Kingship in the Ancient World*. Oslo: Aschehoug, 1953.

Lossky, Vladimir. *In the Image and Likeness of God*. Trans. John Erickson and Thomas E. Bird, intro. John Meyendorff. Crestwood, NY: St. Vladimir's Seminary Press, 1974.

Loulloupis, Michael. *Annual Report of the Director of the Department of Antiquities, Cyprus, for the year 1988*. Nicosia: Dept. of Antiquities, Cyprus, 1990.

Lowden, John. "Illustrated Octateuch Manuscripts: A Byzantine Phenomenon." In *The Old Testament in Byzantium*, ed. Paul Magdalino and Robert Nelson, 107–153. Cambridge, MA: Harvard University Press, 2010.

MacCormack, Sabine G. *Art and Ceremony in Late Antiquity*. Berkeley/London: University of California Press, 1981.

Macrae, C. Neil, Charles Stangor, and Miles Hewstone, eds. *Stereotypes and Stereotyping*. New York: The Guilford Press, 1996.

Macrides, Ruth. "Saints and Sainthood in the Early Palaiologan Period." In *The Byzantine Saint*, ed. Sergei Hackel, 67–88. Crestwood, NY: St. Vladimir's Seminary Press, 2001.

Madrazo, Leandro. "Durand and the Science of Architecture." *Journal of Architectural Education* 48, no. 1 (1994): 12–24.

Madrazo Agudin, Leandro. "The Concept of Type in Architecture: An Inquiry into the Nature of Architectural Form." PhD diss., Zurich ETH, 1995.

Magdalino, Paul. *Constantinople médiévale: Études sur l'évolution des structures urbaines*. Paris: Boccard, 1996.

Magdalino, Paul, ed. *New Constantines: The Rhythm of Imperial Renewal in Byzantium, 4th to 13th centuries: Papers from the Twenty-sixth Spring Symposium of Byzantine Studies, St Andrews, March 1992*. Cambridge: Variorum, 1994.

Magdalino, Paul. "Observations on the Nea Ekklesia of Basil I." *Jahrbuch der Österreichischen Byzantinistik* 37 (1987): 51–63.

Maguire, Henry. *The Icons of Their Bodies: Saints and Their Images in Byzantium*. Princeton: Princeton University Press, 1996.

Maguire, Henry. "The Mosaics of Nea Moni: An Imperial Reading." *Dumbarton Oaks Papers* 46 (1992): 205–214.

Maier, Franz Georg, and Vassos Karageorghis. *Paphos: History and Archaeology*. Nicosia: A.G. Leventis Foundation, 1984.

Mak Daniel, Gordon L. "Prilozi za istoriju 'Života kraljeva i arhiepiskopa srpskih' od Danila II" [Contributions to the history of the life of the kings and the archbishop of the Serbs by Danilo II]. *Prilozi za književnost jezik istoriju i folklor* 46, 1–4 (1980–1984), 42–52.

BIBLIOGRAPHY

Mamaloukos, Stavros V. *To Katholiko tēs monēs Vatopediou, Historia kai arhitektonikē* [The katholikon of the Vatopedi Monastery, history and architecture]. Athens: Ethniko Metsovio Polytechneio, Tmēma Architektonōn, Spoudastērio Historias tēs Architektonikēs, 2001.

Mango, Cyril. "Approaches to Byzantine Architecture." *Muqarnas* 8 (1991): 40–44.

Mango, Cyril. *Byzantine Architecture.* New York: Rizzoli, 1985.

Mango, Cyril. "The Empress Helena, Helenopolis, Pylae." *Travaux et Mémoires. Centre de recherche d'histoire et civilisation byzantine* 12 (1994): 143–158.

Mango, Cyril. "On the History of the Templon and the Martyrion of St. Artemios at Constantinople." *Zograf* 10 (1979): 40–43.

Marinis, Vasileios. *Architecture and Ritual in the Churches of Constantinople. Ninth to Fifteenth Centuries.* Cambridge: Cambridge University Press, 2014.

Marinis, Vasileios. "Liturgy and Architecture in the Byzantine Transitional Period (7th–8th centuries)." In *Transforming Sacred Spaces: New Approaches to Byzantine Ecclesiastical Architecture from the Transitional Period*, ed. Sabine Feist, 189–198. Wiesbaden: Reichert Verlag, 2020.

Marinis, Vasileios, and Robert Ousterhout. "'Grant Us to Share a Place and Lot with Them,' Relics and the Byzantine Church Building (9th–15th Centuries)." In *Saints and Sacred Matter: The Cult of Relics in Byzantium and Beyond*, eds. Cynthia Hahn and Holger A. Klein, 153–173. Washington, DC: Dumbarton Oaks Research Library and Collection, 2015.

Marinković, Čedomila. "Principles of the Representation of the Founder's (ktetor's) Architecture." In *Serbia and Byzantium: Proceedings of the International Conference Held on 15 December 2008 at the University of Cologne*, ed. Mabi Angar and Claudia Sode, 57–73. Frankfurt: PL Academic Research, 2013.

Marinković, Čedomila. *Slika podignute crkve* [Image of the completed church]. Belgrade: PB Press, 2007.

Marjanović-Dušanić, Smilja. *Sveti kralj* [Holy king]. Belgrade: Clio, 2007.

Marsengill, Katherine. "The Influence of Icons on the Perception of Living Holy Persons." In *Perceptions of the Body and Sacred Space in Late Antiquity and Byzantium*, ed. Jelena Bogdanović, 87–103. Abingdon: Routledge, 2018.

Marsengill, Katherine. *Portraits and Icons: Between Reality and Spirituality in Byzantine Art.* Turnhout: Brepols, 2013.

Martin, Jochen. "Das Kaisertum in der Spätantike." In *Usurpationen in der Spätantike. Akten des Kolloquiums "Staatsreich und Staatlichkeit," 6.–10. März 1996, Solothurn/ Bern*, ed. François Paschoud and Joachim Szidat, 47–62. Stuttgart: Franz Steiner Verlag, 1997.

Martindale, John Robert. *The Prosopography of the Later Roman Empire*, II. A.D. *395–527.* Cambridge: Cambridge University Press, 1980.

Matern, Petra. *Helios und Sol: Kulte und Ikonographie des griechischen und römischen Sonnengottes.* Istanbul: Ege Yayınları, 2002.

Mathews, Thomas F. *The Byzantine Churches of Istanbul: A Photographic Survey.* University Park, PA: Pennsylvania State University Press, 1976.

Mathews, Thomas F. "Observations on the Church of Panagia Kamariotissa on Heybeliada (Chalke), Istanbul." *Dumbarton Oaks Papers* 27 (1973), 117–127.

Mathews, Thomas F., and Avedis K. Sanjian. *Armenian Gospel Iconography: The Tradition of the Glajor Gospel.* Washington, DC: Dumbarton Oaks Research Library and Collection, 1991.

Mathews, Thomas F. and Norman Muller. "Isis and Mary in Early Icons." In *Images of the Mother of God: Perceptions of the Theotokos in Byzantium*, ed. Maria Vassilaki, 3–12. Aldershot: Ashgate Publishing, 2005.

Matić, Miljana. "Kivot za mošti svetog kralja Stefana Dečanskog" [Kivot with the remains of the holy king Stefan Dečanski]. In *Srpsko umetničko nasleđe na Kosovu i Metohiji. Identitet, značaj, ugroženost*, ed. Miodrag Marković and Dragan Vojvodić, 414–415. Belgrade: SANU, Kragujevac: Grafostil, 2017.

Matschke, Klaus-Peter. "Sakralität und Priestertum des byzantinischen Kaisers." In *Die Sakralität von Herrschaft. Herrschaftslegitimierung im Wechsel der Zeiten und Räume. Fünfzehn interdisziplinäre Beiträge zu einem weltweiten und epochenübergreifenden Phänomen*, ed. Franz-Reiner Erkens, 143–149. Berlin: Akademie Verlag, 2002.

Matz, Friedrich. "Stufen der Sepulkralsymbolik in der Kaiserzeit." *Archäologischer Anzeiger* (1971): 102–116.

Maulden, Robert. "Tectonics in Architecture: From Physical to the Meta-Physical." MArch thesis MIT, 1986.

Mayer, Wendy. "Introduction." In *St. John Chrysostom: The Cult of the Saints*, intro. and trans. Wendy Mayer and Bronwen Neil, 11–35. Crestwood, NY: St. Vladimir's Seminary Press, 2006.

McClanan, Anne. *Representations of Early Byzantine Empresses: Image and Empire.* New York: Palgrave Macmillan US, 2002.

McCormick, Michael. *Eternal Victory: Triumphal Rulership in Late Antiquity, Byzantium, and the Early Mediaeval West.* Cambridge: Cambridge University Press, 1986.

McVey, Kathleen E. "Spirit Embodied: The Emergence of Symbolic Interpretations of Early Christian and Byzantine Architecture." In *Architecture as Icon*, ed. Slobodan Ćurčić and Evangelia Hadjitryphonos, 39–71. Princeton: Princeton University Art Museum, 2010.

Meister, Michael W., and Joseph Rykwert. "Afterword: Adam's House and Hermit's Huts: A Conversation." In Ananda K. Coomaraswamy, Michael W. Meister, and Indira Gandhi National Centre for the Arts, *Ananda K. Coomaraswamy: Essays in*

BIBLIOGRAPHY

Early Indian Architecture, 125–131. New Delhi: Indira Gandhi National Centre for the Arts, 1992.

Mellinkoff, Ruth. *Outcasts: Signs of Otherness in Northern European Art of the Late Middle Ages*. Berkeley: University of California Press, 1994.

Meyer, Ann Raftery. *Medieval Allegory and the Building of the New Jerusalem*. Woodbridge: Boydell and Brewer, 2003.

Mihaljević, Marina. "Change in Byzantine Architecture." In *Approaches to Byzantine Architecture and Its Decoration*, ed. Mark Johnson, Robert Ousterhout, and Amy Papalexandrou, 99–119. Farnham, Surrey/Burlington, VT: Ashgate, 2012.

Mihaljević, Marina. "Constantinopolitan Architecture of the Komnenian Era (1080–1180) and its Impact in the Balkans." PhD diss., Princeton University, 2010.

Mihaljević, Marina. "Religious Architecture." In *The Oxford Handbook of Byzantine Art and Architecture*, ed. Ellen C. Schwartz, 307–328. New York: Oxford University Press, 2021.

Milanović, Ljubomir. "Encountering Presence: Icon/Relic/Viewer." In *Icons of Space: Advances in Hierotopy*, ed. Jelena Bogdanović, 239–259. Abingdon, Oxon/New York: Routledge, 2021.

Milanović, Ljubomir. "The Politics of Translatio: The Visual Representation of the Translation of Relics in the Early Christian and Medieval Period, The Case of St. Stephen." PhD diss., Rutgers University, New Brunswick, 2011.

Milinković, Mihailo. "Neka zapažanja o ranovizantijskim utvrđenjima na jugu Srbije" [Some remarks on Early Byzantine fortresses in southern Serbia]. In *Niš i Vizantija* 3, ed. Miša Rakocija, 163–182. Niš: Kulturni centar Niša, 2005.

Miljković-Pepek, Petar. *Veljusa*. Skopje: Filozofski fakultet, 1981.

Millet, Gabriel. *L'École grecque dans l'architecture byzantine*. Paris: E. Leroux, 1916.

Miodrag, Grbić. "Vizantijski novci iz Caričina Grada" [Byzantine coins from Caričin Grad]. *Starinar* 14 (1939): 109–110.

Mirković, Lazar. "Da li na freskama u niškoj grobnici (kraj IV) veka imamo portrete sahranjenih u njoj?" [Do we have the portraits of those buried in Nis mausoleum (end of 4th century) represented in its frescoes?]. *Zbornik Narodnog muzeja* 5 (1967): 227–229.

Mirković, Lazar. "Uvrštenje despota Stefana Lazarevića u red svetitelja" [Inclusion of Despot Stefan Lazarevic in the order of saints]. *Bogoslovlje* 2 (1927): 163–177.

Moneo, Rafael. "On Typology." *Oppositions* 13 (1978): 23–45.

Moore, Kathryn Blair. *The Architecture of the Christian Holy Land: Reception from Late Antiquity through the Renaissance*. Cambridge: Cambridge University Press, 2017.

Mouriki, Doula. *The Mosaics of Nea Moni on Chios*, I–II. Athens: The Commercial Bank of Greece, 1985.

Mouriki, Doula. "The Octateuch Miniatures of the Byzantine Manuscripts of Cosmas Indicopleustes." PhD diss., Princeton University, 1970.

Mouriki, Doula. *Thirteenth Century Icon Painting in Cyprus*. Athens: Gennadius Library, 1986.

Mulder-Bakker, Anneke B., ed. *The Invention of Saintliness*. London/New York: Routledge, 2002.

Müller-Wiener, Wolfgang. *Bildlexikon zur Topographie Istanbuls: Byzantion-Konstantinopolis-Istanbul bis zum Beginn des 17. Jahrhunderts*. Tübingen: Verlag Ernst Wasmuth, 1977.

Mundell Mango, Marlia. *Silver from Early Byzantium: The Kaper Koraon and Related Treasures*. Baltimore, MD: Walters Art Gallery, 1986.

Mundell Mango, Marlia, Cyril Mango, Angela Care Evans, and Michael Hughes. "A 6th-Century Mediterranean Bucket from Bromeswell Parish, Suffolk." *Antiquity* 63 (1989): 295–311.

Näf, Beat. *Senatorisches Standesbewusstsein in spätrömischer Zeit*. Freiburg: Universitätsverlag, 1995.

Narkiss, Bezalel. *Hebrew Illuminated Manuscripts*. Jerusalem: Leon Amiel, 1969.

Nenadović, Slobodan. *Bogorodica Ljeviška: njen postanak i mesto u arhitekturi Milutinovog vremena* [The Mother of God Ljeviška: The origin and place in the architecture of Milutin's time]. Belgrade: Narodna knjiga, 1963.

Neumann, Eric. *The Great Mother: An Analysis of the Archetype*. Trans. Ralph Mannheim. Princeton: Princeton University Press, 1970.

Nicol, Donald M. *The Despotate of Epiros, 1267–1479: A Contribution to the History of Greece in the Middle Ages*. Cambridge: Cambridge University Press, 1984.

Nikolova, Bistra. *Monasi, manastiri i manastirski zhivot v Srednovekovna Balgariya*. Vol. 1, *Manastirite* [Monks, monasteries and monastic life in medieval Bulgaria. Vol. 1, Monasteries]. Sofia: Algraf, 2010.

Noble, Jonathan. "The Architectural Typology of Antoine Chrysostome Quatremère de Quincy (1755–1849)." *Edinburgh Architectural Research* 27 (2000): 145–159.

Noll, Rudolf. *Von Altertum zum Mittelalter*. Vienna: Kunsthistorisches Museum, 1958.

Nordenfalk, Carl. *Die spätantiken Kanontafeln. Kunstgeschichtliche Studien über die eusebianische Evangelien-Konkordanz in den vier ersten Jahrhunderten ihrer Geschichte*. Gothenburg: Isacsons, 1938.

Norris, Herbert. *Ancient European Costume and Fashion*. Toronto: J.M. Dent and Sons (1927), reissued Dover Publications, 1999.

Oechslin, Werner. "Premises for the Resumption of the Discussion of Typology." *Assemblage* 1 (1986): 36–53.

Oikonomides, Nicolas. "The Holy Icon as an Asset." *Dumbarton Oaks Papers* 45 (1991): 35–44.

Oikonomides, Nicolas. "St. George of Mangana, Maria Skleraina, and the 'Malyj Sion' of Novgorod." *Dumbarton Oaks Papers* 34–35 (1980–1981): 239–246.

BIBLIOGRAPHY

Olin, Margaret. *The Nation Without Art: Examining Modern Discourses on Jewish Art*. Lincoln: University of Nebraska Press, 2001.

Olkinuora, Jaakko. *Byzantine Hymnography for the Feast of the Entrance of the Theotokos*. Helsinki: Picaset Oy, 2015.

Olovsdotter, Cecilia. "Anastasius' I Consuls: Ordinary Consulship and Imperial Power in the Consular Diptychs from Constantinople." *Valör. Konstvetenskapliga studier* 1–2 (2012): 33–47.

Olovsdotter, Cecilia. "Architecture and the Spheres of the Universe in Late Antique Art." In *Envisioning Worlds in Late Antique Art: New Perspectives on Abstraction and Symbolism in Late-Roman and Early-Byzantine Visual Culture (c. 300–600)*, ed. Cecilia Olovsdotter, 137–177. Berlin/Boston: De Gruyter, 2019.

Olovsdotter, Cecilia. *The Consular Image: An Iconological Study of the Consular Diptychs*. Oxford: John and Erica Hedges, 2005.

Olympios, Michalis. "Resting in Pieces: Gothic Architecture in Cyprus in the Long Fifteenth Century." In *Medieval Cyprus: A Place of Cultural Encounter*, ed. Sabine Rogge and Michael Grünbart, 340–343. Münster: Waxmann, 2015.

Orlandos, Anastasios. "Daniēl o prōtos ktitōr tōn Hagiōn Theodōrōn tou Mystra" [Daniel, the first founder of Saints Theodors of Mystras]. *Epetirís Etaireías Vyzantinón Spoudón* 12 (1936): 443–448.

Ousterhout, Robert. "Architecture as Relic and the Construction of Sanctity: The Stones of the Holy Sepulchre." *Journal of the Society of Architectural Historians* 62, no. 1 (2003): 4–23.

Ousterhout, Robert. "The Architecture of Iconoclasm." In *Byzantium in the Iconoclastic Era (ca. 680–850): The Sources*, ed. Leslie Brubaker and John Haldon, 3–36. Burlington, VT: Ashgate, 2001.

Ousterhout, Robert. "The Church of Santo Stefano: A 'Jerusalem' in Bologna." *Gesta* 20, no. 2 (1981): 311–321.

Ousterhout, Robert. "Loca Sancta and the Architectural Response to Pilgrimage." In *Blessings of Pilgrimage*, ed. Robert Ousterhout, 108–137. Urbana, Chicago, IL: University of Illinois Press, 1990.

Ousterhout, Robert. *Master Builders in Byzantium*. Princeton: Princeton University Press, 1999.

Ousterhout, Robert. "New Temples and New Solomons." In *Old Testament in Byzantium*, ed. Paul Magdalino and Robert Nelson, 223–253. Washington, DC: Dumbarton Oaks Research Library and Collection, 2010.

Ousterhout, Robert. "Originality in Byzantine Architecture: The Case of Nea Moni." *The Journal of the Society of Architectural Historians* 51/1 (1992): 48–60.

Ousterhout, Robert. "Problems of Architectural Typology during the Transitional Period (Seventh to Early Ninth Century)." In *Transforming Sacred Spaces: New*

Approaches to Byzantine Ecclesiastical Architecture from the Transitional Period, ed. Sabine Feist, 147–158. Wiesbaden: Reichert Verlag, 2020.

Ousterhout, Robert. "Rebuilding the Temple: Constantine Monomachus and the Holy Sepulchre." *Journal of the Society of Architectural Historians* 48 (1989): 66–78.

Ousterhout, Robert. "The Temple, the Sepulchre, and the Martyrion of the Savior." *Gesta* 29, no. 1 (1990): 44–53.

Paganes, Georgios. "Ekklesia tēs Panagias tēs Odēgētrias" [Church of Panagia Hodegetria]. At *Koinotiko Symboulio Aredou*—http://arediou.com/portfolio-item /thriskeftiki-zoi/#toggle-id-2. Accessed June 6, 2017.

Pallas, Demetrios. *Die Passion und Bestattung Christi in Byzanz. Der Ritus—das Bild.* Munich: Institut für Byzantinistik und neugriechische Philologie der Universität, 1965.

Panić, Draga, and Gordana Babić. *Bogorodica Ljeviška* [The Mother of God Ljeviška]. Belgrade: Srpska književna zadruga, 1975.

Panofsky, Erwin. *Idea: A Concept in Art Theory*. Trans. Joseph J.S. Peake. New York/ London: Harper & Row, 1968.

Pantelić, Bratislav. *The Architecture of Dečani and the Role of Archbishop Danilo* II. Wiesbaden: Reichert, 2002.

Papacostas, Tassos. "In Search of a Lost Byzantine Monument: Saint Sophia of Nicosia." *Epetiría tou Kéntrou Epistimonikón Erevnón* 31 (2005): 11–37.

Papadopoulos-Kerameus, Athanasios. "Nikēphoros Moschopoulos." *Byzantinische Zeitschrift* 12 (1903), 215–223.

Papadopoulos-Kerameus, Athanasios. *Noctes Petrapolitana* [The nights of Petropolis]. St. Petersburg: Tip. V.F. Kirshbauma, 1913.

Papadopoulou, Varvara. "Amphigraptē eikona tou 14ou aiōna stē monē Gēromeriou Thesprōtias" [A double-sided icon from the 14th century in the monastery of Geromerion, Thesprotia]. *Byzantina* 25 (2005): 375–389.

Papaioanou, Eustratios N. "The 'Usual Miracle' and an Unusual Miracle: Psellos and the Icons of Blachernai." *Jahrbuch der Österreichischen Byzantinistik* 51 (2001): 177–188.

Papamastorakis, Titos. "Epitymbies parastaseis kata tē mesē kai ysterē byzantine peri-odo" [Funeral representations in the Middle and Late Byzantine periods]. *Deltion tēs Christianikēs Archailogikēs Hetaireias* 19 (1996–1997): 290–304.

Papamastorakis, Titos. "Myzithras of the Byzantines / Mistra to Byzantinists." In *Vyzantinés póleis, 8os–15os aiónas. Prooptikés tis érevnas kai nées ermineftikés prosengíseis*, ed. Tonia Kiousopoulou, 277–196. Rethymnon: Panepistiemiou Kritis, 2012.

Papamastorakis, Titos. "Reflections of Constantinople: The Iconographic Program of the South Portico of the Hodegetria Church, Mystras." In *Viewing the Morea: Land and People in the Late Medieval Peloponnese*, ed. Sharon Gerstel, 372–374. Washington, DC: Harvard University Press, 2013.

BIBLIOGRAPHY

Parada López de Corselas, Manuel. "La arquitectura de poder y su recepción: la 'serliana.' ¿Viaje de formas, viaje de contenidos?" In *Ver, viajar y hospedarse en el mundo romano*, ed. Gonzalo Bravo and Raúl González Salinero, 561–582. Madrid/Salamanca: Signifer Libros, 2012.

Parani, Maria. "Defining Personal Space: Dress and Accessories in Late Antiquity." In *Objects in Context, Objects in Use: Material Spatiality in Late Antiquity*, ed. Luke Lavan, Ellen Swift, and Toon Putzeys, 497–529. Leiden: Brill, 2007.

Parani, Maria. *Reconstructing the Reality of Images: Byzantine Material Culture and Religious Iconography (11th–15th Centuries)*. Leiden: Brill, 2003.

Parry, Kenneth. *Depicting the Word: Byzantine Iconophile Thought of the Eighth and Ninth Centuries*. Leiden: Brill, 1996.

Parry, Kenneth. "Theodore the Stoudite: The Most 'Original' Iconophile?" *Jahrbuch der Österreichischen Byzantinistik* (2018): 261–275.

Parry, Kenneth. "The Theological Argument about Images in the 9th Century." In *A Companion to Byzantine Iconoclasm*, ed. M. Humphreys, 425–463. Leiden: Brill, 2021.

Pavlović, Dragana. "Kralj Stefan Uroš III Dečanski" [King Stefan Uroš the Third Dečanski]. In *Srpsko umetničko nasleđe na Kosovu i Metohiji. Identitet, značaj, ugroženost*, ed. Miodrag Marković and Dragan Vojvodić, 382–383. Belgrade: SANU, Kragujevac: Grafostil, 2017.

Pavlović, Leontije. *Kultovi lica kod Srba i Makedonaca* [The cult of individuals among Serbs and Macedonians]. Smederevo: Narodni muzej, 1965.

Pelikan, Jaroslav. *The Emergence of the Catholic Tradition (100–600)*. Vol. 1, *The Christian Tradition: A History of the Development of Doctrine*. Chicago: University Of Chicago Press [1975] 1991.

Pelikan, Jaroslav. *Jesus Through the Centuries: His Place in the History of Culture*. New Haven/London: Yale University Press, 1999.

Pentcheva, Bissera. "The 'Activated' Icon: The Hodegetria Procession and Mary's Eisodos." In *Images of the Mother of God: Perceptions of the Theotokos in Byzantium*, ed. Maria Vassilaki, 195–208. Aldershot: Ashgate, 2005.

Pentcheva, Bissera. *Hagia Sophia: Sound, Space, and Spirit in Byzantium*. University Park, PA: Pennsylvania State University Press, 2017.

Pentcheva, Bissera. *Icons and Power: The Mother of God in Byzantium*. University Park, PA: Pennsylvania State University Press, 2006.

Pentcheva, Bissera. "Rhetorical Images of the Virgin: The Icon of the 'Usual Miracle' at the Blachernai." *Revue des études slaves* 38 (2000): 35–54.

Pentcheva, Bissera. *Sensual Icon: Space, Ritual, and Senses in Byzantium*. University Park, PA: Pennsylvania State University Press, 2014.

Pentcheva, Bissera. "The Supernatural Defender of Constantinople: The Virgin and Her Icon in the Tradition of the Avar Siege." *Byzantine and Modern Greek Studies* 26 (2002): 2–41.

Perera, Sylvia B. *Descent to the Goddess: A Way of Initiation for Women*. Toronto: Inner City Books, 1981.

Perl, Eric D. *Theophany: The Neoplatonic Philosophy of Dionysius the Areopagite*. Albany: State University of New York Press, 2007.

Petković, Sofija, Milica Tapavički-Ilić, and Jelena Anđelković Grašar. "A Portrait Oil Lamp from Pontes—Possible Interpretations and Meanings within Early Byzantine Visual Culture." *Starinar* 65 (2015): 79–89.

Petković, Vladislav R., and Đurđe Bošković. *Dečani*. Vols. 1–2. Belgrade: Academia Regalis Serbica, 1941.

Petrizzopulo, Demetrio. *Saggio storico sull' et à di Leucadia: sotto il dominio de' Romani e successivi conquistatori*. Florence: Stamp. di Piatti, 1814.

Petrović, Damnjan. "Camblakova literarna delatnost u Srbiji" [Camblak's literary activity in Serbia]. In Grigorije Camblak, *Književni rad u Srbiji*, trans. Lazar Mirković et al., 9–45. Belgrade: Prosveta, 1989.

Philip, Grierson. *Byzantine Coinage*. Washington, DC: Dumbarton Oaks Research Library and Collection 1982, 2nd ed., 1999.

Philippa-Apostolou, Maro. "Ē Odēgētria tēs Leukadas, istorikes phaseis" [The Hodegetria of Lefkada, historical phases]. In *Praktika D' Synedriou "Eptanēsiakou Politismou," Leukada 8–12 Septembriou 1993*, ed. P. Rontogiannis, 133–159. Athens: Etaireia Leukadikon Meleton, 1996.

Piccirillo, Michele. *La Nuova Gerusalemme, Artigianato Palestinese al servizio dei Luoghi Santi*. Bergamo: Edizioni Custodia di Terra Santa, 2007.

Pillinger, Renate, Vania Popova-Moroz, and Barbara Zimmermann. *Corpus der spätantiken und frühchristlichen Wandermalereien Bulgariens*. Vienna: Verlag der Österreichischen Akademie der Wissenschaften, 1999.

Platt, Verity. "Framing the Dead on Roman Sarcophagi." In *The Frame in Classical Art: A Cultural History*, ed. Verity Platt and Michael Squire, 353–381. Cambridge: Cambridge University Press, 2017.

Popović, Danica. "Grob arhiepiskopa Danila II" [The tomb of the archbishop Danilo II]. In *Arhiepiskop Danilo II i njegovo doba*, ed. Vojislav Đurić, 329–344. Belgrade: SANU, 1991.

Popović, Danica. "Grob svetog Simeona u Studenici" [The tomb of St. Simeon in Studenica]. In *Osam vekova Studenice. Zbornik radova*, ed. Episkop Žički Stefan et al., 155–166. Belgrade: Sveti arhijereski sinod srpske pravoslavne crkve, 1986.

Popović, Danica. "Mošti Svetog Save" [The relics of Saint Sava]. In *Pod okriljem svetosti, Kult svetih vladara i relikvija u srednjovekovnoj Srbiji*, 75–97. Belgrade: Balkanološki institut SANU, 2006.

Popović, Danica. "Sahrane i grobovi u srednjem veku" [Burials and graves in the Middle Ages]. In *Manastir Hilandar*, ed. Gojko Subotić, 205–214. Belgrade: Publikum, 1998.

BIBLIOGRAPHY   277

Popović, Danica. "Shrine of King Stefan Uroš III Dečanski." In *Byzantium: Faith and Power (1261–1557)*, ed. Helen C. Evans, 114–115. New York: The Metropolitan Museum of Art, 2004.

Popović, Danica. "Srednjovekovni nadgrobni spomenici u Dečanima" [Medieval tombstones in Dečani]. In *Dečani i vizantijska umetnost sredinom XIV veka: međunarodni naučni skup povodom 650 godina manastira Dečana*, ed. Vojislav J. Đurić, 225–237. Belgrade: Srpska akademija nauka i umetnosti, 1989.

Popović, Danica. "Srpska vladarska *translatio* kao trijumfalni *adventus*" [The Serbian ruler's *translatio* as triumphant *adventus*]. In *Pod okriljem svetosti, Kult svetih vladara i relikvija u srednjovekovnoj Srbiji*, 233–253. Belgrade: Balkanološki institut SANU, 2006.

Popović, Danica. *Srpski vladarski grob u srednjem veku* [The Serbian ruler's tomb in the Middle Ages]. Belgrade: Institut za istoriju umetnosti, Filozofski fakultet, 1992.

Popović, Danica. "Sveti kralj Stefan Dečanski" [Holy king Stefan Dečanski]. In *Pod okriljem svetosti. Kult svetih vladara i relikvija u srednjovekovnoj Srbiji*, 143–183. Belgrade: Balkanološki institut SANU, 2006.

Popović, Ivana. "Sakralno-funerarni kompleks na Maguri" [Sacral and funerary complex at Magura]. In *Felix Romuliana—Gamzigrad*, ed. Ivana Popović, 141–158. Belgrade: Arheološki institut, 2010.

Popović, Ivana. "The Find of the Crypt of the Mausoleum: Golden Jewellery and Votive Plaques." In *Šarkamen (Eastern Serbia): A Tetrarchic Imperial Palace: The Memorial Complex*, ed. Ivana Popović, 59–82. Belgrade: Arheološki institut, 2005.

Popović, Ivana. "Inventar grobnica iz Dola kod Bele Palanke (*Remesiana*)" [Inventory of tombs from Dol near Bela Palana (*Remesiana*)]. In *Niš i Vizantija* 7, ed. Miša Rakocija, 55–66. Niš: Kulturni centar Niša, 2009.

Popović, Ivana. "Jewellery as an Insigne of Authority, Imperial Donation and as Personal Adornment." In *Constantine the Great and the Edict of Milan 313: The Birth of Christianity in the Roman Provinces on the Soil of Serbia*, ed. Ivana Popović and Bojana Borić-Brešković, 188–195. Belgrade: National Museum in Belgrade, 2013.

Popović, Ivana. "Kameje iz kasnoantičke zbirke Narodnog muzeja u Beogradu" [Cameos from late antique collection of the National Museum in Belgrade]. *Zbornik Narodnog muzeja* 14, no. 1 (1992): 401–412.

Popović, Ivana. *Kasnoantički i ranovizantijski nakit od zlata u Narodnom muzeju u Beogradu* [Late antique and Early Byzantine golden jewelry in National Museum in Belgrade]. Belgrade: Narodni muzej Beograd, 2001.

Popović, Ivana. *Rimske kameje u Narodnom muzeju u Beogradu* [Roman cameos in the National Museum in Belgrade]. Belgrade: Narodni muzej Beograd, 1989.

Popović, Ivana. "Roman Cameos with Representation of Female Bust from Middle and Lower Danube." In *Glyptique romaine*, ed. Hélène Guiraud and Antony Andurand, 203–224. Toulouse: Presses Universitaires Mirail, 2010.

Pratesi, Alessandro. "Per un nuovo esame della 'Carta di Rossano'." *Studi Medievali* 11 (1970): 209–235.

Price, Simon R.F. "From Noble Funerals to Divine Cult: The Consecration of Roman Emperors." In *Rituals of Royalty: Power and Ceremonial in Traditional Societies*, ed. David Cannadine and Simon R.F. Price, 56–105. Cambridge: Cambridge University Press, 1987.

Pringle, Denys. *The Churches of the Crusader Kingdom of Jerusalem*. Vol. 3, *The City of Jerusalem*. Cambridge: Cambridge University Press, 1993.

Pringle, Denys. *Pilgrimage to Jerusalem and the Holy Land, 1187–1291*. New York: Routledge, 2012.

Radojčić, Svetozar. *Portreti srpskih vladara u srednjem veku* [Portraits of Serbian rulers in the Middle Ages]. Skoplje: Muzej Južne Srbije u Skoplju, 1934.

Raičković, Angelina, and Bebina Milovanović. "Development and Changes in Roman Fashion Showcase Viminacium." *Archaeology and Science* 6 (2011): 77–107.

Raitt, Jill, ed. *Christian Spirituality: High Middle Ages and Reformation*. In collaboration with Bernard McGinn and John Meyendorff. New York: Crossroad, 1987.

Ramphos, Ioannes. "Ta christianika mnēmeia tēs Kimōlou kai tōn perix nēsidō" [The Christian monuments of Kimolos and the neighboring islands]. *Kimōliaka* 2 (1972): 183–299.

Ramphos, Ioannes. *Ta "Sōtēria" tēs Kimōlou eis tēn Hagian Barbaran* [The "salvation" of Kimolos in Agia Varvara]. Athens: n.p., 1954.

Rapp, Claudia. "Old Testament Models for Emperors in Early Byzantium." In *Old Testament in Byzantium*, ed. Paul Magdalino and Robert Nelson, 175–198. Washington, DC: Dumbarton Oaks Research Library and Collection, 2010.

Rautman, Marcus. "The Church of Holy Apostles in Thessaloniki: A Study in Early Palaeologan Architecture." PhD diss., Indiana University, Bloomington, IN, 1984.

Ravegnani, Elisabetta. *Consoli e dittici consolari nella tarda antichità*. Rome: Arcane, 2006.

Restle, Marcell. "Herrschaftszeichen." *Reallexikon für Antike und Christentum* 14 (1988): 937–966.

Revel-Neher, Elisabeth. *L'arche d'alliance dans l'art juif et chrétien du second au dixième siècles. Le Signe de la Rencontre*. Paris: Association des amis des études archéologiques du monde byzantino-slave et du christianisme oriental, 1984.

Revel-Neher, Elisabeth. "On the Hypothetical Models of the Byzantine Iconography of the Ark of the Covenant." In *Byzantine East, Latin West: Art Historical Studies in Honor of Kurt Weitzmann*, ed. Christopher Moss and Katherine Kiefer, 405–414. Princeton: Princeton University Press, 1995.

Ricci, Alessandra. "Reinterpretation of the 'Palace of Bryas': A study in Byzantine Architecture, History and Historiography." PhD diss. Princeton University, 2008.

BIBLIOGRAPHY

Ricci, Alessandra. "The Road from Baghdad to Byzantium and the Case of the Bryas Palace." In *Byzantium in the Ninth Century: Dead or Alive?* ed. Leslie Brubaker, 131–149. (Farnham, Surrey: Ashgate, 1997).

Rontogiannes, Panos. "Ē Christianikē Technē stēn Leukada" [The Christian art in Lefkada]. *Epetēris Etaireias Leukadikōn Meletōn* 3. Athens: Etaireia Laukadikon Meleton, 1974.

Rosenau, Helen. *Vision of the Temple: The Image of the Temple of Jerusalem in Judaism and Christianity*. London: Oresko Books, 1979.

Roth, Cecil. *The Sarajevo Haggadah and its Significance in the History of Art*. Belgrade: Jugoslavija, 1973.

Rumscheid, Jutta. *Kranz und Krone. Zu Insignien, Siegespreisen und Ehrenzeichen der römischen Kaiserzeit*. Tübingen: E. Wasmuth Verlag, 2000.

Rüpke, Jörg. *Domi militae. Die religiöse Konstruktion des Krieges in Rom*. Stuttgart: F. Steiner, 1990.

Rykwert, Joseph. *On Adam's House in Paradise: The Idea of the Primitive Hut in Architectural History*. New York: Museum of Modern Art, 1972.

Šakota, Mirjana. *Dečanska riznica* [Treasury of Dečani Monastery]. Belgrade: BIGZ, 1984.

Salzman, Michele Renee. *On Roman Time: The Codex-Calendar of 354 and the Rhythms of Urban Life in Late Antiquity*. Berkeley/Los Angeles: University of California Press, 1990.

Scarpellini, Donatella. *Stele romane con "imagines clipeatae" in Italia*. Rome: "L'Erma" di Bretschneider, 1987.

Schapiro, Meyer. "The Birds Head Haggada: An Illustrated Hebrew Manuscript of ca. 1300." In *Late Antique, Early Christian and Medieval Art, Selected Papers*, 380–386. New York: George Braziller, 1993.

Schibille, Nadine. "Astronomical and Optical Principles in the Architecture of Hagia Sophia in Constantinople." *Science in Context* 22, no. 1 (2009): 27–46.

Schleißheimer, Bernhard. "Kosmas Indikopleustes, ein altchristliches Weltbild." Diss., Munich University, 1959.

Schreiner, Peter. "Das Hodegetria-Kloster auf Leukas im 11 Jahrhundert: Bemerkungen zu einer Notiz im Vat. Gr. 2561." *Byzantinische Forschungen* 12 (1987): 57–64.

Schrenk, Sabine. *Typos und Antitypos in der frühchristlichen Kunst*. Münster: Aschendorffsche Verlagsbuchhandlung, 1995.

Schwartz, Joshua, and Yehoshua Peleg. "Notes on the Virtual Reconstruction of the Herodian Period Temple and Courtyards." In *The Temple of Jerusalem: From Moses to Messiah*, ed. Steven Fine, 69–91. Leiden: Brill, 2011.

Ševčenko, Nancy Patterson. "Servants of the Holy Icon." In *Byzantine East, Latin West: Art-Historical Studies in Honor of Kurt Weitzmann*, ed. Christopher Moss and Katherine Kiefer, 547–551. Princeton: Princeton University Press, 1995.

Shalev-Eyni, Sarit. "Jerusalem and the Temple in Hebrew Illuminated Manuscripts: Jewish Thought and Christian Influence." In *L'interculturalita dell'ebraismo*, ed. Mauro Perani, 173–191. Ravenna: Longo, 2004.

Shalev-Eyni, Sarit. *Jews among Christians: Hebrew Book Illumination from Lake Constance*. Turnhout: Brepols, 2010.

Shalina, Irina A. *Relikvii v vostochnokhristianskoĭ ikonografii* [Relics in Eastern Christian iconography]. Moscow: Indrik, 2005.

Sharp, Daryl. *Personality Types: Jung's Model of Typology*. Toronto: Inner City Books, 1987.

Sigala, Maria. "Ē Panagia ē Odēgētria ē Enniameritissa stē Chalkē tēs Dōdekanēsou" [Panagia Hodegetria Enniameritissa in Chalki, Dodecanese islands]. *Archaiologikon Deltion* 55, no. 1 (2000) [2004]: 329–381.

Sinkević, Ida. *The Church of St. Panteleimon at Nerezi: Architecture, Programme, Patronage*. Wiesbaden: Reichert, 2000.

Sinkević, Ida. "Formation of Sacred Space in Later Byzantine Five-Domed Chruches: A Hierotopic Approach." In *Hierotopy: The Creation of Sacred Spaces in Byzantium and Medieval Russia*, ed. Alexei Lidov, 260–276. Moscow: Indrik, 2006.

Sinos, Stefanos. *Die Klosterkirche der Kosmosoteira in Bera (Vira)*. Munich: Beck, 1985.

Smith, E. Baldwin. *Architectural Symbolism of Imperial Rome and the Middle Ages*. Princeton: Princeton University Press, 1956.

Smith, Julia M.H. "Relics: An Evolving Tradition in Late Christianity." In *Saints and Sacred Matter: The Cult of Relics in Byzantium and Beyond*, ed. Cynthia Hahn and Holger A. Klein, 41–60. Washington, DC: Dumbarton Oaks Research Library and Collection, 2015.

Snoek, Godefridus J.C. *Medieval Piety from Relics to the Eucharist: A Process of Mutual Interaction*. Leiden/New York: Brill, 1995.

Solovjev, Aleksandar. "Kad je Dečanski proglašen za sveca? Kralja Dušanova povelja Limskom manastiru" [When was Dečanski declared a saint? King Dušan's charter to the Lim monastery]. *Bogoslovlje* 4 (1929): 284–298.

Soustal, Peter, and Johannes Koder. *Nikopolis und Kephallenia*. Vienna: Österreichische Akademie der Wissenschaften, 1981.

Soustal, Peter. *Thrakien (Thrake, Rhodope und Haimimontos)*. Vienna: Österreichische Akademie der Wissenschaften, 1991.

Sox, David. *Relics and Shrines*. London: G. Allen & Unwin, 1985.

Spain, Suzanne. "The Translation of Relics Ivory, Trier." *Dumbarton Oaks Papers* 31 (1977): 279–304.

Spatharakis, Ioannis. *The Pictorial Cycles of the Akathistos Hymn for the Virgin*. Leiden: Alexandros Press, 2005.

Špehar, Perica. "The Imperial Statue from Iustiniana Prima." *Archaeology and Science* 9 (2014): 43–49.

BIBLIOGRAPHY

Spitzer, Moshe, ed. *The Bird's Head Haggadah of the Bezalel National Art Museum in Jerusalem*, 15–19. Jerusalem: Tarshis Books, 1965–67.

Srejović, Dragoslav. "Diva Romula-Divus Galerius. Poslednje apoteoze u rimskom svetu" [Diva Romula-Divus Galerius. The last apotheoses in the Roman world]. *Sunčani sat* 5 (1995): 17–30.

Srejović, Dragoslav. "Felix Romuliana, Galerijeva palata u Gamzigradu" [Felix Romuliana, Galerius's palace in Gamzigrad]. *Starinar* 36 (1985): 51–67.

Srejović, Dragoslav. "Kasnoantički i ranovizantijski portret" [Late antique and Early Byzantine portrait]. In *Antički portret u Jugoslaviji*, ed. Nenad Cambi, Emilio Marin, Ivana Popović, Ljubiša B. Popović, and Dragoslav Srejović, 95–104. Belgrade: Narodni muzej Beograd, Muzeji Makedonije Skopje, Arheološki muzej Zagreb, Arheološki muzej Split, Narodni muzej Ljubljana, 1987.

Srejović, Dragoslav. *Praistorija* [Prehistory]. Belgrade: Izdavački zavod Jugoslavije, 1967.

Srejović, Dragoslav ed. *Rimski carski gradovi i palate u Srbiji* [Roman imperial towns and palaces in Serbia]. Belgrade: Srpska akademija nauka i umetnosti, 1993.

Srejović, Dragoslav, and Aleksandar Simović. "Portret vizantijske carice iz Balajnca" [A portrait of a Byzantine empress from Balajnac]. *Starinar* 9–10 (1959): 77–87.

Srejović, Dragoslav, and Čedomir Vasić. "Diva Romula—Divus Galerius, Imperial Mausolea and Consecration Memorials in Felix Romuliana (Gamzigrad, East Serbia)." In *The Age of Tetrarchs*, ed. Dragoslav Srejović, 141–156. Belgrade: University of Belgrade, Centre for Archaeological Research, Faculty of Philosophy, 1994.

Stefanescu, Ioan D. *L'illustration des liturgies dans l'art de Byzance et de l'Orient*. Brussels: Institut de philologie et d'histoire orientales, 1932.

Stephan, Christine. *Ein byzantinisches Bildensemble: Die Mosaiken und Fresken der Apostolkirche zu Thessaloniki*. Worms: Wernersche Verlagsgesellschaft, 1986.

Stern, Henri. *Le calendrier de 354. Étude sur son texte et sur ses illustrations*. Paris: Imprimerie nationale, 1953.

Stikas, Eustathios. *L'église byzantine de Christianou en Triphylie (Pélponnèse) at les autres édifices de même type*. Paris: Boccard, 1951.

Štkalj, Goran, Aleksandar Bošković, and Željka Buturović. "Attitudes of Serbian Biological Anthropologists toward the Concept of Race." *Anthropologie* LVII/3 (2019): 287–297.

Stout, Ann M. "Jewelry as a Symbol of Status in the Roman Empire." In *The World of Roman Costume*, ed. Judith Lynn Sebesta and Larissa Bonfante, 85–86. Madison: The University of Wisconsin Press, 2001.

Striker, Cecil L. "The Findings at Kalenderhane and Problems of Method in the History of Byzantine Architecture." In *Byzantine Constantinople, Monuments, Topography, and Everyday Life*, ed. Nevra Necipoğlu, 107–116. Leiden/Boston/Cologne: Brill, 2001.

Stuckey, Johanna H. "Ancient Mother Goddess and Fertility Cults." *Journal of the Association for Research on Mothering* 7, no. 1 (2005): 32–44.

Stutzinger, Dagmar. "Das Bronzbildnis einer spätantiken Kaiserin aus Balajnc im Museum von Nis." *Jahrbuch für Antike und Christentum* 29 (1986): 146–165.

Stuveras, Roger. *Le putto dans l'art romain*. Brussels: Latomus, 1969.

Stylianou, Andreas, and Judith Stylianou. *The Painted Churches of Cyprus: Treasures of Byzantine Art*. Nicosia: A.G. Leventis Foundation, 1985.

Subotić, Gojko. "Prilog hronologiji dečanskog zidonog slikarstva" [Contribution to the chronology of Dečani wall paintings]. *Zbornik radova vizantološkog instituta* 20 (1981): 111–138.

Suh, Joori. "An Interactive Generative Abstraction System for the Archetype-Based Pre-Ideation Process (IGATY)." *Design Science* 3, e9 (2017): 1–30.

Sumption, Jonathan. *Pilgrimage: An Image of Mediaeval Religion*. Totowa, NJ: Rowman and Littlefield, 1976.

Sutherland, Carol, and Vivian Humphrey. *The Roman Imperial Coinage* 6. London: Spink and Son Ltd., 1967.

Taft, Robert F. "The Decline of Communion in Byzantium and the Distancing of the Congregation from the Liturgical Action: Cause, Effect, or Neither?" In *Thresholds of the Sacred: Architectural, Art Historical, Liturgical, and Theological Perspectives on Religious Screens, East and West*, ed. Sharon E.J. Gerstel, 27–50. Washington, DC: Dumbarton Oaks Research Library and Collection, 2006.

Talbot, Alice-Mary. "The Relics of New Saints: Deposition, Translation, and Veneration in Middle and Late Byzantium." In *Saints and Sacred Matter: The Cult of Relics in Byzantium and Beyond*, ed. Cynthia Hahn and Holger A. Klein, 215–231. Washington, DC: Dumbarton Oaks Research Library and Collection, 2015.

Tantsis, Anastasios. "Ē chronologēsē tou naou tēs Odēgētrias sto Mystra" [The dating of the Hodegetria Church in Mystras]. *Byzantiaka* 31 (2014): 179–204.

Tatić-Đurić, Mirjana. "Bronzani teg sa likom vizantijske carice" [Steel yard weight with an image of Byzantine empress]. *Zbornik Narodnog muzeja* 3 (1962): 115–126.

Teasdale Smith, Molly. "The Lateran Fastigium, a Gift of Constantine the Great." *Rivista di archeologia cristiana* 46 (1970): 149–175.

Testa, Antonella. "L'affresco dell' Odigitria nella Cappella Palatina di Palermo." *Sicilia archeologica* 28, nos. 87/88/89 (1995): 125–128.

Thacker, Alan T. "The Making of a Local Saint." In *Local Saints and Local Churches in the Early Medieval West*, ed. Alan Thacker and Richard Sharpe, 45–75. Oxford: Oxford University Press, 2002.

Thimme, Jürgen. "Chiusinische Aschenkisten und Sarkophage der hellenistische Zeit." *Studi Etruschi* 23 (1954): 25–147.

Thomas, Thelma K. *Late antique Egyptian Funerary Sculpture: Images for this World and the Next*. Princeton: Princeton University Press, 2000.

BIBLIOGRAPHY

Thümmel, Hans Georg. *Bilderlehre und Bilderstreit: Arbeiten zur Auseinandersetzung über die Ikone und ihre Begründung vornehmlich im 8. und 9. Jahrhundert.* Würzburg: Augustinus, 1991.

Thümmel, Hans Georg. *Die Frühgeschichte der ostkirchlichen Bilderlehre: Texte und Untersuchungen zur Zeit vor dem Bilderstreit.* Berlin: De Gruyter, 1992.

Todić, Branislav. *Gračanica, Slikarstvo* [Gračanica, Painting]. Pristina: Muzej u Prištini, 1999.

Todić, Branislav. "Ikonostas u Dečanima—prvobitni slikani program i njegove poznije izmene" [Iconostasis in Dečani—original painting program and its later changes]. *Zograf* 36 (2012): 115–129.

Todić, Branislav. *Serbian Painting: The Age of King Milutin.* Belgrade: Draganić, 1999.

Todić, Branislav, and Milka Čanak-Medić. *Manastir Dečani.* Pristina: Muzej u Prištini, 2005.

Tomović, Miodrag. "Conclusion." In *Šarkamen (Eastern Serbia): A Tetrarchic Imperial Palace: The Memorial Complex,* ed. Ivana Popović, 107–109. Belgrade: Archaeological Institute, 2005.

Townsley, Ashton L. "Eucharistic Doctrine and the Liturgy in Late Byzantine Painting." *Oriens christianus* 58 (1974): 58–61.

Tradigo, Alfredo. *Icons and Saints of the Eastern Orthodox Church.* Los Angeles: J. Paul Getty Museum, 2006.

Tragomalos, Athanasios. "Naos Panagias Odēgētrias sto Basilopoulo Xēromerou" [The Church of Hodegetria at Basilopoulo Xeromerou] in *Xeromero Press*—https://xiromeropress.gr/εντυπωσιακό-οδοιπορικό-αφιέρωμαναό/. Accessed June 13, 2017.

Trapp, Erich. "Beiträge zur Genealogie der Asanen in Byzanz." *Jahrbuch der Österreichischen Byzantinistik* 25 (1976): 163–177.

Trapp, Erich, Rainer Walther, and Christian Gastgeber, eds. *Prosopographisches Lexikon der Palaiologenzeit.* Vols. 1–12, Add. 1–2, CD-ROM-Version, Vienna: Verlag der Österreichischen Akademie der Wissenschaften, 2001.

Treitinger, Otto. *Die oströmische Kaiser- und Reichsidee nach ihrer Gestaltung im höfischen Zeremoniell.* Jena: W. Biedermann, 1938.

Trifunović, Djordje. "Stara srpska crkvena poezija" [Old Serbian church poetry]. In *O Srbljaku,* ed. Dimitrije Bogdanović et al., 11–17. Belgrade: Srpska književna zadruga, 1970.

Tronzo, William. "L'architettura della Cappella Palatina." In *La Cappella Palatina a Palermo,* ed. Beat Brenk, 79–99. Modena: Panini Editore, 2010.

Underwood, Paul A. "The Fountain of Life in Manuscripts of the Gospels." *Dumbarton Oaks Papers* 5 (1950): 41–138.

Unruh, Frank von. "Unsichtbare Mauern der Kaiserpaläste. Hofzeremonien in Rom und Byzanz." In *Palatia. Kaiserpaläste in Konstantinopel, Ravenna und Trier*, ed. Margarethe König, Eugenia Bolognesi Recchi-Franceschini, and Ellen Riemer, 33–48. Trier: Rheinisches Landesmuseum, 2003.

Valeva, Julia. "Empresses of the Fourth and Fifth Centuries: Imperial and Religious Iconographies." In *Niš i Vizantija* 7, ed. Miša Rakocija, 67–76. Niš: Kulturni centar Niša, 2009.

Vasić, Miloje. *Gold and Silver Coins of Late Antiquity (284–450 AD) in the Collection of National Museum in Belgrade*. Belgrade: National Museum, 2008.

Vasiliev, Alexander A. *Justin the First: An Introduction to the Epoch of Justinian*. Cambridge, MA: Harvard University Press, 1950.

Velmans, Tania. "Quelques programmes iconographiques de coupoles chypriotes du XIIᵉ au XVᵉ siècle." *Cahiers archéologiques* 32 (1984): 137–162.

Verbaal, Wim. "The Vitruvian Middle Ages and Beyond." *Arethusa* 49, no. 2 (2016): 215–225.

Verkerk, Dorothy. "Biblical Manuscripts in Rome 400–700 and the Ashburnham Pentateuch." In *Imaging the Early Medieval Bible*, ed. John Williams, 97–120. University Park, PA: Pennsylvania State University Press, 1999.

Verkerk, Dorothy. *Early Medieval Bible illumination and the Ashburnham Pentateuch*. Cambridge: Cambridge University Press, 2004.

Versnel, Hendrik Simon. *Triumphus: An Inquiry into the Origin, Development and Meaning of the Roman Triumph*. Leiden: Brill, 1970.

Vidler, Anthony. "The Idea of Type: The Transformation of the Academic Ideal: 1750–1830." *Oppositions* 8 (Spring 1977): 95–115.

Vidler, Anthony. "The Third Typology." *Oppositions* 7 (1977): 13–16; reprinted in *Architecture Theory Since 1968*, ed. K. Michael Hays, 284–294. Cambridge, MA and London: MIT Press, 1998.

Vikan, Gary. *Early Byzantine Pilgrimage Art*. Rev. ed. Washington, DC: Dumbarton Oaks Byzantine Collection, 2011.

Vincent, Hugues. "Le temple Hérodien d'après la Mišnah." *Revue Biblique* 61 (1954): 5–35, 398–418.

Vojvodić, Dragan. "Portreti vladara, crkvenih dostojanstvenika i plemića u naosu i pri-prati" [Portraits of rulers, ecclesiastical dignitaries and noblemen in the naos and narthex]. In *Zidno slikarstvo manastira Dečana: građa i studije*, ed. Vojislav J. Djurić, 265–298. Belgrade: Srpska akademija nauka i umetnosti, 1995.

Volbach, Wolfgang Fritz. *Elfenbeinarbeiten der Spätantike und des frühen Mittelalters*. Mainz: Philipp von Zabern, 1976.

Voyadjis, Sotiris. "The Katholikon of Nea Moni in Chios Unveiled." *Jahrbuch der Österreichischen Byzantinistik* 59 (2009): 229–242.

BIBLIOGRAPHY

Vujošević, Žarko. "Hrisovulja kralja Stefana Dušana manastiru Sv. Petra i Pavla na Limu" [The Chrysobull of King Stefan Dušan to the monastery at St. Peter and Paul on Lim]. *Stari srpski arhiv* 3 (2004): 45–69.

Vujović, Miroslav. "Ranovizantijski kanatar iz Beograda" [Early Byzantine steel yard weight from Belgrade]. *Starinar* 64 (2014): 161–183.

Wallraff, Martin. *"Christus verus sol." Sonnenverehrung und Christentum in der Spätantike.* Münster: Aschendorff, 2001.

Walter, Christopher. "New Look at the Byzantine Sanctuary Barrier." *Revue des études byzantines* 51 (1993): 203–228.

Walter, Christopher. "The Origin of the Iconostasis." *Eastern Churches Review* 3 (1971): 251–267.

Warland, Rainer. "Der Ambo aus Thessaloniki. Bildprogramm—Rekonstruktion—Datierung." *Jahrbuch des Deutschen Archäologischen Institut* 109 (1994): 371–385.

Weber, Max. "Objectivity in Social Science and Social Policy." In *The Methodology of the Social Sciences*, ed. and trans. E.A. Shils and H.A. Finch, 50–112. Illinois: Free Press of Glencoe, 1949.

Weber, Winfried. "Die Reliquienprozession auf der Elfenbeintafel des Trierer Domschatzes und das kaiserliche Hofzeremoniell." *Trierer Zeitschrift für Geschichte und Kunst des Trierer Landes und seiner Nachbargebiete* 42 (1979): 135–151.

Weissbrod, Ursula. *"Hier liegt der Knecht Gottes ..." Gräber in byzantinischen Kirchen und ihr Dekor (11. bis 15. Jahrhundert).* Wiesbaden: Harrassowitz Verlag, 2003.

Weitzmann, Kurt. ed. *Age of Spirituality, Late Antique and Early Christian Art, Third to Seventh Century* (Catalogue of the exhibition at The Metropolitan Museum of Art, November 19, 1977, through February 12 1978). New York: The Metropolitan Museum of Art, 1979.

Weitzmann, Kurt. *Late Antique and Early Christian Book Illumination.* New York: Braziller, 1977.

Weitzmann, Kurt, and Barnabo Massimo. *The Byzantine Octateuchs.* Princeton: Princeton University Press, 1999.

Wells, Emma J. "Overview: The Medieval Senses." In *The Oxford Handbook of Later Medieval Archaeology in Britain*, ed. Christopher Gerrard and Alejandra Gutiérrez, 681–696. Oxford: Oxford University Press, 2018.

Wessel, Klaus. "Insignien." In *Reallexikon zur byzantinischen Kunst* 3, 369–498. Stuttgart: A. Hiersemann, 1978.

Weston, Richard. *100 Ideas that Changed Architecture.* London: Lawrence King Publishers, [2015] 2011.

Whallon, Robert, and James A. Brown, eds. *Essays on Archaeological Typology.* Evanston: Center for American Archaeology Press, 1982.

Whitmont, Edward C. *Return of the Goddess.* New York: Crossroad Publishing, 1992.

Whittaker, John C., Douglas Caulkins, and Kathryn A. Kamp. "Evaluating Consistency in Typology and Classification." *Journal of Archaeological Method and Theory* 5, no. 2 (1998): 129–164.

Wilkinson, John. "Early Christian Pilgrimage." In *Egeria's Travels*, ed. John Wilkinson, 4–8. Warminster: Aris and Phillips, 1999.

Wilkinson, John. *Jerusalem Pilgrims Before the Crusades*. Jerusalem: Ariel Publishing House, 1977.

Wilkinson, John. "The Tomb of Christ: An Outline of its Structural History." *The Journal of the Council for British Research in the Levant* 4, no. 1 (1972): 83–97.

Willis, Robert. *The Architectural History of the Church of the Holy Sepulchre at Jerusalem*. London: Parker, 1849.

Wilson, Laurie J. "The Trier Procession Ivory: A New Interpretation." *Byzantion* 54 (1984): 602–614.

Winkes, Rudolf. *Clipeata imago. Studien zu einer römischen Bildnisform*. Bonn: R. Habelt, 1969.

Winkes, Rudolf. "Pliny's Chapter on Roman Funeral Customs in the Light of Clipeatae Imagines." *American Journal of Archaeology* 83 (1979): 481–484.

Wistrand, Erik. *Felicitas imperatoria*. Gothenburg: Acta Universitatis Gothoburgensis, 1987.

Woods, David. "On the Death of the Empress Fausta." *Greece & Rome* 45, no. 1 (1998): 70–86.

Wormald, Francis. *The Miniatures of the Gospels of St Augustine, Corpus Christi College ms. 286*. Facs. Cambridge: Cambridge University Press, 1954.

Wortley, John. "Icons and Relics: A Comparison." *Greek, Roman and Byzantine Studies* 43 (2002–2003): 161–174.

Wortley, John. "The Trier Ivory Reconsidered." *Greek, Roman and Byzantine Studies* 21 (1980): 381–394.

Xyngopoulos, Andreas. "Les fresques de l'église des Sts. Apôtres à Thessalonique." In *Art et Société à Byzance sous les Paléologues. Actes du Colloque de Venise, Septembre 1968*, 83–89. Venice: Institut hellénique d'études byzantines et post-byzantines, 1971.

Zanker, Paul. "In Search of the Roman Viewer." In *The Interpretation of Architectural Sculpture in Greece and Rome*, ed. Diana Buitron-Oliver, 179–191. Washington, DC: National Gallery of Art/University Press of New England, 1997.

Zeitler, Barbara. "Cults Disrupted and Memories Recaptured: Events in the Life of the Icon of the Virgin Hodegetria in Constantinople." In *Memory and Oblivion: Proceedings of the XXIX International Congress of the History of Art*, ed. W. Reinink and J. Stumpel, 701–708. Amsterdam: Comité international d'histoire de l'art, 1999.

Ziebarth, Erich. "Kyriakos o ex Ankōnos en Ēpeirō" [Ciriaco of Ancona in Epirus]. *Ēpeirōtika Chrōnika* 1 (1926): 110–119.

Živić, Maja. "Umetnička ostvarenja u carskoj palati" [Artistic achievements in the imperial palace]. In *Felix Romuliana—Gamzigrad,* ed. Ivana Popović, 107–140. Belgrade: Arheološki institut, 2010.

Index

Illustrations are denoted by italics.

Ablgharib Pahlavid, prince 184
Abrahim Ibn Ezra 146
Aedicula of Christ, church of the Holy
  Sepulchre, Jerusalem 115, 177, 179, 180,
  184, 185
Aetos, Greece 43
Against Heresies (Irenaeus) 218
Agia Triti (Holy Tuesday), church,
  Vasilopoulo 43
Agioi Theodoroi monastery 64
Agitria, church, Mesa Mani 59, 67
Agraphoi, church 63, 67, 71
Akathist Hymn 38n90
Akathistos cycle 58, 70
Alexios Angelos Komnenos 194
Ambrose, Saint 80
Anagnostakis, Elias 56, 66
Anastasius I, emperor 30–31, 109, 134
Andronikos II, emperor 56, 69
Andronikos III, emperor 62n104
Andronikos Palaiologos Asanes 65
aniconism, in Jewish art 147, 150, 161
Annia Galeria Faustina, empress 30
Antiquities of the Jews (Josephus) 158
antitype 1, 2n5, 18, 38, 41, 219, 234
Aphendiko, church, Mystras 202
Apolpaina, church 63–64
apotheosis, symbols of 103, 110n21, 119, 120,
  122, 134
arcade 117, 122, 124–127
Arcadius, emperor 139
arch 103–127, *105, 107, 108, 111, 112, 116, 118, 120,
  121, 123, 125, 126,* 236
  on 'Christ and Mary' diptych 109–110, *111*
  on consular diptychs 104–109, *105*
  in funerary art 117–122, *120, 121, 123*
  passage, symbol of 104, 117
  pediment and 127
  as transcendental gateway 103, 117–120,
    122, 124
  triumph, as symbol of 103, 104–105,
    109–117, 119, 122–124
  over death 120–122, 126–127

archaeological artifacts
  evolutionist approach to architectural
    typology and 8
  typology of 17–18
Archangel Michael on Mount Auxentios,
  monastery 68
arched *fastigium* 137–141
archetype
  of bodily relics, body of Christ as 75,
    77–79, 100
  definition of 2, 12–14, 191, 194, 216–220,
    213, 233–240
  of the divine heiress (empress) 15–42
  five-domed churches 191, 194
  the Great Mother 16–17
  Hodegetria icon as 45, 47, 71
  goddesses as 16–17, 37–38, 41
  Jungian psychology and 16
  likeness and 237
  mental image and 16, 18–19, 42
  primitive hut as 210–232
  Theotokos, the 37, 38, 51
  type and 12–14, 100, 145, 191, 210, 216–217,
    231, 233–239
architectural motifs in imagery 101–103,
    236–237
  See also arcade; arch; arched *fastigium*;
    pediment; portico
architectural types 2n5, 4–11, 103, 168,
    176–177, 188–191, 210, 211, 213–220, 231,
    233–240
  See also planning types
architecture, rhetoric of 145, 168
Arediou, church 53, 67
Areobindus, consul 106, *107,* 109
Ariadne, empress 30–32, *32,* 33n67, 35,
    40–41, 109, 134
Aristotle 210, 216, 238
Ark of the Covenant 12, 146, 150, 156,
    180n37, 218, 219, 220, 224n44, 225, 229
Armenian origins of domed octagon
    structural type 166, 184–185
Arsenius, patriarch 82
Artemis, goddess 38n90
Ascension ivory, Munich 177, *178*

INDEX

Ashburnham Pentateuch   117, *118*
Ashkenazi haggadot, representation of the
   Temple in   153, 159–161
Athanasios I, patriarch   54
Athena, goddess   38*n*90
Augustine, Saint   216*n*20

Babić, Gordana   91
Balaban Ağa Mescidi, mosque   175*n*24
Balajnac, bronze portrait from   33–34, *34*
Bandmann, Günter   101*n*2, 102*n*4
bar Kochba, Simon   149, 180
Bar Kochba Revolt silver coinage   149, *149*,
   180
Bartholomew di Simeri   51
Basil I, emperor   191, 193
basilica, building type   5, 7, 8, 10, 202, 226
Basilakes Nomikos   54*n*55
Bebaia Elpis monastery   69
Bede   1, 215
Bedestan, church, Nicosia   52
Benjamin of Tudela, Rabbi   147*n*10
bilateral icons   49–50
Birds' Head Haggadah   153*n*26, 159–161
Blachernai monastery   55, 60*n*90, 67
Blachernitissa icon   59, 60
Bland, Kalman   146, 147
Boethii, the   131
Boethius, consular diptych of   131, *132*
Bogdanović, Jelena   9, 11, 145, 168*n*8
Brephokratousa icon   59
Brontocheion monastery   54–56, 66, 71
Bruttia Crispina, empress   30
Bryas, Palace of   169*n*10
Buildings (Procopius)   10, 11
Bulgakov, Sergius   79
Busac, Hugues   56
Bynum, Caroline   79

Capernaum, synagogue   180
canopy
   altar   223–225
   dome as   9, 10, 11, 172, 208, 226, 227, 228
   as representative of religious
      structures   217–221, 223–224
   as unit of design   9, 10, 11, 208*n*39,
      217–221, 225–226, 230–232
   See also 'living' canopy
Cappella Arcivescovile, Ravenna   206

Cappella Palatina, Palermo   51, 71
Caričin Grad-*Iustiniana Prima*   36, 41
Carroll, Michael   16
Celestial Hierarchy (Dionysius the
   Areopagite)   216–219, 238 239
centrally planned church type   5, 7, 10, 163,
   168–169, 175–176, 185, 226, 236
Chalke Gate   10
Chalkoprateia, church, Constantinople   55
Choli, church   53, 67
Chorio, church   66–67, 71
Christ, body of   77–79, 100
'Christ and Mary' diptych   109–110, *111*
Christ Pantokrator, church of *See* Dečani
   monastery, church of the Christ
   Pantokrator
Chronography of 354   110–111, *112*, 129, *130*
church buildings
   changes in   6–9
   decorative programs of   7*n*14, 197–200,
      202, 204–208
   evolutionist approach to typology
      of   7–8, 10, 235
   liturgical changes and   6–7, 204–206
   See also planning types
ciborium, as canopy   218–226, 231
Clementinus, consul   106, *108*, 109
coins
   Bar Kochba Revolt silver coinage   149,
      149, 180
   empress imagery on   23, 24*n*31, 25–26,
      27, 28, 35, 36, *36*, 38–41
   images of pediments on   127
Commentary on Mishneh (Maimonides)   160
colonnettes, double
   as architectural feature   163, 165*n*4,
      166–169, 172, 176
   in representations of the church of the
      Holy Sepulchre   176–177, 179–180,
      185, 236
concha, symbolism of   110, 117, 118, 120, 124,
   128, 131, 134
consul, Roman office of   106, 109*n*17, *118*,
   134*n*68
consular diptychs
   arches on   104–109, *105*
   empress imagery on   30–31, 35
   pedimented front on   129, 131–134, *132*, *133*
Constantine VII, emperor   191*n*10

Constantine IX Monomachos, emperor 163, 174

Constantine the Great, emperor 20, 23, 28, 36, 193
 mausoleum of 163

Constantine Lips, North Church of, Constantinople 193

Constantius II *Augustus* 28, 129, *130*, 131

Constantius Gallus *Caesar* 129, 131

Coptic stelae 120, *121*

cross-domed church type 7–8, 10, 193

cross-in-square church type 5, 7–8, 10, 176*n*25, 193, 197*n*22, 202, 226

curtains, symbolism of 110, 117, 124–125, 148, 221, 227

Cybele, goddess 37

Cyriacus of Ancona 63*n*111

Daniel, Russian abbot 50

Danilo II, archbishop 59–61, 62, 68, 83, 88
 Life of 60–61

David, king
 plates 141, *142*
 psalm 226–227, 229

Dečani monastery, church of the Christ Pantokrator 72, *73*, *74*–*75*, *76*, 83–100, *84*, *85*, *86*, *87*, *89*, *90*, *92*, *93*, *94*, *95*, *96*

decorative programs of churches 7*n*14, 197–200, 202, 204–208

della Dora, Veronica 226–227

De Michaele et Andronico Paleologis (Pachymeres) 82

Descent of the Holy Fire 179

De tabernaculo (Bede) 215

De templo (Bede) 215

diadem, in imperial imagery 22, 23, 28, 31, 41, 129*n*58

Didymoteichon, monastery 57, 71

Diocletian, palatial complex of in Split 138

Dionysius the Areopagite 13, 216–219, 238–239

Dionysus 38*n*91

Divine Liturgy, the, in decorative programs of church domes 204–206

dolphin, symbolism of 135

domed octagon church type 10, 163, 165–166, 176

Domentijan, author of Life of Saint Sava 83

domes
 See canopy; cross-domed church type; domed octagon church type; five-domed churches

Domitilla catacombs, 'Passion' sarcophagus 118–119

Dormition of the Virgin, church, Gračanica monastery 197, *203*, *205*

door motif on funerary monuments 117

Dura-Europos, synagogue in 149, *151*, 161*n*51, 180, *182*

Ðurić, Vojislav 60

eagle, symbolism of 119, 120, 122*n*46

Ecclesiastical History and Mystical Contemplation (Germanus) 218

elevatio corporis 81

empress imagery
 antitype 18, 38, 41
 Annia Galeria Faustina 30
 archetypes of 15, 16–17, 37–38, 41
 Ariadne 30–32, *32*, 33*n*67, 35, 40–41, 109, 134
 Christian iconography and 23–26, 35–36
 Christian typology and 18
 on cameos 26, 27, 28, *29*, 30, 38, 40
 on coins 23, 24*n*31, 25–26, 27, 28, 35, 36, *36*, 38–41
 on consular diptychs 30–31, 35
 co-rulers 25, 35–36, 41
 empress as mother 19–25, 36, 38–39, 41
 empress as wife 19, 25–35, 40
 Euphemia 32–34, *34*, 41
 Fausta 26, 28, *29*, 30, 39, 40
 Galeria Valeria 26, 27, 28, 38
 Goddess archetype 16–17, 37–38, 41
 Helena, mother of Constantine the Great 20, 23–24, *25*, 26, 28, 36, 38–39, 40
 ideal type 18, 26, 34–35, 41, 42
 imperial garments on 24*n*31, 31, 33, 41
 as imperial propaganda 15, 19, 25–36, 40–42
 maternal type 15, 17, 38–39, 41
 Mother of God archetype and 16–17, 37–38
 mothers of emperors, glorification of 19–23, 39–40
 on oil lamps 24–25, *25*

INDEX 291

empress imagery (*cont.*)
 as prototype   15, 17, 26, 40, 42
 religious archetypes   15, 16, 18, 37–38
 Romula, mother of Roman emperor
  Galerius   19–20, *21*, 38*n*91
 sculptures of   33–34, *34*, 41
 Sophia   25, 35, 41
 Theodora   15*n*1, 33*n*70, 35
 on steelyard weights   31–32, *32*, 40–41
Eirene Doukaina Komnene, empress   69
Eisen, Charles   211, *212*
Eliezer ben Nathan, Rabbi   161
Empedocles   210
Enniameritissa, church, Chalki   59
Enlightenment, architectural scholars of
 the   211–213, 231
Entry of the Ever Virgin Mary and Most
  Holy Mother of God Theotokos   220,
  222–225, *222*
erotes, symbolism of   134*n*66, *134*, *135*, 140
Essai sur l'architecture (Laugier)   211, *212*,
  216, 220, 229, 231, 232
essentialism, philosophy of   17–18
Euphemia, empress   32–34, *34*, 41
Euphrosyne-Marina, nun   56, 65–66, 71
Eusebius of Caesarea   174*n*18, 179, 190
evolutionist approach in architectural
  typology   7, 8, 10, 235, 240

Fasti consulares   109n18
fastigium
 columned *fastigium See* pedimented front
 palatial *fastigium See* arched *fastigium*
 Syrian *fastigium See* arched *fastigium*
 See also Ravennese *fastigium*
Fausta, empress   26, 28, *29*, 30, 39, 40
Felix, Saint   80
Felix Romuliana, imperial palace   20, *21*
First Temple   145, 146, 150n18
five-domed churches
 approaches to   189–190
 Byzantine perceptions of   190, 197, 198,
  206
 Constantine Lips, North Church of   193
 decorative program of   197–200, 202,
  204–208
 Heavenly Jerusalem as archetype   190–
  193, *192*, 236

Nea Ekklesia church as archetype   191,
  193–194, 197
St. Panteleimon, church, Nerezi   194, *195*,
  196, 198–200, *198*, *199*, 202, 204
 subsidiary domes, placement of   202–
  206, *203*
 symbolism of   190–191, 193, 197, 208
 Virgin Kosmosoteira, church,
  Pherrai   194, *195*, 198, 200, 204
 Virgin of Ljeviška, church, Prizren   197,
  200, *201*, 202, 204
Flavius Anastasius, consul   131–134, *133*
funerary art
 arches in   117–122, *120*, *121*, *123*
 pediments in   134*n*66, 135–137

Galla Placidia, mausoleum of   206
Galeria Valeria, empress   26, *27*, 28, 38
Galerius, emperor   19–20, 23, 26, 38*n*91, 39
Gamzigrad (architectural complex)   20*n*20,
  21, 38*n*91
Gedankenbild   18
Germanus, Saint   77*n*16, 218
Geromeri monastery   57–58, 67
Gonia monastery   58
Gorgon head   135, 137
Gospel Book, MS E.D. Clarke   206, 209
Gračanica monastery   197, *201*, 202–206, *203*,
  205, *207*, *208*
Gradac monastery   83
Great Mother, the, archetype   16–17
Greek octagon church type   165–166
Gregorios, author of Life of Saint
  Romylos   61
Gregory of Kykkos   52
Gregory of Nazianzus   79
Gregory Pachymeres   62, 82
Grigorije Camblak (Gregory Tsamblak)   74,
  88
Gül, church, Constantinople   8

haggadot, illuminated   145, 153–162
Hagia Eirene, church, Constantinople   7*n*17,
  11
Hagia Sophia, church, Constantinople   10,
  11, 82, 138*n*77, 215, 226, 227
Hagioi Apostoloi, church, Chios   165
Hagios Demetrios, church, Thessaloniki,
  'windblown' capitals   *230*

Hagios Georgios, church, Thessaloniki, marble ambo 124, *125*

Hagios Menas, church, Constantinople 175*n*24

Hamilton Psalter 68

Hammat Tiberias, synagogue mosaic floor 150, *152*, 161*n*51

Heavenly Jerusalem 11, 12, 160, 161, 190–193, *192*

Helen, Serbian queen 83

Helena, empress, mother of Constantine the Great 20, 23–24, *25*, 26, 28, 36, 38–39, 40

Helena Palaiologina 64

Hera-Juno, goddess 37, 122*n*46

Heraclius, emperor 25, 36*n*83, 141*n*83

Herodian Temple *See* Second Temple

Hodegetria icon
confraternities of 44, 47, 48, 53, 60, 62–63, 71
foundations dedicated to 43–45, 47–66
Agioi Theodoroi monastery 64
Agitria, church, Mesa Mani 59, 67
Agraphoi, church 63, 67, 71
Apolpaina, church 63–64
Arediou, church 53, 67
Bedestan, church, Nicosia 52–53, 71
Brontocheion monastery 54–56, 66, 71
Cappella Palatina, Palermo 51, 71
Choli, church 53, 67
Chorio, church 66–67, 71
Didymoteichon, monastery 57, 71
Enniameritissa, church, Chalki 59
Geromeri monastery 57–58, 67
Gonia monastery 58
Hodegetria cathedral, Nicosia 52–53, 71
Jerusalem monastery dedicated to the Hodegetria 48–50, 67, 71
Kouklia, church of Panagia Katholiki 53, 67
Kouvouklia, church 64
Maurochorion, church 64
Meronas, church 58
Monembasia, church 56–57, 71
Mušutište, church 61
Mytilene, monastery 64
Peć, church 59–60, 67
Spelies, church 62

St. Nicholas tis Stegis, church, Cyprus 52
St. Sophia, church, Thessaloniki 47, 71
Strumica, church 61
Veliko Tarnovo, monastery 61
Xenophon monastery 65
copies of 44–47, 49, 51, 52, 53, 54, 56, 57, 58, 59, 66, 70, 71, 237
development of the cult of 43–67, 70–71
funerary role of 62
likeness 46
miracle-working powers of 44, 45, 46, 47, 48, 51, 52, 58, 60, 67, 70
mislabeling of 59
patron feasts of Hodegetria-dedicated foundations 67–70
political powers of 47*n*17
as prototype 44–47
veneration transfer and 45–48, 66, 71, 235–236, 237

Hilandar monastery 61, 72*n*5
icon showing the Presentation of the Mother of God in the Temple 220, 222–225, *222*

Hodegon monastery 44, 47*n*16, 61, 62, 68, 235

Holy Apostles, church, Constantinople 163, 190*n*4

Holy Apostles, church, Thessaloniki 202, 204

Holy Sepulchre, church, Jerusalem
Aedicula of Christ and, conflation of 177, 185
Constantine IX Monomachos and 174
copies of 11, 168, 175–177, 183–188
as model for the church of Nea Moni 168, 175–177, 183–184, 236
as prototype 11–12, 168, 236
reconstruction of 174
Temple, associations with 179–180
visual representations of 176–181, *178*, 183, 185

Holy Tuesday 43–44, 70

Homilies of James Kokkinobaphos 191, *192*

Honorius, emperor 104, 105*n*10, 135*n*72

Horreum Margi, cameos from 26, *27*, 38

Horus, god 120

Hosios Loukas monastery 165*n*5, 220, *221*

INDEX

293

Ioannitzopoulos, monk of foundation of the
    Hodegetria in Maurochorion   64
iconoclasm   45–46, 75, 146, 147, 193–194
iconographical studies   2, 4
iconographical approaches to
    architecture   2*n*3, 11–12
iconophiles, visual hierarchy and   45–46
iconostasis
    Dečani monastery   75, *76*, 84, *84*, 86, 89,
        91, *96*, 99–100
    symbolism of   99–100, 237
icons, religious
    architectural representations
        and   181*n*42
    John of Damascus on   45, 75, 98
    likeness and   4, 45–46
    miracle-working powers of   44, 45, 46,
        47, 48, 51, 52, 58, 60, 67, 70, 77
    prototypes and   4, 44–47, 75, 77
    origins of   75
    relics and   75, 77, 98, 100
    typology and   4, 14
    visual hierarchy of   46
    See also aniconism, in Jewish art;
        bilateral icons; Blachernitissa
        icon; Brephokratousa icon;
        Hodegetria icon; Kykkotissa
        icon; Megaspelaiotissa icon;
        Monembasiotissa icon; Presentation
        of the Mother of God in the
        Temple
ideal type   18–19, 42
    church   7
    empresses   18, 26, 34–35, 41, 42
Ignatios, patriarch of
    Constantinople   169*n*10
Ioannes Likinios   56
imaged architecture   101–103
    See also arcade; arch; arched *fastigium*;
        pedimented front; portico
image theory   4, 45–46
imago clipeata   134
inventio crucis See True Cross, legend of the
    Irenaeus, bishop of Lyons   216, 218, 225
Isaak Komnenos   69, 194
Isis-Fortuna, goddess   37, 128–129, *128*

Jacob ben Reuben, Rabbi   146
Jacoby, Sam   239

Jacopo Ruffo/Rosso   63–64
Jerome, Saint   80
Jerusalem
    See Heavenly Jerusalem; Holy Sepulchre;
        Renewed Jerusalem
Jewish art
    aniconism in   147, 150, 161
    Ark of the Covenant in   146, 150, 156,
        180*n*37
    development of   144–148, 150, 152–153
    floor mosaics   150, *152*
    illuminated manuscripts   145, 153–162
    Jewish attitudes to Christians and   150,
        152–153, 160
    perceptions of Jewish artlessness   147
    Temple representation in   148–150, *149*,
        151, 153–162, *155*
    visions of sages and   146
    word-driven imagery   145–147, 162
Jewish Wars (Josephus)   158
John, *ktetor* of St. John the Forerunner
    Phoberos monastery   69
John Chrysostom, Saint   54*n*55
John of Damascus   45, 75, 98
John II Orsini   57
John V Palaiologos   62*n*104
Johnson, Mark   8
Josephus Flavius   156*n*33, 158
Jovan Dragoslav, *kaznac*   61
Judah Halevi   146
Jung, Carl Gustav   16–17
Justin I, emperor   32, 33, 34, 41
Justin II, emperor   25, 35, *36*, 41
Justinian, emperor   10, 11, 33, 34, 41, 106,
    134*n*67, 190*n*4, 215

Kale-e Zerzevan votive bronze *situla*   126,
    126–127
Kalenderhane Camii, church,
    Constantinople   8
Kalligas, Haris   56
Karydis, Spyros   63
Kogman-Appel, Katrin   150, 153*n*26, 159, 162
Koinōnia type   41
Korać, Dušan   74*n*7, *n*8
Kouklia, church of Panagia Katholiki   53, 67
Kouvouklia, church   64
Krautheimer, Richard   2*n*3, 11–12, 175
Küçükyalı, church   169, *170*

Kühnel, Gustav 49
Kutlumus 220 manuscript 56, 57
Kykkotissa icon 52

Laderman, Shulamit 162
Lampl, Paul 102n4
Laugier, Marc-Antoine 2n5, 211, 212, 216, 220, 229, 231, 232
Lavra monastery 65
Lazaros of Galesion, Saint 98, 99n89
Le Corbusier 2n5, 213n11
Leo I, emperor 30–31
Leo II, emperor 30–31
Leonardo III Tocco 63n111, 64
Lidov, Alexei 49
likeness in typology 1, 4, 11–12, 45–46, 71, 98, 236, 237
lion, symbolism of 122
'living' canopy 224–225
Lossky, Vladimir 75
Luke the Evangelist, Saint 44, 46, 51, 68, 79, 114, 208
Luna, symbolism of 110, 119

Machaira monastery 68
Madrazo Agudin, Leandro 2n5, 213, 216n20
Magdalino, Paul 193
Maimonides, Moses 146, 160, 161
Malotaras, bishop of Kernitsa 65–66
Manasija monastery 202
Manouel Kourtikes, Sebastos 64
Manuel, bishop, founder of Theotokos Eleousa, Veljusa 169
Maurochorion, church 64
Maria Regina type of the Virgin Mary 37
Marsengill, Katherine 4, 98
Martina, empress, wife of Heraclius 25, 36n83
Martha, Saint, Life of 56
Mary Latina, church, Jerusalem 49n23
Matejič monastery 226, 228
Maximinus Daia, emperor 20, 23
Megale Panagia, nunnery, Jerusalem 49
Mega Spelaion monastery 66
Megaspelaiotissa icon 66
Mellinkoff, Ruth 147n12
Menologion of Basil II 223n42
mental image, and archetypes 2n5, 16, 18, 42, 183

Meronas, church 58
Metamorphosis, church of the, Koropi 206
Meyer, Ann Raftery 215
Michael, metropolitan of Patras 65–66
Michael IV the Paphlagonian 174n19
Michael VIII, emperor 47n17, 57, 68
Michael Psellos 174n20
Mihaljević, Marina 9
Mihajlović iz Ostrovice, Konstantin 74n8
Mileševa monastery 83
Milica Branković 64
Milutin, king See Stefan Uroš II Milutin
Mishnah Middot 158
Mishneh Torah (Maimonides) 160
Monembasia, church 56–57, 71
Monembasiotissa icon 57
Mother of God archetype 16–17, 37–38
Mother of God in the Temple, Presentation of the, icon 220, 222–225, 222
Mother of God tou Roidiou monastery 69
mothers of emperors, glorification of 19–23
Munich Ascension ivory 177, 178
Mušutište, church 61
Mytilene, monastery, Lesbos 64

naos
impression of circularity of 163, 168–169, 172, 176
placement of domes and 194, 202, 203–204
planning type and 5, 6
Narration of the Hodegon Monastery 68
Nea Ekklesia, church, Constantinople 191, 193–194, 197
Nea Moni, church, Chios 164, 165, 166, 167, 168
double colonnettes of 163, 166, 168, 172, 176, 179
Holy Sepulchre, resemblance to 168, 175–177, 179–184, 236
imperial associations of 174, 183
impression of circularity of 163, 168–169, 172, 176
as prototype for Greek octagon type 165–166
replicas of 165
Neilos, bishop of Tamasia 68
Neilos Erichiotes, founder of Geromeri monastery 57

INDEX

Nemanjić dynasty   72, 91
Nerezi, church of St. Panteleimon   194, *195,
    196,* 198–200, *198, 199,* 202, 204
New Solomon, the   174, 184, 215
Nicholas, Saint   89, 91
Nikanor Gate   156, 157
Nikephoros I, patriarch   45, 46
Nikephoros Moschopoulos   54, 56, 65
nimbus, symbolism of   26, 131, 141

Octateuch manuscripts   159*n*42, 225*n*48
oil lamps, Christian iconography on   24, *25*
On Adam's House in Paradise
    (Rykwert)   213–214
orans position, significance of   24, 25, 38
orb, symbolism of   114*n*28
'otherness', typology of   17
Ousterhout, Robert   145, 148, 174*n*18, 175*n*24,
    176*n*25, 179*n*36, 180*n*39, 197*n*22

Pachomios, founder of Hodegetria church of
    Brontocheion monastery   54, 55
Panagia Krina, church, Chios   165
Panagia Moutoullas, church, Cyprus, icon
    from   52
Panagia Mouchliotissa (Theotokos
    Panagiotissa), church,
    Constantinople   169, 170*n*13, *171, 172,
    173,* 183, 185
Panagia Olympiotissa monastery   204
Panofsky, Erwin   216*n*20, 238*n*7
Pantanassa, church, Mystras   202
Paulinus of Nola, Saint   80
Paulinus of Tyre   174*n*18
Paul, archbishop   56
Paul, Saint   77, 79, 122, *123*
peacock, symbolism of   122
Peć, church   59–60, 67
pediment
    arch and   127
    on consular diptychs   129, 131–134, *132, 133*
    as exemplified by Roman temples   127–
        131, *128*
    in funerary art   134*n*66, 135–137
    on Roman coins   127
    symbolism of   101, 103, 127, 129, 131,
        142–143, 236
Peleg, Yehoshua   156, 157, *157,* 158

Pentcheva, Bissera   229
Perl, Eric   219
personality, typology of (Jung)   17
Pherrai, Virgin Kosmosoteira, church   194,
    195, 198, 200, 204
phoenix, symbolism of   114
pilgrimage, copies of the Holy Sepulchre as a
    response to   177, 180, 183–185
planning types   4–11
    basilica   5, 7, 8, 10, 202, 226
    centrally planned church   5, 7, 10, 163,
        168–169, 175–176, 185, 226, 236
    cross-domed church   7–8, 10, 193
    cross-in-square church   5, 7–8, 10,
        176*n*25, 193, 197*n*22, 202, 226
    domed octagon church   10, 163, 165–166,
        176
    Greek octagon church   165–166
    nine-square grid design   10, 226, *228*
pneuma   227, 229–230
portico   124
Popović, Danica   72
Presentation of Christ in the Temple   220
Presentation of the Mother of God in the
    Temple, icon   220, 222–225, *222*
primitive hut, the   210–232, *212,* 237–238
Probus, emperor   104, *105,* 135*n*72
Procopius
    on architecture   10, 11, 184*n*48
    on empresses   15*n*1, 33
Protoevangelion (Infancy Gospel) of
    James   222, 223*n*42
prototypes
    architectural   2*n*5, 11–12, 101*n*2, *n*4,
        127–128, 237
    Ark of the Covenant as   12, 220
    body of Christ as   77, 98
    definition of   2*n*5, 11–12, 91, 234, 238
    empress images as   15, 17, 26, 40, 42
    Heavenly Jerusalem as   12
    Holy Sepulchre as   11–12, 168, 236
    icons and   4, 44–47, 75, 77
    John of Damascus on   45, 75, 98
    likeness and   12, 45–46, 71, 98
    primitive hut as   213, 216, 238
    relics and   77, 98–99
    Tabernacle as   12, 220
    Temple as   12, 219–220
    type and   14, 98, 238
Pulcheria, empress   57, 67

296 INDEX

Quatremère de Quincy, Antoine-
Chrysostome   2*n*5, 213, 216*n*20, 231, 232

Rabbula Gospels   114–115, *116*
race, typology of   17
Rashi (Solomon ben Isaac)   146, 152*n*25, 160*n*47
Ravanica monastery   204
Ravenna, Cappella Arcivescovile   206
Ravennese *fastigium*   138*n*76, *n*77, 139
Ravennese sarcophagus   120, *120*
Redemption Midrashim   160
relics
   icons and   75, 77, 83, 84, 100
   of saints
      body of Christ and   77–79, 100
      canonization and   74, 81, 82–83, 86–88, 97
      as conduit between heaven and earth   79–80
      development of cult of   78*n*20, 80
      elevation of   74–75, 81
      incorruptibility   77–80
      positioning of   72, 75, 77, 80, 81, 82, 83, 84, 86, 91, 96, 98, 99–100, 237
      translation of   74–75, 80–83, 84–85, 88
Remesiana, cameos from   28, *29*
Renewed Jerusalem   159–161
rhetoric of architecture   145, 168*n*8
Roger II, king   51–52
Romula, mother of Roman emperor Galerius   19–20, *21*, 38*n*91
Romylos, Saint, Life of   61–62
Rudl, nobleman of Strumica   61
Rykwert, Joseph   213–214

Sacred History (Procopius)   15*n*1
saints, establishing the cults of   86–88, 97
saints' relics *See* relics
Santa Maria delle Grazie, crypt of Sicilian Capella Palatina   51
Sarajevo Haggadah, representation of the Temple in   145, 154–162
Šarkamen mausoleum   20, *22*
Satyros monastery   169*n*10
Saul, king   141, *142*

Sava, Saint   72*n*5, 83
Schwartz, Joshua   156–158, *157*
Shalev-Eyni, Sarit   160
Second Temple   144, 148, 150*n*18, 157*n*34, *157*, 158
Seda, Theodorican courtier   120, *120*
Semele, mother of Dionysus   38*n*91
Sephardic haggadot, representation of the Temple in   145, 153–162, *155*
Sepphoris, synagogue floor mosaic   150*n*21, 161*n*51
Septimius Severus, arch of   114
Smyrna Octateuch   225*n*48
Sol, symbolism of   110, 119
solar motifs, symbolism of   113*n*27, 114*n*28, 122, 131
Sol Invictus   113
Solomon, king   174, 193, 215
Solomon ben Meir, Rabbi   146
Solomon's Temple *See* First Temple
Solovjev, Aleksandar   74*n*8
Sophia, empress, wife of Justin II   25, 35, 41
Spelies, church   62
Ss. Sergios and Bakkos, church, Constantinople   11
stag/deer, symbolism of   122
stars, symbolism of   113, 127, 137
St. Augustine Gospels   114
Stefan Nemanja   72
Stefan Uroš II Milutin, king   83
Stefan Uroš III Dečanski, king
   canonization of   74, 86–88, 96–97
   Life of   87–88
   portrait of   88–89, *90*, 91, *92*, 96–99
   prayer of   91, *93*, 96–97, 99
   relics of   72, 74–75, *76*, 83–89, *84*, *85*, *86*, *87*, *89*, 91, 96–100
   reliquary of   84–86, *85*, *86*, *87*, 88, 98
   translation of   74–75, 84–85, 86, 88
Stefan Uroš IV Dušan, king   74, 84*n*54, 88*n*61, 97
stelae   120, *121*, 135, *136*
Stephanos Komnenos   62*n*103
Stephen Protomartyr, Saint   91, *94*
stereotype
   definition of   19, 42, 234
   empress imagery and   15, 19, 39, 40, 42
St. Euphemia, church, Rovini   33*n*66

INDEX

Nemanjić dynasty   72, 91
Nerezi, church of St. Panteleimon   194, *195*,
    196, 198–200, *198*, *199*, 202, 204
New Solomon, the   174, 184, 215
Nicholas, Saint   89, 91
Nikanor Gate   156, 157
Nikephoros I, patriarch   45, 46
Nikephoros Moschopoulos   54, 56, 65
nimbus, symbolism of   26, 131, 141

Octateuch manuscripts   159*n*42, 225*n*48
oil lamps, Christian iconography on   24, *25*
On Adam's House in Paradise
    (Rykwert)   213–214
orans position, significance of   24, 25, 38
orb, symbolism of   114*n*28
'otherness', typology of   17
Ousterhout, Robert   145, 148, 174*n*18, 175*n*24,
    176*n*25, 179*n*36, 180*n*39, 197*n*22

Pachomios, founder of Hodegetria church of
    Brontocheion monastery   54, 55
Panagia Krina, church, Chios   165
Panagia Moutoullas, church, Cyprus, icon
    from   52
Panagia Mouchliotissa (Theotokos
    Panagiotissa), church,
    Constantinople   169, 170*n*13, *171*, 172,
    173, 183, 185
Panagia Olympiotissa monastery   204
Panofsky, Erwin   216*n*20, 238*n*7
Pantanassa, church, Mystras   202
Paulinus of Nola, Saint   80
Paulinus of Tyre   174*n*18
Paul, archbishop   56
Paul, Saint   77, 79, 122, *123*
peacock, symbolism of   122
Peć, church   59–60, 67
pediment
    arch and   127
    on consular diptychs   129, 131–134, *132*, *133*
    as exemplified by Roman temples   127–
    131, *128*
    in funerary art   134*n*66, 135–137
    on Roman coins   127
    symbolism of   101, 103, 127, 129, 131,
    142–143, 236
Peleg, Yehoshua   156, 157, *157*, 158

Pentcheva, Bissera   229
Perl, Eric   219
personality, typology of (Jung)   17
Pherrai, Virgin Kosmosoteira, church   194,
    195, 198, 200, 204
phoenix, symbolism of   114
pilgrimage, copies of the Holy Sepulchre as a
    response to   177, 180, 183–185
planning types   4–11
    basilica   5, 7, 8, 10, 202, 226
    centrally planned church   5, 7, 10, 163,
    168–169, 175–176, 185, 226, 236
    cross-domed church   7–8, 10, 193
    cross-in-square church   5, 7–8, 10,
    176*n*25, 193, 197*n*22, 202, 226
    domed octagon church   10, 163, 165–166,
    176
    Greek octagon church   165–166
    nine-square grid design   10, 226, *228*
pneuma   227, 229–230
portico   124
Popović, Danica   72
Presentation of Christ in the Temple   220
Presentation of the Mother of God in the
    Temple, icon   220, 222–225, *222*
primitive hut, the   210–232, *212*, 237–238
Probus, emperor   104, *105*, 135*n*72
Procopius
    on architecture   10, 11, 184*n*48
    on empresses   15*n*1, 33
Protoevangelion (Infancy Gospel) of
    James   222, 223*n*42
prototypes
    architectural   2*n*5, 11–12, 101*n*2, *n*4,
    127–128, 237
    Ark of the Covenant as   12, 220
    body of Christ as   77, 98
    definition of   2*n*5, 11–12, 91, 234, 238
    empress images as   15, 17, 26, 40, 42
    Heavenly Jerusalem as   12
    Holy Sepulchre as   11–12, 168, 236
    icons and   4, 44–47, 75, 77
    John of Damascus on   45, 75, 98
    likeness and   12, 45–46, 71, 98
    primitive hut as   213, 216, 238
    relics and   77, 98–99
    Tabernacle as   12, 220
    Temple as   12, 219–220
    type and   14, 98, 238
Pulcheria, empress   57, 67

Quatremère de Quincy, Antoine-
Chrysostome 2n5, 213, 216n20, 231,
232

Rabbula Gospels 114–115, *116*
race, typology of 17
Rashi (Solomon ben Isaac) 146, 152n25,
160n47
Ravanica monastery 204
Ravenna, Cappella Arcivescovile 206
Ravennese *fastigium* 138n76, n77, 139
Ravennese sarcophagus 120, *120*
Redemption Midrashim 160
relics
icons and 75, 77, 83, 84, 100
of saints
body of Christ and 77–79, 100
canonization and 74, 81, 82–83,
86–88, 97
as conduit between heaven and
earth 79–80
development of cult of 78n20, 80
elevation of 74–75, 81
incorruptibility 77–80
positioning of 72, 75, 77, 80, 81, 82,
83, 84, 86, 91, 96, 98, 99–100, 237
translation of 74–75, 80–83, 84–85,
88
Remesiana, cameos from 28, *29*
Renewed Jerusalem 159–161
rhetoric of architecture 145, 168n8
Roger II, king 51–52
Romula, mother of Roman emperor
Galerius 19–20, *21*, 38n91
Romylos, Saint, Life of 61–62
Rudl, nobleman of Strumica 61
Rykwert, Joseph 213–214

Sacred History (Procopius) 15n1
saints, establishing the cults of 86–88, 97
saints' relics *See* relics
Santa Maria delle Grazie, crypt of Sicilian
Capella Palatina 51
Sarajevo Haggadah, representation of the
Temple in 145, 154–162
Šarkamen mausoleum 20, *22*
Satyros monastery 169n10
Saul, king 141, *142*

Sava, Saint 72n5, 83
Schwartz, Joshua 156–158, *157*
Shalev-Eyni, Sarit 160
Second Temple 144, 148, 150n18, 157n34,
157, 158
Seda, Theodorican courtier 120, *120*
Semele, mother of Dionysus 38n91
Sephardic haggadot, representation of the
Temple in 145, 153–162, *155*
Sepphoris, synagogue floor mosaic 150n21,
161n51
Septimius Severus, arch of 114
Smyrna Octateuch 225n48
Sol, symbolism of 110, 119
solar motifs, symbolism of 113n27, 114n28,
122, 131
Sol Invictus 113
Solomon, king 174, 193, 215
Solomon ben Meir, Rabbi 146
Solomon's Temple *See* First Temple
Solovjev, Aleksandar 74n8
Sophia, empress, wife of Justin II 25, 35, 41
Spelies, church 62
Ss. Sergios and Bakkos, church,
Constantinople 11
stag/deer, symbolism of 122
stars, symbolism of 113, 127, 137
St. Augustine Gospels 114
Stefan Nemanja 72
Stefan Uroš II Milutin, king 83
Stefan Uroš III Dečanski, king
canonization of 74, 86–88, 96–97
Life of 87–88
portrait of 88–89, *90*, 91, *92*, 96–99
prayer of 91, *93*, 96–97, 99
relics of 72, 74–75, *76*, 83–89, *84*, *85*, *86*,
87, *89*, 91, 96–100
reliquary of 84–86, *85*, *86*, *87*, 88, 98
translation of 74–75, 84–85, 86, 88
Stefan Uroš IV Dušan, king 74, 84n54,
88n61, 97
stelae 120, *121*, 135, *136*
Stephanos Komnenos 62n103
Stephen Protomartyr, Saint 91, *94*
stereotype
definition of 19, 42, 234
empress imagery and 15, 19, 39, 40, 42
St. Euphemia, church, Rovini 33n66

INDEX

297

St. George monastery, Constantinople 8*n*21, 174*n*20
St. George, church, Staro Nagoričino 206
St. John the Forerunner Phoberos monastery 69
St. Louis Psalter 159*n*42
St. Michael, church, Fulda 175*n*23
St. Nicholas tis Stegis, church, Cyprus 52
Stoic philosophy 229
Stoudios monastery 57
St. Panteleimon, church, Nerezi 194, *195, 196*, 198–200, *198, 199*, 202, 204
St. Sophia, church, Thessaloniki 47, 71
Sts. Theodores, church of the Brontocheion monastery 54
structural type *See* planning types
Studenica monastery 72
Surb Prkitch, church, Ani 184–185, *186, 187, 188*
Symbolism of Churches and Church Ornaments, The (Durandus) 219
Synaxarion (Constantinopolitan) 67
Synaxarion of Zakynthos 56

Tabernacle 12, 146, 150, 214–215, 218, 219, 221, 225*n*48, 229
Talmud 153*n*25
Temple
    Ark of the Covenant and 150, 156, 218, 220
    canopy as 220, 221, 223
    Christian church and 215, 218, 219–220
    as model for Byzantine architecture 12, 220
    as primitive hut 220, 229
    representations of in Jewish art 144–145, 148–150, *151, 152*, 153–162, *155*, 180, 234, 237
    Holy Sepulchre and 179–180, 183
    primitive hut and 214–215, 229
    as representation of messianic hope 144, 150, 153, 156, 159–160, 161
    representation of by Schwartz and Peleg 156–158, *157*
    Tabernacle and 214–215, 218
    Virgin Mary as living 223–225
    See First Temple; Second Temple; Third Temple
Theodora, empress 15*n*1, 33*n*70, 35

Theodora, foundress of Bebaia Elpis monastery 69
Theodore Balsamon 62*n*103
Theodore I Palaiologos 55*n*61
Theodore the Studite 45
Theodosius I, silver *missorium* of 139, *140*, 141
Theophilos, emperor 169*n*10
Theotokos Eleousa, church, Veljusa 169, 171, *171, 172*, 183, 200
Theotokos Evergetis monastery 69
Theotokos Kecharitomene monastery 69
Theotokos tou Kouratoros, church, Constantinople 175*n*24
Thessaloniki, Hodegetria icon of 47
Thiofrid of Echternach 77–78
Third Temple 144, 154, 160, 162, 237
Thomas Aquinas, Saint 216*n*20
Titus, emperor 144
Todić, Branislav 91–92
Tosafists 161
Trier ivory plaque 124
triumph, arch as symbol of 103, 104–105, 109–117, 119, 122–124
    over death 120–122, 126–127
triumphal laurel wreath, in imagery 119, 122, 127, 134, 141
triumphal *ornatus* 129*nn*58
True Cross, legend of the 24, 25
Tyche-Fortuna, goddess 38*n*90
type
    in architecture 2*n*5, 4–11, 103, 168, 176–177, 188–191, 210, 211, 213–220, 231, 233–240
    definition of 1, 2, 3, 4, 12, 213, 234, 238
    and archetype 12–14, 100, 145, 191, 210, 216–217, 231, 233–239
    and prototype 14, 98, 238
    and typology 3–4
    See also antitype; archetype; ideal type; prototype; stereotype
typism 19, 42
typology
    approaches to 1–14
    of archaeological artifacts 17–18
    architectural types *See* planning types
    of architecture 2*n*5, 103, 168, 176–177, 188–191, 210, 211, 213–220, 231, 233–240
    biblical/theological 1–3, 11, 18

298 INDEX

typology (*cont.*)
    iconographical studies and   2, 4
    of personality (Jung)   17
    of 'otherness'   17
    of race   17
    visual   1–2
Tyre type sarcophagus   137, *137*

Valentinian II, emperor   139
Vasilopoulo, Greece   43, 70
Vatopedi monastery   64, 172n14
Vavedenije   220, 222–225, *222*
Veliko Tarnovo, monastery   61
Veljusa, Theotokos Eleousa, church   169, 171,
    171, 172, 183, 200
Venus, goddess   38n92
Venus Vitrix   38
Vidler, Anthony   2n5, 176, 177, 213
Virgin Kosmosoteira, church, Pherrai   194,
    195, 198, 200, 204
Virgin of Ljeviška, church, Prizren   197, 200,
    201, 202, 204

Virgin Mary
    life of   222–223, *222*
    as living Temple   224–225
    See also Mother of God archetype
visual typology   1–2
Vita Basilii   191
Vitruvius
    primitive hut   2n5, 210–214, *212*, 220, 227,
      229, 230, 231, 232
    reception of   214–215

Weber, Max   18–19
William Durandus   219
William of Tyre   174n19
'windblown' capitals   229, *230*

Xenophon monastery   65

Zakynthos, *Synaxarion* of   56
Zeno, emperor   30–31
Zoodochos Pege monastery   55
Zosima, Russian deacon   49

Printed in the United States
by Baker & Taylor Publisher Services

Printed in the United States
by Baker & Taylor Publisher Services